INSIGHT GUIDES

Created and Directed by Hans Höfer

PROVENCE

Edited by Anne Sanders Roston
Photography by Catherine Karnow
Editorial Director: Brian Bell

Houghton Mifflin

APA PUBLICATIONS

Anne Roston

I t seems strange that so few guide books have been written on Provence. Once an independent nation, this southeastern part of France possesses volumes worth of history and folklore. And the Provence of today, with its sensuous appeal, has become, thanks partly to the efforts of Peter (*A Year in Provence*) Mayle, one of Europe's most popular destinations.

Anne Roston, this book's project editor and main contributor, first encountered Provence on typical teenage excursions to Avignon, Aix and the Côte d'Azur, and her knowledge deepened after a visit to a friend's home deep in the Var. A US citizen who has lived on and off in Paris and Helsinki, Roston was the project editor for *Insight Guide: France*. Outside France, her non-fiction work has been as disparate as covering sports in Arizona and the politico-economic scene in Malaysia and her credits include the *New York Times*, the *Washington Post* and *Harper's* magazine, but she now spends the greater part of the year in New York.

Karnow

P hotographer **Catherine Karnow** was born and raised in Hong Kong and is now based in San Francisco. France has been a mainstay of her work, and she has held jobs with *Paris Match*, *Le Point* and Magnum

Photo's Paris office. Karnow's interests also extend to the cinema – her film short, *Brooklyn Bridge*, opened the Berlin Film Festival in 1984. She has photographed several Insight Guides, including those to France, Los Angeles and Washington DC.

The chapters on the Vaucluse and the Camargue were written by **Peter Robinson**. A British citizen, Robinson lives near Grasse, and has produced educational television documentaries on the Camargue and Avignon. He also broadcasts on Radio Riviera and has worked on a study of Graham Greene.

Subsequent chapters on the Alpes-de-Haute-Provence and the Var were written by another Briton, **Caroline Wheal**. The years Wheal spent, after graduating from Oxford in French, as a translator of scripts for the BBC and French television were punctuated by periods of residence in her favourite part of France, the Var. She is now a London-based journalist, and has edited Virgin Atlantic's in-flight magazine.

Peter Capella, who covered the Alpes-Maritimes, has been a committed Francophile since spending his teenage years in Toulouse. He headed to Provence after university to live in Toulon, where he worked as a radio producer. He is now a reporter in Berne for Swiss Radio International.

Joel Stratte-McClure was "forced" by never-endingly grey days in Paris to move his Franco-American wife and children down to the sunny Côte. From his nest in the hills behind Cannes, Stratte McClure writes for such publications as *Time*, the *International Herald Tribune* and *People*. He is also publisher of *Sophialet*, a newsletter about the Rivieran science park Sophia Antipolis.

Robinson

Wheal

Stratte-McClure

C. Roston

Ward-Perkins

For someone like **Caroline Roston**, a folklorist from the University of Pennsylvania who specialises in material culture, Provence is nothing less than a wonderland. Formerly the assistant to Henry Glassie, Roston, author of the chapter on Folk Art, has written a thesis on agricultural fairs in Massachusetts.

The feature on Cults was written by **Ward Rutherford**, a French-educated Jerseyman who divides his time between Brighton and Southern France. Rutherford has written several studies on Druidism, the ancient Celtic religion of which he claims to have found relics in Provence. To his credit, also, are 16 books ranging in topic from crime novels to *The Ally*, a work on World War I.

David Ward-Perkins lives in the hilltop village of St-Jeannet just north of the Côte d'Azur, from where he cooks Provençal dishes for his wife and four children. A founding editor of *New Riviera* magazine, he was also the editor of *Seven Adventures on the French Riviera*.

The single-page features to the Places chapters were some of the liveliest additions. This was partly due to Paris-born, Franco-American **Mary Deschamps**, who wrote the pieces on Christian Lacroix and the bikini. Deschamps is a freelance writer in Paris, focusing mostly on fashion and international lifestyles. She edited *A Touch of Paris* and currently contributes regularly to the *International Herald Tribune* and *Vogue Hommes*.

Claire Touchard's family, which has been in the art world for several generations, bought a home in the Vaucluse during the 1950s, making her a natural for the piece on Artist Colonies.

She now works in Paris as a freelance editor and translator.

Although short, **William Fisher's** article on the Cannes film festival is unlikely to go unnoticed. Fisher, the Paris correspondent for *Screen International*, has any number of different projects up his sleeve – including a full-blown book on the festival experience and a "travel" book on Eastern Europe.

On **Rosemary Bailey's** first visit to Provence, she stayed with friends on a rose farm and was immediately fascinated by the flower business. Based in London, she writes for major British publications and has edited Insight Guides to Tuscany, the Loire Valley, Burgundy and the Côte d'Azur.

After securing the text, Roston turned her attention to the illustrative portion of the book. Material from the **Bibliothèque Nationale** in Paris, the **National Gallery of Art**, the **Academy of Motion Pictures**, **Ruth Aebi** of Gstaad, **Gavin Lewis**, and **Jantzen, Inc**. complemented Karnow's photography.

Bailey

This updated edition, checked out on the spot by **Mark Fincham**, was supervised in Insight Guides' London editorial office by managing editor **Dorothy Stannard**. Jill Adam updated the Travel Tips.

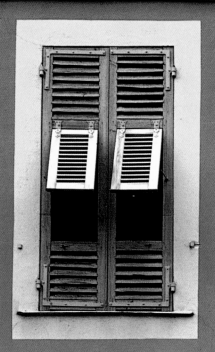
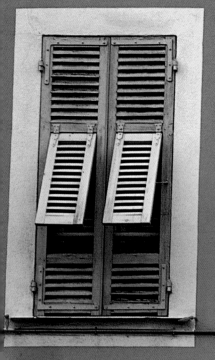
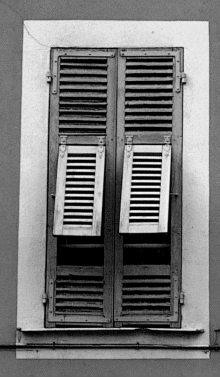

CONTENTS

Located in the sunny southeastern corner of France, Provence has a history is as rich as its soil. Prehistoric Ligurians, classical Greeks and Augustan Romans all left their marks here. Later tyrants included the bloody Saracens and the medieval lords of Baux, who founded the infamous "Courts of Love". It wasn't until the 15th century that the Gauls claimed Provence for their own.

Mary Magdalene is said to have spent her last years in the Var, and several popes made Avignon their home during the 14th century. Impressionist painter Paul Cézanne was born and worked in the Bouches-du-Rhône, where Vincent Van Gogh was driven to madness. More artists arrived from the turn of the 20th century onwards, including Dufy, Picasso, Matisse and Chagall. Writers such as F. Scott Fitzgerald and Graham Greene flocked to the Côte d'Azur, which Queen Victoria and international millionaires had already made famous.

What attracted all these different people? It could be the dazzling light that bathes this intoxicating land of black cypress and crooked olive trees. Perhaps it's the sweet-smelling lavender that sprawls endlessly across its fields and hillsides, and the mouth-watering melons and tomatoes its sun-rich soil produces. Or it might be Provence's strategic position between the Mediterranean Sea, the great River Rhône, the Alps and the Italian border.

Thanks to the strong and independent character of the warm-hearted Provençals, the area hasn't become just a graveyard for invaders' memorabilia. Provence's five *départements* and two subregions each have vivid personalities of their own. Even as children increasingly quit the tiny villages where their grandparents herded sheep, mined ochre or grew vegetables to try their luck in Marseille, Nice and Avignon, they bring with them a deep-rooted respect for the land and its traditions.

Preceding pages: Rue de St Catherine; Abbey St-Michel-de-Frigolet; garlic; shuttered lives; lavender fields on the Valensole Plain; gathering bulls during a feria du cheval; harbour in Cassis; detail from St-Gilles church. **Right**, café patrons.

Originally, the entire southeastern corner of France was covered by the sea. Then, 200 million years ago, a rock continent called Tyrrhenia began to emerge in ever-increasing strata of limestone, shale and clay. It was followed – in another 150 million years – by a second land mass. This area was just slightly further "inland" and would become what is today called Provence.

Submarine forces steadily pressed the Provençal land mass up from beneath the sea and into the high folds running east-west above the modern coastline. It was in this way that Mounts Ste-Victoire, Ste-Baume and Ventoux, the Alpille Ridges, and the Luberon and Baronnies ranges were formed.

This new earth continued to develop side by side with the older continent of Tyrrhenia, until the latter dropped back down into the sea about 2 million years ago. Of Tyrrhenia, all that is now left peaking out above the water is Cap Canaille, the Esterel Massif and several Mediterranean islands such as Sicily and Corsica.

Change of direction: Provence has remained geographically more or less the same since then, although, of course, certain natural changes continued to occur and, indeed, are still slowly taking place. The Rhône Valley began to hollow out, and the Rhône itself was rerouted from its original seaward path, via the Durance east of the Alpilles and down through the Crau Plain, to its current position directly south to the sea from Avignon. Over the centuries, under the gradual process of erosion, some of the oldest coastline reverted back to being submarine, and a little more land is reclaimed by the Mediterranean yearly. Today, Provence officially consists of five different *départements*: the Vaucluse, the Bouches-du-Rhône, the Var, the Alpes-de-Haute-Provence and the Alpes-Maritimes. Its more-or-less natural borders are the Rhône to the west, the Mediterranean to the south, Italy to the east and the Baronnies and Alpine mountain ranges to the north.

Popularly, however, Provence is less

clearly defined, due to the extensive variety it contains. Inhabitants of the western, more traditional areas like the Vaucluse and the Bouches-du-Rhône frequently exclude the Alpes-Maritimes when discussing eastern Provence, and almost no one would describe the Côte d'Azur as Provençal.

The Bouches-du-Rhône is generally considered to be the oldest section of Provence, since the earliest civilised settlements were centred on its shores. Set in the lower half of the western part of the region, this *départe-*

ment is marked by the Rhône to the west, the Durance to the north and the sea to the south, with a less articulated border by the Massif de Ste-Baume to the east. It is in itself so chock-full of variations that it can be taken as a microcosm for the rest of Provence.

The western part of the Bouches-du-Rhône is characterised by an abundance of plains filled with alluvial deposits. To the north are subcomtadine plains cut off from the rest of the *département* by the ragged Alpilles chain. To the south lies the Crau, a vast field of smooth pebbles polished by the river that once ran through it. South of that, along the coastline and to the extreme west,

Preceding pages: vineyard village of Gigondas. **Left,** cherries; and **right,** the Grand Canyon de Verdon.

are the wet plains of the Rhône Delta, commonly known as the Camargue. So unique from the rest of Provence is this latter's sea-level and marshy land that it is often referred to as a region in its own right.

The eastern section of the Bouches-du-Rhône is more mountainous, alternating with synclinal basins. The Ste-Victoire Mountain Range is separated from the Etoile chain by the Arc Valley. Beneath them, the Huveaune Valley and Marseille Basin lean up against the Ste-Baume Massif and the Marseillevey Range.

Most of this area's steep cliffs are composed of limestone, and some peaks reach up to over 1,000 metres. Along the coast, these

vated land, as do wheat fields. Market goods include garlic, tomatoes, courgettes (zucchini) and asparagus.

The Vaucluse bears a certain resemblance to the Bouches-du-Rhône. It also lies along the Rhône to the west and is bordered on one side (the south) by the Durance. Much of its land is flat plain, called the Comtat Venaissin, and it boasts a wide valley, the Coulon, to the south.

But the Vaucluse is also distinctly different from its southern neighbour. The bulk of its area is consumed by the Vaucluse Plateau, which is hemmed in by the imposing Ventoux Massif to the north. Mount Ventoux is, at 6,263 ft (1,909 metres), the highest

mountains create narrow valleys penetrated by the sea and called *calanques*.

Overall, the *département* is dry and rugged, with vegetation ranging from cypress trees to Aleppo and Norway pines and low shrubs to heathland; 256,000 acres (103,600 hectares) are under forest.

A combination of abundant sun and mineral-rich soil have helped to make this *département* France's top producer of fruit and vegetables. Although neither olive nor almond trees are indigenous – the first was brought from Greece, the latter from the Orient – they dominate large portions of the 445,000 acres (180,000 hectares) of culti-

peak in the region.

The Vaucluse Plateau merges into the Albion Plateau to the north. The latter is speckled with miscellaneous fissures that lead down to a vast network of underground caves. Rainwater spills down through these holes, collects in the caves, then runs off into another underground network of rivers. The rivers, in turn, flow along beneath the permeable limestone that composes the plateau, emerging here and there in springs like that at the legendary Fontaine de Vaucluse.

The springs are not all that set the Vaucluse apart. Its land is also, overall, more lush and generous than that of the Bouches-du-Rhône. Equally fertile and as highly cultivated, its premiere products correspond to the *département's* more luxuriant nature: melons, wine, lavender and strawberries.

The Var, on the other hand, shares more of the rougher aspects of the Bouches-du-Rhône. Much of its land is acutely dry, and drought is a constant threat to its residents. Wedged in between the Mediterranean to the south and southeast, the Bouches-du-Rhône to the west and Alpine foothills to the north and northeast, the Var is largely occupied by the deep forests of the Massif des Maures. Indeed, the Var is the most heavily wooded *département* in all of France.

Nonetheless, shrubby grasslands climb up

and down rocky slopes in some parts, making the Var an excellent spot for raising goats and sheep. By the coast, the massif pushes up against the sea creating a natural *corniche* where many of the famed hilltowns of the French Mediterranean waterfront are perched. Offshore are a number of islands included within the Iles d'Hyères.

Lying to the north of the Var, in between the Vaucluse to the west and the Alpes-Maritimes to the east, are the Alpes-de-Haute-Provence. This is an interesting region that wavers between being Provençal and Alpine. It also possesses one of the greatest natural wonders of the Provence region, the Grand Canyon de Verdon, which is, as its name suggests, an enormous canyon filled with turquoise-blue water from the Verdon River.

As soon as you enter the Alpes-de-Haute-Provence, you know it. Although it grows much the same products as the rest of Provence and is dominated to the south by a plateau (the Valensole) much like the Vaucluse, this region possesses an unmistakably Alpine feeling of physical remoteness. The further north you go, the more Alpine the land becomes, as it gradually assumes the flat-coloured, treeless folds of the Massif des Ecrins in the Alps proper.

The Alpes-Maritimes oscillate between the parched and rocky plateaux of the Var and the full-fledged ridges of the Alpes-de-Haute-Provence. On the eastern side, it is equally influenced by the mellowing Italian Alps. Its coastline is the most individual: first cliffs, then pebbles, then widening out into flat sandy beaches.

Along with the Var, the Alpes-Maritimes lives in constant dread of fire. In August 1987 alone, one fire ravaged more than 20,000 acres of forest, killed two and injured 100, and drove some 2,000 inhabitants from their homes. The dry shrub land makes unfortunate but excellent tinder.

One thing that all the *départements* share is dazzling light from a potent sun that never seems to stop shining. Farmers delight in the long growing season, and painters revel in the magical glow that surrounds the land. Another unifying characteristic is the infamous mistral. This wild and indefatigable northern wind sweeps down over almost the entire region between late autumn and early spring, although the western and central sections are generally the worst hit. Fittingly, its name is derived from the Provençal word for master, *mestre.* Its violent, chilling gales are created whenever a depression develops over the Mediterranean.

Learning about all the different geographies contained within Provence demands diligence, but the information is essential to understanding the Provençal world. Everything – the history, the economy, the characters of the people – centres around the land in this region where the earth is all.

PROVINCIA.
La Provence.

MARIS MEDITERRANEI

Petrus Kærius Cælavit

Provence has never lacked new admirers eager to conquer its land. Ligurians, Celts, Greeks, Romans, Teutons, Cimbrians, Visigoths, Saracens, Franks – they all had their day under the warm Provençal sun.

The region's strategic position along the Mediterranean, providing the northern Europeans with access to the sea and the southern Europeans, Africans and Middle Easterners with access to the northern Europeans, brought century after century of new colonisations and settlements before France

vence with Mesolithic development. The nearby coastal shell-midden and fishing sites of Ile Maire and Ile Riou have offered up pottery belonging to the middle Neolithic period of the fifth millennium BC.

Unfortunately, further study into the earliest settlements faces an unsurmountable obstacle, for most of the Stone-Age sites were submerged during the post-glacial rise in sea level. Scientists, nonetheless, are able to agree on two interesting facts.

The first is that – like their descendants –

became the stable entity it is today.

The great Rhône, which rushes down through Provence and tumbles out into the Mediterranean, offered added incentive to settlers. The Greeks supposedly used the river as a trade route to tin-producing Cornwall, and the Romans were quick to recognise its value as a means of communication between their many conquests. Not until the invention of the railway did the Rhône's attraction to traders and travellers diminish.

Even in prehistoric times, the area was popular. Archaeological sites at Châteauneuf-les-Martigues and the Baume Longue within the Bouches-du-Rhône area link Pro-

these early Provençals were as involved in growing cereals as they were in hunting. All the elements of an agricultural economy were in place by 5000 BC, although it was probably not until 4000 BC that agriculture became the firm subsistence base.

Secondly, also like their descendants, communications between different settlements around the area were fluid. These early inhabitants were remarkably mobile. Most Stone-Age settlements were found in the arable lands of the Provençal basins and on the coastal plain of Languedoc, but caves discovered further inland that seemed to have been used as transit sites suggest that there was a well-spread economic system.

More evidence of early human habitation, in the form of rock carvings and skeletons, has turned up in the region, dating back to over a quarter of a million years BC. Curious tourists can visit the lagoon-surrounded spot of St-Blaise, near Martigues, where excavations have revealed a parade of inhabitants from 700 to 50 BC. For those less inclined to wandering around half-ruined spots in the hot sun, the Sault Museum has a fine collection of Stone-Age artifacts.

disparate village settlements and scratched whatever living they could from the rocky land around them. Early cultural bonds between the different Ligurian outposts, which stretched from Catalonia through Provence to the base of the Swiss Alps, can be whittled down to a propensity for flat burial graves and a special skill with razor design. Eventually, however, the Ligurians were "Celticised," although genetically they were related to neither the Gauls nor the Celts.

Even if the shape of their heads may elude

Historically, however, the area didn't become active until the advent of the Ligurians. It's difficult to pinpoint the origin of these people. Some believe all Ligurians descended from the Iberians in Spain, others insist that only some were linked to the Iberians. The term usually refers to anyone living around the Mediterranean as the Neolithic Age spilled over into the Iron Age.

The Ligurians certainly didn't act like a structured group. They lived in small and

historians, we do know that these later Ligurians were a tough people whose taste for piracy annoyed the Romans. Posidonius, the 2nd-century BC historian, said of them: "...daily hardships are such that life is truly difficult for these people whose bodies, as a result, are skinny and shrivelled. It sometimes happens that a woman gives birth to her child in the fields, covers the little one with leaves, and then returns to her work so that a day will not be lost."

One thing the Ligurians did enjoy was a fair amount of anonymity from outside influences. The Phocaean Greeks would change that, however, in the 6th century BC.

Preceding pages: Provence under the Romans. Left, prehistoric graffiti in the Mercantour. Above, Ligurian and Roman ruins at Glanum.

Pl. VII.

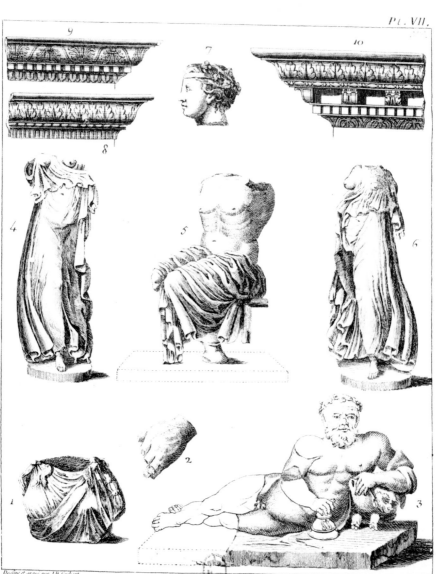

FRAGMENS DÉCOUVERTS, en 1788 et 1789, DANS LE THÉÂTRE ANTIQUE D'ARLES.

THE ARRIVAL OF CIVILISATION

Ici
Vers L'An 600 Avant J.C.
Des Marins Grecs Ont Abordés
Venant De Phocée
Ils Fonderent Marseille
D'Où Rayonna En Occident
La Civilisation
– Plaque on Quai des Belges, Marseille

Marseille, it might be argued, was the birthplace of Western civilisation on the European continent. It was to this marshy bay that Ionian Greeks from Phocaea set sail in the early 6th century BC.

According to legend, the Phocaeans cemented their interest in what was to become Marseille with a marriage. Gyptis, the daughter of the local Ligurian king, was in the process of choosing a husband when they arrived. A gathering of hopeful suitors waited as she decided to whom she would give the cup of wine that indicated her choice. When Protis, the captain of the Greek sailing party, stepped forward, she handed him the chalice.

The Phocaeans formed a happy alliance with the locals. They had come for economic purposes, not battle, and quickly set up a successful trading post. Their new colony, Massalia, soon became the most important commercial centre along the coast and a flourishing republican city-state in its own right. During its heyday in the mid-4th century BC, the Phocaean presence spread throughout the area. Some of the cities founded were Nikaia (Nice), Antipolis (Antibes), Citharista (La Ciotat), Olbia (Hyères) and Athenopolis (St-Tropez).

Pytheas, the Greek responsible for our modern method of measuring latitude and for explaining the tides, was actually a 4th-century Massalian. He expanded the Phocaean world view by visiting the British Isles and the Baltic. Another Massalian navigator, Euthymenius, explored the west coast of Africa around 350 BC.

During this period, Massalia was still very much a Greek city, although independent in nature. The late 3rd century BC, however,

witnessed a budding relationship with Rome. When Hannibal, making his way up from Spain towards the Alps, appeared on the plains of Provence with his elephants, the Phocaeans were quick to join forces with the already outraged Romans. This alliance grew steadily to the point where, in 212 BC, Massalia switched over to the Roman form of municipal government.

For the moment, the friendship with Rome proved beneficial. The northern and warlike Celts, Ligurians and Celto-Ligurians had been watching the prosperous Phocaeans with envy for some time and banded together in 125 BC to seize the Massalian riches. Overwhelmed, the Phocaeans were able to turn to the Romans for help.

In response, Caius Sextius Calvinius marched over a whole Roman army. A particularly bloody three-year war ensued but, in the end, the Romans prevailed. By that time Marius had discovered that he liked the area. He stayed on to found a city called Aquae Sextiae (Aix-en-Provence) on what was formerly a Celtic stronghold.

The Romans, as a sign of generosity, decided not to disturb the Massalian control of the coastal strip that reached from the Rhône to what is now Monaco. They increased their own interest in the region, however, and went on to defeat in 102 BC some more northern barbarians, the wild Teutons and savage Cimbrians.

Before too long, the Romans had replaced the Phocaeans as lords of the region, which they called Provincia Romana and from which the modern name "Provence" is derived. Massalia, however, continued to thrive and to operate fairly autonomously. Now no longer just a trading post, the city became famous as an intellectual centre, whose universities rivalled those of Athens.

The good times were not to last. Massalia made the fatal error of siding with Pompey against Caesar during Rome's civil war. After his victory, in 49 BC, Caesar punished the city by making it a Roman vassal. He further crushed the colony by strengthening the port of Arelate (Arles) and using its inhabitants to besiege Massalia.

Arles was not a new town, having been

Left, Roman fragments from Arles.

founded back in the 6th century BC by the Greeks. During the 2nd century BC, Marius had built a canal that connected Arles's position on the Rhône to the Fos Gulf, making the city a handy river and maritime port.

The waterway had helped exploit the Arlesians' particular talent for building rafts supported by goat bladders. To add to its fortunes, this city was situated beside the highway that linked Italy with Spain, the Roman Aurelian Way.

With the fall of Massalia, Arles became the most important city in the area. Rome converted the whole south of France into a Roman province and made Arles its capital, with a secondary city at Cimiez above Nice.

the arrival of The Word in the northern Mediterranean. Many believe that it was to these shores that Mary Magdalene and Martha – along with her resurrected brother Lazarus; Mary Jacoby, sister to the Virgin Mary; Mary Salome, mother to the apostles James and John; Saints Maximinius and Sidonius; and the servant Sarah – fled after the crucifixion of Christ.

Buffeted by the waves, without sail or oar, this saintly company arrived on the sandy shores of the town now called, appropriately, Les-Stes-Maries-de-la-Mer. Supposedly, they erected a small chapel to the Virgin, then went their separate ways. Mary Magdalene, for one, found a cave up in the hills of

The Romans would remain in Provence for another 600 years. Mostly these were years of peace and prosperity. Temples and bridges and baths and theatres were built, to the delight of modern-day tourist associations. During the reign of Augustus in the latter half of the 1st century, culture and the arts as well as trade expanded considerably. Slowly, due to their firm control and imposing political machine, the Romans managed to unite what had once been a scramble of disparate trading posts. One sign of this was the growth of a regional language, Provençal, derived from Latin.

As legend tells it, the 1st century also saw

Ste-Baume where she lived as a hermit until her death 30 years later.

Whether or not Saint Trophimus was among this group differs according to the source, but he is widely credited with the introduction of Christianity to the northern countries. Presumably sent by his friend, Saint Peter, he headed up to Arles where he built the first Christian church in Gaul – named St-Trophime and still standing today.

By the time the Roman Empire fell in AD 476, Roman civilisation had left a permanent

Above, Charles Martel squashes the Saracen army.

mark on the land. For one thing, the entire region had been Christianised. The frugal and industrious character of the Provençal people today is also widely accredited to their Roman ancestry. The Phocaeans, and more specifically the Massalians, were enthusiasts for the joys of the flesh. The Romans, however, were much more attentive to cultivating the hard dry soil and building up sufficient fortifications, which probably had something to do with their ability to dominate the area for so long.

But the fall did come – and with it the Visigoths. Their interest in Arles came as no surprise, since they had been routinely attacking the city since the earlier part of the fifth century. They quickly assumed all of the area south of the Durance River, while the Burgundians took over to the north.

The Visigoths didn't do much for the region, but they weren't to last long either. In 507, they were firmly trodden upon by the Franks. To escape these northern strongmen, they ceded their Provençal conquests to the Ostrogoths from Italy, who also appropriated all the Burgundian lands for themselves.

The Franks did not agree that the Ostrogoths deserved Burgundy and proceeded to make it their own in 534. The Ostrogoths incurred further problems by alienating the Byzantine Empire. In return for Frankish neutrality, these early Italians had to hand over their Provençal territory in 536.

The Franks now had an awful lot of land to supervise – too much for one authority to manage. They decided to split up the territory, uniting northern Provence with Arles, Toulon and Nice to Burgundy but giving the strip including Marseille, Avignon and much of the coast to the kings of Austrasia.

Representatives, known as *patrices*, were appointed within each region by the central Frankish ministry. The *patrices*, however, proved more interested in promoting their own independence and didn't hesitate to bond with foreign elements if it would protect their own autonomy.

One such group were the Saracens. For the first couple of centuries under Frankish rule, Provence had fared pretty well commercially. Nonetheless, their integration with the rest of France was minimal at best, and when the Arabs arrived in Provence in 732, not all of the natives complained.

In 732, two Saracen armies besieged Arles. Encouraged by their victory, they continued northward until they encountered the famed French hero Charles Martel in Poitiers. He expelled these heathen intruders from all of Provence in 729.

Martel was less than happy with the Provençal ambivalence towards the Saracens, and throughout the battle against the Moors, he treated the region as hostilely as an enemy. Between his armies and those of the Saracens, countless Provençals were slaughtered and whole cities were destroyed. Avignon was virtually wiped out.

Pepin the Short succeeded his father, and after him came Charlemagne. Each was careful to keep Provence under strict Frankish rule, but this did not prevent the return of the Moors in 813. Their new tactic was to approach by sea rather than via Spain, and it proved to be an effective strategy for about two more centuries.

Meanwhile, in the north, Charlemagne had created the Holy Roman Empire. With the Treaty of Verdun in 843, Provence was turned over to his grandson, Lothair I, as part of the "Middle Realm." When Lothair died, the region was labelled a separate kingdom and passed through the hands of several unmemorable rulers: his son Charles; the emperor Louis II, ruler of Italy; Charles the Bald; Boso, ruler of the Viennois; Boso's son Louis, who was to become king of Italy in 900; then Hugh of Arles, who handed it over to Rudolf II of Jurane Burgundy in the mid-10th century.

All these kingships and dukedoms did little to secure the area. As if they hadn't suffered enough under the Saracens, the Provençals soon had to deal with the Normans, who set out, in 859, to stake a claim in the south land. They levelled both Arles and Nîmes as well as much of the countryside before the fierce opposition of Gérard de Roussillon made them decide to head back to Scandinavia.

The departure of the Normans didn't give the region much respite, however, since the Saracens were soon to return. During the last part of the 9th century, the Saracen hold reached its apogee. The entire coastal area fell to their powers, and they marauded right on up into the Alps. Not until 1032 did William the Liberator – abetted by an attack of plague – finally eliminate the Saracen menace from Provence once and for all.

Although contained within the Holy German Empire, Provence was a fairly independent entity by the year 1000. Threats from outsiders subsided, giving the major cities of Arles and Avignon a chance to smooth their feathers and the entire region the opportunity to cultivate an identity.

The departure of the Saracens and Normans also left the Provençals with time and energy for internal squabbles. When Boso, Count of Arles in the mid10th century, died, he left control of Provence to his two sons, Rotbald and William. The former was Count of Arles and the latter Count of Avignon, and they ruled jointly over the region from their respective seats. By 1040, however, Rotbald's male line was extinct, and his inheritance moved into the female side of the family. This was the beginning of a long and unfortunate pattern. If Emma, the first lady in question, had known just what future troubles she was bringing by marrying into the house of Toulouse perhaps she would have opted for virginal sainthood instead. Unfortunately, she didn't.

When Bertrand of Arles died in 1093, with him passed the last direct male heirs from the line of Boso. Gerberge of Arles, sister of Bertrand, stepped forward to claim control, followed by Alix, heiress of Avignon. They were soon joined by Raymond IV, grandson to Emma of Toulouse.

The previously intact countship of Provence fell into turmoil. First, the countship of Forcalquier was carved out of the region and given to Alix. Then, in 1112, Gerberge turned her rights over to her daughter Douce. Not one to forsake family tradition, Douce complicated matters by marrying Catalan Ramon Berenguer III, count of Barcelona.

Within a year, Ramon had changed his name to the more-Gallic Raymond Berengar I and assumed the title of count-marquis to Provence. The Toulousians, outraged at his usurpation, contested his claim. They were soon joined by the house of Les Baux, whose own Raymond had married Douce's younger sister, Stephanie.

Left, ruins at Les Baux. **Above**, fresco from Pope's Palace in Avignon.

The Baux family was no insignificant enemy. The Provençal poet Mistral would later describe them as "eagles all – vassals never." Not known for their modesty, they traced their genealogy back to Balthazar, the Magi king, and implanted the star of Bethlehem on their arms. Before they got around to claiming control of Provence, *grâce à* Stephanie, the Bauxs had already subjugated, during the 11th century, some 80 towns and villages. As their power increased, they gathered up such titles as Prince of Orange,

Viscount of Marseille, Count of Avellinoad and Duke of Andria.

At the height of its splendour, the airy perch of the Baux fortress, which rises from a bare rock spar at 650 feet, was famed for its "Court of Love." Here, troubadours milled among the inhabitants – as many as 6,000 – composing passionate poems in praise of well-bred ladies. In return, the poets would receive a peacock's feather and a kiss.

But being hosts to the Court of Love didn't stop the Bauxs from being the bloodiest, cruellest group around. Their history is an unending catalogue of savagery. One prince suavely massacred the entire town of Courthézon; another was carved up in prison by his own wife; a third besieged the castle of his pregnant niece for the purpose of violating her bedchambers.

Perhaps most famed was the husband of Berangère des Baux who slew the poet Guillem de Cabestanh and gave his heart to his wife for dinner. Unknowingly, she ate the sweet meat and drank a goblet of his blood. In a rare show of conscience, after discovering the ingredients of the meal, she declared that so lovely were that meat and that drink that none other would defile her lips again – and threw herself off the top of Les Baux.

No one wanted to parley with the Bauxs, but the Barcelonians and the Toulousians did dating from that time. The lack of stern central authority promoted the rise of the feudal system. Grandiose castles were built, and the arts found ready patronage within courts other than Les Baux's.

The troubadours emerged as a direct result of feudalism. Wealthy heiresses, daughters to territorial lords, were married off for political and economic reasons rather than those of mutual lust. Once wed, they were left mostly to their own designs and, not unnaturally, welcomed the attentions of their husband's courtiers. The songs of love they inspired were considered a mere convention and harmless – although the courts were far from being models of chastity.

manage to sign an amicable treaty among themselves in 1125. This agreement gave everything south of the Durance River to the former and everything north of the river to the latter, with Avignon, Sorgues, Caumont and Le Thor to be shared. They seemed content with this solution, but the Bauxs continued to challenge the Barcelonians.

Throughout this period, the German kings – who, after all, were the real rulers of Provence – were in a constant state of confusion about whom they should recognise as vassal for the region. The greatest still visible evidence of the era's rampant instability are the numerous defensive *villages perchés*

The arts were not all that flourished within this period of lean control. Towns such as Arles, Avignon, Nice, Tarascon and Marseille reorganised as communal regimes under consular government and became independent forces in their own right. The opening up of the Levant by the Crusades and the disappearance of the Arab threat provoked a revival in commerce that added to their well-being.

A succession of Raymonds from Barcelona and Raymonds from Toulouse and

Above, St-Michel's 12th-century tympanum in Salon. **Right**, the Provençal language.

40

THE LANGUAGE OF THE TROUBADOURS

Never content to go along with the crowd, the people of Provence early on developed their own dialect and stuck with it even after the rise of the French-speaking Gauls. Provençal is a Romance language derived closely from the Latin spoken by the Roman conquerors of the 1st century BC.

In fact, the staying power of the language is good evidence of the profound cultural effect of the Romans. Many centuries after they had faded from power and had been replaced first by varied Germanic invasions then by the Franks, the Provençal language clung to its Latin attributes. Hardly any of the Germanic traits evident in French can be found in Provençal.

The feudal organisation of the Midi during the Middle Ages resulted in the fragmentation of Provençal into a variety of related but individual dialects. Nonetheless, a unified literary language, "Classical Provençal," was recognised from the 11th to 15th centuries. It was in this language that the poems of the troubadours were written.

The oldest piece of Provençal verse still extant is a 10th-century refrain attached to a Latin poem in a Vatican manuscript. But the earliest complete works to have survived the centuries are a set of poems by William IX, duke of Aquitaine. These poems consist of 11 different pieces, each written in stanzas and meant to be sung.

Almost certainly, William did not pioneer such work. More likely, his noble rank helped preserve his poetry when that of his predecessors and contemporaries fell into oblivion. The true creators of the troubadour-style literature were probably of much more modest social standing.

It is widely believed that the troubadours developed from the lowly class of jugglers. First they combined poetry with their acts and then, evolving into a more refined group of court residents, composed and recited their poetry unaccompanied by tricks. These poets were encouraged by the lonely wives of their noble patrons to develop the love songs that became the mark of the troubadour, and they eventually created the medieval convention of "courtly" love. Naturally, it's to be expected that some of the devotion lavished on the ladies of the court by the poets did not go unreturned. In general, however, the poets' lesser rank forced them to couch their words of praise in the most respectful manner, and their attentions were considered innocent – even convenient – by the men of the court, who more often than not had married for economic and territorial reasons rather than for those of love.

By the end of the 11th century, the troubadours had become a vital institution of a much higher status than their ignoble predecessors. Among the most famous were Bernart de Ventadour, patronised by Eleanor of Aquitaine; Arnaut Daniel, inventor of the sestina; Jaufre Rudel de Blaye, poet of the *amor de lonh*, or "love from afar"; Giraut de Borneil, creator of the *trobar clus*, or "closed" style; Folquet de Marseille, a troubadour who became a monk, then an abbot, and finally bishop of Toulouse; Bertran de Born; and Peire d'Alvernhae. All in all, the works of over 460 troubadours have been preserved.

With the rooting out of the Cathares during the earlier part of the 13th century came the rise of the French Crown's control over Provence and the fall of the feudal lords. The troubadours were no longer able to make a happy living, and the use of Provençal as a literary language declined drastically.

Over the next few centuries, a handful of valiant artists continued to write in Provençal, and the literature saw a mild revival during the 16th century in what is generally referred to as the Provençal Renaissance. Nothing, however, could compare with the glory of the medieval period.

Nothing, that is, until the advent of the chauvinist society of the Félibrige, established by Frédéric Mistral and a handful of concerned Provençal writers in the mid-19th century. Mistral was influenced by the schoolmaster and poet Joseph Roumanille – a native of St-Rémy, who turned to composing in his dialect so that his mother would be able to read his work – and he dedicated his enormous talent towards "stirring this noble race to a renewed awareness of its glory." His devotion was rewarded in 1905 with a Nobel Prize for literature.

Raymonds from Provence, plus a Spanish Alfonso, traded the countship throughout the 12th century. Eventually, the three claimant parties decided to split the region up definitively. Toulouse became Languedoc, Barcelona was named Catalonia, and Forcalquier evolved into a new, more limited Provence.

In 1209, just to add a little more spice, a huge French army stormed down south to rout out the Albigensians. Also known as Cathares, these ill-fated people supported a radical departure from traditional Christian dogma and were considered dangerous heretics. They also possessed a fair amount of widely coveted treasures. Although the Albigensians were located within Languedoc,

enced a greater taste of authority with the advent of Raymond Berengar VII. In between proving his might, this Raymond begat a bevy of daughters, all of whom made brilliant and fateful matches. The eldest, Marguerite, became queen of France after marrying the prince who would later be known as Saint Louis. The second, Eleanor, landed King Henry III of England. The third, Sancie, married Richard, Duke of Cornwall, who would eventually become the Germanic emperor. This left Beatrice, the youngest.

Although her three older sisters must have had ample charm to marry as they did (some credit must be given to the stature of their homeland, Provence, at the time), Beatrice

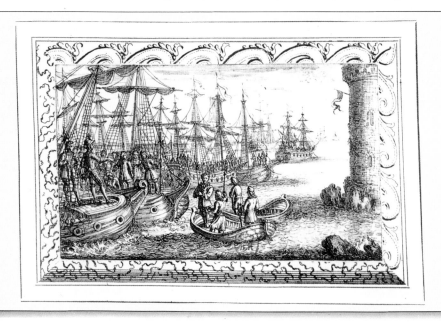

the Toulousian connection to Provence and, more particularly, Avignon caused that city to be besieged and belittled by Louis IX of France in 1226.

After the Albigensian episode, the Toulousians were eager to get back on the good side of the French kingdom. In 1229 Raymond VII of Toulouse wed his daughter to Louis IX's brother, Alphonse of Poitier. By way of additional placation, the Toulousian territories, including the Comtat-Venaisson region north of the Durance in Provence, also were passed along to the French.

Unlike the area under Toulousian control, that under the Provençal countship experi-

was considered to be the sweetest and most beautiful of all. Crowned suitors flocked to her side. Yet, in the end, she chose Charles of Anjou, brother to the French king.

Beatrice's sisters ridiculed her unadorned pate until 1265, when Charles was crowned king of Naples and Sicily. He also became king of Jerusalem and, when Raymond VII left Provence to Beatrice, he was named Count Charles I of Provence. The sisters were no longer laughing. Even less pleased were Charles's new subjects, who considered him a foreigner – ever a dirty word in Provençal. In between embarking on Crusades, Charles had to concentrate on squashing rebellions, with Marseille the first to go.

Marseille, that sturdy determined city, had prospered during the Crusades. Its citizens had established new trading centres in Asia Minor and North Africa that resulted in increased revenues, and Saint Louis's departure in 1248 from nearby Aigues-Mortes on his seventh Crusade had bolstered the economic activity back home. They held out against Charles the longest but eventually were subdued along with fellow rebels Arles and Avignon. Charles's final triumph in 1257 marked the end of the era of quasi-autonomy.

The new French dynasty provided long-missing stability. Charles's involvement with Naples and Sicily also heralded a revived link with Italy. Most of the succeeding noble families set up housekeeping in Italy and appointed administrators to lord over the state in their stead. In 1271, Philip III of France turned over the Comtat-Venaisson – inherited after the Albigensian Crusades – to the Rome-based Holy See. And Charles II, who took over in 1285, instigated many legal reforms based on Italian models. His successor, Robert, king of Naples and count of Provence from 1309 to 1343, installed *syndicats* or municipal councils.

Another example of the new link with Italy is the visit of Petrarch. The famous Italian poet made his residence in Fontaine de Vaucluse from 1337 to 1353. During that time he composed the 366 poems and sonnets of the *Canzonière*, inspired by the beloved Laura. He had already caught his first glimpse of her in a church in Noves while visiting Provence 10 years earlier.

When Robert died in 1343, his granddaughter Jeanne took over. Jeanne is alternately known as "the Good Queen" and as "the Wicked Queen." She appears to have possessed some of that old Massallian attitude towards free love and to have exercised it liberally during her lifetime. Married first to Andrew of Hungary, it is believed she had him assassinated. She soon moved on from her second husband, Louis of Tarento, to wed the Adonis-like Jaime II of Mallorca. Eleven years her junior, Jaime was unfortunately mad, due to having been imprisoned

in an iron cage for 13 years. Her fourth spouse, however, Otto of Brunswick, seems to have lived and died normally.

Despite her many opportunities, Jeanne never did come up with a male heir. Her cousin Charles of Durazzo became the logical successor but, based on a deep-rooted dislike for him, she adopted Louis of Anjou, brother to King Charles V of France, and named him heir instead. This created new possibilities for internal strife. It also incited Charles of Durazzo to live up to her estimation of him. In 1382, he had her kidnapped to a lonely castle in the Apennines and, tied to her bedposts, strangled. Another war for control of the dukedom ensued.

FRANCESCO PETRARCA
FIORENTINO CELEBRATIS.^{MO}
POETA *nacque nel MCCCIV* *Laureato nel CAMPIDOGLIO*
L'Anno MCCCXLI. mori in ARQVA nel *Distretto di PADOVA nel MCCCLXXIV.*

Meanwhile, the region was in the process of recovering from an invasion by Languedoc armies, who took Tarascon and besieged Arles and Aix before Neapolitan forces finally overcame them. To pay for these wars – and some say to be pardoned for killing her first husband – Jeanne had had to sell Avignon to the Holy See in 1348. Avignon had already been the seat of the papacy for some 40 years.

In 1309, Pope Clement V, a native Frenchman, had decided that he had had enough of the constant bickering of Rome. When King Philip the Fair of France invited him to return home, he quickly gathered his robes and

Left, Saint Louis leaves for the Crusades from Aigues-Mortes. **Above**, Petrarch found love in Provence.

headed for the Comtat Venaisson on the lower Rhône. His removal and that of his court to Avignon began what would be called the "second Babylonian captivity of the church." Five more popes would follow in his lead. The third, Benedict XII, was widely criticised for being avaricious, egotistical, uncharitable and prejudiced. He also instigated the erection of the famed Palais de Papes with its large number of secret escape routes. The enormous Palais was well over an acre in size, supposedly to exemplify the absolute power of the church. But Benedict's successor, Clement VI, decided that it still didn't properly represent the grandeur of the church. He added a more ornate section,

bringing the total size up to 2.6 acres (1 hectare). Clement VI was also the one to purchase Avignon from Jeanne for 80,000 gold florins.

In 1376, the Florentines sent a Dominican sister from Siena to intercede with the Pope in their favour, having perpetrated a failed attempt at annexing the papal territories. Saint Catherine succeeded not only in gaining their pardon but also in convincing Gregory XI, last in this string of French popes, to return to Rome. Gregory agreed to the homecoming in the belief that reinhabiting Rome would improve negotiations with the Byzantine church, thus increasing the possibility of holding onto the papal territories. He may well have been right, but this didn't mean that the Palais des Papes would remain empty for long.

The next elected pope, Urban VI, an Italian, so displeased a large number of French cardinals that they decided to call for a new vote. They selected a new Pope, a native of Geneva to be called Clement VII, in 1378. The next year, Clement VII retreated to Avignon, and the Great Schism, lasting from 1378 to 1417, was born.

Now there were two popes – one in Avignon and one in Rome. This confusing situation continued for several bitter decades, although not all of these years were spent in Avignon. Benedict XIII was driven out in 1403, and the city withdrew from the controversy and fell back into a peaceful life. Its heightened stature as the seat of the papal court, however, never diminished.

Meanwhile, the rest of Provence had degenerated into a state of constant civil war following the death of Jeanne. The area was already reeling from the arrival of the first great plague in 1348. A semblance of peace and order was restored only after the fortuitous murder of Charles of Durazzo and some skilful manoeuvring on the part of Louis of Anjou's widow, Marie of Blois, in 1348, whose son, Louis II, proved to be a capable ruler. Louis also fathered the most beloved count of Provence, René of Anjou, popularly known as "Good King René."

To this day, René is remembered with love and admiration by the Provençals. A self-styled philosopher and humanist, he devoted himself to promoting the economic revival of Provence and its ports and to reinstating interest in the arts. He showed himself to be a tolerant, amicable leader, whose steady control permitted cultural life to flourish.

René's talents, however, did not extend to the martial arts. He failed so miserably in battles elsewhere that he was impelled to relinquish his right to designate his own heir. Instead, he was forced by the crown to name the unlikely Charles III, comte de Maine and chronic invalid.

Charles assumed the throne in 1480 but died a year later. He left his countship to Louis XI of France.

Above, Pope Benedict XII's palace in Avignon. **Right**, the beloved "Good King René".

RENATVS DEI GRATIA. SICILIÆ. etc REX.

The first steps towards unification with France were taken when the three Estates of Provence (the Clergy, Nobility and Commoners) accepted Louis XI, King of France, as their ruler in 1482. Five years later, their union was cemented by a treaty supposedly designed to protect the autonomy of Provence. The constitutional equality of the countship and the kingdom was ratified, and the formerly independent state was allowed to retain a substantial number of individual liberties and traditional customs.

it as a capital. Not surprisingly, it was in Aix that the treaty of 1487 was signed.

It was also in Aix that Louis XII decided to establish a parliament, of French origin, 14 years later. The Parlement de Provence was introduced as a supreme court of justice with limited political authority and as a place where all the estates would meet. Most of the native Provençals, however, felt that its real purpose was to impose stiff tax increases.

The affiliation with France may have finally brought a firm authoritarian command

Marseille had had its day under the Greeks, as had Arles under the Romans. With the advent of the counts of Provence and the papal residency, Avignon had sprung forth in glory. Under Good King René, however, Aix-en-Provence emerged as the star city of Provence. After losing Anjou to Louis XI, René and his beloved second wife, Jeanne, retired to this lovely town, remaining there until his death in 1480.

A metropolitan see since the beginning of Christianity and home to a venerable university, Aix did not diminish in importance with the passing of the good king. The French chose to recognise its eminence and treated

to the region, but it did not usher in any new-found peace. The martial escapades of Francis I engendered the invasion of Provence by German Emperor Charles V in 1524 and then again in 1536. Meanwhile, annoyed by constant friction with Provence, Francis I increased the curtailment of the region's independence. In 1535, he issued the Edict of Joinville, which severely limited the freedom of the Estates, squashed the Provençal-originated *conseil éminent* and strengthened the control of the hated Parlement over the local judiciaries.

In the end, Provence was left with more or less the same status as any other French province. But even this did not satisfy Francis: four years later he unfurled his Edict of Villers-Coterets, which introduced a new tactic in the suppression of Provence. This decree installed French as the language to be used in all administrative laws in Provence, supplanting the native Provençal dialect. Although the ancient language was hardly wiped out by this one action, the new law did initiate its eventual decline.

Despite the repression by France, individual families continued to thrive. Large numbers of châteaux, still standing as silent witnesses today, were built, and small fortunes amassed. Concerned that these wealthy inhabitants might try to rival the French nobility, the Parlement turned its Gallic eye towards their belittlement. Deciding that the châteaux, with their rounded corner towers, were potentially aggressive as well as presumptious, they commanded that all towers be truncated to the level of the main roof. The stunted leftovers are still visible, dubbed *poivrière* (meaning literally "pepper pots") by the locals.

The arts and intellectual life also continued to prosper. The troubadours had faded from eminence, although the 16th century saw a certain revival in native literature, mostly in the form of religious mystery plays, and the period is sometimes called the Provençal Renaissance. New champions sprung up in their place, often pioneering more scientific fields.

Nostradamus (Michel de Notredame) was born in St-Rémy-de-Provence in 1503. He first studied medicine and, after extended travels, developed a successful remedy against the plague. He kept the cure a secret, however, which proved unpopular with his colleagues. They voted to have him expelled from the medical profession.

Nostradamus next turned to astrology. In 1555, he produced the famed *Centuries*, a book filled with predictions on the future of the world, written in cryptic quatrains. Interpreters claim that he foretold such 20th-century events as World War II and the holocaust, as well as the 1963 assassination of US President John F. Kennedy.

A second, less sensational but equally productive Provençal was Adam de Craponne (1527–76). Born in Salon-de-Provence amid the dry Crau plains, De Craponne was the gifted civil engineer largely responsible for bringing fertility to the region. He designed and had constructed the irrigation canal that diverts water from the Durance River through the Lamanon Gap.

Up north, the French continued to devise ways to fetter Provençal activity. Not content to concentrate on local legislation or the lives of the up-and-coming, Baron Megnier d'Oppède led one of the bloodiest campaigns in the history of France against a religious sect called the Vaudois.

The unfortunate Vaudois were descendants of the Waldensians, who had originally formed in protest against the growth of papal wealth and property under Pope Sylvester. Waldensian dogma related vaguely to the Manichaean system of duality with its emphasis on severe asceticism. An earlier branch had already been literally

Left, Adam de Craponne brought water to the Crau Plain. **Above**, Provençal astrologer and prophet Nostradamus.

burnt out of existence – in the form of the Cathares.

Most offensive among Waldensian tenets were their beliefs that any layman could consecrate the sacrament and that the Roman church was not the true church of Christ. Nonetheless, up until this point, the Vaudois had managed to escape the iron arm of the Church by living quietly and fairly inaccessibly amidst the Luberon mountains. The French did not let this deter their zeal, and the Vaudois fell victim to endless massacre. They had been virtually decimated by the year 1545.

The slaughter of the Vaudois was only a trial run for what was to come. The brutal

Wars of Religion, brought on by the Reformation and occurring between the Catholics and the Protestants, consumed the greater part of the second half of the 16th century. The region witnessed countless atrocities until finally the arrival of a second, equally horrible enemy – the second plague, in 1582 – caused the Provençal "heretics" to weaken. Under that devastating epidemic, even argumentative Marseille finally submitted to Henry IV of France.

Marseille had steadily added to its wealth and significance since the profitable years of the Crusades. The port city reached new heights during the early 1500s. Being the

bullwark of France's Mediterranean coast, it had been virulently threatened by Charles V of Germany but had managed to summon up a successful group campaign against him. Even the fair damsels of the city are said to have participated in the defence, as commemorated by the Rue des Dames.

Triumphant in its resistance to Charles, the city's pride, infused with an inherent spirit of determination and independence, found new fodder. Again and again during the next couple of centuries, Marseille would emerge as the most vociferous of political entities, generally leading the other main cities of Provence in revolt.

With the Protestants under control, with many dead and with Marseille temporarily enfeebled, the 17th century rolled in on a more closely aligned Provence. Local authorities, however, displayed no sudden affinity for the Crown. Minor rebellions continued to flare up, often led by the bull-headed Marseillaises. Then, when in 1630 the French government tried to abolish the Estates' control over taxation, the parliament at Aix simply refused.

Under the threat of overwhelming Gallic violence, the parliament voted in an extraordinary subsidy the following year, but the Estates had already sounded their own death knell. After a particularly obstreperous showing in 1639, the Estates were simply no longer invited to attend the assemblies of parliament. Not until a century and a half later was their voice reinstated.

New dissension against the French emerged in the form of the Provençal Fronde. Unlike its northern brother, which pitted itself against royal absolutism from 1648 to 1653, the Provençal Fronde concentrated its venom on hostilities between the parliament and the governor. Only later did the struggle become one between the Sabreurs (adherents of the Rebel princes) and the Canivets (royalists).

The Southern Fronde was supressed in 1653, but discontent persisted in Marseille. The defiant city revolted in 1659, only to be stripped of all its remaining rights after its defeat the following year. To ensure his control over the uppity Marseillaises, Louis XIV personally ordered the construction of Fort St-Nicholas, from which both the town and port could be closely monitored. A year later, undaunted by their neighbour's lack of success, the citizens of Nice also took up arms. The town was subsequently occupied by the royal army as well.

In 1673, the beleaguered Louis XIV established the *généralité* of Aix, under a superintendent whose job it was to manage the province. From 1691 on, this office was united with that of the premier presidency of the parliament, giving the Crown effective legal control over the region.

The French king also continued his interest in Marseille, ironically to that city's ultimate benefit. He expanded the urban area threefold and encouraged the growth of seaborne trade by making it a free port. Marseillaise commerce continued to blossom during the 18th century, reaching its peak just before the Revolution of 1789.

It is probably due to the greatly broadened status of the Marseillaise port that the third and deadliest of the plagues hit Provence in the early 1720s. It was brought by trading ships from the east, and more than 100,000 people died – half of them from Marseille alone. Whole towns disappeared. Traces of an enormous wall built in the desperate effort to contain the disease can still be seen near Venasque in the Vaucluse.

The newly organised authority under the *généralité* led to improved relations between Provence and the French crown during the early 18th century. Invasions into the region by Austria and the Savoyards in 1707, then again in 1746, also helped force internal squabbles to a back burner. Toulon and Nice suffered particularly badly during the foreign incursions. Both ports were hardily ravaged by the Austro-Sardinian maritime forces before their final defeat in 1747.

By this time, the Crown was facing more serious upheaval than that provided by the arrogant Provençals. The discontent that would lead to the permanent removal of monarchical rule in France was brewing throughout the country.

The people of Provence embraced the ensuing Revolution with open arms and an extraordinary excess of blood-letting, even for that violent era. Their interest in the new constitution stemmed not so much from a desire for social reform as the hope that it might offer a chance to regain lost powers.

Left, protective clothing against the plague. Above, bust of "La Marseillaise."

Marseille was an especially enthusiastic adherent. Before long, a guillotine graced the city's main street of La Canebière, and the cobblestones ran red with spilt blood. As many supposed Royalists were decapitated in Marseille as in Paris itself.

On 11 April 1789, the Société Patriotique des Amis de la Constitution was formed on the Rue Thubaneau in Marseille, and it was there that Rouget de Lisle's *Le Chant des Marseilles* – now the bloody national anthem for all of France – was first sung. Meanwhile, it was from the small nearby town of Martigues that the *tricolore* – now France's national flag – originated. Martigues consists of three boroughs, each with

its own standard. Ferrieres's is blue, Ile St-Genest's is white, and Jonquières's is red. United, they created the red, white and blue flag adopted by the Revolutionaries.

The French Revolution in 1789 did not, however, return to Provence its autonomy of earlier centuries. Instead, the region lost what little independence it had been able to retain. The local government was completely dissolved in 1790, and the region was divided into three *départements*: the Bouches-du-Rhône, the Var and the Basse-Alpes. The Vaucluse was added three years later, after the French annexation of the papal territory in the Comtat-Venaisson.

THROUGH AN IMPRESSIONIST'S EYE

Among Provence's greatest contributions to the Revolution was the young Corsican captain, Napoleon Bonaparte. The famed Napoleon first came to notice in Toulon, when he managed to wrest that important port city from an occupying Royalist-Spanish-British force in 1793. Three years later, as a commanding general at the age of 27, it was from Nice that Napoleon set off on his first glorious Italian campaign.

Although the Provençals had embraced Napoleon the military genius, they were

in 1814–15 following Napoleon's defeat. It was not until 1860 that Napoleon II managed to return these lands to France.

Nonetheless, the 19th century brought Provence the most peaceful period it had ever experienced. The subsequent revolutions of 1830 and 1848 and the new regimes that each heralded roused little interest from the southern regions. Provençals concentrated on expanding their economic structure.

The martial lull also permitted the arts to flourish in a way that they hadn't since the

much less enthused about Napoleon the Emperor. This same people, such eager participants in the early years of the Revolution, soon became staunch supporters of the returning Bourbon monarchy. Once again, blood flowed in the streets, as those suspected of being anti-Royalist were slaughtered with the same intensity as the anti-Revolutionaries had been under Jacobinism.

The Provençal antipathy towards Napoleon proved to be justified, for his ever-escalating wars finally resulted in the bequeathal of much of the eastern territory – Nice and the land up as far as the Var River – to Sardinia during the Congress of Vienna

days of Good King René. Poetry was rediscovered, and painters from colder climates became aware of the advantages of the Mediterranean environment. It was amidst this atmosphere that the Félibrige arose.

Founded in 1854, the Félibrige was created by the literary masters of the region out of concern for the preservation of their native tongue. Stripped of any political autonomy, the people of Provence had been further slighted by the removal of their dialect as Provence's official language. Unsurprisingly, the language had since then begun to slide into oblivion.

The idea behind the Félibrige was to encourage a revival of the language through the promotion of literary works written within the dialect rather than French. They also compiled a vast dictionary of Provençal called *Lou Tresor dóu Félibrige*.

At the head of the Félibrige was the renowned Provençal poet Frédéric Mistral. In 1859 he published the verse romance, *Mireio*, later set to music by Gounod, whose depiction of Provençal life gained recognition for the Félibrige. A half-century later, in 1905, Mistral was awarded the Nobel Prize

famous son of the south was Paul Cézanne. The child of a wealthy hatter-turned-banker and one of his work girls, Cézanne was born in Aix-en-Provence in 1839. He was educated at the local Collège Bourbon, where he developed a close friendship with another student, novelist Emile Zola. Although Zola was not born in the area, he also spent much of his youth in Aix.

While Zola committed himself to artistic pursuits, Cézanne struggled to become his father's successor. Eventually, his family

for literature. Ever true to the cause of artistic revival in Provence, he used his prize money to resuscitate the ethnographic Museon Arlaten in Arles.

Aside from Mistral, the original Félibrige included Joseph Roumanille who had been Mistral's own teacher and inspiration, the well-respected Avignonais printer Théodore Aubanel, and four contemporary Provençal poets of slightly lesser talent. Native painters also brought glory to the region. One most

Preceding pages: *Farmhouse in Provence* by Van Gogh. **Left**, *Houses in Provence* by Cézanne. **Above**, the poet Frédéric Mistral and his wife.

came to the realisation it would be better to allow him to pursue his painting. In 1863, he ventured north to join Zola in Paris. Once there, Cézanne's distaste for the "old school" soon led to his association with the revolutionary group of painters now known as the Impressionists. However, he eventually split from that group as well, believing their work to be too casual and lacking in an understanding of the "depth of reality."

Cézanne returned to Aix in 1870, where he would spend the rest of his years until his death in 1906. Some of his most celebrated works were completed during that time, based on Provençal models. Among these paintings are the series after Mont Ste-Victoire, which stands some 20 miles (32 km) east of Aix, and the portrait of Geffroy. His studio in Aix has been preserved exactly as it was and is open to the public.

A second painter to immortalise the beauty and simple lifestyle of the south was not a Frenchman, much less a Provençal. Tired of the dark and dreary lands of the north, Dutch-born Vincent Van Gogh became possessed by the dazzling light and colours of the Mediterranean.

Van Gogh first arrived in Arles in 1888. It was in this ancient city that he would paint such masterpieces as *The Arlesienne, The Starry Night* and the series of *Sunflowers,*

Rémy. He was soon allowed to paint once more and continued with his studies of the area. At first, his work was confined to the asylum garden, but even these are among some of the greatest works of the modern age. In May of 1890, however, he chose to return north to be closer to his brother, Theo, and farther from the blinding sun, which he was convinced had contributed to his mental fragility. Two months later, he committed suicide by shooting himself in the breast.

The turn of the century witnessed many more painterly visitors. Martigues hosted Corot and Ziem, while Cassis boasted a long list of luminaries, including Dérain, Vlaminck, Matisse and Dufy.

each of which offers a vivid account of some aspect of Provence. It was also here that he drove himself to madness through too much sun and absinthe and too little temperance.

After convincing Paul Gauguin to join him in what he hoped would become a working community of "Impressionists of the South," Van Gogh's health deteriorated drastically. The two exceedingly strong-minded men clashed constantly and worked with equal fervour. Finally, after a particularly violent argument, Van Gogh suffered the first of his "fits" and sliced off his earlobe.

In April of 1889, Van Gogh voluntarily repaired to a mental asylum at nearby St-

Less artistic types were also busy. The industrial revolution, which came fairly late to France, did not leave Provence untouched. By the 1870s, industrialisation had carved a distinct foothold in the region. Between 1876 and 1880 alone, the primarily rural *département* of the Vaucluse lost some 20,000 inhabitants to the cities. Although still overwhelmingly agricultural in nature, the economy was changing.

The onslaught of phylloxera, which destroyed half the vineyards of the Ardèche and massive numbers of orchards in the Rhône Valley in 1880, contributed to the imminent overhaul of local economies. New economic avenues were explored and exploited. By 1901, extensive mining of the red and yellow cliffs of upper Provence for ochre was underway and, by 1914, the Vaucluse was exporting 56,000 tons of ochre a year. This, in turn, changed the population by encouraging the immigration of potential labourers, many of them Arabs.

Another new industry that encouraged, indeed thrived on, foreign interests was that of tourism. A scattered number of English aristocrats had begun wintering on the Riviera during the late 1700s, but not until Lord Brougham took a fancy to the town of Cannes did tourism become a profitable staple in the gross regional product.

Nonetheless, agriculture remained the backbone of society. The size and distribution of fields changed little since the beginning of the 19th century. Even today they closely resemble the patterns begun in the 1500s. Most farms are fairly small. Generally, one central tract circles a farmhouse while other fields are interspersed among the holdings of other farmers.

World War I drained the countryside of its manpower, adding to the decay of the agricultural society. It also damaged the blossoming ochre-mining industry by immediately cutting off the Russian market. By 1917, all foreign markets had disintegrated, leaving the industry in dire trouble.

After the war, bauxite and ochre mining both climbed back to their former levels of production. Then a new catastrophe hit: the Depression. Much of the ochre had been used for house paint, and the collapse of the construction industry meant that demand plummeted. The ochre industry never managed to recover. World War II closed off foreign markets again and, shortly after its conclusion, the United States developed a synthetic ochre. Although still active, the mines of the Vaucluse would never again be the source of bounty they had once been.

World War II destroyed more than the ochre industry. Although a greater proportion of youths were killed during the first war, the region had remained physically untouched. But during World War II the Provençals found themselves living on a battlefield for the first time in over 150 years.

On 21 June 1940, Mussolini struck out against the thin Alpine guard. Encouraged by the collapse of the French army under the Germans, the Italian dictator felt confident of his own victory, but the general armistice of 25 June cut short his onslaught. The region fell into an unoccupied zone during the ceasefire, but this semi-independence did not last. When the allied North African landings were launched in the winter of 1942, the Germans marched on Toulon and Marseille. Eager to get in on the deal, the Italians took over the Côte d'Azur. After the collapse of the Italian regime 10 months later, the Germans took possession of the entire area.

The Provençals were swept into the thick of things. Those who had not already been conscripted into the French army banded into fierce local Resistance groups. Particularly active in the mountainous regions, their guerrilla tactics brought relentless reprisals from the occupying forces. Meanwhile, the American Air Force began to mount counter-attacks against the Germans, causing additional damage to the once peaceful towns and destroying numerous historical monuments. While this went on, many innocent civilians lost their lives.

Finally, General de Lattre de Tassigny's 1st French and General Patch's 7th United States armies landed on the Dramont beaches just east of St-Raphael on 15 August 1944. By 15 September, most of Provence had been freed from the occupational armies and by April of the following year, the enemy had been eliminated completely.

Economic recovery came quite rapidly after the end of the war. The coastal areas, in particular, enjoyed a new rush in tourism, brought on by the sun-starved years of the war. But the bitter emotional scars caused by the years of occupation and by the widespread loss of life and limbs were not so quick to evaporate.

The Provençals had long become accustomed to their little niche in the southeastern corner of France and, even after losing all political autonomy, had felt fairly safe and separate from the crazy doings of the rest of the world. World War II shattered their sense of security and anonymity, resulting in an attitude of "who cares because who knows if tomorrow will even come?" – similar to the response that the threat of nuclear war produced in many of the next generation.

THE CÔTE D'AZUR SWINGS INTO ACTION

Today, the Côte d'Azur conjures up images of movie stars and suntans, roadsters and Monaco's royal family, casinos and pleasure boats. But the Riviera, as the Italians affectionately dubbed this strip along the Mediterranean, was not always considered so glamorous.

When English novelist Tobias Smollett came to Nice in 1764 to cure his bronchitis, he wrote home that it was a land of little but rude peasants and persistent mosquitoes. Nonetheless, he admitted, the gentle climate was remarkable. His praise for the weather encouraged a few brave Englishmen to visit, but the French stayed clear away, preferring the fashionable spas of Normandy.

The region remained more or less ignored until the advent of Napoleon I several decades later. His unsuccessful martial escapades resulted in the annexation by the King of Sardinia of everything east of Nice and south of the Var River. However, his construction of the *grande corniche,* which linked Nice to Italy, would bring the area its greatest break. In 1834, Lord Brougham, the English Lord Chancellor, and his daughter were forced to wait in Cannes while their favourite Italian winter playground struggled with a bout of cholera. Brougham was less than thrilled by the detention, but his tune changed drastically after spending a little time in the tiny fishing village. Eight days after his arrival, he bought land and ordered the construction of a villa.

The rage had begun. Within a year, a tiny but extant winter colony had sprung up in Cannes. Within three years, 30 new villas had been built and, the following year, the harbourside avenue now called La Croisette was created. Five years later, the appropriately named Promenade des Anglais was constructed in Nice to facilitate the newcomers' morning constitutionals.

The second half of the 19th century saw a Côte d'Azur in full swing. Any halfway fashionable Briton knew to winter in Nice, Cannes, Menton or Beaulieu. The elaborate Belle Epoque villas for which the Côte is still famous sprung up all over.

Russian society joined the throng. In 1856, King Victor-Emmanuel of Sardinia, still ruler of Nice, invited Empress Alexandra for a visit. Her approval encouraged the Russian nobility to add their own mansions to the coastline. So hectic did the waterfront become that a municipal order had to be decreed in May of 1856 forbidding anyone to bathe without underwear.

On 24 March 1860, the signing of the Treaty of Turin finally returned Savoy and the county of Nice to France. Although this made little difference culturally, it did have a huge economic impact, as tourism in the region was fast becoming one of Provence's most profitable businesses.

Until this time, the Côte had been appreciated mostly for its therapeutic virtues. This was long before Coco Chanel had made sunbathing chic and instead, "taking the waters" was the rage. But, in 1863, when Charles III of Monaco agreed to inaugurate the now-famous Monte Carlo casino, the serenity disappeared. The rigid morality of the Victorian Age proved to be no match against the seductive powers of the Riviera. Even the presence of Queen Victoria herself, who often vacationed along the Côte, didn't stop the mounting excesses of the wealthy Europeans who had made it their favourite home away from home.

Stories of the era are legion. One night, for example, the Russian Princess Souvranoff won 150,000 gold francs at the Niçoise casino. To celebrate, she rented a villa for 7,000 francs, but when her invitees contin-

American actress Grace Kelly.

ued to party past the witching hour of 7am, she simply bought the house for an additional 120,000 francs.

Along with the rich, the turn-of-the-century brought painters to the area. Signac, Matisse and Renoir all found inspiration on her shores. Earlier, the composer Berlioz, the violinist Paganini and the writer Guy de Maupassant had already discovered the delights of the sea air.

The Roaring Twenties brought newly made millionaires from the United States to the Côte, as well as the infamous Gertrude Stein and the wild F. Scott Fitzgeralds. The arrival of the Americans marked another change in atmosphere. Jazz clubs popped up all over, and its spirit encouraged Fauvists like Dufy and Bonnard to move in.

Perhaps the biggest revolution came in 1925 when Coco Chanel hit the Côte and created three of what were to become mondial institutions: the tank-style bathing suit, her now-classic Chanel No. 5 perfume, and the suntan. Until then, most people had come to winter on the Riviera. With Coco's help, summer tourism began.

When the stock market crashed in 1929, American visitors declined, but the French increased and the British remained faithful.

The area thrived until World War II. It took something as momentous as a world war to dissipate the power of the Riviera, and dampen things it did. Afterwards tourism picked up again, but things never would be exactly the same.

Chic artists and glamourous movie stars replaced aristocrats as the new lords of the Côte. The first official International Film Festival of Cannes was held in 1947, the same year as Picasso moved to Antibes. Between 1948 and 1951, Matisse decorated the Chapel of the Rosary in Vence, and from 1957 to 1958 Jean Cocteau worked on Menton's town hall. French starlet Brigitte Bardot made history (and St-Tropez's name) when she appeared in the then-racy *And God Created Woman* in 1957. Prince Ranier of Monaco married the American movie star Grace Kelly.

This trend has continued up to the present. Nowadays, only movie moguls and oil tycoons are able to afford the sky-high prices of the good life on the Riviera. But, a new element has appeared, along with dozens of unimpressive condominiums and modern hotels. The Côte has become a place for tourists from all walks of life. And come they do, in droves.

The Belle Epoque Grand Hotel of Nice.

COPING WITH MODERNISATION

World War II heralded a new attitude throughout all of France, not just in Provence. What was once a boastfully agricultural country hardly embraced industrial expansion, pursuing such advances as the Concorde supersonic aircraft and nuclear power. Even agriculture became industrial in practice, and farmers were encouraged to modernise their operations with new equipment.

The change in attitude towards farming had no small effect on the already poor region of Provence, which had historically centred its economy around agriculture. The very essence of the Provençal character was – and is – to be found in the earth. Suddenly, they discovered their pride as well as their security threatened.

Some farmers tried to adapt, going deeply into debt to buy the new equipment. But the new tools proved effective only for extensive farms and not the mom-and-pop type that characterise those of Provence. These same farmers found themselves abandoned by the government, which was more interested in pumping funds into industrialisation then propping up Provençal farmers. Some tried to band together in cooperatives, but their independent natures proved unable to bear joint planning on a large scale.

In the 1960s, a few groups of French-style hippies made the move to the country. Most, however, became disillusioned and returned to their urban lives after a number of years. With them went many of the dissatisfied offspring of farmers, hoping to find "better lives" in the cities. Provence remained agricultural at its core, but for the next couple decades that core struggled.

By the early 1980s only 10 percent of the natives worked the land, compared with 35 percent 40 years earlier. Nonetheless, the decade rejuvenated hope for the Provençal farmer. The mondial back-to-nature trend has filtered into the French mentality, and people have returned to using natural substances. Now, in the 1990s, importers around the world are looking for pure high-quality goods that may cost more but taste better, are healthier or carry more prestige.

Vintners have always fared the best, since no substitute has ever been found for the intensive human care required in wine-making. Now, the small Provençal farmer seems optimistic that demand for other "specialised" products – such as fresh-pressed olive oil and all-organic herbs – will rise.

Despite continuing problems in several areas, Provence continues to be the top producer and exporter of fruits and vegetables in France, with 445,000 acres (180,000 hec-

tares) of land under cultivation. Animals are also raised locally – particularly sheep, whose high-quality wool is greatly prized.

Close to the farmer is the fisherman. Methods may have changed in some areas, but along the coast at dawn you will still see plenty of locals readying their small boats for sail. The famed fish market of Marseille continues to convene each morning, and popular Mediterranean specialties like sardines, tuna, eel and red gurnet are caught by large trawlers and small-time anglers alike.

The coastline has also become extremely profitable in the areas of shipbuilding and oil refining. The latter, which is centred around

Left, corporate offices in Sophia Antipolis. **Above**, fishing is still an occupation in Marseille.

the wide Berre Lagoon, has in turn led to a large quantity of dependent petrochemical facilities in Fos-sur-Mer, Lavera and Mède.

Industrial expansion in the Berre Lagoon area may have gained for the locals a prosperity unknown to their inland brethren, but it's been done at a great price. The countryside resembles no other part of the earthy Provence, as industrial estates consume the horizon. Also, local critics claim, no new jobs were actually created by the expansion. Instead, they say, the jobs simply changed from the more traditional and appealing ones of the past, such as boat-building and fishing, to the more impersonal ones connected with big industrial plants.

The industrialisation of Fos has brought the sea in about 1½ miles (2 km) closer. Meanwhile, even more ominous changes hang over this city. When Dutch engineers came down to help build the Port-de-Bouc they had to undertake massive dredging of the sea floor. While doing so, they discovered giant holes lining it, and it is believed that the whole city will eventually and inevitably drop down into the sea.

The enormous Berre Lagoon itself has remained quite beautiful, but it is surrounded by ugly row houses and low-hanging smog. It has been France's principal petroleum port for the past 60 years, but the construction of a new port in Martigues and the South Euro-

The effect on the environment is unarguable. In 1965, you could swim or fish happily in two of the lagoons that lie between the Berre Lagoon and Fos-sur-Mer: the Etang de Lavalduc and the Etang d'Engrenier. Then the waters of the Lavalduc Lagoon, which come from Manosque, were discovered to be incredibly salty, 60 percent in fact. Profit-minded engineers drained its waters and placed them within the Engrenier Lagoon, from which they could more easily produce liquid industrial salt. Both were blocked off from the canal that linked them to the grand *étang*. Now, they are so polluted that you can see their filth from miles away.

pean Oil Pipeline during the 1960s even furthered its eminence. It now pumps more than 65 million tons of oil a year.

Of course, not all industrialisation in Provence has produced such dire results as have those surrounding the Berre Lagoon. In 1952, the Donzère-Mondragon Power Station was inaugurated and, four years later, France's first nuclear reactor began operating in Marcoule. More power was created by the hydroelectric installations at Avignon, Caderousse and Vallabrègues along the Rhône, and St-Estève, Jouques, Mallemort, Slaôn and St-Chamas along the Durance.

As seems appropriate, most of the industrialisation of Provence has focused on using already existent local products. Cork is gathered from the Maures Forest. Ochre and bauxite continue to be mined, although their contribution to the economy is less than it once was. In the Camargue and by Hyères, salt is pumped from seawater between March and September and, once crystalisation has been completed, gathered between September and October. Olives are used not only in making martinis and salad oil, but lamp and oven fuel, soapmaking and, at its most extreme, fertiliser. The production of soap in France continues to be dominated by the *savonniers* of Marseille, although generally within large factories rather than the old-

more effort into wooing tourists as well.

Meanwhile, as unskilled, factory-type jobs have grown and discontent in North African countries has come to the fore, the number of illegal or, at least, immigrant workers has also swelled. In a parallel movement, protectionism against the new foreigners has reared its head in the form of National Front leader Jean-Marie Le Pen.

Le Pen was not born in Provence, nor does he embody any particularly Provençal attributes. Nonetheless, this controversial political leader has found a remarkably large following in the region, especially in the area around Marseille. His policies, viewed by many as outrageously bigoted, are centred

fashioned soap *ateliers*.

Lighter industries also depend on local raw materials. Almonds are used by the confectioners of Aix-en-Provence to make *calissons*, and fruits, especially berries, and vegetables are canned. The chic sparkling mineral water of Perrier is tapped from an underground spring near Nîmes.

Tourism continues to dominate the economy of the Côte d'Azur region and some of the more famous cities. In recent years, however, some smaller towns have begun to put

around using all "foreign" elements in France as scapegoats; they struck a chord with some disgruntled Provençals, and in recent elections, Le Pen has received an especially strong show of support from the southern regions.

Despite the many problems of modern Provence, however, the area does appear to be on the upswing. It has taken a bit longer for this region, deeply rooted for so long in the agricultural life, to come to terms with modernisation. But recent years have seen a more optimistic Provence learning to adapt to the changes – on its own terms, of course, and without losing its identity.

Left, flamingos mingle with factories in the Camargue. Above, the Cadarache power station.

What is a *vrai* Provençal? Everyone has their own opinion. One person says it is someone whose grandparents were native to the region. Another says it is someone who lives and works in the same village where he was born and where his parents and his parents' parents were born, lived and died.

The explanations become more complicated. An Avignonais is different from the rest of the Provençals – "they are more stuck in their own world, prosperous, cosmopolitan." The people from the Alpilles are "both more conservative and more open than those from the Luberon," due to their greater poverty and dependence on outside markets. And those from the Alpes-Maritimes, even the Var, are they really Provençals at all?

Certain characteristics are true for the entire region. The Provençals are overwhelmingly a rural people with enormous respect and love for the land on which they live. Even the city dwellers know how to cultivate an excellent garden and can sense the oncoming change of weather.

Also, many Provençals are distant and, one might even say, suspicious at first encounter. But, if the visitor persists in trying to be friendly, he or she will find that the Provençals will quickly turn into the most generous and hospitable people imaginable.

Other similarities can be found in their appearance. Provençals come in many guises, especially since today many are sunseekers from the north or returned colonists from Algeria. For the most part, however, you can expect them to be on the smaller side, perhaps stocky, and darker than a typical northern Frenchman. They are, after all, Mediterraneans.

However, if there is one thing that marks the Provençals, it is the richness of their traditions – and their pride in them. Centuries of complicated history, foreign invasions and determined independence from the rest of France have left their mark.

Provence is one of only four areas in France to retain its own regional dialect. Not everyone speaks Provençal, but it is taught as an option in most schools, and in 1987, for the first time, a *faculté* in the Provençal language and literature was created at the University of Aix-en-Provence. The push to preserve the language is on, begun by the determination of the Noble Prize-winning native poet Mistral at the turn of the century.

Religion plays a big role in the life of the Provençal, although at times it may seem almost paganistic in interpretation. Harvest spirits and the beneficence of God, storytale

monsters and Christian saints walk hand-in-hand, often enough combined within the very same legend or *fête*. Superstition also rages, even in the homes of the sophisticated. Never leave an iron out on the table of a Provençal hostess – it will undoubtedly bring her bad luck.

Traditions are taken seriously in this region. Consider the example of Christmas. Whether it be that of a poor rural farmer or a wealthy urban banker, nearly all Provençal homes still follow certain Christmas rituals that are unique to the area.

Christmastime begins on 4 December with *le jour de St-Barbe*. On this day, the

Preceding pages: festival participants in Arles. **Left,** farmer sells his produce in Vaison. **Above,** young girl of North African descent.

children of each household plant a grain of wheat (or a lentil or chickpea) in a saucer. If it sprouts, this predicts good fortune for the coming year; if it doesn't, the household should prepare itself for a rocky time.

Originally, of course, the *blé de St-Barbe* was a purely agricultural ceremony. But, like many other Provençal customs, it has evolved to combine a curious blend of ancient agricultural rites with more recent Christian concerns. The superstition of St-Barbe itself is derived from a pre-Christian Middle Eastern ritual that referred specifically to the harvest year ahead. Today, however, when other lifestyles exist, it has been adapted to offer a more general omen.

Alegre!
Dieu nous alegre!
Cacho-fio ven
Tout ven ben!
De veire l'an que ven
Se sian pas mai
Sieguen pas men.

which translates roughly as:

Joy!
God gives us joy!
Cacho-fio comes
Everything goes well!
Let us see the year which is coming
If we are no more
Let us not be less.

The way the log lights is considered a portent

Around the same time as the planting of the grain of wheat, the crèches and *santons* are brought out of storage. These beloved clay Christmas cribs are set up in a specially designated corner, where they will remain for the rest of the season.

All this is just a preliminary for the rites of Christmas Eve. On that night, 24 December, everyone in the family gathers around for the *cacho-fio* (more or less, "hidden flame"). The very oldest and very youngest members of the household bless, with an olive branch soaked in wine, a log cut from a fruit tree. The elder then lights it, speaking the following words in Provençal, when they can:

for the year to come, and it should continue burning until the *jour des Rois*.

After the *cacho-fio*, the family regroups around the *gros souper* in the same room as the crèche has been set up. The table is set with three cloths, commemorating the Birth, the Circumcision and the Epiphany, and is lit by three candlesticks, each containing one sole candle, which represents the Holy Trinity. In the middle are the saucers of germinated wheat from the day of St-Barbe, surrounded by a ribbon.

Although *gros souper* translates as "large supper," it is, in fact, a lean meal that traditionally included no meat, although only the most religious families still respect that stricture. It is followed by the *treize desserts* (13 desserts) after the 13 who attended the Last Supper. These desserts generally include raisins, almonds, dried figs, plums, apples, pears, candied lemon, quince jam, oranges, *nougats noirs* and *nougats blancs*, small round cakes, *pompes à huile* and wine.

Afterwards, Christmas carols may be sung – in Provençal if possible – and then those who are still practising Christians head off for Midnight Mass. Before going to sleep, the adults place presents by the crèche to be opened on Christmas morning.

The most dedicated Provençal families will don traditional clothing for the festivi-

ingly, connected to the earth around them: flower, olive and wine festivals, rites that beckon rain (such as the pilgrimage of St-Gens) or which give thanks for the harvest (such as the "sacrifice of the last blade"). Whole books have been written on the mythology of the Provençal calendar.

Of course, not every Provençal cares for gardens, crèches and traditional costumes. After World War II, many young Provençals left their home towns, rejecting the lifestyle of their parents for the ways of the big cities. In turn, they either lost interest in, purposefully shed or simply forgot the old ways.

But the traditions and costumes and festivals are far from being a specialised matter.

ties of Christmas Eve. This "costume" recalls the style of the 18th-century bourgeois and is also worn during some of the many annual folkloric festivals. The colourful and lively festivals are a joy for the tourist trade, but Provençals are quick to remind that the *fêtes* are not "shows" or "charades" put on for the entertainment of visitors but something that they take seriously.

A large number of the festivals for which the Provençals are so famous are, unsurpris-

The continuation of an independent and individual regional life is a very live issue among many Provençals. Groups are forming yearly with the specific purpose of protecting the Provençal traditions. In Arles, a "queen" is chosen every three years on the basis of her ability to uphold these traditions (i.e., speak the language) rather than her beauty or long legs. The phrase "a true Provençal" will be spoken with pride.

So what is a *vrai* Provençal? Perhaps the best description is this: "A true Provençal is someone who holds dear the traditions of Provence – its language, legends, costume – and actively works to preserve it."

<u>Left</u>, rice grower in the Camargue. <u>Above left</u>, St-Tropez denizen and <u>right</u>, a former "Queen of Arles" in costume.

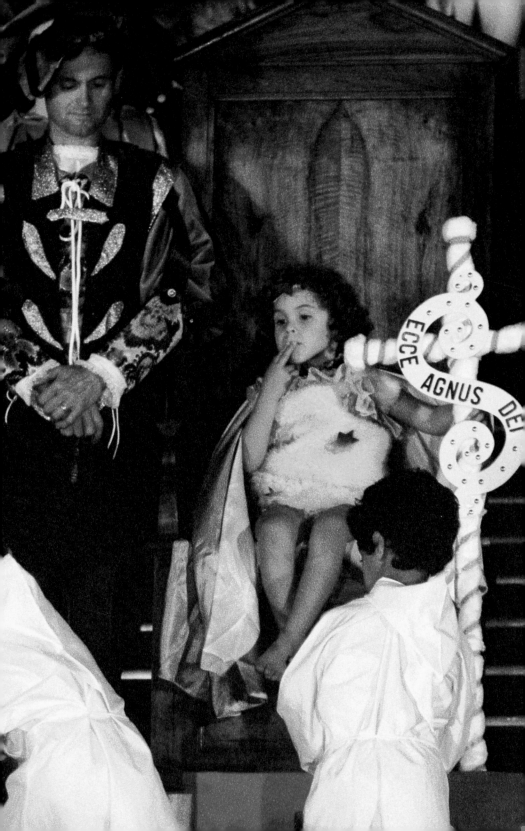

So strong are religious feelings in Provence that belief in divine will and miraculous intervention can be found behind even the most mundane activities.

In most places, for example, the decision to build a bridge would be made by local elders. At Avignon, however, the 12th-century bridge spanning the Rhône – the *Pont d'Avignon* of the song – came to be built after a shepherd-boy, Bénézet, claimed he had been commanded to do so by a voice he recognised as Christ's. Overcoming initial ecclesiastical hostility by singlehandedly lifting a stone big enough to form one of the bridge's piers, he set to the task. He was soon joined by a band of volunteers who called themselves the Brotherhood of the Bridge; together they completed the structure in a record eight years.

Other stories emphasise the religiosity of the Provençals by associating their region with the *dramatis personae* of the New Testament. Thus, Mary Magdalene, fleeing persecution in Judea with her (presumed) sister Martha and brother Lazarus – as well as Mary Jacoby, mother of Saint James the Less, Mary Salome, mother of John and James the Great, and their Egyptian servant, Sarah – were said to have been washed ashore in an open boat at the place now known as Les-Stes-Maries-de-la-Mer.

They celebrated deliverance by erecting a rough stone oratory dedicated to the Virgin. It was replaced in the 12th century by a fortified church that today houses a carving of the boat with the two Marys standing in it. In the carving, Mary Magdalene holds a chalice-like object often taken to be the Holy Grail, which she is credited with having brought to France, but which may represent the "precious ointment" with which she anointed the feet of Christ. This would link it with St-Baume on whose mountainside she passed the last 33 years of her life in a cave. Though *baoumo* is the Provençal word for a cave, in the high French used by ecclesiastics *baume* means "balm."

Meanwhile, Mary became a cave-dweller,

and Martha is said to have journeyed inland along the course of the Rhône until she reached the town of Tarascon. She found its inhabitants terrorised by the dragon-like Tarasque, who made a habit of dining off anything that crossed its path. Undaunted, she singlehandedly sought it out and, confronting it with the Cross, reduced it to docile submission.

In 1474, Count René of Provence decreed that the miraculous conquest of the monster should be commemorated with an annual fête. Still held on the last Sunday in June, its climax is a procession in which a representation of the Tarasque, jaws snapping and tail whipping like a Chinese New Year dragon, parades through the town.

Appropriately enough, Saint Martha's remains lie in the town's church. They are, as one might expect, by no means the only holy relics to which the Provençals lay claim. The body of Saint Anne, apocryphal mother of the blessed Virgin, lies in the Apt Cathedral and that of Mary Magdalene in the Basilica of St-Maximin. The remains of Saint Sarah, adopted as the patron saint of gypsies, are to be found in Les-Ste-Maries, whose church has become the focus of a mass pilgrimage of gypsies each 24 and 25 May.

Most relics are credited with miracle-working properties, but the most powerful of all is the Holy Bit, made at the order of Helena, mother of the Emperor Constantine, out of two nails believed to have been extracted from the Cross. It is reputed to drive out evil spirits and cure eye disease, neuralgia and haemorrhages. Now kept at the Church of St-Siffrein (or Siegfried) in Carpentras, it is brought out on Good Friday and on 27 November.

Pagan whispers: Despite all this piety, the visitor, chancing upon a local festival, may well notice some startlingly discordant elements. Why are masked and costumed mummers permitted to intrude on so solemn an occasion as a Corpus Christi procession? Isn't the noisy explosion of blunderbusses during the *bravades* (the typical saint's-day processions on the Côte d'Azur) reminiscent of the means used as far away as Africa and China to frighten away evil spirits?

Preceding pages: Fête de St-Jean in Valréas. Left, traditional offering to a newborn baby.

The suspicion that one is witnessing something that owes little to orthodox Christianity becomes even stronger at feasts such as Saint Marcellus at Barjols. Each 16 January the reliquary of this stern 4th-century pope is taken from the church to oversee celebrations that include the ritual blessing and slaughter of a garlanded ox. Its carcass is then paraded about the town before being roasted whole as the townsfolk dance round the fire to the sound of flutes, tambourines and, as at the *bravades*, volleys of shots.

These are, of course, survivals from a distant pre-Christian past, also to be found in innumerable Provençal folk customs. Take for example the practice of preserving half-found mixed in with pious legend. Saint Martha, on reaching Tarascon, was taken for the goddess Diana, which provides good evidence that a cult to the pagan deity existed there. Another old story tells how Saint Trophime, who came to convert Arles, consigned the goddess of love, Venus, to the nether regions.

Even edifying stories like that of Avignon's Bénézet contain their primitive themes. One is that of the shepherd as a link to the divine. Naturally, Joan of Arc hearing heavenly voices as she tended her sheep springs to mind; but Apollo, the most mysterious of the Greco-Roman gods and the inspirer of oracles, expiated his slaughter of

burned logs from the bonfires lit on Midsummer Eve – itself a pagan tradition – as protection from lightning.

Or consider the custom of giving the newborn an egg, some salt, a piece of bread and a matchstick. The egg as a symbol of the continuity of life can be traced back to the ancient Middle East and survives both in the Jewish Passover meal and the Easter egg. The same archaic tradition regarded salt as the symbol of prosperity and bread as the staff of life. The matchstick, undoubtedly a later addition, is said to ensure that the infant grows straight.

Hints of a pagan heritage are often to be the Python by serving as a shepherd in Thessaly and thereafter acquired the title of "protector of flocks." The popular Mesopotamian Shamash, with whom Apollo has many similarities, played a similar role.

Another prominent pagan theme is that of the hero proving himself through supernatural strength and, in particular, by lifting a heavy stone. It was by this means that Theseus asserted his right to the Athenian throne and that King Arthur did the same for the British one. The antiquity of this theme is proven by the fact that the Norse Odin underwent the same test and that something very like it is shown on a Hittite stone carving.

Celtic links: How did such patently alien ideas originate? The principal answer is that, perhaps more than any other region of France, Provence has always been a crossroads. From the 6th century BC, its first inhabitants, the Ligurians, played hosts to Greeks who crossed the Mediterranean to establish trading posts along the coast from Marseille to La Ciotat. Not long afterwards invading Celts swamped the Ligurians, and then in the 2nd century it was the turn of the Celts themselves to be invaded, this time by the legions of Rome.

Each visitor left a legacy. The bullfighting found here, as in Spain, may well have come from the Greeks. The ox sacrifice at the Feast temple dedicated to the Phrygian Great Mother, Cybele, whose practices, forbidden to Roman citizens, included self-castration by her male devotees.

But, of all the very ancient pre-Christian peoples, those who left the most indelible paganistic footprints wherever they trod were the Celto-Ligurians. Their remains, too, have been found at Glanum. Among them is a lintel supported by pillars, which, as is typical of Celtic sacred places, lies close to a natural spring. Skull niches cut into the lintel itself are testimony to the custom of head-hunting.

Similar discoveries have been made at other sites, such as Mouriès, Roquepertuse

of St Marcellus suggests Mithraism, the Persian cult popular in the Roman army up to its conversion to Christianity.

Concrete evidence for this mixture of religious influences comes from excavation sites, such as that on the Glanum plateau, a short distance south of St-Rémy-de-Provence. Artifacts found there include the remains of temples, baths, a forum and a triumphal arch erected in the time of Caesar Augustus (31 BC to AD 14) as well as a

Left, votive statuary to the Virgin Mary beside Mt. St-Victoire. **Above**, reliquary of Mary Magdalene in Maximin-Ste-Baume.

and St-Blaise. At Entremont, 15 male skulls have been uncovered, some retaining the nails by which they had been affixed.

Celtic traces to be found throughout Provence also include linguistic ones. For example, the word *aven*, used to describe the holes bored into the calcareous rock by rainwater, means "a well." The *esprit fantastique* bears a striking resemblance to the British Puck and to those mischievous fairies, the *sidhfolk*, descendants of ancient gods, to be found in rural Ireland.

But most Celtic of all is the very ability to absorb outside influences, Christian as well as pagan, and make them their own.

THE CUISINE

The traveller to Provence is faced with a delightful choice when looking for a restaurant. After eliminating the obvious tourist-traps, only two kinds of restaurant remain: cheap and excellent – and out of this world. If you are wondering how to recognise the former, don't worry. Just look for the paper tablecloths, hard wooden chairs and hand-written sign that says something like:

Chez Claude
Cuisine Provençale
Menu 70F et 90F
Tomates Farcies ou Soupe de Poisson
Dorade Grillée ou Daube Maison
Fromage Dessert

Such signs, with appropriate variations, hang over 100 restaurants from Marseille to the Italian frontier. Inland, towards Avignon or Sisteron, the soup will be vegetable, the fish will be trout, and the prices will be slightly cheaper. In all cases, however, the service will be warm and friendly, the portions generous and often the meal will be served on a sunny terrace, under the vines or in view of the sea.

In selecting a meal, the first-time visitor to Provence should choose a dish containing tomatoes. If any vegetable or fruit symbolises Provençal cuisine, it is the tomato, the term for which, in Provençal, can be literally translated as "love apple." Anyone who has had more than three meals in Provence can attest to its local popularity.

In addition, if any method of cooking symbolises Provence, it is the stuffed vegetable – the *farci*. Like everyone else, the Provençaux stuff meat, fish and fowl, but the *farcis* they do with vegetables are special. They stuff eggplants with onion and tomato, onions with garlic, and cabbages with sausage and parsley. A traditional recipe, adopted by the fashionable chefs of the *nouvelle cuisine*, is courgette flower *farci* – stuffed with the flesh of the courgette itself. As for the tomato, it is the queen of the *farci*.

The *farci* may be a fairly simple dish to prepare, but the *soupe de poisson* (fish soup) is not. The latter is a dirty unappetising brown liquid, served in a big white tureen from which escapes the delicious, inimitable smell of myriad tasty sea creatures that go into its making. These are all the *poissons de roche* (literally "rock fish") that hide in the shadow of the indented Mediterranean coastline – including the *rascasse*, the ugliest fish on God's earth, bony *girelle* and *rouquier*, crabs and eels – and are caught at night from the little wooden boats called *pointus*. Until dawn when the nets are pulled in, not even the fishermen know which of the 20 or so varieties they will bring to shore. In towns like Beaulieu-sur-Mer, where the fishing fleet cater to at least a dozen restaurants, the competition is fierce. As the boats chug home around the headland, the restaurant chefs position themselves on the quays, to get the pick of the night's catch.

A first-rate *soupe de poisson* can take hours to prepare. In the traditional manner, the fish is crushed, then hung in linen sheets from the kitchen's rafters to squeeze out the rich juice. Nowadays, some cooks have replaced the sheet with a sieve that presses the juice out more efficiently. But many fishermen's wives, the acknowledged experts, refuse to believe that the taste is the same. They prefer to stand on chairs in their kitchens twisting linen sheets rather than make changes to a recipe handed down through several generations.

Another controversy is that of the *rouille*, a thick red spicy sauce whipped up into a kind of mayonnaise and served in most restaurants with *soupe de poisson*. You spread the *rouille* on the croutons that you float in the soup before sprinkling grated cheese on top. Most diners look forward to the *rouille* and consider it to be an integral part of the soup. However, the supporters of linen sheets claim that the *rouille* is a recent addition and clashes with the rich taste of the fish. In older recipes, they point out, you just rubbed a little garlic on the croutons to bring out the taste.

This may not seem of great importance to the traveller, but it is a subject of heated discussion in all the seaports of the French Mediterranean. Indeed, it is almost as heated as the rivalry between the supporters of *soupe de poisson*, as served in Nice and the eastern ports, and those of *bouillabaisse*, the speciality of the Marseille coast. The great difficulty in this comparison, however, is that *bouillabaisse* is not strictly speaking a soup. The fish are served whole on a side plate, and the liquid they were cooked in is placed in a dish in the centre of the table for all the diners to dip their hunks of bread into. (Or, in some kitchens, the broth will be ladled into each diner's bowl, then large pieces of fish will be carved up and placed within the bowls.)

Bouillabaisse is a dish to be tasted in the restaurants just off the old port of Marseille, where the cook struts past the tables in his

with bargain-priced all-inclusive menus buy it frozen from wholesalers in Toulon or Nice who prepare it in the traditional way but on a large scale.

It takes a connoisseur to tell the difference between the fresh and the mass-produced *bouillabaisse*. However, that little difference is the one that separates the cheap and excellent from the out of this world. For the Provençal, the restaurant that serves frozen soup *manque de coeur* (literally "lacks heart"), an accusation that lies heavily against him.

Simple and fresh: So, what makes a real Provençal dish? On one level, it's the choice of the ingredients: the best olive oil, from a

undershirt and the clients wear striped jerseys or heavy black suits with a bulge under the armpit. Unfortunately, most of the restaurants of Pagnol's old port are slowly being turned into dry-cleaners or croissant-bars. The modern visitor has to go a little more out of his or her way, perhaps to one of the creeks or beaches where you can sit at a terrace, watch the boats and smell the sea – such as the Vallon des Auffes – to enjoy a good old-fashioned *bouillabaisse*.

Wherever, it doesn't come cheap. A good *bouillabaisse* or *soupe de poisson* is rarely billed at under 80F a head – even in the cheapest restaurants. And most restaurants

first pressing of the olives; good firm cloves of garlic – preferably from the little heads that are purple ("like wine stains," as they say in the markets), not the white lumpy ones that look like potatoes; little tasty courgettes (zucchini) and tomatoes, not the big watery vegetables imported from the north. Then come the traditional herbs – thyme and rosemary in sprigs and fresh basil in season.

All this is prepared *avec coeur* ("with heart"), which means the willingness to take extra pains and to work hard for little material reward. The cuisine explains something basic about Provençal life – about the precarious climate where the summer months may go by without a drop of rain and where an exceptionally cold winter may bring to nothing five generations of back-breaking labour. The Provençaux are small cultivators that fish and farm mostly in family units, and the produce of the land is valued tree by tree and row by row. When the Provençal family gathers around the table, the exact origin of each dish is known.

The purpose of Provençal cooking is not to disguise but to accentuate the flavours and to make the diners aware of each ingredient. Consequently, the cuisine includes none of the rich creamy sauces of central and northern France. The ultimate example of this emphasis upon freshness and simplicity is

Mougins, return again and again to the simple side dishes of Provence.

Vergé is also aware of the influence of time and place on how a meal is received. "It is particularly important to serve the wine cool and abundantly," he says, "and to place the table in the shade of a large tree. The dish is already suffused with sunshine, leading to thoughts of a siesta."

Just as the rosés of the south are dependent on hot summer days to bring out their flavour, so are the local dishes. It is no doubt for this reason that Provençal cuisine is less well-travelled than that of Lyon and Paris. A *ratatouille* in London or New York is little more than a limp vegetable stew. In Prov-

the Christmas meal that culminates in the *treize desserts*. The 13 desserts are actually 13 simple little side dishes, most composed of a single ingredient such as apples, figs, raisins, pears, almonds, walnuts, candied quinces or prunes. To mix all these ingredients, in the spirit of the English Christmas pudding, would be considered a kind of sacrilege. Even today, the spirit remains the same. The great chefs of southeastern France, such as Roger Vergé of Le Moulin de

ence, however, *ratatouille* is an explosion of rich vegetable tastes.

Storytelling meals: The Provençal *ratatouille* is also the memory of a bustling market under the parasols, where you elbowed your way towards the piled heaps of aubergine and tomatoes. It is the sprig of thyme that your neighbour passed you over the garden wall, in exchange for a couple of freshly laid eggs. In other words, each dish in Provence is a story, something you can recount over dinner to your guests.

"Tante" Jeanne is the greatest storyteller of all. Jeanne runs a kind of restaurant near Apt, 30 miles (50 km) east of Avignon and

Left, the ubiquitous Provençal tomato. **Above left**, pompes à l'huile from Marseille; **right**, herbes de Provence.

just north of the Montagne du Lubéron. She lives not far from the hamlet of Bouaux, at the end of a small dirt road which has no name, and she has no telephone. Nevertheless, on Sundays, the field beside her house becomes a parking lot for Mercedes and Porsches, as well as many more-modest vehicles. These cars will have come from as far away as Nîmes or Aix, and their owners will be there by personal introduction only. Jeanne is – by choice – in no directory or guide of any kind.

Lunch will begin precisely at 11.30, and latecomers will not be served. No choices will be offered: what is served to one is served to all. There will be only one wine: a

it out. The Provençaux learned long ago that the best way to ensure a discerning, appreciative clientele is to open your shop or restaurant on the top of a mountain or in a shady backstreet. Those willing to follow the clues in this article and read between the lines will be able to find Jeanne's. On the other hand, if you are willing to go to that much trouble, you will make your own discoveries in Provence, which will be even more wonderful in that they are your own.

Choosing a restaurant: The casual tourist will do fine eating "Chez Claude" in excellent, moderately priced restaurants close to the town centres: in Nice, on the sunny Cours Saleya; in the old town of Antibes; in the

Côtes du Lubéron bottled at the vineyard, and with great delight Jeanne will announce that only she and the owner's family have access to this *cuvée*. She will also narrate how she negotiated a certain vegetable out of season or a cut of beef that no butcher this side of the Rhône serves over the counter. The diners, in their Sunday finery (casual dress is not approved of), sit on hard wooden chairs at a single long table and respond in kind, praising each ingredient or comparing dishes with their own family recipes.

Jeanne's restaurant is a Provençal secret, but one that nobody bothers to keep because only the initiated will take the trouble to find

Suquet of Cannes, behind the port; in the back streets of St-Tropez; in Arles, in the quarter running west of the Roman Arena; in Avignon, south of the Palais des Papes. In fact, in any town or village, in the plains or the mountains, where the tablecloths are clean and the waiters look cheerful, you can be guaranteed an honest meal and often one far beyond your expectations.

Those who are more demanding should ask advice of the locals they meet. They should talk to butchers and grocers, who know where the fresh produce is served. They should watch for the restaurants that need no advertising – little doorways in shady streets with small signs, packed with local diners and accompanied by chalk boards announcing the day's special – and consult departing diners, who are always glad to give an opinion.

Finally, once they've found a spot, they should put themselves in the hands of the waiter and defy him to produce a meal that will delight and surprise. Few waiters thus addressed will be prepared to disappoint. They may even serve you dishes that are not on the menu. As elsewhere in France, restaurant management is not so much a means of livelihood as a profession of faith.

Departmental variations: In Nice, a best-selling publication is *La Cuisine du Compté*

de Nice by the former mayor Jacques Médecin, and one of the best known personalities of the city is probably "La Mère Barale". This *restaurantrice extraordinaire* once threatened to stop serving the author of the famous Gault et Millau gastronomic guide if he continued to include her in the guide. "I am getting old," she said, "and I have enough customers." The honest critic took the risk and printed her name once again on his list of top recommendations.

Mme. Barale can even make a gourmet dish of stockfish (*estocaficada*, in dialect).

This terrifying Niçois speciality is based on dried cod, soaked in water for several days, then cooked with onions, leeks and tomatoes. From an incompetent kitchen, it can smell of boiled manure and taste of glue. *Chez* Barale, it has a delicate flavour that sets off the taste of the vegetables.

Barale's other speciality is ravioli. Some readers may assume that ravioli is a typically Italian dish. Anyone in Provence will put you right: *au contraire*, it is a Provençal dish exported to Italy, originally called *ralhola*.

The ravioli of Provence is stuffed with all manner of vegetables, meats and cheeses. The flavour will vary from town to town, subtly different according to the vegetables grown or the animals raised in each region. In the Camargue, the land of cowboys, you can get an excellent beef ravioli, served in a thick meaty sauce. In the rich plains between Nîmes and Aix, the stuffing is an assortment of vegetables. In St-Tropez, you can taste a *ravioli aux sardines*. As in Italy, the dishes of Provence are essentially local, reflecting the everyday reality of generations of farmers, traders and fishermen.

In the Alpes-de-Haute-Provence, on the high plateaux between Sisteron and Gap where the grass is frozen in winter and burnt away in summer, the shepherds drive their flocks across rocks and scree. The sheep, with their long legs and hard bitter eyes, have little in common with their fat complacent cousins in the lush valleys below.

In taste, also, there is no comparison. An *agneau de Sisteron* has a spicy herby flavour and is never oily or heavy. A southern chef will choose no other kind of lamb for his *gigot de mouton à la Provençale*, a leg of lamb that is boned then stuffed with herbs, garlic and sausage, cooked in white wine, and served in a sauce made of tomatoes, aubergines and green peppers.

Variants of the *gigot* can be tasted at most of the better restaurants in the foothills of the Alps, such as the excellent Auberge de Reillanne. In the mountains, lamb tends to be served stuffed or in a garlic sauce. In the plains near Nîmes or Arles, it is more often cooked on a spit or in a stew with potatoes and parsley.

The truth is that the roots and emotional connotations are what make the Provençal cuisine. The landscape, the love, the struggle and the victory are part of the recipe.

When you bring home a piece of craftwork from Provence, you bring home more than just a pretty pot or well-made belt. Most Provençal artisans rely on local materials and regard their work as pieces of art. And more importantly, just as with so many other aspects of Provençal life, folk art has emerged from long-time regional traditions and is pursued and respected as such.

No folk art displays the importance of tradition more strongly than *santons* (little saints). These symbolic clay figures are used in a crèche, the scene that is laid out in Catholic homes at Christmas to represent the Nativity. Formed out of plaster-cast moulds and baked, their clothing and other details are then painted on with acrylics. They generally range in size from less than an inch (two cm) to five inches (13 cm), and differently sized figures are commonly placed in the same crèche to create perspective.

The most important figures, as in any crèche, are those of the Nativity itself: the infant Jesus, Mary, Joseph, the angel and the three wise men, all clothed in their Biblical costumes, plus the ox and ass. However, instead of Jerusalem, the Provençal crèche places the birth of Jesus in a typical and bustling 19th-century Provençal village. Clay models of stone houses are set up around the central stable. Moss and pebbles are used for the hillside; rosemary and thyme twigs act as trees.

A supporting cast of figurines represents all the tradesmen and society that one would find in a 19th-century Provençal town. They wear the traditional clothing of the period and carry a tool or product that symbolises their trade or social position: the garlic farmer; the fish merchant; women carrying newly drawn water; the gypsy; the coquette; the parish priest. In some *ateliers*, more than 100 subjects are created.

The original *santonniers* (or santon makers) came from Marseille in the beginning of the 19th century. They modelled their figurines after the village characters that were portrayed in *pastorales* (the popular Nativity plays) and in *crèches parlantes* (talking, mechanical marionette crèches), which were commonly staged in the streets of Marseille during the Christmas season. The famous Pastorale of Maurel, written in 1844, is still played at Le Cercle de la rue Nau in Marseille, and you can see a wonderful collection of crèche marionettes at the Musée du Vieil Aix.

Unsurprisingly, Marseille and the nearby cities of Aix-en-Provence and Aubagne remain the *santon*-making centres of Provence. The great *Foire aux Santons* takes place in Marseille for two weeks each December. This fair has become an integral part of the Christmas festivities, and most towns in the Bouches-du-Rhône have their own smaller version each year.

Although the figurines can be bought inexpensively from craft shops and at summer craft fairs, the best place to buy them is at the workshops of the *santonniers* themselves. Almost all have an attached boutique, and you can often take a look at the workshop too. There are a handful of recognised *maître santonniers* working today, whose work can be distinguished by all connoisseurs based upon their individual styles and repertory. The two best known, both winners of the prestigious *"Meilleur Ouvrier en France"* medal, are M. Paul Fouque, who works with his gifted daughter, Mireille, in Aix-en-Provence, and has the largest number of models in his repertory; and M. Marcel Carbonel, who heads the largest workshop in France and has a fun museum of crèche figures from around the world attached to his Marseille workshop.

Brilliant fabrics: Another traditional decoration that has kept a strong contemporary following are the printed cottons of Provence. Known as *indiennes* when they were first produced throughout France during the second half of the 17th century, they were made following the methods and designs of the imported *toiles peintes* of India. In 1686, the Royalty declared a halt to the importation and production of the Indian fabric. However, as part of the Comtat-Venaissin, Provence was not on royal land. The industry, therefore, grew in this region throughout the

Preceding pages: tilemaker beside his jeep of tiles in Salernes. Left, Collet pottery in Vallauris.

17th and 18th centuries, with factories in Orange, Avignon, Tarascon and Aix.

These fabrics, which formerly served as women's shawls and are now mostly used for interior decoration, are brilliantly multi-coloured prints in kaleidoscopic floral and geometric patterns. Originally, the dyes were obtained from natural materials and each colour in a design was applied with separate woodblock impressions.

Only one factory has survived the mechanisations of the textile industry: a company based in Tarascon and owned and operated by a member of its founding family, Charles Demery. It trades under the name of Souleiado – a Provençal term taken from the

in the 19th century, factories began to open in answer to the ever-growing demand for thrown or moulded cookware and for building materials such as tiles and bricks. The 20th century's economic and martial turmoil and the advent of aluminium and plastic, however, led to the eventual closure of these factories.

In Aubagne, formerly a centre for earthenware manufacturing, one such factory (called Poterie Provençale) still runs, turning out the kind of handmade, mass-produced casseroles and coffee pots made in the 19th century. But generally the days of utilitarian cookware production are gone. Now, most pottery is primarily decorative.

works of poet Mistral and meaning "the rays of sun that pierce through clouds."

Decorative pottery: The region has produced earthenware since the days of the Romans. Pottery workshops complete with kilns dating from the 1st century AD have been excavated in La Butte des Carnes, near Marseille. A model of one of these kilns can be seen at the Musée de l'Histoire de Marseille, along with examples of amphoras and urns from the same period.

Over the centuries, pottery continued to be made in individual workshops, both for domestic purposes and for international export through the Mediterranean seaports. Then,

Three basic types of pottery are now produced. *Terre rouge*, the coarsest and humblest, is made primarily from the red clay of the region. This type of pottery can be recognised by its reddish-brown colour (if it is covered with an opaque glaze, look at the underside of the base to see the material from which it is made), its rough texture and its weight – it is never thin and fine, for this kind of clay cracks easily.

Objects such as unglazed moulded flower pots and tiles are still made in *terre rouge* for household use, while a wide variety of thrown forms such as jugs, bowls and mustard pots are sold as partly decorative, partly useful objects. Be careful, however, to check that they are really hand-done.

Roadside pottery stores, where they exist, are usually outlets for small family-run workshops. One such store is La Ceriseraie, in Fontvieille, a modest establishment where M. Monleau makes *la cuisinerie* (cookware) as well as *santons* out of *terre rouge*, and his prize-winning daughter Chantal creates *la décoration*, or *faïence*.

Traditionally, if *terre rouge* was the poor man's pottery, faïence was the rich man's. *Faïence* is made from the finest indigenous clays combined with various mineral elements to produce a greyish-white body that is formed in moulds, covered with a (gener-

infusers, which had been put into use by the aristocracy, joined figurines as decorative pieces displayed on walls or mantlepieces.

Faïence can also be found in simple utilitarian forms, but you can always distinguish it from plain pottery by its enamel porcelain-like finish. Good collections of Provençal *faïence* are owned by the Musée Arbaud in Aix-en-Provence, the Musée Cantini in Marseille and the Musée de la Faïence in Moustiers-Ste-Marie.

The town of Moustiers-Ste-Marie, in the Alpes-de-Haute-Provence, has been a centre of *faïence* since the 16th century. The "Moustiers-style," which is now made throughout Provence as well as in its name-

ally milky-white) enamel shell, decorated with engraved or painted designs and glazed to a high sheen. The drawings will depict anything from entire hunting tableaux with garlanded rims to a simple initial.

Faïence, introduced to France by Italian ceramicists during the 16th century, was originally the unique province of aristocrats. By the 18th century it had become available to all as a popular form of decorative pottery. Elaborate tableware forms such as scalloped plates and platters, pierced bowls and tea

sake town, follows the patterns created by the grand 17th and 18th masters who lived and worked in the small town.

Perhaps the most distinctive motif in the "Moustiers-style" is the 18th-century *décor à grotesques* that represents fantastic monsters, the donkey musicians, monkeys and plumed birds. To find it, you might want to visit the town's most celebrated *atelier*, Segriès, which is regularly frequented by the fashion house of Hermès and other members of the modern-day aristocracy.

The third type of pottery is *grès*, made out of grey clay from central France. Contemporary artists introduced it to the region be-

Left, Camarguais cowboys wear shirts of traditional fabric. **Above**, Biot glass.

cause its harder consistency lends itself better than *terre rouge* to art pottery.

Grès comes in a wide range of original forms and is decorated with a rainbow of polychrome glazes that range from gentle variegated green-pink to earthy brown-speckled blue. The artists who use this medium draw inspiration from the pottery of the Orient as well as Provence and strive to reinterpret the classic beauty of traditional craftsmanship with originality.

Two leading exemplars are P. Voelkel, who works in St-Zacharie and displays his work both there and in Cassis, and Roger Collet of Vallauris. Although long a pottery centre, Vallauris became internationally fa-

mous after Picasso joined the local workshop "Madoura" in the 1940s, and it is now crammed with cheap tourist ware. Collet, a master of both *grès* and porcelain, was a colleague and friend of Picasso and is one of only a handful of reputable potters left in the town. However, you can always go to the Musée Nationale de Ceramique, situated next to the church, to see the products of Vallauris's illustrious past.

The bubbles of Biot: The nearby town of Biot offers a refreshing contrast to the shoddy tourism that has overwhelmed Vallauris in recent years. In Biot, a unique system is used to create swirls of bubbles in clear or iridescently coloured blown glass.

Founded in 1956 by Eloi Monod, a potter and engineer who wanted to revive the craft of glass-blowing in Provence, the original Biot glass factory has grown from one blower, Raymond Winnowski, and one glassmaker, Fidel Lopez, to 70 workers. The workshop where all the glass is blown is open to visitors, with the lusty bare-chested Winnowski presiding amidst the glowing coals. The adjoining store offers an array of beautiful yet surprisingly sturdy glassware in more than 100 different forms: glasses and goblets, jugs, vases and bowls, as well as many miscellaneous items such as decanters, oil lamps and knife stands.

Creating new traditions: Today, most handicraft artisans working in Provence are not natives of the region. In the 1950s, artists as well as movie stars were drawn to the Alpes-Maritimes. The 1960s, a period of social upheaval in France when many sought a "return to nature," brought an even greater wave of artists – known as the "Romantics of '68" – to the entire region.

Trained in art schools, the new artisans freely experiment, creating new decorative forms and introducing innovations to the traditional utilitarian ones. Visiting art galleries in towns such as Aix-en-Provence, Avignon, Marseille and along the Côte d'Azur, walking through the many craft fairs such as the *Foire aux Croutes* on the Cours Mirabeau in Aix, or stopping by communal workshops scattered around the countryside, such as Visse and Rosen's San Francisco-style *atelier*, Li Mestierau, at the foot of the Alpilles, one will find an eclectic variety of forms and styles. Many have no specific link to traditional Provençal folk arts: painted silk, woven murals, mobiles, olivewood sculptures, jewellery, watercolours and pastels, leather goods and wooden toys, as well as more traditional Provençal handicrafts such as pottery and puppetry.

Despite the great changes brought on by the industrial age and the advent of the new artists, the traditional handicrafts of Provence have not been lost to the present, and the richness of the craft tradition continues to be both a foundation and source of inspiration for the Provençal artisan.

Above, Moustierware motif. **Right**, M. Fouque, **master santonnier, at work.**

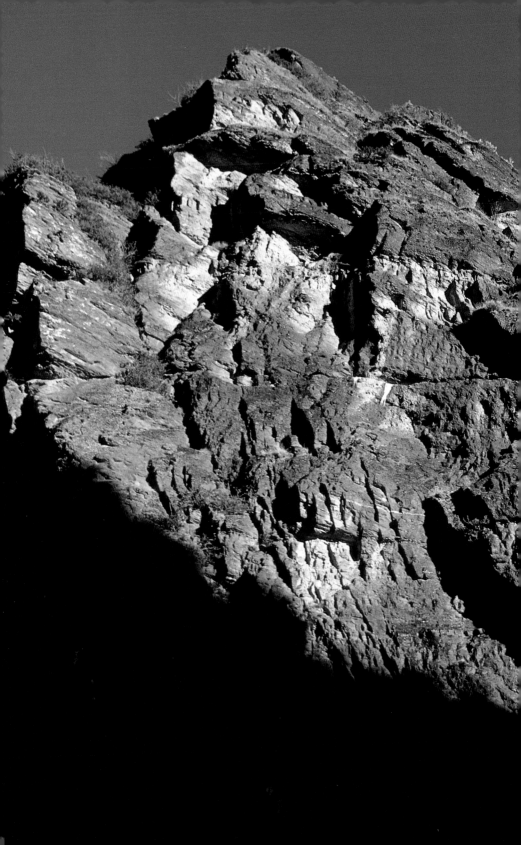

Provence consists of five departments with two sub-regions. Of them, the Vaucluse is known for lush landscapes, fruits and the sophisticated papal city of Avignon. The ancient Bouches-du-Rhône combines dry wide plains of olive trees and cypress with a Mediterranean coastline and includes the distinctly Roman city of Arles, the fountain-bedecked university town of Aix-en-Provence and the seaside metropolis of Marseille. Within it, the Camargue is an ecologically fascinating mixture of marshland, salt plains and beaches, populated by flamingoes and French-style cowboys.

Crowned by the naval capital of Toulon, the southern reaches of the Var also lie along the Mediterranean, while massive inland forests make it the most heavily wooded *département* in France. To the north, the Alpes-de-Haute-Provence rises to Alpine heights, with fortified villages clinging precariously to mountainsides. Its neighbour, the Alpes-Maritimes, is equally renowned for its hilltowns, becoming increasingly Italian in character towards its eastern border. As one nears the sea, one enters a different world: beaches and harbours, yachts and villas – the Riviera.

Along with disparities, certain very Provençal characteristics can be found all over. Summer festivals abound, as do fresh produce and a hearty but delicious cuisine. All year round, the legendary light of Provence, which has long lured artists here, dazzles mountains, plains and seaside alike. The people are warm and down-to-earth, and a love for folkloric tradition is reflected in much of their daily lives.

There is no question that where you spend your time will colour your impression of the region. But, wherever you go, you can find a little bit of the magic of Provence.

Preceding pages: the Gorges de Cians; evening on the Cassis waterfront; hilltown in the Var. Left, Niçois flower seller.

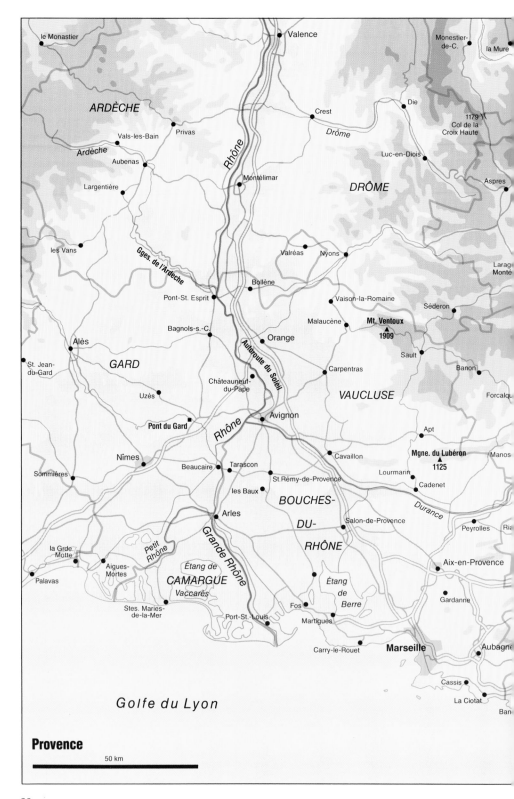

Provence

50 km

du cadavre
d'une femme à Bollène
Les colis étaient
bourrés de bijoux
Vaucluse Matin
La rupture

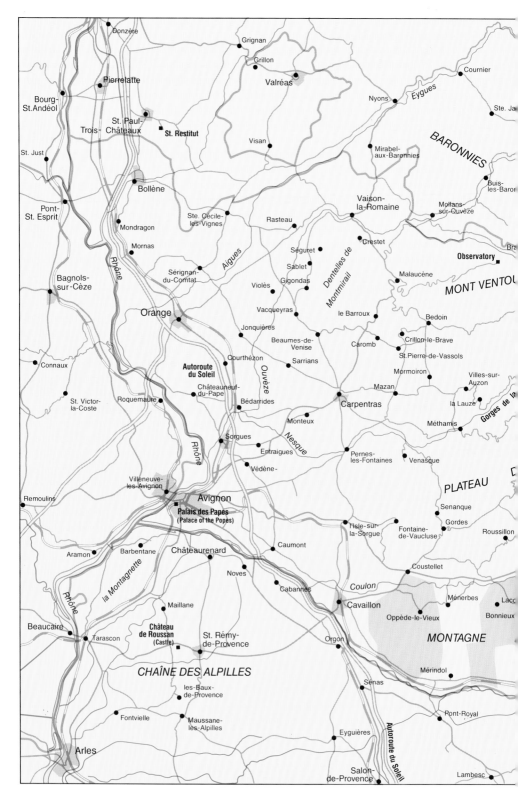

THE VAUCLUSE

In a recent survey conducted by *Le Point* magazine, the **Vaucluse** topped the list of 95 *départements* in France for cultural activities, second only to Paris. However, any traveller journeying through this region's beautiful country-side will quickly become aware of a richness far beyond staged events.

Each town and little village within the Vaucluse guards its own special character, overtly expressed through unique and traditional *fêtes* and customs. More intriguing differences exist between mountain and valley people, town and rural life, and even the Provençal and French mannerisms, all contributing to the joy of discovering the region.

A similar diversity in terrain provides the visitor to the Vaucluse with a real choice of things to do. You can go mountain climbing or bird watch, pony trek or canoe, taste some of France's finest wines in Châteauneuf-du-Pape or indulge in a cuisine that draws on an abundance of locally produced herbs, fruits and vegetables. Or you can simply sit back and, as you drive, let the fragrance of lavender, the freshness of rosemary and the softness of pine waft through your open car windows.

It is important to choose your season carefully in keeping with your plan of action, for – unless you intend to visit one of the many summer festivals – there are good reasons to go in early spring or late autumn. During those seasons, the region is less hot, less crowded and more naturally "Provençal." Both the blossoming of spring-time and the autumnal greens and browns have a magic that is a feast for the eyes and does wonders for the soul.

Whenever you go, the colour and texture of a land that embraces the snow-capped peak of Mt-Ventoux, the cherry blossoms of Malaucène, the ochre cliffs of Roussillon and, of course, the light that has inspired so many painters should be sufficient in-

Preceding pages: catching up on the news.

centive to wander away from the main cities and motorways to explore. And, as a general rule in the Vaucluse, the adventurous spirit is rightly rewarded. Some of the best finds are still tucked away along mountain tracks or forest-lined backroads.

From the north in Valréas to the west along the banks of the Rhône, southwards to the Durance River and east through Mt-Luberon, the Vaucluse has virtually natural borders. Historically, the region has always been a sort of crossroads. For centuries a trampling ground of marching armies, it has seen conflict between Romans and Gauls, Saracens and Christians, Catholics and Protestants and, more recently, between French Resistance groups and Germans. These many different conflicts have come together to shape the rich architectural heritage of the region.

Nowhere is this more apparent than in the papal city of **Avignon**, *préfecture* of the Vaucluse and gateway to Provence. Strategically situated near the junction of the Rhône and Durance rivers, Avignon was first established by the early Gauls as a tribal capital, and it was known to the Greek traders of Marseille. During the Roman period, however, it was overshadowed by Orange and (although some Roman artifacts can be found in the **Musée Lapidaire**, a former chapel of a 17th-century Jesuit college), most buildings that you can see today belong to a medieval past.

Avignon is, in every sense, a walled city, and 3-mile fortifications enclose its inner core. A walk along these ramparts, broken up by 39 towers and seven gates, reveals a cornucopia of historic buildings, churches and palaces.

Rabelais called Avignon "*la villa sonnate*," because of the number of steeples that adorned its skyline and, today, buildings of a religious character still outnumber the secular. On a less lyrical level, the battlements now also bear witness to the modern growth of the city. Factories and modern suburbs extend outwards from under the shadow of the wall to accommodate the city's population of over 100,000 inhabitants.

The Pont St-Bénezet.

The **tourist office** provides information on two good methods of getting to know the **old town**. The first is via a miniature train, which covers all the key points and the shopping zone. Later, having saved your energy, you can return on foot to explore in greater depth the buildings that most interest you.

Alternatively, the tourist office also offers an excellent guide service that takes you on either a half-day or full-day walking tour of the town, with commentary available in most of the major European languages. For the tour, it is best to book in advance as space is restricted. If you are travelling as a family or small group you can arrange to have your own guide.

Whether you go by bus or by foot, you must not miss the famous bridge, **Pont St-Benezet**, immortalised in the popular children's song ("*Sur le pont d'Avignon...*"), although today only four of its original 22 arches remain. Inspired by heaven, St-Benezet built the bridge at the end of the 12th century, but it was destroyed during the Albigensian War and reconstructed in 1234. The little **St-Nicholas Chapel**, which still stands on one of its piers, was also altered during this period and a Gothic apse was added to it in 1513.

There are four other places in Avignon that every visitor should see: the Papal Palace, the Cathedral of Notre-Dame-des-Doms, the Church of St-Didier and the Calvet Museum.

The **Palais des Papes**, symbol of the papal residency in Avignon (1309–77), is easy to find. As they say in Avignon, all roads lead to the Papal Palace. The Route Rapide, Rue Vieille Porte and Rue de la Monnaie all merge into its frontal square. Seen from this spot, the off-yellow stone, set against a clear blue sky, makes an imposing picture.

When you face the facade, with its two flanking towers, it becomes immediately clear that the palace was built for defensive purposes as well as residency. The former aspect of the structure was necessary, because the original city walls, which were built by Innocent VI and Urban V, were not enough to prevent the bands of wandering knights

that plagued the countryside from attacking the palace.

You enter the palace through the **Porte des Champeaux**. Once you step into the **Grande Cour** (or "the great courtyard"), this fortress palace will quickly take on the sense of being a city within a city. Already you will be able to feel all the splendour that once belonged to Avignon.

The immense inner courtyard also acts as a link to the splendour of contemporary Avignon. It is here that many of the open-air theatre performances of the famed summer festival are staged.

It takes about an hour to walk through the palace, which is divided into two sections: the **"old" palace**, built by Pope Benedict XII between 1334 and 1342, and the **"new" palace**, begun under his successor, Pope Clement VI, and completed in 1348. You may want to buy a simple map at the little shop that stands by the entrance, but you won't need any help to recognise the extreme difference in style between these two popes. The old palace has a monastic

simplicity and austerity that reflect the sombre character of Benedict XII. The new palace, on the other hand, is brightly decorated with fantastic fresco work and flamboyant ceilings, which have much to say about Clement VI, who was a patron of the arts and lover of the high life.

It is easy, almost fun, to get lost in all the rooms, but there are some slightly obscure things that shouldn't be missed. Be sure to look in on the row of portraits of the popes who resided in Avignon that hang in the **Aile du Consistoire** (Hall of the Consistory). Try to decide which one you would like to be seated next to at a sumptuous feast, such as were held upstairs in the **Grand Tinel** (Banqueting Hall).

Photographers might also want to note the great shot of the old town that can be taken from the window on the stairs that mount to the kitchen tower.

The most fascinating room in the new palace is the **Chambre du Cerf** (Deer Room). There your eyes will feast on the frescoes of Giovanetti, painted in

1343. These superbly colourful scenes of hunting, fishing and falconry, and of fruit-picking youths bathing in what looks like a modern swimming pool, give a valuable insight into life at the papal court in the 14th century.

If you were in any doubt about Clement VI's sumptuous tastes, the star-studded ceiling of the **Aile de Grande Audience** (Audience Hall), done in shades of blue and old gold, should dispel any last reservations. And, if it doesn't, the magnificent walls and windows of the **St-Martial Chapel** will.

Eventually, you will find the guardroom that leads back to the entrance. Before leaving, it is worth taking one last glimpse across the great courtyard. Now that you have experienced the interior, the definitive contrast in style between the old and new palaces should really take hold. It does not take an architectural expert to recognise which is which.

However, both parts of the palace are far from modest, although each in their own way. Their grandeur was received

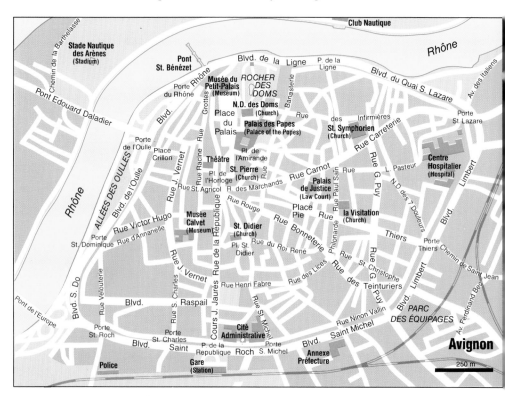

not without controversy. Petrarch, no lover of the court of Clement, called the palace "the habitation of demons," while Froissart, the well-known medieval chronicler, praised it as being "the finest and strongest in the world."

By way of contrast, the **Cathedral of Notre-Dame-des-Doms**, where John XXII is buried, is strictly a serious affair. This Romanesque, 12th-century building has undergone many architectural changes, but it still retains its original spiritual simplicity. Unfortunately, the addition in 1859 of a gilt cast-iron statue of the Virgin gives it something of the look of a wedding cake.

A church that hasn't changed much, since its consecration in 1359, is the **Eglise St-Didier**. It was the largest church to be built in the town during the Avignon papacy and owes much of its clean-lined attractiveness to the influence of ("old" palace) Pope Benedict XII. The elegant restriction of internal decoration is a reflection of the "purity" that Benedict supported.

Upon entry into St-Didier's first chapel, you will come upon one of the church's vantage points: an early Renaissance work by Francesco Laurana called *The Way of the Cross*. In 1953, more 14th-century wall paintings of the Crucifixion were uncovered, which are now slowly being restored. Another interesting feature is the hexagonal Gothic pulpit that stands in the centre of the church, a certain indication of the important role sermons played during the 14th century.

Shopping facilities in this area are good, and there are several spacious pedestrian zones that are lined with boutiques as well as open-air bars and cafés. As a general rule, the prices become more reasonable the further you go from the Palais des Papes. However, in July and August, all the streets of the old town (as in most of Provence) are hot and crowded, and even the smarter restaurants hereabouts do not offer the quality of menu or service that their exteriors promise.

During any month, a visit to the **Musée Calvet** will be rewarding. The

museum, which can be found on the Rue Joseph Vernet, was named after a doctor who was also an archaeologist and bibliophile. When he died, he left his large library, art collection and funds to start the museum.

Inside, you will discover a comprehensive study of the French and Avignon schools of painting and sculpture from the 14th to the 20th century. David, Gericault, Delacroix, Corot and Manet are just a few of the important painters whose works hang in this nicely lit museum. (Canvases from other painters of the Avignon school can be found in the **Petit Palais**.)

Musée Calvet's archaeological collection is a treasure trove of objects from the neo-Gothic period. Its holdings include finds discovered in the 1960s that have changed theories about the origins of Avignon and have suggested that its culture has much earlier roots than was previously believed.

A cultured city: Avignon's past is in many ways celebrated by the city's renowned summer festival. Started in 1947 by Jean Vilar, it continues Avignon's long-time tradition of cultural excellence. With the exception of Petrarch, who quite openly hated the city, many writers have sung its praises. For Stendhal, it was "*la ville de jolies femmes*" (the city of pretty women). The British philosopher John Stuart Mill chose to be buried within its walls. Frédéric Mistral, the great Provençal poet, was educated at the Old Lycée in Avignon and began his most famous poem, *Mireille*, while living here. So, it seems natural to find dramatists, actors, poets and musicians flocking to the city during the 20th century.

The festival runs from the first week of July to the end of August. Performances include classical theatre such as Shakespeare and Racine, modern theatre such as Becket, "off-Broadway" or fringe-type productions, street theatre, puppets and marionettes, dance, mime and café cabarets. Some orchestral concerts are held and, recently, a French-American film workshop was added to the agenda.

Cherries.

Given their own dramatic flare, the Avignon popes would undoubtedly have approved of the festival as well. At any rate, many of the shows are given in the court of their one-time residence. Other performances make imaginative use of local churches and cardinals' houses to stage their productions.

Don't be surprised, however, while sitting in a boulevard café during July or early August, to find yourself suddenly surrounded by a troupe of strolling players in colourful medieval costumes, carrying drums, pipes and lyres and acting out a full-blown drama. This is part of the charm of the summer festival. Gaiety exudes from every quarter of the city, and modern-day troubadours (who often sound more like Bob Dylan than Raimband d'Orange) will unannouncedly serenade your table and then, with the jingle of silver, move on to the next restaurant.

The town has a busy, but breezy and relaxed, atmosphere during this period. The serious productions arranged by the festival mix comfortably with more in-

formal and often quite satirical street theatre. Just wandering around the old town will probably give you a couple of opportunities for entertainment, and a few minutes on the central **Place d'Horloge** is sure to gain you some sort of impromptu performance.

A good way for visitors to find out what, where and when is officially going on is to visit the **English Bookshop**, on the second floor of 23, Rue de la République. Here you can pick up a free copy of the *Langue Provençal Journal*. Despite its name, this small paper is written in English, and it gives a brief breakdown of events. In the same building is the **French-American Centre**, so Anglophones who opt to stay for the season and want a crash course in French will be all set. Francophones should head over to the tourist office, where there are hand-outs that list the festival productions and programmes of events in French.

During other times of the year, there are still plenty of things happening in Avignon. January welcomes an eques-

trian fair, February an antique fair and mid-November heralds the Baptème des Côtes du Rhône, which is the festival celebrating the yearly first tasting of the regional wine. And regularly, throughout the year, there are musical soirées at the **Minit Conservatory**, open markets, up-tempo disco at the **Embassy Club** and quiet entertainment at the **Piano Bar** of the Hotel Mercurie next door to the palace.

Sporting types will enjoy a swim in the olympic-size pool at **Ile de Barthelasse**. Two other spots that welcome day visitors for a refreshing dip on a hot day are the **Squash-Racket Centre** and the **Golf Club** at Châteaublanc. Boat cruises along the Provençal waterways can be arranged at Allées de l'Ouile and 32 Boulevard St-Roch. Both places offer regular trips.

Across the Rhône: If you want to escape the hustle and bustle of Avignon altogether, you may prefer to stay across the river at **Villeneuve-les-Avignon**. This much smaller city has a rich and celebrated history all its own but lacks the hectic frenzy of its neighbour.

Towering over the attractive little town is **Fort St-André**, which guarded the frontier of France when Avignon was allied to the Holy Roman Empire. The structure is everything a fortress should be. Built in the second half of the 14th century by John the Good, it still retains a military prowess so palpable that you feel it the moment you pass through its magnificent defensive entrance with its strong powerful twin towers. The massive crenellated walls represent one of the finest examples of medieval fortification extant.

The other militaristic building in Villeneuve is the isolated **Tower of Philip the Fair**, which was once the starting point of the St-Benezet bridge. Both the St-André fort and this tower give excellent views over the papal city. On a clear evening you can see some magical twilight colours, as the sun sets on golden stone and the hefty silhouette of Mt-Ventoux in the distance.

Villeneuve rose to splendour during the Avignon papacy. As the papal court

Herbes de Provence at market.

grew in glamour, the number of adjunct cardinals also rose. Finding that Avignon had no more suitable space available, many of these cardinals chose to build their magnificent estates in Villeneuve. At one point, there were as many as 15.

Ironically enough, the one structure to survive from that period is the simple and austere **Chartreuse de Val de Bénédiction**. This Carthusian monastery was founded in the mid-14th century by Pope Innocent VI (whose tomb lies in the adjacent church) to commemorate the general of the Carthusian Order, who had himself been elected pope in 1352 but had refused the position out of a sense of humility.

Although you can't visit any of the cardinals' homes, you can treat yourself to a feast for one at the **Hostellerie La Magnaneraie**. This hotel's quiet restaurant can be found on the terrace, set against the fragrance of pines. Equipped with a swimming pool and tennis court, the hotel also provides a comfortable and convenient base from which to tour the region. Otherwise, Villeneuve offers a reasonable choice of smaller hotels, and there is an excellent campsite on the outskirts of town.

Itineraries: There are three basic journeys that can be easily made from Villeneuve. The first is towards **Châteauneuf-du-Pape**. This trip involves crossing the busy bridge to Avignon, but you can avoid the main-town traffic by joining N7 immediately and heading off in the direction of Sorgues. At Sorgues, join D7 going west.

On either side of the road, rows of green vines rise out of what looks like a beach of pebbles. In fact, this land was once washed by the waters of the Rhône. Today, the curious landscape marks the beginning of the villages whose vineyards are permitted to call themselves under the Châteauneuf-du-Pape appellation.

The legal history of the area is interesting, for it marked a major change in the history of French wine. In 1923, the local wine-growers applied to the courts for exclusive use of the Châteauneuf-

Medieval St-André Fort at Villeneuve-es-Avignon.

du-Pape designation. Until that time, there were no such restrictions on the labelling of wines. After a slow legal process, six years later, judgement was passed in their favour by an Orange court. The action gave rise in 1935 to the *appellation contrôlées* that appears on French bottles of wine today.

The vineyards of Châteauneuf-du-Pape are planted with 13 different grape varieties. The best wines achieve their complexity and character from blends of these grapes. Most red wines are the result of a blend of at least four grape types. Grenache is the dominant red-wine grape, followed by Mourvèdre, Syrah and Cinsault.

The end-product is what Alphonse Daudet nicknamed "the king of wines and the wine of kings." Châteauneuf-du-Pape is a supple, warm and full-bodied wine (made into reds and whites but no rosés) that goes well with strongly flavoured dishes like game, red meat and pungent cheese. This noble wine, perfumed with the scent of the Garrigues, can be sampled at any of the local vineyards. Particularly impressive are the cellars and vineyard of **Domaine de Mt-Redon**.

Above the village of Châteauneuf-du-Pape itself are the ruins and tower of the 14th-century **château** built by Pope John XXII as a summer residence. From here, you can look right down the valley of the Rhône over the red-tiled roofs of the village all the way to Avignon. Unfortunately, the château's strategic importance led to its almost total destruction in 1944, when German troops fought a scathing battle against the Resistance forces.

More opportunities to visit *caveaux de dégustation* (wine cellars where tasting is available) lie along D92 towards the market town of **Courthézon**. One valuable tip to remember about visiting the wine cellars is that it's always a good idea to offer to pay. This indicates to the proprietors that you are a serious taster, so you will be offered the better wines. And chances are the owners will refuse payment anyway.

Real wine lovers should head a little

112

further along the route to **Beaumes de Venise**, whose wines are excellent. This is the spot made famous by troubadour Raimband d'Orange, who wrote and sung about medieval life in its castle. You'll enjoy the drive, for it is an especially pretty one, on a road lined with vineyards and neat rows of cypress.

Jews, truffles and wagoners: Back in Courthézon, it's about 5 miles (8 km) to **Sarrians**, where there is a fine example of late 18th-century architecture in the eccentric **Château de Toureau**. From here it's a straight run along D950 to **Carpentras**. Along the way, any of the side roads that lead in the direction of the **Auzon River** will take you to beautiful shady groves perfect for escaping the heat of the midday sun and enjoying a picnic.

Carpentras's strange collection of different architectural styles – from Roman to rococo – reflect its history. The town's name is said to have been derived from the Latin word "*karpenton*," meaning a two-wheeled cart drawn by horses. And, indeed, for cen-

turies it was famous for its wagoners. Even before it was conquered by the Romans, however, it was called Carpentoracte and was the tribal capital of the Celto-Ligurian Memini. The conquest itself is recorded in the carvings on the **monumental gate** in the courtyard of the **Palais de Justice**.

By the 4th century, Carpentras had become a bishopric. Then, from 1274 until 1797, it was elevated to the position of capital of the Comtat Venaissin, and as such it was a part of the Holy See. During the first couple of centuries of this period, a thriving Jewish population enjoyed a liberal freedom of worship and were known as the "*juifs du pape*" (or, papal Jews). In testament to this singular period of religious tolerance, France's oldest **synagogue** stands behind the town's Hôtel de Ville. Built in the 15th century, one floor of the building now acts as a museum, but you may have to request permission from the curator to gain entry.

Also dating from the 15th century, the Romanesque **St-Siffrein Cathedral** is

further evidence of the church's good relationship with the Jewish community of that time, for the south portal is known as the **Jew's Gate**. Note the marble sphere that is depicted as being gnawed by rats and stands above the gate. Historically, the sculpture is interpreted as connoting God's anger, for the rat was considered the spreader of plagues. And, over the centuries, the Vaucluse was no stranger to the dread arm of the plague.

One man who was a good deal less than kind to the Jewish population was the Bishop d'Inguimbert. In the 18th century, he decreed that the Jews had to remain within their own ghetto and couldn't traffic with the better houses. Nonetheless, he played an important role in the cultural and architectural development of Carpentras.

D'Inguimbert ordered the building of the elaborate rococo **Chapelle Notre-Dame-de-Sainte** and founded the **Ho-tel-Dieu Hospital** in 1750. He also left the city a famous collection of books, on view at the **Musée des Beaux-Arts**.

This is by far the most important library collection in all of Provence. It contains over 150,000 books and 2,300 manuscripts, including rare editions of Petrarch and an autographed score by J.S. Bach.

Music is further remembered in Carpentras during the Offenbach Festival. This exciting event not only stages operas but also includes visits from international ballet companies. The delightfully cool, open-air theatre where the concerts are held is a pleasant extra in the hot summer.

During intermission, you can enjoy some of Carpentras's sweet specialities. The town makes its own sort of caramel candy, called *berlingots*, and is also known for its strawberries. But most of all, Carpentras is rightly famous for its truffles, which some call "*les perles noires du comtat*" ("the black pearls of the county").

On the return journey along D942 towards Villeneuve and Avignon, make a short detour at **Monteux**, southwest along D13, to the **Saule Pleureur**. Set

Picnickers.

in the Quartier Beauregard, this restaurant has established a well-deserved reputation for gastronomic delight, using mostly local produce.

Back on the main road of D942, you will pass through **Entraignes-sur-Sorgue**. This village was a stronghold of the Templars during the 12th century, and one tower still stands of the fortress that this powerful group once commanded there. From here, the road leads directly back to Avignon, from where you simply cross back over the Rhône to reach Villeneuve.

A visit to Roman Gaul: The second journey you might take from the Villeneuve-Avignon area is to **Nîmes**. Although this will take you technically outside the borders of the Vaucluse and, actually, even Provence, it's a great introduction to Roman Gaul and is generally included in tours of the area.

To reach Nîmes you pass the **Pont du Gard**. This bridge and aqueduct are a testament to superlative Roman technology. The aqueduct spans the Gardon Valley; 2,000 years after its construction it remains in excellent condition

Vineyards slope away on either side of the route, and it is here that the Tavel wines are grown. However, modernity is the prevalent force in the area. Even as you approach the outskirts of the city, you will become aware of the emergence of modern architecture.

Urbanisation had already taken a firm hold of Nîmes 100 years ago. When Henry James sojourned here in 1884, he described the square where he stayed as having "the air of Brooklyn and Cleveland." When you gaze at the readily visible skyscrapers to the southwest, it is easy to agree with him that Nîmes's "only treasures are its Roman remains, which are of the first order."

The Roman ruins in Nîmes are wonderful. Nîmes was the first French city to be colonised by the Romans and for many years was their link with Spain. As a result, a number of impressive structures were built in the city by the Romans, several of which still stand.

The most outstanding monument is the **Amphitheatre**, built in AD 50. Just

The Pont du Gard.

slightly smaller than its counterpart in Arles, it was originally capable of seating 21,000 spectators at a time. It also possessed a gallery where slaves could sit and was designed so that it could be flooded for aquatic events.

Over the centuries, the amphitheatre experienced a variety of indignities. Visigoths substantially altered its form for use as a fortress. Then, it suffered further changes to accommodate a village for 2,000 poor people, including the addition of many houses and a chapel. Finally, during the 19th century, attempts were begun to unearth the original structure, which was by then hidden under 25 ft (8 metres) of rubble.

Today, the amphitheatre has been returned to something of its early glory. It now welcomes Spanish, Mexican and Provençal matadors in both traditional bull-fighting (where they do kill the bull) and Provençal-style (where they don't). During the summer, its stands are filled with eager fans.

Like the amphitheatre, the **Maison Carrée** had to go through a variety of different incarnations before arriving at its present state. This 1st-century BC temple was even used as a stable for a while, as well as a town hall and a monastery church. Although its original dedication is a matter of discussion – some say to Juno, others say to Jupiter or to Minerva – it is generally considered to be the best preserved of all Roman temples still standing.

The building, which has for centuries been known as the "Square House" despite the fact that it is twice as long as it is wide, now houses a **Museum of Antiquities**. Among its many Roman holdings is the lovely Venus of Nîmes.

On a hot summer day in Nîmes, you may well have found yourself quenching your thirst with a bottle of Perrier. This natural mineral water comes from a spring just a little distance southwest in the direction of Vauvert. To find out more about the strange and wonderful history of what is now one of the most popular drinks in the world, you should visit the plant at **Vergèze**.

It was Hannibal and his 30 elephants

Vineyard owner.

who supposedly first discovered the spring here, in 218 BC. Some 300 years later, the Romans also were enchanted by the cool, naturally sparkling water. Then, in 1863, Napoleon III took up its case. He decided the water should be bottled "for the good of France."

However, it was an Englishman, St-John Harmsworth, who, in 1903, first put the water in a bottle and marketed it, spurred on by a meeting with a Dr Perrier in Vergèze. What they did was to collect the abundant natural gas, found in the underground lake formed by the spring, and reinsert it into the water under pressure.

For a striking contrast to the modernity of the Perrier plant, take a look at the adjacent château with its Louis XIV architecture and its attractive gardens.

More of Rome: The last excursion from Avignon is a full-day's outing and brings together two of the most important Roman towns in France: Orange and Vaison-la-Romaine. This trip is sure to make you realise just how extensive was the culture and civilisation brought by the Romans and how it was adapted to fit the region.

Take the N7 direct for 15 miles (24 km) to **Orange**. In the 2nd century, this southern city was of much greater importance even than Avignon. Today, it is still a busy place, partly because of the autoroute that passes by and brings a lot of through-travellers stopping the night, and partly because of the large daily market that is held between mid-April and mid-October.

The city's name actually has nothing to do with the fruit but, rather, is connected with the Royal Dutch House of Orange, who inherited the city in 1559 from the Chalon family. Its three most outstanding monuments – the **Arc de Triomphe**, the **Ancient Theatre** and the **Forum** – however, date back to the earlier days of the Romans, and each, in its own way, represents the force of Roman colonisation.

The Arc de Triomphe comprises three archways. The decorative friezes and carvings tell a proud tale of Roman success on land and on the sea, but their message is subtle. The weaponry, shields and helmets depicted on the lower part of the side arches are Celtic, and their positioning suggests Rome's triumph over Gaul.

The Ancient Theatre, which at one time could hold up to 10,000 spectators, is still in use. Orange's summer theatre festival and other cultural events all year long are staged here, while the statue of Emperor Augustus sits in the central alcove overseeing things as though nothing had changed. The acoustics are excellent in this well-preserved auditorium, but don't forget to bring a cushion, because the stone seats are hard and cold.

The Forum stands next door to the theatre. It is one of only three Roman gymnasiums still extant. Unfortunately, it suffered some drastic changes during the period of William of Orange, but you can still get a fairly good idea of its original size and shape.

For a clear explanation of how Roman colonial policy worked in Gaul, visit the **Musée Municipal** just opposite the Forum on the Rue de Pouillac.

Tiled roofs of Beaumes-de-Venise.

Inside is a marble tablet, discovered during an archaeological dig in 1963, on which were recorded land holdings. This AD 77 example of land registry has markings that entend some 510 sq. miles (850 sq. km) from Bollène to Auzon. It not only reveals what areas were settled but also to whom the better plots belonged. This finding has given archaeologists a superb avenue for investigating the nature of early property ownership, on both a geographical and sociological scale.

The museum also has two other sections. One specialises in the history of Orange and the other in paintings. Of special note are the gallery's portraits of members of the Royal House of Orange and the paintings of British artist Sir Frank Brangwyn.

At the treaty of Utrecht in 1713, Orange was yielded to France. When Louis XIV said that the city's theatre possessed "the most beautiful wall of the kingdom," it is quite likely he was expressing his joy in having finally won over this valiant town as much as his wonder at the survival abilities of Roman architecture.

There is much more, however, to Orange than its Roman heritage. If you take the time to stroll through its streets, you will stumble upon some delightful old houses on attractive tree-lined squares and avenues. A particularly pleasant walk leads you up the hill behind the theatre, where the ruins of the **château** built by the Orange family can be found. It is easy to understand why they chose to locate their castle here, for it offers a magnificent view of the town.

Peaks of lace: The drive on D975 to Vaison-la-Romaine passes one large vineyard after another and encompasses some of the most picturesque countryside in the Vaucluse. On the way are several short detours well worth taking, for they will rapidly transport you to another century.

D8 brings you down to the hamlet of **Vacqueyras**, near to the already mentioned Beaumes-de-Venise. Before reaching it, however, you might prefer to switch onto D7 towards the beautiful

Wine château in Gigondas.

118

medieval village of **Gigondas**. The excellent wines produced here are well-enough established to be pricey, but there are still several lesser *caves de dégustation* were you can pick up a bottle or two without feeling you've spent a fortune.

Continuing along D7 will head you towards the prototypically Provençal village of **Sablet**, which in turn leads into **Séguret**. This charming village, with its steep streets and old gate, fountain, belltower, church and castle, looks like a film set for *Ivanhoe*.

In the village is a nice terraced restaurant called **Le Mesclun**. From it you can look down into the valley and point to the vineyard whose wine you would like to try. The lavish portions and mouth-watering desserts are as good an excuse as any for lingering in this calm and tranquil spot. As an added surprise, the owner has his own collection of Belle Epoque paintings.

The sharp limestone peaks that frame the area are **Les Dentelles de Montmirail**. *Dentelle* means lace in French, which should give you a good hint as to this rock formation's appearance. The jagged edges that jut into the clear blue sky present an attractive challenge to climbers, many of whom make special trips here just to tackle the slopes. The less energetic will also find the area great for rambles through the surrounding pine and oak woods and over the wild but beautiful countryside.

From Séguret take D88 back to D977 and you will soon reach **Vaison-la-Romaine**. By a direct route Vaison is only 17 miles (28 km) from Orange but, unlike Orange, Vaison's Roman past is very much a 20th-century discovery. Excavations only began in 1907. Vaison is divided into two distinct parts. The Roman town was built on a flat area of land on the east bank of the River Ouvèze. This is where the bulk of Vaison is located today. Walk down through the town and cross the Roman bridge and you will see the medieval village perched on a rocky outcrop. Clearly with the fall of the Roman empire the villagers no long found it safe to live on the exposed river bank and re-

treated to the more easily protected hill across the river.

The digs in the ancient part of the city have been done in such a way that you can begin to visualise something about life in Roman Gaul. There are two open sites. The first lies within the Puymin Quarter and is composed of a park dotted with attractive cypress trees and a handful of buildings. Uncovered have been the **House of the Messii**, the **Portico of Pompey** and the **Nymphaeum**. The portico is a type of pillared hall, and the Nymphaeum is the source of the town's water supply.

Reproductions of the statues that are housed in the adjacent **museum** decorate the park's **promenade**, bringing it some life. Actually within the museum are the originals, plus a helpful historical map of the province of Gallia Narbonensis and a variety of antiquarian exhibits such as jewellery, weapons, coins and ceramics. The imposing statue of Tiberius and two larger-than-life marbles of the Emperor Hadrian and Empress Sabina have a lot to say

about the one-time arrogance of Rome.

The second excavated spot lies to the southwest of the Puymin site. Here, the ruins of a **Roman villa** and a well-restored and paved **Roman street**, whose mosaic floor leads to the arch of a former **basilica**, give the visitor an impression of the size and layout of the commercial part of the town during the Roman times.

The last major ruin in Vaison is the **Roman Theatre**. Like the one in Orange, it provides the stage for much of the town's summer festival, although it is much smaller in size. Cut out of rock from the north side of the Puymin Hill, it has been appreciated by theatre lovers for over 25 years for its dramatic, operatic and balletic productions. The festival begins during the first week of July, usually with a colourful and expensive folkloric and international gala, and runs through August.

Vaison's **Cathédrale de Notre-Dame-de-Nazareth** is a well-preserved, 12th-century church whose arcade pillars possess beautifully deco-

rated capitals. Other attractions include a walk through the maze of the old streets to the **haute ville** (upper town), where you will find an interesting if dilapitated church and a ruined château that was once the country seat of the counts of Toulouse. Looking east from the top of the upper town will give you one of the best views out over the valleys and foothills that lead to Mt-Ventoux. This spot is slowly becoming an artists' colony and might be a good place to purchase local pottery and paintings.

A day-trip from Vaison will take you across the Aigues River north to **Valréas**. Valréas marks the northernmost frontier of the Vaucluse, in which department it is included for historical reasons despite the fact that it is surrounded by the Drôme River. The witty and literary Madame de Sevigné spent considerable time in this old Roman town and eventually built a château in nearby **Grignan**. There is more than a slight ring of truth to her criticism of the climate, since the mistral wind is par-

Girls' club of Vaison in local costume.

120

ticularly virulent here. However, she did have much praise for the local food and the immediate countryside, which is brightened with fields of bright yellow sunflowers.

Valréas and **Grignan** are still small, medieval-seeming towns, but the network of roads and number of trucks that roll down them are grim reminders that you are returning to the very different lifestyle of the 1990s.

As you drive back south towards Vaison, you will pass a number of new communities like those of **Pierrelatte** and **Bagnols-sur-Cèze**. These settlements have sprung up as a result of the construction of nuclear and military centres (which, of course, you won't be able to see from the road). All the original locals that know a thing or two have moved out.

After a hot and exhausting day amidst the ruins of Vaison or the secret industrialisation of the north, you may want to stop the night at **Les Terres Marines**, the local health spa. To reach it, take D98 south in the direction of Ma-

laucène, go west onto D76 then look out for a right-hand turn about 2½ miles (4 km) along the road for Crestet.

Les Terres Marines may be difficult to find, but once there you will discover that it offers just about everything a weary traveller could desire. It is set in a truly peaceful spot, with a refreshing swimming pool shaded by oaks and a selection of magnificent walks. It also has a sauna, solarium, hot tub with jet streams and fully equipped gymnasium. If your back is sore from too much driving, a soothing massage by the resident physiotherapist will get you feeling back to normal. And if you feel that you've been appreciating the wines of Châteauneuf-du-Pape too liberally, you will be rejuvenated by the restaurant's tasty health-food menu.

Hilltop villages: After a visit to the spa, you should be ready for a few days in the nearby mountains. This part of the Vaucluse is worth devoting a good piece of time to, for there is a lot to see concentrated in a relatively small amount of land. Among other things,

the **Mt-Ventoux** area gives you the chance to do some horseback riding, climbing or hiking, any of which can easily run into a full-day activity. Moreover, driving around here takes a little longer than elsewhere, because many of the attractions involve fortified hilltop villages that often can only be reached by winding roads, followed by a walk on foot to a lofty castle or church.

Crestet, south of Vaison, is just such a hilltop village. It is set above olive groves and has both charm and a ghostly quality. Upon first entering, you may think that this 12th-century village has no inhabitants. Then, at twilight, you will see the odd light or two in a window – but, still, you won't hear a sound.

To visit the town, you have to leave your car at the outlying park and set out on foot. A climb up the cobbled alleyways brings you to the **church** and, after a further ascent, to the town's **castle**. From the lookout point on top are some stunning views across the valleys and the peak of Mt-Ventoux. Walks around other parts of the village will also offer some green and ferny spots to picnic.

Get back on D938 and head south to **Malaucène**. The fun main street bustles with cafés and restaurants where, during the season, you can sample some of the cherries for which this town is a capital. Malaucène also produces some delicious local honey.

The town's **church** offers a good example of how closely connected war and religion have been in this part of France. Built by Clement V in the 14th century, it is both fortified and castle-like in appearance from the exterior. As the iron-plated front door suggests, the church was the place of refuge for the townspeople during the times of war. Today, it functions on a more traditional level, and you will have to attend a service to hear the tone of the impressive 18th-century organ.

If you head out west from here in the direction of Mt-Ventoux, you will be following the route that Petrarch took in 1336 when he undertook to climb the legendary mount. First, however, you might want to make a quick dip south to

Horseback riding in the northern Vaucluse.

Caromb. This route, D938 to D13, will take you over a scenic backroad. Even if you don't stop along the way, you will be able to see, on both sides of you, a series of little fortified villages. Almost unchanged from the time they were first built, they crown the surrounding hills.

Caromb is another traditional example of the medieval hilltop village of this region. Long a vineyard haven, the town's well-preserved exterior walls enclose another typical feature of the area: a bell-towered **church** with an 18th-century wrought-iron cage for the bell, designed to protect it from the mistral. Inside, the church is furnished with frescoes and woodcarvings. Don't forget, however, if you elect to stay in the town's hostel, that the church's bell chimes all night long!

Another fortified town in the Mt-Ventoux area is **Le Barroux**, whose **château** and fine Romanesque **church** illustrate the locale's transition from royal to country seat.

Lunch along the Ouvèze. The base of Mt-Ventoux is surrounded by many more pretty villages.

Mazan, **Crillon-le-Brave**, **St-Pierre-de-Vassols** and **Bédoin**, to name a random few, are all charming in their own individual ways, and many are wine-tasting centres for the produce of the Mt-Ventoux vineyards. A good number of these *villages perchés* (literally, "perched towns") are best investigated on foot. Because of their defensive physical characteristics and dramatic locations, they fire the imagination with colourful pictures of knights, sieges and other scenes from the Vaucluse's turbulent past. A visit here will bring to life the songs of the troubadours.

Mt-Ventoux: After you've had your fill of picturesque hill villages, rejoin D974 for the best route to Mt-Ventoux. Placed along the immediate ascent, the small, Romanesque, 11th-century **Chapelle de Notre-Dame-du-Grosseau** is worth a look. On a hot day, drink from the nearby Source du Grosseau. The taste of the fresh water in this mountain pool far exceeds the promises of the average Coca-Cola television commercial.

Mt-Ventoux divides into two very

distinctive sections: the lower area, which lies below the ski resort and is ferny and forested and full of beautiful spots where one can stop to enjoy a packed lunch; and the upper, very harsh, limestone area that approaches the summit. When the sun reflects off the white of this higher part, the glare is so great it can leave you momentarily blinded. The peak is snow-capped for about three-quarters of the year.

There are two interpretations of the origin of the mount's name. One suggests that it is a derivation of the Celtic phrase "*ven top*," which means "white mountain." The other associates it with the French word "*venteux*," or "windy." And, indeed, there are always winds blowing around the Mt-Ventoux area. In fact, it is wise to be wary of this, for the gusts can become quite powerful as you climb, and lighter cars can easily be pushed all over the place.

The peak is ever-white, whether it be from snow or limestone, and has a certain science-fiction quality about it. This is emphasised by the placement of a radar station from which protude numerous television aerials and next to which is an observatory.

However, a stop in the **Chapelle de la Ste-Croix**, which stands nearby, should give you the chance to spend a moment meditating on the glories of nature rather than the intrusions of man. From up here, at 2,000 feet, it is also easy to appreciate why the Vaucluse has always been such an important crossroads. On a clear day – although mist and haze are more the norm – you can see the Rhône, the Alps and the Mediterranean. Some even claim to have spotted the Pyrenées.

The drive downhill towards **Sault** takes you through a nature reserve of particular interest to botanists. The 19th-century Provençal entomologist Jean-Henri Fabré discovered a rare species of yellow poppy growing here as well as a collection of other plants to which he attributed unusual medicinal qualities. One hundred years after his death, practitioners of various forms of alternative medicine – generally of the

The misty heights of Mt-Ventoux.

homeopathic variety – are now proving his theories to be correct.

Fabré also was influential in re-foresting this area, and the region is a paradise for nature lovers. As Fabré observed at the turn of the century, "half a day's journey, in a downward direction, brings before our eyes a succession of the chief vegetable types, as we should find in the course of a long voyage from north to south along the same meridian." And it is true. Pine trees give way to oak, then you spot fields of wild thyme and, eventually, in the lower valleys, the resilient mauve of lavender.

A benign statue of Fabré overlooks the main thoroughfare of **Serignan**, well to the west by Orange. The unassuming home and rocky outdoor "laboratory" where this celebrated scientist, affectionately dubbed by the public *L'homme des insectes* ("the insect man") conducted his research are also here and are open to visitors.

Not surprisingly, the Ventoux area is equally popular with ornithologists. They come in early summer with an eye to spotting sub-alpine warblers, sea crossbills and mountain thrushes. However, the decline in species of all sorts of wildlife, due to the rash of forest fires in Provence, is unmistakable. Campers, climbers and picnickers should take extra care not to leave matches or cigarettes smouldering.

The climate of **Buis-les-Baronnies** (actually in the *département* of the Drôme), nestled between Mt-Ventoux and the Baronnies Ridge to the north, is especially suitable for growing apricots, olives and almonds. And, in early July, the fragrance of lime blossoms fills the town. Not surprisingly, in the old quarter, many of the shops sell excellent samples of Provence's most genuine souvenirs: lavender soap, lime-blossom *eau de toilette* and olive oil.

The Gorges de Nesque: If you don't want to go north from Mt-Ventoux, you should probably head southeast towards **Sault**. During the 15th century, Sault was a baronial seat, but now the only remnants of glory are the towers of the 16th-century castle. The Roman-

Mountain life in Buis-es-Baronnies.

esque **Eglise de St-Saveur** stands guard over the town, which acts as a market-place for the surrounding lavender mills.

The drive along D942 to **Monieux** is lush and green and lined with fields of lavender. If you stop in the town to lunch at the delightful **Les Lavandes**, you will be able both to enjoy a spectacular view from the terrace and mingle with the riders coming in fresh from the mountains. Watch as they tie up their horses in the square adjacent to the restaurant. There is a very pleasant feeling about the buzz of this village as it continues a time-honoured existence.

The Monieux road takes you through the **Gorges de Nesque**, which at all times of the year offer breathtaking views and a sensational cascade of colours. In some spots, the gorge plunges to depths of over 300 metres, and scrub and rocks camouflage profound caves. Despite the fascination of the mountain views, the driver should be sure to pay attention for tunnels and hairpin bends.

The Nesque Gorges have their own share of attractive Provençal villages. **Villes-sur-Auzon** has, like Mazan, had its fair share of disasters in the form of invaders, sieges and outbreaks of the plague. On top of that it bore being the battleground of Baron des Adrets. Nonetheless, it managed to survive and, today, has a steady if small population of a little less than 1,000 inhabitants.

The close-knit community lives off the cultivation of the vineyards that surround the town. You may want to stop at one of the town's *caves de dégustation* to try the local Côtes du Ventoux, a light-coloured "café" wine, which is best drunk when young and which, since 1974, has qualifed to bear an *appellation contrôlée*.

Like many mountainous areas in Provence, the Nesque Gorges make for great climbing and hiking country. An excellent starting point for these activities is **Le Hameau de la Lauze**, but you may well have to ask directions to find this rustic hostel. Located approximately 4 miles (7 km) from Villes-sur-Auzon, its turn-off is most obscurely

Festival in Valréas.

marked and at first looks like no more than a path.

Once you find the way, the winding drive down rough pebbled road, through woods, scrub and gorse brush, gives a clue to the adventure in store. And, indeed the owners of this *ferme-auberge* (literally, "farm-inn") mean what they say when they describe themselves as having a "*cadre rustique*" ("rustic setting").

La Lauze supplies guides, maps and excellent advice for hiking and pony trekking. Local walks through the wild fauna, flowers, herbs and oaks, olives, beeches, cedars and pines that dot the mountainside are sensational. You will find that often, on a hot summer's day, the temperature is just a little bit cooler than that of the valleys and villages of lower altitudes and that the air is fresh and invigorating.

The menu at La Lauze is strictly mountain men's food, and sleeping conditions would probably better appeal to an overnight commando unit. Nevertheless, the spirit is great, and the experience and expertise of the hosts have saved many an amateur explorer from spending an unexpected night on an exposed cliff face.

To the South: As the descent from Mt-Ventoux will have revealed, the countryside of the Vaucluse can change rapidly. Further proof of this will come along the journey south and slightly west to **Venasque** through the **Plateau du Vaucluse**.

Venasque stands quietly tucked away between two small but steep hills, cupped to the east by a deep and dense forest, in which it is easy to become lost. The village has a pleasant and unaltered charm that offers a good example of the benefits of careful restoration. Once the capital of the Comtat Venaissin, to which it gave its name, it still retains an identity of its own, although rather drastically subdued. In the early summer, it comes alive as a market centre for cherries and during the rest of the year has a couple of buildings worth viewing.

The **baptistry** within the **Eglise de Notre-Dame** is one of France's oldest religious buildings. Built during the 6th century and remodelled during the 11th, it still causes dispute among historians as to its specific function.

Also worth noting is the **Chapelle de Notre-Dame-de-Vie**. Constructed in the 17th century on top of a 6th-century site, it houses the tomb of Boetius, bishop of Carpentras and Venasque. The tombstone is an excellent example of Merovingian sculpture.

From Venasque, follow D4 to D177 south through the plateau. Looking down over the **Valley of the Senancole** will reveal the path to the **Abbé de Senanque**. The curved road at its side leads to an area for parking your car, about 1¼ miles (2 km) away from the abbey itself.

The 12th-century Cistercian abbey stands at the edge of a grey mountainside and is surrounded by oak trees and lavender. Its one curiosity is the manner in which the limestone from which it is constructed changes colour as the day heats up. The buildings seem to change from grey to a deep yellow.

Senanque possesses a natural serenity. Although there have been no monks living in it since 1969, it still has the feel of an abbey, and there is a remarkable quietness reflected in the pastoral setting, the simplicity of the building and the austerity of its interior. If you find the mood persuasive, you can retire to a room that has been set aside for meditation. This room also happens to be the coolest spot in the monastery, so you can emerge from it with both the spirit elevated and the body refreshed.

Now a cultural centre, the abbey has established a permanent exhibition on comparative religions. Among its holdings are a fascinating series of detailed photographs of the nomadic tribes of the Sahara and clear documentation of the origins of monasticism. During the summer months, musical concerts are held here. The acoustics are excellent, and Gregorian chants echo through the building as though nothing has changed since the abbey was founded in 1148.

The nearby town of **Gordes** is linked to Senanque by a narrow, winding and bleak road. But don't expect to find it deserted. During the summer, this town is one of the most popular tourist spots in the Vaucluse.

At first glance, the village of Gordes looks as though it is about to slip off the small mountain on top of which it is spread. Over the centuries, however, this peculiar location has contributed to the village's natural defence. Gordes has had a turbulent history, especially during the 16th-century Wars of Religion and then again during World War II when the town was a stronghold for the Resistance movement.

Most of the tourists come to see the "ancient" village of 20 restored *bories* (drystone huts) that lies just beneath the central town. This group of curious, wind-resistant dwellings in round or rectangular shapes are believed to date from the 17th century, but don't be surprised to find 19th-century tools and furniture in some. Others are privately owned and have been modernised for use as holiday homes.

As a bridge to the contemporary world, stop in at the **château**. The castle itself is Renaissance and old but, in more recent times, five rooms were set aside for the contemporary artist Vasarely. Within them, he established a study centre for the "interaction of the arts and sciences."

Overall, the château has a sobering effect. First built during the 12th century, it was radically altered during the 16th century to emphasise the strength of its fortifications. Moreover, within the **Vasarely Museum**, some of the kinetic objects on view have a disturbingly mesmerizing effect. It is with relief that one returns to the sunshine.

Summer homes, artists and pastis: From here, the drive south along D104 will take you into the foothills of the **Lubéron**. This third, and last, mountain range in the Vaucluse is also a general favourite. It is an increasingly popular spot for well-heeled Britons and Parisians to have summer homes. Appreciation for its natural beauty spurred the creation of a 247,000-acre (100,000-ha.) **Regional Park** in 1977.

Outside the park, the foothills make for great walking country. But remem-

Playing boules beneath the plane trees.

ber, come autumn, that the hunters here take their sport most seriously. Once a "boar drive" is under way, it's like driving in Paris – pedestrians are considered fair game. After the hunting season has opened, be sure to walk with your eyes and ears open.

On a lighter note, *pastis*, the legendary drink of the Provençal, had its origin in this part of the Vaucluse. First blended within the small villages of the Lubéron, this herbal brew is supposed to be the secret of the Provençal people's reputation for good health. It is nowadays usually associated with Ricard, a licorice-flavoured drink commonly referred to as the "good-natured thirst quencher."

The force of tradition is strong in the Lubéron. The mountain village of **Lacoste**, where stone quarries are still worked, is a good example of how slowly change comes to some parts of the Vaucluse. Rural life here very much resembles that depicted in the Pagnol films, and Lacoste's major acknowledgement of the 20th-century comes in the form of the floodlit *boules* court behind the local church.

Elsewhere in the village, traditional life continues much as it has for the last few decades: hanging out in the cafés, sipping *pastis*, playing the popular card game of *belote*. Perhaps all that is missing is the Marquis de Sade, who lived here from 1774 until his arrest in 1778. The ruins of his huge **château** look down on the village and, as the guide is wont to say, "If walls could talk..."

From the heights of **Bonnieux**, southeast along D109 to D3, you can see the junction of the Vaucluse Plateau and Mt-Ventoux. On one side of you, through an attractive mist, you'll look out over a forest of cedars and, to the other, south towards the Crau Plain, you can catch the glimmer of the Beise Lake and, beyond it, the Mediterranean.

The easternmost section of the Vaucluse, from Bonnieux to **Oppède-le-Vieux**, has the distinct touristic advantage of being less crowded during July and August than many other parts of the *département*. Yet, the area is as

Church in Lacoste.

rich in both natural beauty and historical interest as many of the more accessible parts of the Vaucluse.

Many of the stories written by the renowned Provençal novelist Jean Giono (1885–1970) dwelt upon the dying out of local villages in the 1920s and 1930s, and the "Petite Lubéron" could easily have gone that way. In recent years, however, a new brand of year-round resident has brought a fresh spirit to these small villages.

Writers and artists from all over the world, attracted by the tranquillity and the climate, have undertaken the careful restoration of many of the houses. Their tasteful work shows a great understanding and respect for the Lubéron's past, and their appearance has done much to improve the region's economic future.

All over, the soft yellow and red shades of the houses are both startling and attractive. Magic descends with the setting of the sun, as the colours become illuminated with unearthly light.

Particularly beautiful is the southerly **Roussillon**. This hilltop village, just east of Gordes, is constructed of an incredibly brilliant red, set off by the grey-green landscape that surrounds it. First made known as the subject of sociologist Laurence Wylie's *Village in the Vaucluse*, under the pseudonym of "Peyrane," Roussillon became the site of a real-estate boom in the 1960s. Although it is still charming, visitors of today will have to read the book to find its impoverished heritage.

The capital of the Luberon is **Lourmarin**. The countryside that surrounds this small "city" is colourful all-year-round, because the large variety of trees, wild flowers and vegetables that thrive in the region benefit from having the longest growing season in France.

Lourmarin could also claim to be a sort of cultural capital for the Vaucluse. On the west side of town, and open to the public, is the house where that most famous French author Albert Camus (1913–60) once lived. He also chose to be buried here, and his grave lies amidst a tangle of wild rosemary. The Provençal writer Henri Bosco (1888–1976)

Herbal vinegar.

130

is buried here as well. Reading his novels is a good way of understanding the area, for they often draw nostalgically on his memories of the childhood he spent here.

More art is still produced at the 16th-century **château** just outside the village. It was restored in 1920 by Laurent Vibert, and today acts as a study centre for artists, musicians and writers. Musical concerts and exhibitions are held here regularly, and an organised tour of the château is available. If you take the tour, be sure to ask for an explanation of the graffiti, scrawled on one of the walls, that depicts a small sailboat surrounded by mysterious birds with human faces. Before the château was taken over by Vibert, it had acted for many years as a stopping place for gypsies on route to Les-Stes-Maries-de-la-Mer. Many people say that the graffiti is a curse put on the place by them after their expulsion.

A little detour 6½ miles (10 km) east will bring you to the delightful 10th-century village of **Ansouis**. Like many of the tiny Provençal towns, its narrow, twisting and climbing streets were certainly not designed for motorised traffic. Unless you are driving an ultra-compact car, you may want to park in the central square and do your exploring by foot.

Ansouis's **château** is an interesting combination of styles, for it has been in the same family for centuries, and each member to live there has left his or her own mark. It commands the top of the hill where the town stands. Also a novelty is the **Musée Extraordinaire**, dedicated to marine life and, in particular, to the underwater creatures that once occupied the Vaucluse.

A market town: From Ansouis, follow the bank of the Durance west along D973 to **Cavaillon**. On the way, you may be tempted to buy fresh melons from a roadside vendor. Cavaillon is the melon capital of the Vaucluse – indeed, its justly famous melons are appreciated all over Europe.

The fertile fields that surround this town contrast with the rocky terrain of

Picking tilleul, which is used for tea.

much of the land that you have been passing through and make for an excellent crop of fruits and vegetables. A typical morning sight is that of the farmer on his Velosolex motorcycle with a sidecar carrying huge baskets of some type of produce, as he heads for Cavaillon's marketplace.

Outdoor markets are a year-round feature of life in this *département* where so many of the fruits and vegetables are grown that feed the rest of France. Far from a side attraction, the markets remain the centre of business as well as social activities for many of the area's towns and villages.

Whether you speak French or not, you can gain real insight into the Provençals and their way of life by visiting their markets. These people take their food seriously, and the beginning of any good Provençal dish invariably involves fresh tomatoes, peppers, herbs and garlic. Colourful fruits decorate the stalls, and you can generally find specialised stands selling local spiced sausage and goat's cheese.

Cavaillon's market is far from an exception, and people travel from all over to shop here. But melons are not all that is legendary about the town. Popular mythology suggests the area around Cavaillon was once flattened by a monster called "the Coulobie." Basically an oversised lizard, he later either flew away to the Alps or was chased away by St-Véran, the patron saint of shepherds.

The Coulobie is the subject of a painting by Mignard to be found in the **Notre-Dame and St-Véran Cathedral** at Place Joseph d'Arrard. The building itself is an unhappy mixture of styles with a 16th-century facade and some unfortunate 19th-century additions. However, its little 14th-century side chapel was nicely restored after the Wars of the Religion in the 17th century and has a particularly attractive interior.

Like Carpentras, Cavaillon "tolerated" a significant Jewish community during the time of the Papal residency in Avignon, although the number of its members never exceeded 300. A first **synagogue** was built during the 16th

Below, the red dirt of Roussillon. Right, sketching in Lourmarin.

ARTIST COLONIES

The first artist colony in the Vaucluse dates back to the 14th century, when Petrarch informed his readers of an enclosed valley where "water sprang from the mountain." This magic spot has since been named the Fontaine de Vaucluse.

The valley of the Calavon lies north of the Luberon Mountains, along with a score of famous hilltowns such as Roussillon, Gordes and Ménerbes. Although seemingly calm, this same valley has been the site of frequent wars and invasions since before the birth of Christ. The local population was, therefore, not too surprised when, in the 1940s, the region underwent a full-blown invasion by foreign artists and intellectuals.

The locals watched these painters and writers at first with amazement and then with curiosity and commiseration. Indeed, the humble native residents found themselves able to relate to the barely marginal existence of the artists. Little by little, they allowed their mountains to become the heart and inspiration of an entire new subculture in the area.

The transformation really began with World War II. Many artists and intellectuals took refuge in Provence, where they could find beauty, peace and affordable housing. One such artist, Consuelo de St-Exupéry, wife of the novelist Antoine and an exile from Paris, wound up with a group of artists and architects in Oppède.

This small village had fallen into deep decay, and its original inhabitants had all left to make new homes further down the valley. Undaunted, the colony set about turning the ruins into studios. Although, after the war, the group dispersed and the buildings fell back into ruin, it was not long before other artists took their place in Oppède and neighbouring villages.

Painters were not the only artists to take refuge in the Vaucluse during the war. The playwright Samuel Beckett spent from 1942 to 1945 in the red village of Roussillon, where ochre and iron had been mined for more than 1,000 years. Unfortunately, his visit wasn't as successful as that of his peers. He was so bored by village life that he had a nervous breakdown. He returned to Paris the minute peace was declared.

Meanwhile, Gordes was also being discovered by artists. The hilltop village had been abandoned in 1904 after an earthquake changed the water table but, to the wartime artists, the love of the site superceded the need for water or electricity. In 1943, the famous artist and theoretician André Lhote moved to the town and tried to start an art school. Then, a few years later, painter Jean Deyrolles saw Gordes on his way to Collioure. He decided to stay and was soon joined by his students from the Berlin Academy of Art.

Deyrolles's connection with the Denise René art gallery attracted even more artists, including Hungarian-born Vasarely, one of the most famous of the "op-artists." Vasarely leased the château that stood in Gordes from the town and took responsibility for its restoration. Once it had been returned to its original glory, he transformed it into a museum.

Even though the Lubéron region never really produced an artistic movement, it continued to be a hotbed of inspiration and to attract many artists long after the war had ended. Among these was the surrealist painter Bernard Pfriem who founded an art school in Lacoste in the 1950s that is now affiliated with the Cleveland Institute of Art. The school's dedicated outlook has drawn some of the best instructors to be found in the US. Visiting lecturers have included such personalities as Man Ray, Max Ernst, Henri Cartier-Bresson, Ernst Haas, Peter de Francia, John Rewald and Stephen Spender.

In more recent years, photographers have also discovered the advantages of the Lubéron. Denis Brihat started a school of photography in Bonnieux, Jean-Pierre Sudre founded another in Lacoste, and the French National School of Photography is now in Arles. The region's exceptional light causes the number of shutterbugs steadily to swell.

In addition, many traditional crafts can be studied from masters living in the Lubéron. Among these are pottery, weaving, lacemaking, basketmaking and iron work. Music is also represented by the Deller Academy of Early Music, located in Lacoste and open in summer.

century, but it later fell to pieces, and the elegant building that now stands was constructed in its place in 1772.

A small **Musée Judeo-Comtadin** occupies what once was the bakery where the Jews made their unleavened bread. It stands on the ground level of the synagogue and contains, as well as the original oven, Jewish prayer books and Torahic relics.

Cavaillon's newly constructed **cultural centre** has its feet firmly planted in the 20th century. Apart from staging jazz concerts during the town's annual summer festival, it boasts a lively yearlong programme of performing and visual arts.

Also striving to keep up with modern times is the bustling little city of **Apt**. Its particular contributions to the economy of the region are crystallised fruits and preserves, the making of truffles and the bottling of lavender essence. In addition, it is one of the few places in the region still to mine and refine ochre.

On a more spiritual level, Apt is the seat of the **Ancienne Cathédrale Ste-Anne**. The main structure dates from the 12th century, but the Royal Chapel, which is also the major point of interest, was erected in 1660, the year that Anne of Austria arrived in pilgrimage. It is now the destination of an annual pilgrimage by Catholic devotees that takes place on the last Sunday in July.

All over Provence, you will see the word "*mas*," a regional dialect word meaning "farmhouse." Many of the most convivial places to stay are renovated *mas*, for they are often conveniently and pastorally located, personably run and give a nice feeling for the traditional lifestyle of the area.

A good example of the *mas* hotel is in **Gargas**, just outside Apt. The **Mas de la Tour** waits at the end of a winding, dusty road off route D101. This 12th-century farmhouse has been converted into a more-than-comfortable hostel with a swimming pool, a restaurant and 12 clean rooms.

Before leaving the area, you will probably want to visit **Fontaine de Vaucluse**. It's a physically delightful

Markets are the centre of activity.

but busy spot – over a million tourists visit each year. It also is a good place to begin or end a trip to the Vaucluse, for it brings together many of the different aspects of the region's history, geography and mythology.

The town's main architectural sights – a war museum, ruined castle and 11th-century church – don't add up to anything very startling, although the Romanesque **Eglise de St-Véran** possesses the coffin of the 6th-century bishop of Cavaillon, said to have freed the area of the Coloubie monster.

The real attraction is the "**fountain.**" Fed by rainwater that drains through the Vaucluse Plateau, it is thought to be the source of the Sorgue River. It emerges from within a cave and, in winter and spring, the flow can rise to 32,985 gallons (150 cubic metres) a second. Needless to say, it is one of the most magnificent natural spectacles in Provence, indeed, all of France.

Emerald green water gushes forth from the underground river believed to be its source. Such noble investigators as Jacques Cousteau have come to try to substantiate this claim, but by far its most celebrated observer was Petrarch. The poet lived here from 1337 to 1353, between stays in Avignon, and it was here that he composed his celebrated sonnets to Laura. As with so many places in the Vaucluse, poetry and legend play large parts in the village's popularity.

Two-and-a-half miles (4 km) from the fountain is the quintessentially Provençal *village perché* of **Saumane-de-Vaucluse**. Once again, some of the key names from Provence's past crop up in this town's history. The village was a papal gift by Pope Clement V to the de Sade family. Restoration has begun on their impressive, pine-enclustered **château**.

Nature, however, seems to have had the last word here, for all the trees have been permanently marked by the fierce gusts of the mistral. But this is true for so many places in the Vaucluse, where the real wonders are natural ones that owe nothing to human beings.

Left, fruit vendor; **right**, peaches.

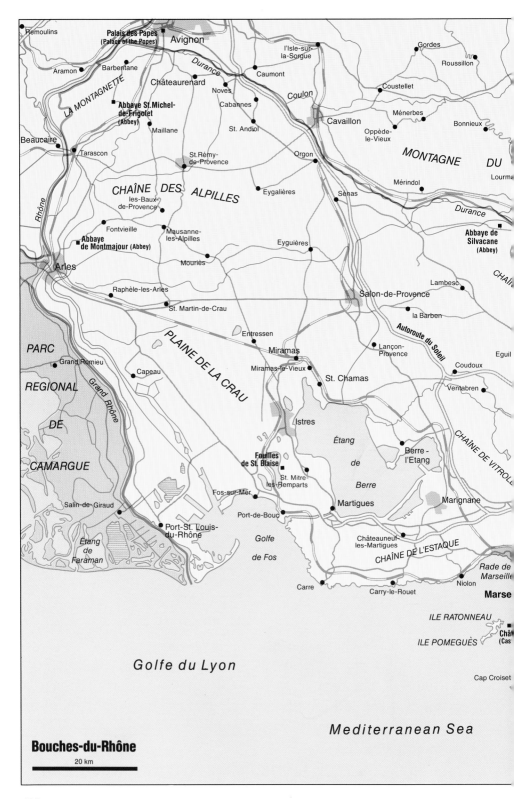

Remoulins · Palais des Papes (Palace of the Popes) · Avignon · l'Isle-sur-la-Sorgue · Gordes · Roussillon

Aramon · Barbentane · Châteaurenard · Durance · Caumont · Coustellet

LA MONTAGNETTE · Novès · Cabannes · Coulon · Ménerbes · Bonnieux

Abbaye St.Michel-de-Frigolet (Abbey) · St. Andiol · Cavaillon · Oppède-le-Vieux

Maillane · Beaucaire · Tarascon · St.Rémy-de-Provence · Orgon · MONTAGNE DU

CHAÎNE DES ALPILLES · Eygalières · Sènas · Mérindol · Lourma

les-Baux-de-Provence · Durance

Rhône · Fontvieille · Mausanne-les-Alpilles · Eyguières · Abbaye de Silvacane (Abbey)

Abbaye de Montmajour (Abbey) · Mouriès · CHAÎ

Arles · Raphèle-les-Arles · Salon-de-Provence · Lambesc

St. Martin-de-Crau · la Barben

PARC · Entressen · Autoroute du Soleil · Eguil

Grand Romieu · PLAINE DE LA CRAU · Miramas · Lançon-Provence · Coudoux

REGIONAL · Capeau · Miramas-le-Vieux · St. Chamas · Ventabren

Grand Rhône · CHAÎNE DE VITROLL

DE · Istres · Étang de · Berre-l'Etang

CAMARGUE · Fouilles de St. Blaise · Berre

Salin-de-Giraud · St. Mitre-les-Remparts · Martigues · Marignane

Fos-sur-Mer · Port-de-Bouc · Châteauneuf-les-Martigues

Étang de Faraman · Port-St. Louis-du-Rhône · Golfe · CHAÎNE DE L'ESTAQUE

de Fos · Rade de Marseille

Carre · Niolon · Marse

Carry-le-Rouet

Golfe du Lyon · ILE RATONNEAU · Châ (Cas

ILE POMEGUÈS

Cap Croiset

Mediterranean Sea

Bouches-du-Rhône

20 km

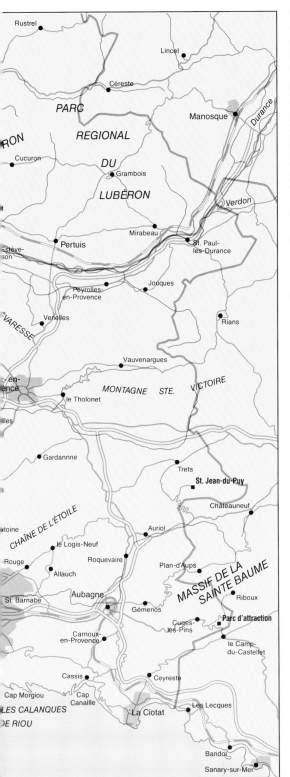

THE BOUCHES-DU-RHÔNE

The privileged position of the Bouches-du-Rhône (literally, "mouths of the Rhône") between the Mediterranean and one of France's greatest rivers has made it a virtual museum of European history. But visitors shouldn't expect to see the Parthenon or the Villa di Borghese gleaming on a distant hilltop. Instead, they will encounter acres of arid land dotted by crooked olive trees and dark vineyards, alternately scorched by a merciless sun and threatened by the violent gales of the mistral.

It takes an informed eye to appreciate the historical bounty of the Bouches-du-Rhône. Many of the monuments are either in ruins or hidden amidst the desolate countryside. Other sites become interesting only after learning the myths and traditions that surround them. Nonetheless, a visit to the right place at the right time with the right information can transform a mass of rock into a touchstone for the magical, mystical world of this *département*.

Although a fairly small *département* in size, the Bouches-du-Rhône can be divided into at least three distinct areas. The divisions centre around the major cities: Marseille, the second largest city in France, and its industrialised coastal territory; Aix-en-Provence, an elegant and bourgeois university town, and its slightly mountainous and fertile surroundings; Arles, ancient and distinctly Roman, set in the midst of dry, flat and poor plains with menacing Alpilles Ridges to the north. A fourth area, the marshy Camargue, is so individual that, although administratively a part of the Bouches-du-Rhône, it deserves (and has been given) a chapter of its own.

Provence's oldest city: It was 2,600 years ago that Greek sailors from the Ionian city of Phocaea first sailed into the natural harbour of **Marseille**. According to legend, they arrived just as Gyptis, the local Ligurian princess, was selecting a husband. Suitors stood in a

Preceding pages: splash of sunflowers.

circle awaiting her decision when, eschewing local blood, she handed the chalice that marked her choice to Protis, captain of the Greek entourage.

From their union flowered a prosperous Greek trading post, called Massilia. Over the centuries, the Massilians knew numerous high and low points of fortune, all the while developing a strong and independent character still apparent in their modern descendants.

Today, the city continues to be a major sea port and harbour – with a somewhat salty reputation. The latter is due to the fact that, as a centre for trade and commerce, a certain amount of drug traffic and black marketeering inevitably passes through its ancient waters. Also, the city is one of the major French entry points for North African immigrants. Their emergence as an integral part of the French work force has engendered a strong local following of the reactionary National Front party headed by Jean-Marie Le Pen.

To make matters worse, the proud Marseillaises have wasted little effort in

trying to refute their well-publicised problems. The overall result is that most visitors to Provence consider Marseille a spot either to avoid or to pass through as quickly as possible, looking over their shoulders and clasping their wallets all the while. In truth, however, Marseille is a quite fascinating city, with its pale colours and strong personality, and no more dangerous than any other major urban centre.

Any visit to Marseille should begin at the **Vieux-Port**. Here, pleasure boats share the waters with fishing rigs, and a lively fish market heralds each morning along the wharfs. Although the city's other harbours now handle incoming commerce, the Vieux-Port is Marseille's original and oldest harbour – and still its most picturesque.

At the very base of the Vieux-Port docks a ferry that taxis visitors out to a tiny rock island just off the coast. This is the site of the **Château d'If**, from where the legendary Count of Monte Cristo was fabled to have made his escape. The castle is currently empty and, in truth, not terribly interesting, but Marseille's city council has decided to give it some spice by recreating its interior, complete with furnishings and wax figures. Until the project has been completed, visitors can enjoy a great view of the city, a little swim off its rocky shores or one of the nighttime performances held here during the summer.

On the northern side of the port is the **Quartier Panier**. Many of the city's immigrants live in this, the oldest, quarter and, as there is no public nightlife, it is not a wise place to wander around after dark. During the day, however, it is an interesting (and safe) area to explore, with its narrow climbing streets and colourful inhabitants – as long as you don't mind getting lost at least once.

Within the Quartier Panier are several of the city's museums. Not to be missed is the **Musée de Vieux-Marseille**, which will give the newcomer a fine introduction to the folk life of Provence. Housed within the remarkable Maison Diamantée (1570–76), this museum is dedicated to Provençal culture, with entire rooms of traditional cos-

Left, the Old Port in Marseille.

tumes, tarot cards, crèches etc. Also on display are a variety of engravings and models of Marseille over the centuries.

As long as you are in the area, you might as well look in on the **Musée des Docks Romains**, which shelters a series of uncovered Roman docks on the very spot where they were excavated. The open amphores once stored grain, olives and wine for the Romans.

On a more modern scale, and also in the neighbourhood, is the **Galeries de la Charité**. Built in the 17th century as a hospital by the grand architect of Marseille, Pierre Puget, the recently restored buildings are now the site of several galleries of contemporary art. In the very centre stands a chapel with an interesting oval-shaped domed ceiling, and behind the chapel is a small outdoor theatre active in the summer.

Ancient walls: Much of Marseille's ancient ramparts were destroyed during the continual battles of the centuries – and most of whatever was left was decimated by the Germans during World War II. But, among the modern buildings and bobbing shipmasts, a few ancient walls still stand.

Recent excavations at the **Centre Bourse** have unearthed fortifications, wharfs and a road, dating from somewhere between the 3rd century BC and the 4th century AD. Called the **Jardins des Vestiges**, the remains now form a public garden beside the Centre Bourse shopping mall and the **Musée d'Histoire de Marseille**.

The museum is itself a fascinating place, filled with an excellent selection of Ligurian, Greek and Roman artifacts found over the ages in Marseille. Everything is extremely well-documented, such that Francophones can read all about the restoration of the ancient Bateau de Lacydon while examining the boat or the Greek method of firing ceramics while viewing a Hellenic kiln.

Be sure to note, directly on the left when you first enter the museum, the terrifying "Gros Repasse." Once the doorway to a Ligurian sanctuary, frontal ledges are filled by the skulls of unlucky enemies. Also worth an extra

minute, for French speakers, is a stop in the *videothèque*, where videotapes concerning Marseille, on anything from soapmaking to World War II newsreels, can be requested and viewed free.

Running straight up from the centre of the harbour is the **Rue de Canebière**. Despite its fame, this is an unattractive street, lined with cheap department stores and unsavoury characters. The cool crowd should head right past it to the **Cours Julien**, where the young hipsters hang out. Around this square are the prerequisite cafés, numerous second-hand bookstores and a number of alternative clothing shops.

Equally *branché*, but a little less youthful, is the pedestrian area around the **Place Thiars**. Located on the south side of the harbour off the Quai de Rive Neuve, its streets are lined with galleries, shops and outdoor cafés. Newly installed parks and fountains make it a sympathetic spot to lunch or take an afternoon stroll.

Also on this side of the harbour, at 47 Rue Neuve St-Catherine, is a small shop

of special interest to the *santon* enthusiast. At the **Atelier Marcel Carbonel**, visitors are welcome to watch some of the best-regarded crèche figures being made and view M. Carbonel's personal collection of Christmas cribs from around the world.

Just down the street, at 136 Rue Sainte, is another enclave of Marseillaise tradition, **Le Four des Navettes**. First created in 1781 in this very shop, *navettes* are biscuits cooked in the shape of the boat that is said to have brought Mary Magdalene and a host of other saintly Marys to the shores of Provence 2000 years ago. Made according to a secret method, they are the special mark of the Fête de la Chandeleur, which takes place on 2 February annually. But biscuit fanciers can buy them for two francs each all year round.

The Rue Sainte ends at **St-Victor's Basilica**. In the 3rd century BC, the site was a Greek burial ground and, in the 1st century, it became a Roman monument. Then, during the 3rd century AD, a Christian cemetery began to develop

Mansion on the Corniche J.F.K.

around the tombs of two martyrs who were slain during the persecution of Dece in AD 250.

The church itself was built in the 5th century by St-John Cassian, an Egyptian monk who named it after a third local martyr, Saint Victor, the patron saint of sailors, millers and Marseille. Saint Victor had been ground to death between two millstones. The primary structure now standing is an 11th-century reconstruction, whose high Gothic arches resound with distant taped music. Deep below, in the crypt, lies the aptly solemn original church. Ancient sarcophagi, some hidden in candle-lit coves, line the walls; in the centre stands the sombre tomb of the two martyrs.

Even more eerie, in a rocky alcove to one side, is the 3rd-century tomb of Saint Victor himself. His grave image, carved into the wall on the right as you enter, watches over the shadowy corner. This is not a place for those with a fear of ghosts, for they command the dark and hollowed crypt.

Once back on the port, if you still have an appetite, you might want to try the *bouillabaisse* dining experience. Anyone seeking to understand Marseille should attempt this traditional fish stew – but be fair warned. Only a few restaurants still offer an authentic *bouillabaisse*, and it won't be inexpensive. At the same time, don't expect a refined meal. *Bouillabaisse* was created by fishmonger's wives trying to use up the catch their husbands hadn't sold, and in basic ingredients and recipe it hasn't changed much.

If you can still stand after three bowls of fish soup and are in the mood for some night-time panorama, climb to the site of **Notre-Dame-de-Garde**. No matter where you go in Marseille, you can't miss noticing the airy 19th-century basilica. Erected on a bluff of 530 feet (162 metres), it offers, without question, the best view over the city.

But the most beautiful view in Marseille is to be found along the **Corniche President-John-F.-Kennedy**. No one should miss taking a drive along here. Following the coastline, this 3-mile (5-

THE UNDERWORLD AND MARSEILLE

As a thriving port, Marseille has long had to bear the associations that come with trade and the passing sailor. By the 1930s, such was its tough reputation that every employee in the town hall was said to have a criminal record. The statistics were far from conclusive, but the city nevertheless cemented its reputation as France's capital of organised crime and corruption.

Today, the town hall and the *milieu* (underworld) coexist in an unconcealed loathing that, admittedly, sometimes gives way to pragmatism. This is because, although Marseille has traditionally produced strong mayors, they have little control over a feature that permeates society in southern Europe: clientelism. A favour rendered is a favour returned. A *milieu* "businessman," for instance, will during an election campaign be approached for favours by candidates from all sides. Yes, perhaps he can help, he tells his supplicants – in return for guarantees of protection and a job for a friend.

If the circumstances sound like New York in the 1920s, then there will be no surprise to find that connections between the two cities abound. Marseille was a transit port for Sicilian emigrants on their way to New York. Many never reached Ellis Island and, instead, found hope in France's second

largest city. Some brought the code of the mafia; it was to mix with the traditions of the native Marseillaises and the Corsican clans which had come to the mainland in search of jobs. Over generations, this heady brew took to an extreme the Phocaean city founders' vision of Marseille as a trading post.

In 1971, the "French Connection" was broken up, exposing a huge web of drug smuggling with Marseille as the linchpin. The process had been for the illicit raw materials to be hidden in cargo ships from Pakistan and the Middle East, refined in the south of France and shipped out to New York. By then, much of the money had been laundered, finding its way to bars, nightclubs and casinos all the way up the coast.

Of course, busting the French Connection didn't put an end to all criminal activity in Marseille. The *milieu* continues to function with panache. Several years ago, the police seized 40 fruit machines in a clampdown on illegal gambling. Their faith in the security of local warehouses was minimal, so the evidence was stored overnight in the main police station. When they returned the next morning, 36 of the machines had been meticulously stripped down, the mechanism removed for further use elsewhere.

And the dashing brigands of one day frequently turn into blood-thirsty killers the next. *Règlement de comptes* (literally, the settling of accounts) spill into the street, from one-off assassinations to massacres like that of 10 people in the Bar du Téléphone in 1977.

Attempts are often made to strip the core from the *milieu*. The imprisonment in 1983 of one of the gangland bosses, Gaetan Zampa, was thought to have ended the *guerre des clans*, a war of underworld families. Instead, the *milieu* restructured. Its vocabulary now has taken on the jargon of business efficiency, and the *parrains* (godfathers) have virtually disappeared. Five groups are said to share Marseille, occasionally cooperating on joint ventures. Operations aim to maximise revenue with the lowest possible profile. Labour-intensive prostitution and racketeering are out; fruit machines and bank robberies – the *milieu* pioneered the technique of tunnelling in through the sewers – are in.

When the "new" underground does come out of its shell, it is ruthless. An examining magistrate, Juge Michel, was shot dead in 1983 as he rode home on his motorcycle. It was the first time anyone had dared to touch a senior judicial figure in the city. Two people were sentenced for the murder five years later, but the identity of whoever ordered the killing remains unknown. However, Michel's investigations into drug smuggling, and the massive surge in local drug addiction, leave the police in little doubt that the drug trade has come back to roost in Marseille.

Yet, it would be unfortunate for tourists to fear the darker side of the city. Visiting the Louvre is potentially a more dangerous pastime; for despite its reputation, Marseille actually has a far lower crime rate than Paris.

km) road looks out over the sea, the offshore islands, the surrounding *massif* and the winding shore ahead. It also is adorned by some of the most beautiful war memorials to be found anywhere. Of special note is the one that commemorates the Oriental troups of World War II. Even the staunchest of hearts will heave a little beneath its outstretched arms.

The road eventually leads to the **Plage de Marseille**. The beach here has been split into two parts, the first half being pebble and the second sand, and the water is quite clean. Bearing a striking resemblance to Southern California, this area is a lively and chic place to dine at night.

Not just a fishing town with fjords: Hardcore beachgoers may want to continue down the coast another 15 miles (23 km) to **Cassis**. First of the Rivieran resorts, Cassis possesses none of the glamour or urbanity of St-Tropez or Cannes – and therein lies its special charm. It also is blessed with the coolest water along the French Mediterranean,

.eft, heroin. Below, the Vallon des Auffres boasts bouillabaisse and crime.

thanks to a series of mainland streams.

Modern painters once spent many summer days in this delicate port, and it is easy to see why. For sheer natural beauty, it is hard to beat – especially at dusk, when irridescent shades of light dust over the harbour.

Nonetheless, it would be stretching it to call Cassis a simple fishing town. The fact is, during the high season, it is as crowded and overbooked as any of the Mediterranean resorts. The trick is to come before or after the rush, in May, June or September, when the sun's still very hot and the masses are gone.

The end-all of any visit to Cassis has to be a bathing holiday on one of its beaches. The town possesses three, the best being the **Plage de la Grande Mer**. But most visitors make at least one trip to the town's spectacular *calanques*.

The first inlet, reachable by car, is **Port Miou**, and it is dedicated to harbouring yachts. The second is **Port Pin**, so named for the shrubby pines that decorate its rocky walls. It must be approached either by boat or foot, as

must be the last and most incredible of the *calanques*, **Port En-Vau**.

Port En-Vau is breathtaking. Similar in appearance to a Norwegian fjord, sky-high white cliffs cut directly down into water of the deepest blue-green imaginable. A sandy white beach adorns one end. The view from the top is something never to be forgotten, but be warned – getting there isn't easy and neither is getting down. The paths that lead to both of the last two *calanques* are more or less unmarked, and *ingénues* may find themselves lost on arid clifftops.

In the long run, all but the most adventurous would be better off taking a native guide or a boat to Port En-Vau. And remember, if you're there during the high season, none of these places are going to look like paradise – unless you like naked Scandinavians and countless families with little dogs and picnic baskets. Even the waters start to float with empty wrappers.

Cassis has a casino and a couple of little nightclubs, but don't expect to find a wild nightlife here. This is a resort mostly for families or young marrieds, and after-dark activities centre around the harbourfront and its row of excellent restaurants. While enjoying a meal along here, be sure to sample the delicious local white wine.

Friendly and unpretentious: Dominating the little village is **Cap Canaille**, which at 1,400 feet (416 metres) is the highest cliff in all of continental Europe. For a panoramic thrill, take a drive along the **Route des Crètes**, which climbs up, over and down to the neighbouring city of **La Ciotat**. From summer homes to clinging vineyards to rubble, the road seems to disappear up into the sky. The view is fabulous, as is the lightheadedness it gives the viewer.

Down on the other side of the cliff, La Ciotat has a very different character. First called Citharista and an outpost to Marseille, its harbour now rather resembles a resort in Florida. The people carry a friendly unpretentious air about them, and the long flat beachfront is lined with souvenir shops.

On vacation in Cassis.

Some of the town is quite pretty – in particular, around the old port and 17th-century **Notre Dame de l'Assomption**. Unfortunately, the huge shipyards that build oil and methane tankers at one end of the waterfront keep La Ciotat from achieving ultimate picturesqueness.

Like Cassis, La Ciotat possesses a set of *calanques*, but **Muguel** is not for swimming and **Figuerolles** is polluted and ugly. A more enjoyable tourist attraction is the beachfront monument to the Lumière brothers. These two illustrious sons of the city were the inventors of the moving picture.

Travelling inland along A50, north of La Ciotat and east of Marseille, will bring you to the hometown of another inestimable Provençal native: Marcel Pagnol. The renowned writer and film director was born in **Aubagne** in 1895. But, unless you are a real Pagnol aficionado or are seeking out one of the crèchemakers who have settled here, avoid this town. It is dirty and unattractive, and the inhabitants seem to carry a chip on their shoulders about it.

Movie fans would do better to drive through Cuges-les-Pins and up to **Riboux**, where the pastoral scenes of the films *Jean de Florette* and *Manon des Sources* were shot. One can easily imagine Manon tripping along the wild and rugged mountainside with her goats – and, even if not, you'll enjoy a great view and hair-raising drive.

Afterwards, you might make a stop at the **O.K. Corral Amusement Park**, set at the base of the road that leads up to Riboux. Here you will find France at its tacky best. The entire park has been done around a Western motif, including, of course, a "genuine" Wild Wild West show.

An elegant university town: Although physically but a stone's throw north of the coast, Aix-en-Provence is a million miles away in character. Bastion of culture and bourgeois niceties, seat of one of France's finest universities since 1409, Aix embodies grace and gentility.

The Romans first founded Aquae Sextiae – so named for its hot springs – in 122 BC, after conquering the nearby

The Calanque de Port-Miou.

Ligurian settlement of **Entremont**. It was overshadowed, however, by Massilia and Arles until the 12th century when the beloved "Good King René," count of Provence, made it his city of preference. René's death brought Provence under the rule of the French crown, and Aix was made the seat of a parliament designed to keep the region under Gallic control. By the 17th and 18th centuries, it had become the leading city in the Bouches-du-Rhône.

Much of Aix's renowned architecture dates from this period of prosperity. Buildings erected during the 17th century can be distinguished by the single iron balcony placed over their central front door, frequently embellished by a corniche underscored with little teeth. The 18th-century structures, on the other hand, have iron balconies on all the windows and the door on the right.

The architecture also bears witness to the eventual decline of the city's power. All over you find homes whose windows were closed in, because taxes were assessed according to the number of windows a house possessed and owners gradually were unable to pay them. Eventually, most of the grand homes were repossessed by the banks.

During the Industrial Age, Aix fell back under Marseille's shadow. Over the past century, some new industry has managed to find a niche here – it remains the European capital for prepared almonds (some of which can be sampled in the local specialty: white iced diamonds of almond paste, called *calissons*) – but mostly, now, Aix is a university town. Of its 150,000 inhabitants about 40,000 are students.

City of fountains: The best time to visit Aix is May, and the worst time is July. But whenever you choose to come, the best place to begin your investigation of the city will be at the **Cours Mirabeau** with its famed fountains.

The Cours Mirabeau is a long and wide avenue, lined with cafés on one side and venerable old addresses on the other. Four rows of benevolent and stately plane trees run down the centre of it, punctuated by three 19th-century

The Fontaine de la Rotonde.

fountains. The most celebrated of these is the **Fontaine de la Rotonde**, which dominates the western entrance to the avenue. It is a source of joy to all viewers – and of terror to any motorist battling the roundabout where it stands.

The avenue's original purpose was to separate the southerly **Quartier Mazarin** from the northerly Quartier Ancien. Only parliamentarians and nobles were allowed to grace the Cours Mirabeau's elegant thoroughway, and the Mazarin Quarter was designed specifically to accommodate them. Unsurprisingly, many lovely parliamentarian homes can be found within this quarter.

Of these homes, the **Hotel Arbaud** is generally considered the most beautiful. It was built in 1730 directly on the Cours by the first president of the parliament. A good runner-up, however, is located within the quarter, at the corner of Rue Joseph Cabassol and Rue Mazarin. The only house in Aix aside from the Hotel Arbaud to have been designed by a non-local, the **Hotel de Caumont** was constructed in 1720 by the illustri-

ous architect of Versailles. It is now the Ecole Superior d'Art et de Danse de Milhaud. Go inside to see the foyer fountain and the Atlanteans that hold up the ceiling. Many of the older houses in Aix possess similar interior fountains, remembrances of the city's aquatic origins, and the Atlanteans are a popular local motif, borrowed from the Genoans.

East down the Rue Cardinal lies the sweet **Fontaine des Quatres Dauphins** (Fountain of Four Dolphins). Built in 1667, it was the first fountain in Aix to be placed in the middle of a street rather than against a wall, giving it an unprecedented decorative purpose. Alain Delon fans will be interested to know that the beloved French celebrity owned the home on the northeast corner until the mid-1980s.

The **Musée Paul Arbaud** stands close by the Fontaine des Quatres Dauphins, at 2a, Rue du 4-Septembre. Immediately as you enter its large foyer, you will be struck by a plethora of reliefs and capitals from different ages.

Be sure to check out the "Seven Deadly Sins," hanging directly on your right.

The first room in the museum has one of the most important collections of Moustiers-Ste-Marie-style *faïence* to be found in Provence. Among the numerous examples of traditional work are such whimsical pieces as that marking the hot-air balloon ascent of 1783.

Going up the stairs, note the 18th-century, hand-painted, ornamental trimming. This was clearly not the home of a miser. Indeed, the house itself might be considered the most interesting exhibit. The detail upstairs is incredible, with acorns and leaves carved directly out of the wood portals and exquisitely handcrafted fireplaces.

Another museum within the Mazarin Quarter is the **Musée Granet**. Its main and first floor are devoted to a great deal of fairly unremarkable paintings. Even the eight Cézanne canvasses, of which the museum is so proud, look rather like leftovers. Its true interest lies in its basement where an excellent collection of lengthily documented Celto-Ligurian artifacts have been assembled, with maps and text describing early geological and prehistoric activity.

Next door is the 13th-century **St-Jean-de-Malte**, former priory of the Knights of Malta and the oldest Gothic building in Aix.

Old but lively: When you cross over the Cours Mirabeau to the **Quartier Ancien**, you will instantly notice a change in atmosphere. Whereas the Mazarin Quarter oozes a sense of serenity, the streets of the Old Quarter are filled with the lifebeat of the city.

This part of town also possesses a lion's share of interesting museums and splendid architecture. The **Hotel Boyer d'Eguilles**, about two blocks in from the Cours, at 20 Rue Espariat, combines both. Dating from 1675, the architectural plan is Parisian while the exterior decor is Italian. The **Museum of Natural History** lies inside, with a number of large dinosaur eggs as its star attraction.

Unfortunately, internal political turmoil during the 1980s and the lack of a sturdy mayor to champion the upkeep

Aix's Hôtel de Ville and clocktower.

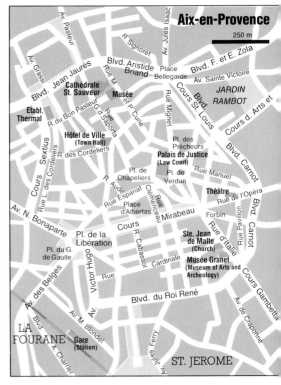

of Aix's landmarks have begun to tell on the Hotel Boyer. But, down the street at the charming **Place d'Albertas**, there are no such signs of decay.

When the parliamentarian Albertas built his home in the 1720s, he also bought all the land in front of it – to "protect his view." This land, over time, came to be called the Albertas Square. The four contiguous buildings that enclose it were not constructed until 1740. The fountain was added in 1912.

The Place d'Albertas lies at the base of the **Rue Aude**, home to many of Aix's most fashionable stores and best-loved tourist sites. However, the first square that you come upon when heading up it, **Place Richele**, may seem slightly incongruous. Young rockers and their impromptu concerts have claimed the Place Richele for their own, and the square is more or less the centre for illegal substances in the city. But, remember, Aix is primarily a town for university students.

Gentility is restored at the **Place d'Hotel de Ville**, just up the Rue Aude.

The liquid fare at the many little tables that fill the square is strictly a nice cup of tea or harmless *ballon de rouge*, and it makes for a relaxing place to pass some of the afternoon.

On the western side of this square is the **Town Hall**. When going in, be sure to glance up at the beautiful wrought-iron work above the entrance, which fans out in a representation of the sun. Crossing the pretty paved courtyard will lead you into the foyer, whose elegant staircase was the first to be built in the double style in France.

To the south side of the square is the **Post Office**. It was first begun in 1718 as a granary, but work was shut down two years later because of the plague. Another 40 years passed before work was resumed, and by then it had been designated as a public structure. For this reason, it possesses windows and decorations such as one wouldn't ordinarily find on a lowly granary. Particularly engrossing are the cavorting figures, intended to represent the Rhône and Durance rivers, that drape themselves

M. Fouque's *santons*.

into the stone beneath the central eave.

On the north side of the square is the whimsical **Tour d'Horloge**, dating from 1510. This tall clock tower houses four different statues, each of which marks a season and appears alone for an appropriate three-month stretch. In the summer, you will see a woman holding wheat. Autumn shows the wine harvest. Winter has a wood bearer, and spring appears as a woman carrying fruit and a young salmon.

Passing under the arch of the Tour d'Horloge and up the Rue Gaston-de-Saporta will bring you to the **Musée de Vieil Aix**. This is a funny little museum, badly lit with what at first seems like an odd collection of riff-raff. Don't let this put you off. To the left is a fun hall of mechanised crèche marionettes, and to the right is a fascinating room documenting the *jeux de la Fête-Dieu*.

The Fête-Dieu, half-religious and half-profane, takes place during June and is a long procession in honour of the battle of Christianity against paganism. Its origins lie in the 13th century, but it

wasn't until 1836 that the marionettes of Bontoux, displayed within the museum, were created. Also shown are some of the participants' masks and a large painted screen. Don't miss the emphatic devil masks hanging up on high or the devil puppets with red faces, white teeth and pitchforks.

The **Cathédrale St-Sauveur** heads the Rue Gaston-de-Saporta. At first on this site there was just a small Roman church. Then, in 1170, after the Crusades had caused the population of Aix to swell, the little church was deemed no longer big enough. This led to the planning of the cathedral.

Soon after work had begun, however, the plague struck, and it was closely followed by the 100 Years' War. All in all, 140 years went by before construction could be continued and, as a result, the cathedral is an eclectic structure. Its facade combines the 12th century with the 16th, the belfry belongs to the 15th and the Gothic nave to the 16th.

Slightly more coherent is the cathedral's 5th-century **baptistry**. It encompasses all that is left of the initial Roman settlement in Aix and is one of only three original baptistrys (the others are in Fréjus and Riez) left in France.

The baptistry is a fascinating example of symbolic architecture. The exterior plan and cupola are cubic to represent the four apostles. The interior pool is octagonal with eight marble columns for the "eight" days of the week. Water flowed in from the west and exited to the east, in keeping with the direction of the sun and its light. Similarly, the two westernmost columns were formed of black granite (for the darkness of unenlightenment), and it was between these that the to-be-baptised would enter the pool. The other six columns, through which the newly baptised exited the pool, were of green marble (for the light of redemption).

Country cottages: One last – but definitely not least – local architectural feat is the **Pavillon Vendôme**. To reach it, you must quit the central city, if just barely, and head down the Rue Célony. Its original owner, Louis de Mercoeur, duke of Vendome and governor of

Atlantean holds up the Pavillon Vendôme.

Provence, had it built in 1665 outside the central confines of Aix – for very specific reasons.

Louis de Mercoeur had the good fortune to be the grandson of King Henry IV and the nephew-in-law of Cardinal Mazarin. After his wife died, however, he had the misfortune to fall madly in love with Lucrèce de Forbin-Soliers, "La Belle du Canet." Although Lucrèce was available, being a widow, she was not of a high-enough social stature to become the official consort of the duke. Desperate, Louis had this second home built outside the town, so that they might continue to rendezvous in secret. Eventually this wasn't enough, and he decided to marry her anyway, at which point an outraged Mazarin made him a cardinal and thereby elevated his status to a place where any legitimate union was forever impossible.

Outside, the Pavillon looks much like an English country home, enhanced with *quatrepartite* formal gardens. The only disturbance to the symmetry of the grounds and building is the unfortunate

third floor, which was added during the 18th century.

The house itself is replete with memories of the starry-eyed couple. Groaning Atlanteans hold up front portals that are decorated by the figure of Spring – said to have been modelled after Lucrèce. Inside, portraits of the lovers hang side by side.

A small room in the back of the first floor is equipped with a video that tells the entire story of the Pavillon in French, German and English. The ceiling of this same room bears a gay fresco of giggling and naked cherubs. It was only revealed recently, having been covered over during the days when the home was a convent school. Apparently, the nuns that ran it considered such frolicking inappropriate for their students' dining room.

Artists in Aix: The **Atelier Paul Cézanne** lies behind a little wooden gate, just north of the Old Quarter. The renowned modern artist was born in Aix in 1839 but left during the 1860s to join the Impressionists in Paris. He soon

The Vasarely Foundation.

became disenchanted and returned to his hometown in 1870, where he remained until his death in 1906.

Cézanne had his studio built in 1900, and it was here that he painted his last works. The large windows are testimonials to the fact that he himself designed the building. Inside are a couple of reproductions, his easel, a rucksack, a cape, his books and many of the objects that he used in his still lifes. Cézanne fans will enjoy matching the models with the paintings, but anyone with a knowledge of Cézanne should find a visit here fascinating.

To see more of his inspiration, drive out of the city along the Route de Tholonet, D 17. This will bring you to the foot of Cézanne's perhaps most-famous model, the huge and silvery **Mont St-Victoire**.

Another artist who left his mark on Aix was Paul Vasarely. A museum to his work (which he himself built, named the **Fondation Vasarely** and donated to the city) stands just to the southwest of Aix on the Jas de Bouffan. The building

is unmistakeable – for it was designed in geometric shapes with black dots on white squares and vice-versa.

Even the rooms inside are hexagonal. All of the 42 works, which the artist described as "mural integrations," were painted directly onto the high walls in 1975. Also on view are some 800 "experiments" and a gallery of contemporary exhibits. Visiting this incredibly dated museum is like wandering into a wonderland of 1970s op-art.

Painting is not the only art on display in Aix. During the summer festival, original productions of opera and chamber music can be seen almost every night. The Met it isn't, but the offerings are earnest and entertaining and sometimes even quite good.

The Aix festival is just one source of nocturnal distraction. Jazz clubs, encouraged by the large student population, swing all year round, as do a number of rock clubs and discos. Restaurants abound, and the cafés that line the Cours Mirabeau are always full of people-watching pastis drinkers.

It's easy to fall into being a night owl in this young city. Be sure, however, not to sleep through the market that overtakes the Old Quarter every Tuesday, Thursday and Saturday morning.

The *marché d'Aix* is undoubtedly one of the largest and most colourful markets to be found in all of Provence. In front of the Hotel de Ville are the flower stands. Over by the Palais de Justice are produce on one side and second-hand goods on the other. In between, the narrow stone streets spill over with additional merchants selling everything from kitchen utensils to underwear.

North of Aix: On days when there is no market and you feel like getting out of the city, you may want to head up north towards the **Durance River** and the solemn **Abbaye de Silvacane**. Built by the Cistercians in 1144, Silvacane's name is derived from the Latin for wood *(silva)* and reed *(cane)* after its marshy surroundings.

True to the Cistercian spirit, this abbey is anything but frivolous in appearance. No stained glass, no statues and no decoration whatsoever were allowed.

Mt. St-Victoire.

Add to its original austerity an empty interior and a poor job of exterior reconstruction and Silvacane makes for a rather bleak destination.

The area up along the Durance, however, does provide a nice break from the dry plains of Aix. As you head north, the land begins to rise, coniferous trees appear and green surrounds you. Occasional meadows, deep reservoirs and distant mountains are a welcome sight. You are now heading into wine country.

Those with a yen to visit a working wine château from the *Côteaux d'Aix* should follow the river east to the cute little town of **Jouques**, with its gay central fountain. The young owners of the **Château Revelette**, who speak French, German and English, are happy to offer the curious a tour of their *cave* and a taste of their grape.

Afterwards, head south on A11 through the **Forest of Peyrolles**, past numerous fields, vineyards and sheep-crossing signs, and you will find a number of shaded groves suitable for picnicking. You'll need some fortifica-

Inside the Château Revelette.

tion before embarking on the climb up over the mountains and back down towards Aix. The curvy, shoulderless road resembles nothing more than a goat path that has been mildly picked over to accommodate modern civilisation. Even its surface undulates.

Once you've hit the crest of the **Col de St-Buc**, the road begins to wind down through cliffs of sheer rock, cut into natural tiers. At the bottom, head just west and you will come upon the **Château de Vauvenargues**. Perched on a little hill, but within a deep valley and surrounded on all sides by green mountains, the château is heartbreakingly picturesque. Apparently, Picasso thought so too, for it was here that he chose to spend his final years. His tomb lies within the park, but the grounds are not as yet open to the public.

Continue west, in the direction of Aix, and you will pass the **Barrage de Bimont**. This dam makes for a nice afternoon trip of its own, with its tremendous James Bond waterworks and large nature reserve. Hikers will find

numerous trails to choose from, several of which lead to the **Barrage Zola**, designed by Emile Zola's father in 1854.

Heading West: Another day trip from Aix lies to the west of the city on the road to Arles. However, a visit to the impressive **Château de Barben** and its **zoo** best serves to show the public the perils of tourism in Provence.

Physically the château is a lovely place. Originally built in the Middle Ages, it was enlarged during the 14th and then the 17th centuries. The formal gardens were designed by Versailles's own Le Nôtre, and in their centre is a sweet fountain, which Napoleon's little sister, Pauline, liked to bathe in *au naturel*. To protect her modesty as she frolicked, servants would hold sheets of black cloth up around it.

Inside are a number of rooms worth seeing, such as Pauline's delicate boudoir, with its hand-painted wallpaper. Unfortunately, however, management of the château is atrocious, and unpleasant guides rush eager visitors through with all the warmth of prison guards.

On the other hand, the guides seem delightful in comparison to the adjacent zoo. Go only if you feel like climbing dozens of perilous stone steps to find some ill-looking animals, plopped down in bare cages with no attempt to create a "natural habitat."

Olive country: Situated on the edge of the arid Crau Plain, **Salon-de-Provence** likes to call itself the "crossroads of Provence." And, indeed, it lies within 30 miles (50 km) of Arles to the west, Avignon to the north, Aix to the east and Marseille to the south.

The town is also at the heart of the olive-growing country, making it France's number-one marketplace for that silky oil. Add to this the 50-year-old presence of the officer's training school for the French Air Force, and Salon comes up as a fairly *puissant* spot.

In fact, however, Salon is a very laid-back city with a warm, small-town feel. Gay standards hang from the 17th-century **Town Hall**, and more flags decorate the heavy arches that give passage-

Life at the Barben Zoo.

way into the cobbled streets of the central **old town**. Above the arches, imposing towers mark what remains of ancient ramparts.

The old town is dominated by the grim **Château de l'Emperi**, built between the 10th and 16th centuries and around which Salon originally sprang up. Inside, the **Musée de l'Emperi** showcases France's largest collection of military art and history. Under the vaulted Gothic ceilings await copious exhibits of saddles and sabres, guns and medals, toy soldiers and life-size figures. The tour culminates with several rooms dedicated to the Napoleonic era, including among its treasures the brilliant general's short blue bed.

The museum has been marvellously arranged, with great attention to presentation and documentation. And, while only a quarter of the collection is on view at any given time (all objects date between 1700 and 1918 and pertain to French – not just Provençal – history), the tour still seems gargantuan. Serious military history buffs would make the trip to Salon just to visit this museum.

Spiritualists, on the other hand, should come to see the **home of Nostradamus**. The renowned physician-turned-astrologer settled in the town, birthplace of his wife, in 1546, and it was here that he both wrote his famous book of predictions, *Centuries*, and spent the last 20 years of his life.

Salon has made much of this famous inhabitant but, if truth be told, he wasn't so warmly welcomed during his lifetime. The townspeople held him in suspicion, partly because of his star-watching and partly because of his conversion to Judaism. Indeed, he was only saved from condemnation as a sorcerer by his ties to King Charles IX.

His house is a modest affair, recently turned into a museum but without any objects to exhibit. All his original manuscripts are under lock and key in the mayor's office, and most of his household objects were lost in a fire. Restoration, however, is at long last under way, and the authorities intend eventually to move the priceless manu-

eft, mural of Nostradamus in Salon. Right, statue of Adam de Craponne.

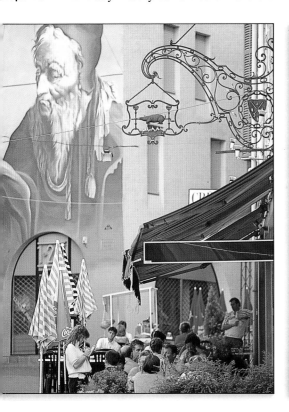

scripts into their rightful home.

Also within the ancient ramparts of the old town is the beautiful **Eglise St-Michel**, dating from 1220 to 1239 and built in the Roman Gothic style. The church possesses two belltowers, one a delicate 15th-century addition, the other contemporary to the construction of the building. Inside, cobwebs hang from the skylights above a tiny cool chapel. Be sure to note the stone tympanum, which shows Archangel Michael killing a snake above the paschal lamb, that decorates the wooden front door. It pre-dates the church, having been carved in the 12th century.

A second church lies just outside the ancient walls of the original citadel. **St-Laurent** was built between 1344 and 1480 and presents a much grander spectacle than its forerunner. Done in true Provençal Gothic, its exterior presents a simplicity that its sombre and majestic interior reiterates.

Only the largest of chapels within is lit. Placed directly across from the entrance, it is dedicated to the Virgin. A smiling, 16th-century alabaster statue commemorates her maternal piety.

The **tomb of Nostradamus** stands beside the statue of the Virgin. On the wall behind it is an inscription worth translating: "Here lie the bones of Michel de Nostradamus, alone at the judgement of humans worthy of knowing the stars of the future. He lived 62 years, 6 months and 17 days. He died in Salon in 1566. May future times not trouble his repose. Anne Ponsard, his wife, wishes him true happiness."

A second famed inhabitant, Adam de Craponne, has been remembered with a statue on a small square across from the Town Hall. De Craponne was the gifted 16th-century engineer who brought fertility to the region by building an irrigation canal from the Durance River down through the dry plains of the Crau and out into the sea.

Although Salon has served as a centre for the olive trade since the 15th century, insiders flock to three neighbouring towns to buy their oil. You may want to also but, before going off in

Olive country.

search of that perfect bottle of olive oil, it is important to know what to look for. First, check whether the bottle is marked *premier pression à froid vièrge extra*. If it isn't, don't buy it. If it is, then hold the bottle up to the light. The best oil will be a delicate green in colour.

South of Salon is the first town, **La Fare**, which many say offers the best oil in all of France. The local oil mill and wine cooperative are open to the public, and products can be bought on site. If you can, of course, it is best to go during the harvest season.

Other locals swear by the olives of **Aureille**, a half-forgotten town on the road westward to Avignon in the midst of grassy plains and vast expanses of olive trees. Aureille is a poor town, without any of the gussied-up look of most of the touristic circuit. At the same time, it is a pleasant enough place with a friendly central bar and a ruined 11th-century castle rising up on a hill above it that is only accessible by foot. For those in search of the "real" Provence, it can be both a relief and point of interest.

Its olive mill, just off D17, can also be visited by the public.

A third town with a claim on the olive market lies more within the jurisdiction of Arles than Salon. Like Aureille, **Mouriès** gives the outsider an opportunity to generalise about the Provençal character. Although hardly more than a village, with just one main street, Mouriès boasts several cafés, a handful of markets and two hotels. It also has two olive oil mills, one of which is a local cooperative. The other, on the Cours Paul Revoi, is open to the public with on-premise sales.

Since Mouriès is just outside Arles, it's a good place to remember if you have a car and can't find a room in the city during one of its festivals.

Bastion of tradition: For many, Arles *is* Provence. No other city in the region offers a more colourful atmosphere or possesses a greater awareness of its Provençal heritage.

The proud inhabitants of this old city are the first to tout themselves as not only "*vrai* (true) Provençals" but "*Ar-*

Landowner and daughter outside Arles.

lesiens," said with a special emphasis to drive home the significance of the phrase. Societies dedicated to upholding local customs flourish, and a "queen of Arles" is selected every three years on the basis not of her beauty but of her knowledge of Provençal traditions and her ability to speak the regional dialect and dress in its costume.

There is something almost otherworldly about Arles. It bears none of the shrewd urbanity of Marseille or the cultured sophistication of Aix. Instead, it seems to live in its past, haunted by the spectre of the Romans, populated by fierce upholders of tradition and deeply affected by its proximity to the wild marshes of the Camargue.

Founded by the Massilians as a trading post in the 6th century BC, Arles's position at the crossroads of the Rhône River and the Roman Aurelian Way made it a natural choice for development by the Romans.

It grew slowly for several hundred years, with some special help from Marius in the 2nd century BC. Then, during the struggle for power between Caesar and Pompey, Arles got its lucky break. Marseille made the fatal error of showing friendship towards the latter, and Caesar turned to Arles, which was already known for its skilled boatmakers, with the request that 12 war vessels be built for him within 30 days. The city complied, and Arles's good fortune was sealed. After squelching the claims of Pompey in 49 BC, Caesar squelched Marseille and designated Arles as the first city of Provence.

The city continued to prosper and under Honorius in 418 was made the administrative capital of the territory for Gaul. Although its predominance would waver over the following centuries, Arles remained a central maritime and river port up until the advent of the steam engine, when transportation by train overtook the tugboat method.

Train travel spelt disaster for the Arlesian economy, which had from the very beginning depended on its port activity for importance. As gateway to the Camargue (the top producer of rice

The old town lies along the Rhône.

in France), Arles has managed to recoup some of its value as a trading centre, but its days of eminence are long gone.

Lacking any major industry or university, the Arles of today relies heavily on the glorious Arles of yesteryear for its livelihood. Tourism abounds, and nary an ancient monument exists without a cardtable and guardian beside it demanding 10 francs. But don't let this dissuade you. The ghosts of the past are far more powerful than the souvenir sellers, and a feeling of mystery and romance still surrounds the city.

At the heart of Arles is the **old city**; a maze of narrow stone streets that mingle crumbling Roman edifices with sturdy medieval stonework. It is bordered to the south by the wide Boulevard des Lices, to the east by the remnants of ancient ramparts and to the north and west by the grand pathway of the Rhône. Surrounding all of this is the fairly innocuous spread of the more modern city, including the large Trinquetaille section.

Most visitors will first arrive in Arles via the **Boulevard des Lices**. If you have a car, it might be a good idea to leave it right away in the municipal parking garage to be found on this street's south side. Almost all of the city's touristic sites are within easy walking distance of each other, and the narrow lanes of the old town are not hospitable to automobiles.

The Boulevard des Lices is a busy spot with many cafés and the local tourist office, but it lacks both the charm of the Cours Mirabeau and the commerciality of the Rue Canebière. Its highest points come on Saturday morning during the extensive produce market and every first Wednesday of the month when a wonderful flea market spills over its sidewalks. At other times, it serves mainly as a thoroughfare past the ancient part of the city.

Before heading into the old city, take a quick detour south along the **Avenue des Alyscamps** to the site of the same name. Not much is left of this ancient necropolis, but no first-time visit to Arles is complete without having taken a stroll down the leafy **Allée des Sarco-**

phages, painted so vibrantly by Vincent Van Gogh. As you walk down the tomb-lined lane, notice the plaque that reads: "Van Gogh. Here, struck by the beauty of the site, he came to set up his easel."

The cemetery was begun by the Romans but by the 4th century had been taken over by Gallic Christians. Its fame spread during the Middle Ages, but the necropolis gradually fell into decline as its stone began to disappear; some of it went towards the building of other religious structures, some to antique dealers, some as presents to illustrious guests of the city.

All the tombs are now empty, and the stone shells that are left bear an uncanny resemblance to a long line of molars. Nonetheless, there is a peacefulness under the poplars that guards the solemnity of the spot and makes it a favourite for meditative afternoon talks.

At the very end of the lane stands what remains of **St-Honorat des Alyscamps**. Once upon a time, a large Romanesque church, St-Honorat now functions mainly as a backdrop for

The reigning "Queen of Arles."

some of the city's theatrical activities.

To enter the old city, return to the Boulevard des Lices and walk a block inwards, up the cobbled Rue Hôtel de Ville. This will bring you to the spacious **Place de la République**. The Town Hall stands at one end, but more impressive is the **Eglise St-Trophime**. Its front portal dominates the eastern side of the square with a beautiful severity befitting a church dedicated to the saint who is credited with having brought Christianity to France.

The doorway of St-Trophime's is itself a glorious example of Provençal Romanesque style. Constructed between 1152 and 1180, its intricate tympanum shows the Last Judgement being overseen by a barefoot and crowned Jesus. He is flanked by the four apostles (Matthew with wings, Mark as a lion, Luke as an ox and John as an eagle). To the left of this group, the elect are presented to Abraham, Isaac and Jacob by an angel. To the right, the damned are refused admission to Heaven by an angel brandishing a sword of fire.

Inside, the lofty tone continues. The church's broken-barrel vaulted nave is, at over 60 feet (20 metres), the highest in Provence. By the left of the entrance, a fourth-century sarcophagus serves as a baptismal font. Further in, the life of the Virgin is depicted on a huge 17th-century d'Aubusson tapestry.

The **St-Trophime Cloisters**, which stand to the right of the church, are more cheerful. The sound of birds fills the air as you enter, and in warm weather pink flowers dot its bright courtyard, which is enclosed by solemn 14th-century figures posted as columns.

Work began on the cloisters during the second half of the 12th century, but was interrupted for about 100 years and they were not completed until the 14th. The northern and eastern galleries belong to the earlier period, the western and southern to the later.

Be sure to climb up to the very top before leaving. As you step out onto the "roof," you will be struck by the brilliant sun, reflected off the white stone. Look down into the courtyard, then to

Festivities in the Roman amphitheatre.

the lofty belltower circled by birds. Delicate columns and the stone tiles that were used for eaves complete the exquisiteness of this lofty perch.

Across from St-Trophime is the **Musée d'Art Païen** (pagan art), housed in an unconsecrated 17th-century church that, despite its date, appears curiously Gothic in style. Its logical counterpart lies around the corner; the **Musée F.-Benoit d'Art Chrétien**. This museum of Christian art stands within a 17th-century Jesuit chapel and is particularly replete in sarcophagi.

A third museum, the **Museon Arlaten**, waits a couple of blocks away down the Rue de la Republique. Native-born poet Frédéric Mistral founded this ethnographic museum with the money he received for winning the Nobel Prize in literature, with the stipulation that it be dedicated to all that is Provençal. Accordingly, the name is Provençal (for "Musée d'Arles"), all the documentation within is in dialect (as well as in French) and even the *gardiennes* are dressed in traditional costume.

Room after room lead you through the world of the Provençal. One hall is filled with costumes and explanations of how they should be worn, others have amulets and magic charms, *tambours* and other instruments, nautical and agricultural equipment, wallhangings and paintings. There even are several life-size re-enactments of Provençal domestic scenes. It is the sort of place where you can easily spend a lot of time.

The *museon* is not the only mark left on the city by the poet. A formidable **bust of Mistral** looks down over the **Place du Forum**, just a stone's throw away. Most of the nightlife that doesn't involve a festival or cinema takes place in this lively square that overflows with a variety of cafés. Grab a table, if you can find a free one, but don't expect the food you are served to be gourmet. Bullfighting aficionados may prefer to head into the Tambourin, where the local champions patronise; the walls are lined with their autographed photos.

If you continue towards the river, you will hit the **Thermes de la Trouille**.

Barmaid.

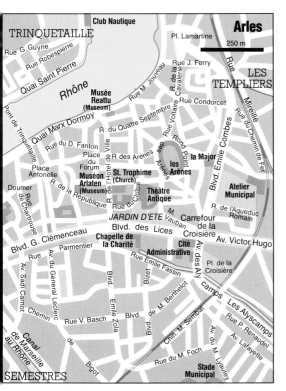

These 4th-century baths were once the largest in Provence, but little of them still exists. The **Musée Réattu**, across the street, is far more interesting.

The Réattu Museum bespeaks eclecticism. It isn't worth paying the entrance fee of 13 francs to see most of the paintings, many of which are badly in need of restoration and some of which have not even been attributed. However, the collection does include some intriguing modern sculpture from the region, including one fascinating metallic piece with "living beads," and a collection of 57 Picasso sketches. The latter, dating from 1971 and donated by the artist himself, shows a somewhat more personal Picasso than one normally gets to see. The sketches may not be great art, but as free-form drawings they are a good deal of fun. Also of interest are the Salle Henri Rousseau and an extraordinary chapel-like room, vaulted by stone megaliths and containing a 1975 hanging-rope sculpture by Joseph Gran Garriga.

If the inevitable press of tourists has begun to get to you, steal a quiet moment walking down the ramparts that line the Rhône. Here, with the wide river on one side of you and crumbling stone facades on the other, you may recapture a sense of the Roman spirit that once dominated this city. (Try not to look at the new five-storey tenements on the facing bank.)

The **Amphithéâtre** is another place to chase Roman ghosts. Enormous in size – 440 by 345 ft (136 by 107 metres), 11,500 in total, and capable of accommodating more than 20,000 spectators – this Roman arena is both larger and older than its cousin in Nîmes, having been built in the 1st century AD. A visit to its tower offers a view out over the expanse of the red-roofed old city, its modern environs, the Rhône and the Alpilles Ridges to the north.

Bullfights of various types are still held here. Saturday afternoons find locals munching peanuts and drinking sodas as they watch their favourite *co-carde* champions cavort in front of snorting bulls. The first of May wel-

Local painter.

comes the Fête des Gardians, when cowboys from the Camargue gather for a yearly spectacle. More annual bullfights take place during the Feria Pascale of Easter and the Prémices du Riz in mid-September.

Chances are that, if you enter the old city on a warm summer night, you will be greeted by the sound of flamenco, opera or jazz wafting out from within the walls of the neighbouring **Théâtre Antique**. During the summer days, this 1st-century-BC theatre is little more than some piles of rubble, a siding of worn stone seating and two half-standing columns. At night, however, the Théâtre is transformed into a magical backdrop for the Festival d'Arles.

Like all the other cities of Provence, Arles puts on a special cultural festival during the summer. The Festival d'Arles is particularly successful, wisely taking advantage of Arles's many antiquities as ultra-atmospheric stages for everything from folkloric dance to classical music to high-fashion shows.

The festival is accompanied in July by another widely applauded annual event: the **Rencontres Internationales de la Photographie**. This "festival" brings together photographers from around the world to compare techniques, peruse exhibits and enjoy nightly spectacles. Workshops with respected masters are also available. Like the festival, the Rencontres use many of the Arlesian monuments and museums to enrich their productions.

Artists who come to Arles with the intention of making a pilgrimage to the haunts of Van Gogh may be disappointed, however. The house where he and Gauguin once lived, worked and argued no longer stands, and not much has been done elsewhere to commemorate his days down south. Devotees will have to content themselves by seeing some of the sites he once painted, the fabulous light he once saw and the copious fields of sunflowers from where he once gathered bouquets for still lifes.

Into the Alpilles: The dry flat land that surrounds Arles, circled by jagged, white stone peaks called **the Alpilles**, is

Fields of sunflowers surround Arles.

CHRISTIAN LACROIX

When a creation by *haute-couture* designer Christian Lacroix is modelled down the catwalk, a great gust of sunshine goes through the room. For it is no secret that Lacroix, one of the fashion market's most innovative and eclectic modern talents, is strongly inspired by his native region of Provence. Indeed, Lacroix's madcap designs are a pure reflection of his love for the sunniest area in France. His magic paintbrush is reminiscent of the colours one finds in Van Gogh's paintings: bright sunflower yellows, poppy reds, hot pinks, purples and blues, as well as swirling prints.

Since the mid-1980s, the outlandish decor of Christian Lacroix's *cou-*

ture house – designed by Elizabeth Garouste and Mattia Bonetti – at number 73 of the very trendy Faubourg St-Honoré in Paris, has welcomed the *crème de la crème.* International names such as Ivana Trump and Lucy Ferry (wife of rock star Brian) are just two among the host of cosmopolitan beauties to cross its threshold. And, in 1987, the designer, atill in his mid-thrities, made the cover of *Time* magazine. But, even with his new-found fame, Lacroix admits he often feels the need to go back to his childhood Provençal roots and draw breath.

"I've always been crazy about terracotta floors, primitive people, sun and rough times," says the 37-year-old designer. "This is my real side – goat cheese and bread, elementary things. I am fascinated with Paris, its elegance, its women, even its artificiality. But with my heart and skin I love the south – bullfighting, pleasure, music, nature, the sea."

As an adolescent, Christian Lacroix grew up in Arles, which he still speaks of with a feverish nostalgia for his golden youth: the now-deserted Rue de la Roquette, then alive with gipsies; the Rue des Porcelets, where he bought the *fougasse aux gratillons*, a delicious bread that Marcel Pagnol often talks about in his novels; the Rue de la République, where he used to be fascinated by the shop of *santons.*

Some of Lacroix's favourite landmarks around Arles include the entrance hall of the Hôtel de Ville, the St-Trophime Cathedral and the Notre-Dame-de-la-Majour Church near the Arena. Following the sinuous Rue Parade leads to the Musée Réattu, in the former palace of the Maltese knights. When the young Lacroix played truant from school, it was often to go and look at *L'Arlésienne* and *L'Atelier de couture en Arles*, painted by Antoine Raspal in the 18th century.

"Our local hangout was Le Mallarte," remembers Lacroix. "It was the bourgeois café in town, where we liked to spend long hours practising the art of conversation, seated at smoky tables in our navy pea coats and long hair." Nowadays, he is more likely to dine at Vaccarès, a popular local restaurant whose terrace overlooks the Place du Forum and whose other famous patrons include writers Michel Tournier and Yvan Andouard.

When he can escape from his numerous obligations as the new darling of *haute couture*, Lacroix can generally be found somewhere in the golden triangle of Provence – and not just in Arles. The little towns he so cherishes are scattered along the bright road of the Apilles, from Maussane to Mouriés, from Les Baux to St-Rémy-de-Provence, and eventually down into the Camargue region.

"In fact, Arles is really a passage between my two worlds: Provence and the Camargue," the designer says. "On the one side, the laughing universe of the Alpilles commemorated by Alphonse Daudet; on the other, as soon as one crosses the Rhône and enters the Trinquetaille, where my grandparents lived, it is already the door to the Camargue and its flat countryside. Since I am both Cévenol and Provençal, I am very sensitive to this double aspect."

It's just a short drive south to the region of the Camargue and the town of Stes-Maries-de-la-Mer, where Lacroix remembers with great fondness spending long lazy summers. "I have always loved the swampy landscapes of the Camargue," he says. Proof of this is the lovely *mas* (the local name for a traditional Provençal farmhouse) that he bought once he had established himself in Paris. "I come here as often as possible with my wife Françoise and renew my relationship with my friends, to whom I am just Lacroix, the old pal from 20 years ago."

filled with sunflowers – not to mention cypress groves and olive orchards. Arles holds reign over this region, generally referred to as the Pays d'Arles.

Although most are extremely poor, the natives of this dusty land bear the mixture of pride and generosity intrinsic to all that is Provençal. It is a rewarding area to travel in, filled as it is with anecdotes and reminiscences.

If you don't have a car and are energetic, you can try cycling, but be wary of the hot midday sun in summer and the steep inclines of the Alpilles. Local buses will get you where you want to go, but they will take both time and money. As a final choice, try hitchhiking. It's never the best idea but probably safer and easier here than in most places.

Just 4 miles (7 km) northeast of Arles, past a long field of peppers, lies the **Abbaye de Montmajour**. Founded in the 10th century by Benedictine monks, on an island amidst a swamp that was passable only by raft, the monastery fell into decline by the 1600s. Total collapse came during the next century when the head abbot, Cardinal de Rohan, became entangled in a scandal concerning Marie Antoinette.

In the 1790s, the property was bought and then stripped by antique dealers. Restoration was begun in 1872, but there is still something like a movie facade about the abbey: grand from the front, empty at the back. To add to its problems, it was occupied by foreign forces in 1943 and burnt a year later.

Nonetheless, the plan of the abbey is fabulous. In fact, it is touted as being, along with the Abbé St-Gilles, the most elaborate of any Romanesque church in Provence. The central crypt, which is above ground and inscribed with cryptic inscriptions, forms a perfect circle with five evenly radiating chapels. And the enormous 12th-century **Eglise de Notre-Dame** possesses a never-completed nave that is considered one of the masterpieces of Romanesque art. Its thick echoing walls and floor would have made a perfect stage for the dances of Isadora Duncan.

Stepping out of the cloister and onto the ruins offers a wonderful view of the outlying countryside, with the city of Arles in the distance. For an even grander panorama, climb to the top of the imposing tower erected by the Abbot Pons. From there, you can see the nearby village of **Fontvieille**.

Following the road just northeast will take you right into this pleasant little town. As you enter, note the modest oratory, erected in 1721 in thanks for the end of the plague. Similar oratories mark each corner of the town.

Fontvieille is a charming spot, but one that has clearly been marked for tourism, with prices to match. Its primary attraction is the **Moulin de Lettres**, as they call the mill where Daudet presumably wrote *Letters from My Windmill*. The fact that the windmill actually belonged to friends (not the author) and probably witnessed little penmanship (although Daudet did visit it) has done little to deter the hordes of tourists that crowd its tiny interior.

Set in a picturesque spot, the mill does contain some interesting features, such as a round ceiling marked in compass fashion with the names of the winds that sweep the hill. Unfortunately, you can't hear these winds over the din of tourists. The narrow subterranean museum is equally disappointing.

Today, a number of literary immigrants continue to make Fontvieille a writer's enclave. Most notable among them is the (once-Parisian) author Yvan Audouard. Other artists have also found the town an amenable haunt, such as the Swiss painter Carl Liner. The photographic community is admirably represented by the Rockport Workshops held in town every September.

Fontvieille is also a popular spot for summer homes, and quite a few Germans, with some Swiss and English, have found a niche here. But weekend visitors won't find the town lacking for traditional charm, and if you arrive on the first Sunday of August or on Christmas Eve, you can indulge in some true-blooded folkloric revelries.

Another place to indulge is the

Plane trees line many roads in the Pays d'Arles.

Château d'Estoublon Mogador on the outskirts of the village. This traditional 14th-century wine château, complete with geese and kittens playing in the front yard, welcomes visitors. The Lombrage family sell their own red and rosé wines, plus their prize-winning olive oil, right on the property.

Alphonse Daudet also left his mark on the neighbouring town of **Tarascon**. This small city was founded by the Massillians in the 3rd century BC and became a Provençal legend in AD 48 when its horrible resident monster, the amphibious Tarasque, was tamed by the sweet Saint Martha. Widespread fame came in the personage of Tartarin, fictional "hero" of the book of the same name by Daudet.

Tartarin was Daudet's revenge against what he saw as the smallness of the provincial spirit. Despite a superficially sympathetic aspect, the character was a liar, a braggart and an all-in-all ridiculous figure. The people of Tarasque, from where Tartarin was supposed to have come, have never been able to live this reputation down. Without too much prodding, they'll tell you just how little they appreciate being known as the compatriots of Tartarin.

This hasn't prevented them from creating a tiny museum to the character, the **Maison de Tartarin**. Opened in 1985, the Tartarin House features wax figures in re-enactments of scenes from the book. It's kind of a silly place, really only for those who know the book well.

All visitors to Tarascon will want to stop by the **Collegial Ste-Marthe**. Like many other churches in the region, this imposing edifice presents an interesting eclecticism of architecture, for one half was built during the Romanesque 12th century and one half during the Gothic 14th century. Unfortunately, most of the bas-reliefs that once decorated its doorway were destroyed during the Revolution.

Nothing, however, has touched its remarkable crypt. Descending into its tiny alcove, you are immediately overwhelmed by the cool hush. A button on one side illuminates the oratory just

long enough to expose the relics of the saint, hostess to Christ at Bethany, passenger on the *navette* from Jerusalem and tamer of the menacing Tarasque. Her crypt is one of those unique places where the unseen overtakes the everyday. From the moment you enter its dark and damp confines, you feel a shroud of sanctity fall over you. It's not grandiose – but it is convincing.

Grandiose would more accurately describe the feudal **Château du Roy René**. Built directly on the banks of the Rhône during the first 50 years of the 15th century, it proudly rivals the Château of Beaucaire, which stands across the river on the opposite shore.

The interior of the castle is mostly empty. In the first gaping hall, a changing exhibition of modern abstracts creates a striking effect against the severe medieval walls. Aside from that, the castle has no furnishings but six magnificent 17th-century tapestries that recall the glory of Scipion.

The city puts on several *fêtes* each year but none more celebrated than that of the *Tarasque*. Among the activities that accompany this festival, which takes place during the last weekend in June, is a colourful parade led by a *papier-mâché* fascimile of the monster.

From Tarascon, travel north along D35 to reach the 10th-century **Abbaye St-Michel de Frigolet**, where a handful of monks still dwell. The land seems slightly less forbidding here, as the Alpilles meld into the gentler **Montagnettes**. These hills cover the area between the curve of the Rhône and the east-west stretch of the Alpilles and harbour numerous alcoves of cypress and poplars, olive and almond trees, straggly pines and fragrant herbs.

Barbentane is a friendly little town just north of the abbey, with a warm and comfortable atmosphere. Despite its modesty, a wonderful **château**, built in 1674 and still occupied by the marquis of Barbentane, stands right off its main street. Step through the gates and you'll wonder whether you have suddenly been transported to the Ile-de-France.

Luckily for the public, the marquis and marchioness have fallen on hard times, forcing them to open their doors to the curious. Guided tours are now available at scheduled times.

Outside, the subtle evidence of decay is everywhere. The lawns are slightly overgrown, and moss sprouts from the heads of classical statues. The backyard is lost in weeds. And, somehow, this only adds to the château's charm.

The interior is one-in-a-million. The grandson of the first owner spent 20 years as ambassador in Florence and brought home from his Italian voyages masses of marble and 18th-century furniture. Everything within is original, and many items, such as the wrought-iron bannister, are handmade.

Among the most amazing articles are: the marble floor and circular mosaic ceiling of the "statue" salon; the hand-painted 18th-century wallpaper of the "Chinese" sitting room; the Italian-style wall fountain in the parlour (it was once the dining room, but lack of servants and distance from the kitchen forced the marquis to switch their uses); the Provençal-style library and upstairs

Column from the Abbaye St-Michel-de-Frigolet.

bedroom, also with original hand-painted wallpaper. The beds were short because people never lay on their backs (considered the position of death). Above the stairwell is a stone-carving of the blustry mistral.

From the front door you can see the ominous **dungeon**, but it is not open to the public. Also within sight is the crumbling **Notre-Dame-des-Graces Church**. A more contemporary attraction on the outskirts of town is the **Provence Orchidées Greenhouse**. Here, you will find an extensive offering of prize-winning orchids for sight and for sale. It is best to come between October and May.

Before heading back south, you may want to make a quick sweep east through **Noves**. The town today boasts little to attract tourists (all that remains of its château are segments of the 14th-century ramparts), but it does have an almost mythic past. Founded in the 5th century BC, it was here that Petrarch first laid eyes on his beloved Laura, about whom he would later write some of the world's most famous love poems. The wine grown on the neighbouring hillsides is called, most appropriately, the *Cuvée des Amours* (Love Vintage).

Another town of literary significance lies south along D5. **Maillane** was both the birth and burial place for Frédéric Mistral. The house where the poet lived from 1876 until his death in 1914 has been turned into a museum, containing his desk and gloves as he left them, many of his books, and portraits of him, his wife and friends. In the cemetery down the street rests his tomb.

D5 runs directly into **St-Rémy-de-Provence**, the mini-capital of the area. St-Rémy makes a fine base for any vacation in the Alpilles, especially for those wishing to avoid the greater bustle of Arles. It is right in the middle of the region, possesses many attractions of its own and is, all-in-all, an extremely pleasant place to be.

St-Rémy is also the place to come for those interested in herbalism, for which it is the recognised centre. During the 1960s and 1970s, the number of *herbo-*

Young monk.

ristes in Provence declined, due to the growing popularity of chemical substitutes, but recent years have seen a resurgence in the use of natural products. Locals are optimistic that this will, in turn, help boost regional economy.

Wholesalers head for the **Herboristerie Provençale**, just outside the old town on Avenue Frédéric Mistral. Amateurs are welcome there too but might prefer one of the town's many "herb boutiques." An excellent one exists on Boulevard Mirabeau. Called **Les Herbes de Provence**, this pretty little store offers a variety of luxuriant herbal and flowery bath products as well as sacks of freshly dried basil, thyme, rosemary, etc.

Herbs are only one aspect of St-Rémy's popularity. Like most of the larger towns in the Bouches-du-Rhône, at the heart of the (relatively) new city lies a rather older city built in a round and criss-crossed with narow stone streets. In St-Rémy, these streets are labelled with names in Provençal as well as French, and several of the houses have been turned into museums.

One old house that hasn't been converted but is still worth taking a peek at stands along the Carriero di Barrio de l'Espitau. The building has long been boarded up, but an exterior plaque proclaims its significance: "Here was born, on the 14th of December in 1503, Michel de Nostradame, alias Nostradamus, astrologer."

The cavernous **Collegiale St-Martin** is less modest. The ceiling of this church is decorated with faded blue paint and a sprinkling of gold stars and lit by numerous stained-glass windows. What really catches the eye, however, is the enormous organ that dominates the church's anterior. Known to be outstanding among its peers, free concerts are given on it every Saturday.

Crossing behind the church leads you to the **Musée des Alpilles**, arranged within the 16th-century mansion of Mistral de Mondragon. This ethnological museum contains scores of photographs, portraits, costumes and household objects linked to the surrounding

Herbal bath oils from St-Rémy.

region. One room features the minerals mined within the Alpilles: bauxite, limestone, sandstone, etc. The building, which extends over an old alley as a courtyard, is also remarkable.

Next door, the venerable 17th-century **Hôtel de Lubières** offers informal exhibitions. One side is filled by modern paintings, and the other shows local works and sculptures in wood and other natural materials.

Across the street stands the **Hôtel de Sade**. Built during the 15th and 16th centuries, it is now an archaeological museum, housing all the objects discovered at the nearby site of Glanum. Its contents include everything from votive altars to pottery to bones.

Glanum and **Les Antiques** lie just outside the city. Once the site of a major Phocaean trading post, constructed beside a sacred spring, they are the town's top tourist attractions.

Les Antiques stands on the right-hand side of the road and comprises a commemorative arch and a mausoleum. The arch, situated across what once was the road connecting Spain to Italy, was built during the reign of Augustus to indicate the entrance to the city of Glanum. The mausoleum is a funereal monument of three levels that was dedicated to Caius and Lucius Caesar, the two grandsons of Augustus who died prematurely. The mausoleum has been particularly well-preserved, and both it and the arch are amazing pieces of Roman stonework such as you would more expect to find in an Italian city than upon an Alpilles plain.

Glanum, across the road, is slightly less approachable. Originally Celto-Ligurian, a sanctuary city and then a flourishing point of commerce during the Gallo-Greek years and later Roman times, it was virtually destroyed by invaders in the 3rd century. Excavations continue to uncover archaeological treasures, but the layman will need a good text and plan of the site.

Posted in between Glanum and the centre of town is the **Clinique de St-Paul**, where Van Gogh commited himself after slicing off his earlobe in Arles.

oman
ieze on
es
ntiques.

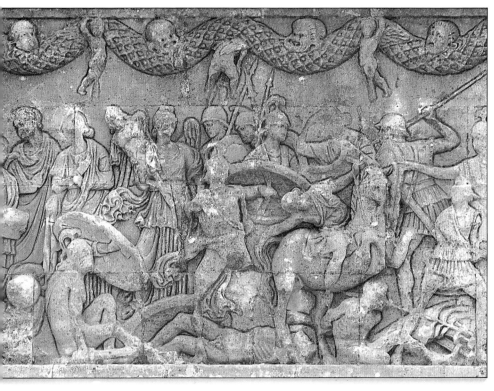

The tiny cloisters of the medieval **St-Paul-de-Mausole Monastery**, which houses the clinic, can be visited, but the still-active rest home can not.

One pleasant way to spend a meditative afternoon in St-Rémy is fishing. Follow the Avenue Antoine de La Salle, just down the road from the clinic, until you see the sign for Le Lac on the Chemin de Barrage. At its end lies the **Peiroou Lake**. The Lac de Peiroou, which means chauldron in Provençal, is reserved for fishing – you're not supposed to swim there – and behind it is a nice park for picnicking.

Or, if you are feeling really lazy on a hot afternoon, stroll up to the sandy square in front of the *syndicat d'initiative* and you will find the spot where the locals gather daily to play *boules*.

A feudal city like no other: When you're ready for a little change of scenery, take D99 west and switch on to D27 south. This perilous route climbs up into the peak of the Alpilles, overlooking the aptly named **Val d'Enfer** (Valley of Hell). Narrow stone cliffs cut into the winding road on one side, and on the other you will find a sheer drop. If possible, keep both hands on the steering wheel, and pray you don't meet another car.

From the **Cave de Sarragon**, the aerie peak dominated by Les Baux comes into view. But first, before making the prerequisite tour of this Provence-style ghost town, stop in on the **Cathédrale d'Images**. Movie buffs will recognise the spot as the site of both Cocteau's *Orpheus* and *Antigone*.

Even as you near the huge covered quarry-turned-theatre, the cool air of its interior reaches out to envelop you. When you step inside its darkened caverns, cold blackness surrounds you. Then, as your eyes begin to adjust, you realize that continually changing slides are being projected in monumental sizes over the rocky crevasses of the walls. Some photos even drape across the floor, so that you feel as though you are walking upon whatever they portray. Meanwhile, music echoes through the hollowed chambers. The whole ex-

The heights of Les Baux.

hibit will belong to a single theme, say Saharan Africa one year, Van Gogh another. No one should miss a visit to the "Cathedral."

Originally, the quarry belonged to the fabled citadel of **Les Baux**. Set on an imposing site way above rocky outcrops that tumble into deep valleys, the site of Les Baux has been occupied for the past 5,000 years. Its fame, however, comes from the period, between the years 1000 and 1400, when the bold and arrogant Lords of Baux made their presence felt throughout the region.

The feudal life of Les Baux offers a fascinating paradox. Here, "amidst this chaos of monumental stones and impregnable fortresses, inhabited by men whose roughness was only matched by that of their suits of armour, the 'Respect of the Lady' and ritual adoration of her beauty was born." The patronage of the troubadours by these violent lords engendered the first "Court of Love," and much of France's literary tradition emerged from their bloody citadel.

Today, more than a million and a half tourists a year come to see where once the poets roamed and the lords raged, with July and August being close to unmanageable. Craft shops and ice-cream boutiques spill out of many of the old buildings, and even parking costs ten francs. The impenetrable Les Baux has become the ultimate in tourist traps.

The spot divides into two parts: the ancient city, containing the ruins of the feudal court, and the village, where some 60 people still live and the shops and galleries now stand. In winter, the number of inhabitants drops to about 40, and ice and snow ravage the exposed peaks. Over the years, Les Baux has become somewhat of a retreat, but the number of year-round artisans is currently on a decline.

The village boasts three museums. The **Hotel de Manville** is a good place to start, since it contains the historical museum of Les Baux. The three rooms offer thorough documentation (in French) on the annals of Les Baux from neolithic times to more modern days. The last room shows photographs of

The good life at the Oustau de la Baumanière.

Princess Grace and Prince Albert Grimaldi of Monaco to whose family Les Baux belonged from 1642 to 1791.

Down the street, the **Hôtel des Porcelets**, built in the 16th century, houses a museum of fairly unremarkable contemporary art. But, next door is the best-preserved of all the monuments in the old city: the **Eglise de St-Vincent**. Its central nave dates back to the 12th century, and its stained glass is a striking *mélange* of the very ancient and the ultra-modern. Across the way is the charming 17th-century **Chapelle de Penitents Blancs**, decorated by Brayer. The apt theme of its mural, painted in 1974, is the shepherds of Provence, with an Alpilles Nativity. Finally in this little corner, cut directly into the rock face, is the **Galerie St-Vincent** with more modern paintings and sculptures.

A last museum, of archaeological and lapidary objects, occupies the **Tour de Brau**. Built at the end of the 14th century, the tower also marks the entrance into the **Cité Morte** (the ancient city).

A tour of the Cité Morte begins with the 12th-century **Chapel de St-Blaise**. Beside it lies a small modern cemetery filled with lavender and butterflies. Continue further up to the top of the ruins where stands a round tower from which the Baux family must have surveyed the valley with watchful eyes. The view is incredible. In the distance, the Alpilles sweep across the countryside. Pepper fields, olive groves and tiny hillside swells, all framed by white stone outcrops, nestle below.

More of the ancient city can be found along the northern ramparts. The energetic can climb them to attain even wider views or to investigate what is left of the 15th-century castle, the 10th-century keep and the Paravelle Tower.

Hugging the cliffs below the old village, the world-renowned **Oustau de la Baumanière** restaurant can compete with any dining establishment in Provence – or Paris – for quality. The proud chef uses mostly local produce and much of the menu is regional, but that doesn't mean the fare is peasant style. On the contrary, if you want to dine here, make a reservation, pack your pearls and *stuff your wallet.*

If the Alpilles have left you hot and thirsty, you may want to head back towards the Mediterranean. One choice would be the area around the **Etang de Berre**. Most of this section is highly industrialised, but the old port of **Martigues** still possesses some of the charm that enticed such painters as Corot, Renoir and Dufy to sojourn there. It makes a nice place to lunch.

Martigues is also near one of the most important archaeological discoveries in the Bouches-du-Rhône. Excavations at **St-Blaise** have uncovered several superimposed Celto-Ligurian cities as well as Greek ramparts. The site is open to the public, but it isn't well-marked and the uninitiated may easily lose their way (and understanding).

Another easy excursion from the Pays d'Arles is the **Camargue**. Indeed, many young Arlesians drive down nightly to enjoy its discos. Daytime visitors will find plenty of distraction as well when they are transported into what seems like a whole new world.

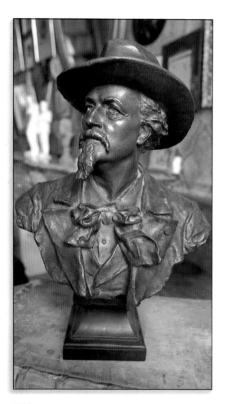

Left, bust of Mistral in Maillane; right, cooling down at a café.

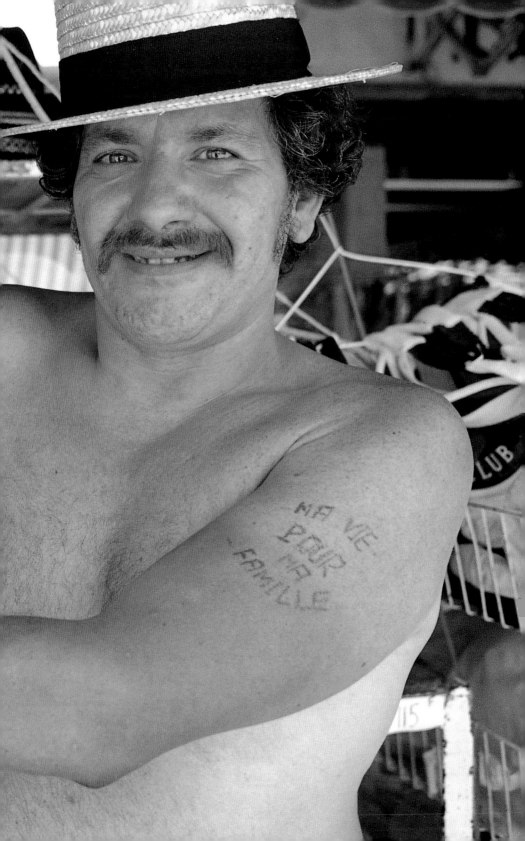

THE CAMARGUE

The **Camargue** lies directly to the south of the Pays d'Arles and, although officially a part of the Bouches-du-Rhône, is very much in a world of its own. Almost triangular in shape, bordered to the west by the Petit-Rhône, which flows to the sea past Les-Stes-Maries-de-la-Mer, and to the east by the Grand-Rhône, which runs down from Arles, its unusual natural environment has helped create for it a unique history.

Most of the region is marsh and lagoon, creating a perfect setting for one of France's greatest wildlife reserves. The area also provides a spiritual home for the country's gypsies, stages a national windsurfing championship, offers the joy of riding across beaches and salt plains, and provides the tourist with a choice of historic castles and churches to visit. It can be an equestrian's dream, a birdwatcher's paradise, a historian's treasure chest, a gourmet's delight or a windsurfer's playground.

At the same time, without advance reservations, the Camargue can turn into a tourist's nightmare. The famous horizons that inspired the Provençal poet Frédéric Mistral and the stunning light that fascinated Vincent Van Gogh also have encouraged an onslaught of touristic commercialism, resulting in the construction of simulated-rustic hotels and brash campsites and leaving behind a pile of left-over debris generated by summer holidaymakers.

To get the best from the Camargue, which covers over 480 sq. miles (800 sq. km), takes careful planning. Bear two things in mind. First of all, it is not always possible to wander off the main track without special permits. Secondly, the multiplicity of attractions makes it exceptionally popular with tourists, particularly families with children, in both July and August. During the high season, demand frequently exceeds both space and services available.

Preceding pages: vacationing couple. **Left,** white horses graze beside a *mas*.

Despite the growth of tourism, there is still much worth seeing in the Camargue and, with a little forethought, you can get around most of its downfalls. Any exploration of the region entails a certain amount of unavoidable zig-zagging, due to the layout of the land, so some people may prefer to stay on its edge near Arles and visit during a series of day trips.

Once within the region, travellers will find themselves with a wide selection of ways to get around. The curious blend of marsh, swamp and salt plain, which have in turn led to the establishment of copious wildlife parks, means that one can either journey by boat, by jeep, by horseback or on a bicycle. Real nature lovers will probably find that some areas can best be discovered on foot.

Even if you decide only to spend a few days in the region, visits to two or three well-chosen spots can reveal an amazingly rich variety of wildlife. And the real appeal of the Camargue lies in its wildlife: white horses, black bulls, wild birds, salt-water vegetation and swamps and lakes.

Getting to know the area: For a good, over-all introduction, take N570 west from Arles to the **Mas du Pont du Rousty**. This combination sheep farm and regional museum contains a permanent exhibition illustrating the history and traditional way of life of the Camargue. Best of all is its explanation of the different terrains in the region, which describes how the wildlife of fresh-water marshes is dissimilar from that of the salt lagoons and that of the coastal dykes. (At the same time, as you actually start to move around, don't be surprised to see a flock of pink flamingoes – inhabitants of the marsh – in full flight over an industrial salt plant in the southeast sector. It may seem incongruous, but it will just be another one of those startling contrasts that make the Camargue such an exciting region.)

For a hands-on look, take the sign-posted footpath that lies to the rear of the museum and leads to the beginning of the marshes. The walk will take you

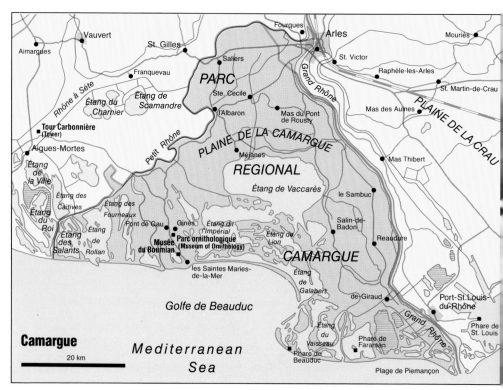

about an hour and give you a personal feel for these strange flatlands.

At first, you will be struck by the loud croaking of frogs, then the colourfulness of the flowers, which comprise everything from alofile plants to tamarisk and, during the warmer six months of the year, daisies, irises and asphodels. In addition, you will see a wide selection of birds: the curious black-winged stilts with their long pink legs, herons and all sorts of wading birds such as the ringed plovers.

The Camargue is a great place for birdwatchers. If you happen to be one, remember that you will find a lot more feathered activity in the early morning – which also is much the most pleasant time to be out rambling, especially during the hot summers. Springtime, of course, is the ideal season, for you will both get to hear their singing and see the large variety of migrants that visit the Camargue during their trip back north.

Once you've left the Mas, continue west along N570 towards **Albaron**. This route will take you past both paddy and wheat fields, land that has been recovered from the swamps over the past 40 years. Along the way, you will notice constant advertisements for a roadside ranch, complete with a wagon wheel and mock "western" frontage. This is just one of the many places in the Camargue that run pony trekking and safari trips into the marshes. The trips last from an afternoon to a full day.

At Albaron, a right turn onto D37 will lead you into **St-Gilles**. The carvings on the western front of this busy little agricultural town's 12th-century church are mild masterpieces. Upon entering the structure, you will find a remarkable stone spiral staircase, which has managed to survive despite extensive destruction during the Wars of Religion.

French cowboys and white horses: If you had taken a left-hand turn in Albaron onto D37, you would have entered the **Rhône Delta**, where lies the **Etang de Vaccarès**. Going in this direction, even from a car, will provide you with excellent views of pink flamingoes and other water fowl. On foot, a

Wedding at St-Gilles.

perceptive eye should be able to spot a beaver or a turtle or a scampering little lime-green tree frog. Here, too, the famous black bulls of the Camargue roam, and sometimes (but not as often as postcards may lead you to believe) you will catch a *gardien* (the French-style cowboy) astride his white horse.

Some say that the famouse white horses of the Camargue are the descendants of the wild horses that populated prehistoric Gaul and are depicted in the ancient cave paintings at Lascaux. Others claim that they are of North African origin, and even others suggest that they were first introduced from Tibet.

To get a closer look at them, you may want to check in at one of the Camargue's "ranches," where the *gardiens* take you out on horseback to visit the marshes. Extensively publicised is the *mas* belonging to Paul Ricard at **Méjanes**. Here, they've set up a well-organised trekking centre, and the *gardiens* who accompany you are particularly knowledgeable and authentic, for they work during the winter months as herdsmen. However, Ricard's is extremely commercial, and the bullfights and equestrian displays staged there are strictly for the tourists.

If you choose to travel without a guide, remember that the lagoon is a protected area. Any kind of hunting or fishing and even the picking of plants and flowers is prohibited.

Motorists will find few alternative routes once in the area beside the lagoon. This shouldn't matter for, as one follows the curve of the *étang* east, the view over seascapes, sandbanks and lagoon is magnificent. Butterfly lovers will be delighted to discover a rich variety of brightly coloured little creatures, including the Southern White Admiral, Swallowtails and Spanish Festoons. Don't be surprised, however, to learn that this (and all of the Camargue) is also the land of the mosquito.

Eventually, you will start to see powdery white hills and salt pans decorating the landscape. This southeastern corner of the Camargue, leading down to **Salin-de-Giraud**, is the French capital

Flamingos on the *étang*.

for salt production, and over half of the country's supply comes from right here. As might be expected, salt is a major industry for the region.

This area is also the gateway to the Camargue's beaches. After a long hot drive, few things are more refreshing than racing into the Mediterranean, cooling off in its inviting waters and then collapsing behind a sand dune for an afternoon's siesta. One word of caution, however, if you've parked your car out of sight. Sadly, the last few summers have witnessed a deplorable increase in thefts by seaside resorts. Best is to leave your car visibly empty and to carry any valuables with you.

Continue along D36 to what becomes a much narrower track, and you will reach the **Plage de Piemenson**. This beach represents a different sort of "natural" paradise, for its frequenters are all *"naturistes"* or nudists. Anyone familiar with beaches along the Côte d'Azur may well wonder why the local authorities have bothered to make any distinction between "nudist" beaches and "normal" beaches, but they do. And, it's true, there is something startling about watching middle-aged couples barbecuing in the nude. But you will soon get used to it. Besides, playing *boules* in the nude is more than fashionable, it is positively trendy.

If you don't feel up to baring all, you will find plenty of other sandy stretches without nudists along the same coastline. The **Plage d'Arles** will give you more chances to glimpse sea birds, such as the yellow-legged gulls, slender-billed gulls or the tern as it dives into the water for a fish. A fine breeze blows across these waters, making them particularly good for windsurfing.

If you are lucky, you may be able to find, along one of these beaches, a private boat operator who can take you directly over the sea to **Les-Stes-Maries-de-la-Mer**.

However, if you prefer to drive here, return by D36 to D37 up to Albaron, then head back south on the other side of the Etang de Vaccarès along D570. At twilight this journey is a bewitching

Camargue experience: the setting sun casting its colours over the lagoon.

A saintly city: Les-Stes-Maries-de-la-Mer is one of those places that has been very much influenced by its natural environment. During the Middle Ages, it stood several miles inland, and even as recently as 100 years ago its outlying borders were still a good 600 ft (200 metres) from the sea. Today, however, it is a flourishing resort, right on the border of the water.

The encircling seas have also brought scores of eastern visitors over the centuries. The town owes its name to an early group of these, who were by far the most famous of its settlers: Mary Jacoby (sister of the Virgin Mary), Mary Magdalene, Mary Salome (mother of Apostles John and James), Martha and risen-from-the-dead Lazarus, along with their Egyptian servant Sarah.

According to legend, in about AD 40, these early Christians had set out to sea from Palestine in a small boat without sails. They were miraculously washed ashore at this spot, safe and sound. In thanks, they built a chapel to the Virgin, and Mary Jacoby, Mary Salome and Sarah remained in the Camargue as evangelists.

After their deaths, the two Marys that had stayed in the Camargue and Sarah became the subject of pilgrimage. During the 9th century, a **church** was built in place of the simple chapel and fortified against invading Saracens. Excavations beneath this structure, begun in 1448 under the behest of Good King René, led to the discovery of a still-extant well and a spring filled with "the fragrances of sweet-scented bodies." In this same spot were uncovered the remains of the saints.

Their tomb was placed in the the church's **High Chapel of St-Michel**. The stones on which the bodies had rested are kept below in the crypt and have become "miracle" stones. They are said to heal painful eyes and to have the power to cure sterility in women.

The servant, Sarah, has attracted a cult all her own. Considered the patron saint of gypsies, she is remembered on 24 and 25 May each year with two special nights of celebration. Gypsies from all over the surrounding regions descend upon the town for horse racing, running of the bulls and a whole variety of other festivities.

In the evenings, the fiesta spirit runs wild, and the frenzied excitement of gypsy music and dancing fills the air. At the same time, during this period, the town has become a rendezvous spot for the bullherders of the Camargue. Needless to say, in recent years, the festival has become a major media event, attracting television teams, film crews and even some politicians.

Another day of celebration comes on the last Sunday of October. This is the special feast day for Mary Salome, and it is commemorated by colourful processions around the **Church of Notre-Dame-de-la-Mare**. During the summer months, when there isn't a festival but lots of tourists around, this church is still very crowded. If you decide to visit it anyway, climb to the roof for a stunning panoramic view across the sand hills and down to the waves as they splash against the sunlit shore.

During the holiday season, Les-Stes-Maries-de-la-Mer is unquestionably a commercial resort. Its busy pedestrian zones are lined with souvenir shops, and the many reasonably priced hotels and camping sites do well. There are many places where you can rent horses and boats, swim or play tennis during the day and, at night, some of the area's hottest discothèques swing into action. Bullfights are held in the local arena.

A less strenuous attraction is the **Baroncelli Museum**, housed in the one-time domicile of the Marquess of the same name. Inside is her collection of varying types of literature on the Camargue. Also on display are examples of local furniture, fauna, artwork and *gardien* paraphernalia.

If the bustle is starting to get to you, escape by booking a boat trip along the Petite Rhône. Go down to the landing stage near **Baroncelli-Jauron's Tomb** to join one of these excursions, which leave at regular intervals. Photographers will be thrilled by the action shots they can take of Camargue wildlife from the water, especially of the marsh birds. Everyone will enjoy a new opportunity to see the herds of bulls and horses that run along its banks.

If you would prefer to find some quiet beaches in the area and are willing to challenge weathered tracks off the main road, head west out of town. Along here you will be able to find a place to park. Leave your car and climb the sand dunes, and you should be rewarded with some clear and empty spaces far away from the crowds.

Van Gogh, who was fascinated by the light in this region, painted the famous *Boats of the Stes-Maries* on these beaches. Of course, that was before campsites, caravans and water scooters had intruded on the seascape. If he arrived today, Frédéric Mistral, who set the tragic end of his famous Provençal work *Mireio* on these sandy shores, would no longer be able to write of it "no trees, no shade and not a soul."

As you leave Les-Stes-Maries-de-la-Mer area by the main route of D570, you will pass by the **Musée Boumian**. Its much-touted waxwork tableau, which attempts to recreate a romantic version of the Camargue, is actually well-worth missing. You may, however, want to stop in on the **information centre** at **Ginès**. An informative sideshow here explains about the indigenous flowers, plants and fauna that grow in the outlaying land.

Western Camargue: Continue north on D38, then turn left onto D58, and you will enter the plain of **Aigues-Mortes**. The drive along here will take you across a part of the Camargue that has not radically changed for years and years. From time to time, you will spot an authentic *mas*, single-storey cabins with thatched roofs that over the years still defy the mistral.

The plain borders on a rich agricultural area that produces grapes and cereals. The **Tower of Carbonnière** at the end of the drive along D58 will give you the chance to look out over these fields, to the foothills of the Cévennes in the northwest, the Petite Camargue in the east and across the salt flats of Aigues-

Enjoying a game of *boules* at the plage de Piemançon.

Mortes to the south. Built as an outpost to the garrison of Aigues-Mortes during the time of the Crusades, the tower guards what once was the only route in and out of town.

The area around Aigues-Mortes is made up of salty lagoons and water channels where the Rhône meets the sea. The town itself was built amidst the marshes, salt flats and lagoons in 1241. It was named for its location (Aigues-Mortes means "dead waters") as it contrasted with a town, **Aigues-Vives** ("living waters"), that lay in the hills about 12 miles (20 km) north of it.

Good fortune from an architectural point of view has limited the town's growth, and there has been little expansion beyond its walls. What stands today is a well-preserved medieval town that has changed little on a superficial level. The ramparts remain intact and still readily dominate the surrounding countryside. With a little concentration, it is easy to imagine this town as the springboard from which Saint-Louis (King Louis IX) launched the Seventh Crusade in order to liberate Jerusalem.

When photographed at twilight from the southwest, the **battlements** at Aigues-Mortes make a fabulous picture, as sharp silhouetted shapes emphasise the strategic position of this curious medieval garrison town. If by now you have become adept at bird-spotting, climb up and take a look out over them. It is not uncommon to see kestrels, marsh harriers and the colourful bee-eaters with their blue, yellow and green plumage as they somersault after tasty insects.

Once you've passed through the gateway, you will find a number of attractive narrow streets criss-crossing the town. They lead to the **central square**, which is overlooked by a statue of Saint-Louis, the patron of the town who granted it its special rights and privileges. Although you will find the square lined by cafés and restaurants, you can get a better meal by wandering down the adjacent and more secluded side streets. Look for a restaurant that specialises in local dishes like *Gardiane de Taureaux*

Preparing for the *feria du cheval*.

(a delicious type of beef stew cooked with olives) or local seafood dishes.

After dining, you may want to climb the **Constance Tower** and **ramparts**. They provide an excellent overview of Aigues-Mortes. Look down to the northeast sector of the town, and you will see what originally was all one farm owned by the Knights of St-John until the Revolution.

The town has a population of 5,000 and, although its importance as a seaport has diminished, it is still a centre for salt production and vine growing. Visits to "Les Salins du Midi" (The Salt Marshes of the South) are organised in July and August on Wednesday and Friday afternoons by the **tourist office**, which stands in the central square.

The local wine, Listel, is grown commercially and is remarkable for being a *vin de sable*. This means that it is made from vines that grow directly out of the sand. The white is called *gris de gris* and the red *rubis*. Nearby *caves* offer free wine-tasting.

The horses that play such an important part in the life of the Camargue have also been woven into one of legends that surround Aigues-Mortes. Young children are told that if they misbehave they will be dragged off by "Lou Drape," a horse that is supposed to hover over the ramparts at night. It is said that its body can lengthen to carry away as many as 100 naughty children on its back into the marsh, where it will then devour them. Even today myths, legends and popular superstitions are an integral part of life in the Camargue.

A little bit of Languedoc: Le Grau-du-Roi and Port-Camargue, although only 6 miles (10 km) west of Aigues-Mortes, actually belong to the region of Languedoc-Roussillon, but they may well be of interest to travellers who wish to discover the Camargue from the sea. The lagoons and mooring facilities of these two ports make them attractive harbours, with excellent opportunities for watersports and fishing.

Le Grau-du-Roi is a narrow coastal strip that separates the Etang du Repausset from the sea. It has two very different identities that contrast old and new architectural styles. The eastern quay is an active fishing port with canal connections to Aigues-Mortes some 3½ miles (6 km) away, and it can be a useful mooring for people entering the Camargue by boat. The quayside cafés serve excellent fish, and you can actually see the clams being shovelled out of the water before they arrive on your table. Across the bridge to the west lies a new development of holiday apartments that manages to blend into the old town without making too much of a sharp contrast. Despite modernisation, Le Grau-du-Roi is still a pleasant town to stroll through on summer evenings.

The **Port-Camargue**, which lies to the south, has excellent boating facilities and broad sandy beaches. It is also extremely practical for sailing parties as boats can be tied up outside the front doors of the recently constructed holiday apartments. A first-class sailing school is based at the marina and offers instruction for complete beginners or for advanced students interested in competitive sailing.

The
oceanfront.

Alpes-de-Haute-Provence

20 km

St. Bonnet
Pont du Fossé
St. Etienne-en-Dévoluy
le Cros
Ancelle
Château d'Ancelle (Castle)
St.Julien-en-Beauchène
Romette
la Bâtie-Neuve
Creyers
Montmaur
Gap
Chorges
Beaurières
la Beaume
Veynes
Savines-le-Lac
Aspres-sur-Buech
Lac de Serre Ponçon
St. V les-F
Taillard
le Lauzet-
MON
Serres
Barcillonnette
MONTAGNE DE ST. GENIS
Turriers
Rosans
La Motte
Seyne (1200)
Durance
Orpierre
Laragne-Montéglin
Esparron-la-Bâtie
Clues de Verdaches
Laborel
MONTAGNE DE CHABRE
Châteaufort
MONTAGNE DE GACHE
St. Géniez
Pierre Ecrite
Barles
Verdaches
le
Défie de
CRÊTE DE GÉRUEN
Lachau
Ribiers
le Castellard
CRÊTE DE LIMAN
Séderon
Sisteron
la Jav
Thoard
Signal de Lure
1826
Volonne
Pic d'Oise
1140
Digne
MONTAGNE DE LURE
Redortiers
Château-Arnoux
Tar
St. Etienne-les- Orgues
St. Donat
Peyruis
Bléone
St. Christol
Banon
Les Mées
Mézel
Clue de Chabrières
N.D. de Ganagobie
Limans
Simiane-la-Rotonde
Forcalquier
la Bégude-Blanche
Barrême
Observatoire de Haute Provence (Observatory)
Mane
S
Oppedette
Sauvan
Oraison
Reillanne
Dauphin
Moustiers-Ste. Marie
Céreste
Valensole
Riez
Su
PARC
Roumoules
REGIONAL
Manosque
Grand Canyon du Verdon
DU
Allemagne-en-Provence
Ste. Croix-de-Verdon
Lac de Ste. Croix
LUBÉRON
Grambois
Gréoux-les-Bains
St. Laurent-du-Verdon
Verdon
Mirabeau
Vinon-sur-Verdon
Pertuis
Quinson

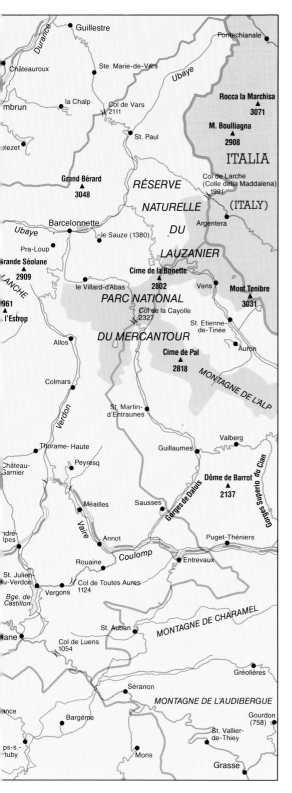

ALPES-DE-HAUTE-PROVENCE

Perhaps Provence's least-known *département* and certainly the least densely populated, the **Alpes-de-Haute-Provence** seem at first glance to miss out on much that makes the rest of Provence so attractive. Bypassed by the main artery of communications down the Rhône Valley, this vast region lacks the beaches and glitz of the Côte, the gems of art and architecture of the Vaucluse and the fertile vineyards and perfect *villages perchés* of the Var.

Instead, the Alpes-de-Haute-Provence show a wild, rugged face. The turbulent sweep of the Durance and the desolate Valensole Plain, brought to life in summer by countless rows of lavender bushes, dominate the western region. Vertiginous gorges to the south rise to heady Alpine heights as you move north and east. In between are azure lakes, bizarre rock formations and inaccessible mountainous terrain.

Simplicity and practicality characterise the region's architecture. Stark defensive citadels crown many towns, and villages are constructed to give maximum protection against the elements. The much-vaunted climate – balancing on a happy axis of Provençal warmth and cool Alpine clarity – can turn to harshly low temperatures in winter.

Ask any local to sum up life in the Alpes-de-Hautes-Provence, and he or she will give the same answer: "*pauvre*" (poor). Like its architecture, the region's cultural heritage is marked by simplicity and austerity. Until recently, the inaccessibility of much of the country meant that progress arrived slowly and ancient traditions endured. Life followed the rural rhythms of the movement of sheep herds (known as *transhumance*) and was characterised by constant battles against the elements.

Nonetheless, the Alpes-de-Haute-Provence have witnessed a surprising amount of migration in the past 100 years. In common with the rest of inland

Preceding pages: the famed Alpine sheep.

Provence, the 20th century has left many villages abandoned, as locals move south to work in the more prosperous areas around the coast.

In the past 30 years, the Alpes-de-Haute-Provence have changed beyond recognition. The Durance River has been tamed by an elaborate system of dams, providing fertile ground for fruit cultivation along the valley, and is soon to be served by a new autoroute along its length. New jobs in hydroelectricity and at the Cadarache nuclear research centre have been created.

Tourism, though a good deal slower to develop here than in the more obviously enticing parts of Provence, has gained impetus. The spa towns of Digne and Gréoux-les-Bains attract health-cure seekers, the northern Alpine resorts lure skiers throughout the winter, and wind-surfers and hikers swarm over the vast lakes and austere peaks.

The French press have devoted considerable space to the Alpes-de-Haute-Provence as the next region waiting to be "discovered." Wealthy Parisians now spend the summer in Manosque and increasing numbers of city-dwellers from Marseille buy holiday homes in the mountains. The *pauvreté* that has marked the lives of many of its inhabitants is still in evidence, but the impressive, singular beauty of the Alpes-de-Haute-Provence is increasingly attracting profitable new visitors.

Border town: Sisteron, the natural gateway to Provence, seems hardly Provençal at all. This pretty, tidy town, dominated by a stark towering citadel, has a definite air of Dauphiné about it. Just to the north, the olive trees stop and, to all intents and purposes, you say goodbye to Provence.

Sisteron's setting is impressive – on the left bank of the Durance and looking across at the craggy **Rocher de la Baume**. For centuries, people have passed through this strategically placed "gateway," lending it a feeling of lively, if not exactly cosmopolitan, activity. A bustling market, some light industry and a steady wave of tourists along the N85 maintain that atmosphere today.

Tending the flock.

In the past, such comings and goings brought Sisteron both good times and bad. Plague and typhus, carried by passing travellers and armies, decimated the population in the 14th, 17th and 18th centuries. Napoleon stopped here for lunch on a misty March day in 1815, when returning from exile on Elba. Still standing in the Rue Saunerie is the now-private **Bras d'Or Inn**, owned at the time by the grandfather of the Sisteron novelist Paul Arène. A plaque commemorates the site where the imperial lunch was quaffed.

The town's **citadel**, originally built in the 13th century then redesigned by Henri IV's military engineer Jean Erard in the 16th, is Sisteron's most obvious crowd-puller. An impressive collection of keeps and dungeons, watchtowers and crenellated battlements stands on a massive rock topped by a small chapel.

Its complex, fascinating history as a fortress and prison pales next to the blow dealt by our own age. On 15 August 1944, the Allies bombed it in an attempt to speed up the retreat of the German occupying army that had taken refuge there. More than 300 people died, and a quarter of Sisteron's fine medieval town was destroyed.

Visitors to the citadel today can listen to a dramatised version of the fateful day, relayed through small speakers dotted round the ramparts. The questionable quality of the sound effects does nothing to dim the poignancy of the tragedy.

Fortunately, a good deal still remains of the **old town** that sits huddled at the foot of the citadel rock. A mixture of modern boutiques and pleasant old-fashioned shops line its narrow streets, known here as *andrônes*, from the Latin word for "alleyway" or the Greek term for "between two houses," depending on which linguist you ask.

The town's bakers sell the local speciality, *fougasse à l'anchois*, a delectable bread dough smeared with anchovies and sold by the kilo. Butchers display the justly famous Sisteron lamb, given a fragrant herbal flavour by the wild thyme and rosemary culled from

Sisteron.

pastures of the upper Durance Valley.

North of Sisteron, on the D3 to **St-Geniez**, look out for a rock slab covered with Roman inscriptions. The **Pierre-Ecrite**, carved in the 5th century, records the conversion to Christianity of Claudius Dardanus, prefect of the Gauls. Tantalisingly, it mentions a nearby "city of God," which apparently was founded by Claudius, though archaeologists have been unable to fix its exact setting.

For centuries, the Durance was known as one of the "three scourges of Provence" (the *mistral* and the Parlement at Aix completed the triumvirate). In recent years, its unpredictable surges have been harnessed by a series of major dams beginning at **Serre-Ponçon** on the northern border of the Alpes-de-Haute-Provence. Apple and pear orchards, created over the past 30 years on the newly irrigated alluvial plains, have brought a refreshing vigour to the once-ailing economy hereabouts. And hydro-electric power, nicknamed by locals *la houille blanche* (white coal), has brought added prosperity to the region.

Nonetheless, the Durance remains tortuous, complex and peppered with islets. It is one of the few rivers in Provence that contains more than a thin trickle of water in summer.

Limestone penitents: As the Durance snakes its way south and meets the Bléone arriving from the west, a sprawling collection of light industrial plants appears. Across the apex of the confluence, south of Château-Arnoux, the rocks of **Les Mées** stand eerily over miles of flat maize fields.

The village of Les Mées itself does not tempt much, but the staggering **"Pénitents,"** the name given to the curious row of limestone pinnacles outside it, do. The smooth, dolmen-shaped formations, some as high as 330 ft (100 metres), rise sheer and bare out of what seems like a dwarfed, stunted forest – some alone, some clustered in groups – until they close ranks to form a single mini-*massif*.

The legends that surround them have a sadness that echoes their lonely as-

Serre-Ponçon.

pect. During the Saracen invasions, a group of monks from the Montagne de Lure are said to have been attracted by the beauty of some Moorish girls. As the cowled, disgraced figures were banished from the village, Saint Donatus turned them to stone, in punishment for their impropriety.

The religious theme continues on the opposite bank of the Durance, in the foothills of the **Montagne de Lure**. The evocative ruins of the **Church of St-Donat**, reached by the narrow D101, sit isolated in thick oak woods. Formerly the retreat of Saint Donatus, a sixth-century monk from Orléans, the church is today in a sorry state, its floor covered with rubble and graffiti etched into its venerable stone. The eight mighty pillars that support its ancient vaulting and a faded-white apse, decorated with pale terracotta-coloured stars, hint at its former glory. It is one of Provence's few remaining examples of early medieval Romanesque architecture.

More obviously impressive is the nearby medieval **Priory of Ganagobie**.

Like St-Donat, it was in a sad dilapidated state, until restoration work began in the 1960s. Now its principal attractions, other than the wonderful view of the Durance Valley, are its magnificent zig-zag west portal and the stunning 12th-century mosaics, in red, black and white, that decorate the interior.

Alpine summits: The vast, forbidding Montagne de Lure is a continuation of the vine-rich Ventoux Range to the west and is bordered by the Lubéron Mountain to the south. Its heights are reached via the little town of **St-Etienne-les-Orgues** that lies at its feet. The prosperity of this pretty village was traditionally based on medicinal remedies concocted from mountain herbs and sold by travelling pedlers.

A road lined with fir trees and, in summer, purple fields of lavender leads out of the village. Soon, the lavender stops, and the dense oak and fir forest of the mountain proper appears. Though seemingly deserted, this route becomes an animated pilgrims' way in August and September each year, as locals con-

A core crop.

tinue the centuries-old tradition of pilgrimage to the isolated **Chapel of Notre-Dame-de-Lure**, located halfway to the summit.

Also founded by the reclusive Saint Donatus, Notre-Dame-de-Lure has none of the architectural distinction of the Eglise de St-Donat, but its setting is ample compensation. In summer, local people and tourists picnic in the shade of the splendid lime trees that shelter the church's entrance.

The familiar pattern of decay of so many of Provence's ancient religious sites has in this instance been broken by the restoration work currently being carried out by a religious group called the Community of Jerusalem. Groups of young Christians, camped in the only building adjoining the church, chisel enthusiastically at the stonework or sit in circles reading the Bible. The purity of the air, which seems positively cool here even in the height of summer, adds to the healthy atmosphere.

Somewhat less wholesome is the fact that one of the church's few pieces of ornamentation, a statue of the Virgin, was stolen in 1985. A rather sad photograph, propped up on the statue's empty plinth, is all that remains.

After Notre-Dame-de-Lure, the road to the summit rises in steep curves, edged in summer by seas of purple larkspur. The **Signal de Lure**, the mountain's summit (5,990 ft/1,826 metres) boasts an undistinguished *station de ski* and some of the most impressive panoramas to be found anywhere in Provence. Views of the Cévennes and Mt-Ventoux are interrupted only by the sight of soaring black buzzards.

The wild isolation of the Lure inspired many of the novels of Jean Giono. A native of Manosque, Giono made his name in the first half of this century with a series of novels on village life – and death – in the Alpes-de-Haute-Provence. Giono's Provence has little in common with the smiling, sunny nostalgia depicted by Pagnol or even Daudet. His central themes were the progressive abandonment of the small mountain villages of the region,

Young goatherd girl.

the inexorable destruction of the traditional patterns of rural life and the rough sensuality of man's communion with nature. In *Regain* (1930), the fictional village of Aubignane, already reduced to just a handful of inhabitants, eventually houses just a solitary man, determined to stay in his native village.

Many have tried to locate Giono's settings, mostly without success. Nonetheless, it is widely believed that Aubignane is based on the ruined village of **Redortiers**, north of **Banon**. Whether or not intimations of Giono appeal, it is worth making a visit to Banon to sample its renowned goat's cheese wrapped in chestnut leaves and to Redortiers to see an example of Giono's reality.

A 1980s angle on Giono's literary theme is provided by the changes that have taken place in the beautiful, remote village of **Simiane-la-Rotonde**. Simiane, dominated by the strange "rotunda" that gives the village its name, is today almost entirely composed of *maisons secondaires* (second homes).

Goat cheese of Banon.

Outside the summer months, its closed shutters and deserted streets have more than a little in common with the desolate ruins of Redortiers.

An unshaken heritage: No such cultural instability dogs the everyday life of one of the most appealing towns of the *département*, **Forcalquier**. The locals here happily welcome visitors during the summer months but don't allow the brief invasion to disrupt the rhythm of their prosperous lives.

Forcalquier is at its best on Monday – the day of its wonderful weekly market. Countless stalls, groaning with local produce or stacked high with better-than-average *objets artisanaux,* crowd the spacious **Place du Bourguet** and the labyrinth of streets around it. The market acts as a magnet to people from the region who come to buy, sell or simply gossip in the pleasant marketplace cafés.

Forcalquier's air of independence has its roots in the 12th century when the town was an independent state. During this period, the town served as the capital of Haute-Provence, making it a centre for culture and trade and a favourite residence of the counts of Provence.

The origin of the town's name, however, goes back much further. Situated on the Via Domitia, one of the three great Roman roads in Provence, Forcalquier is said to be derived from *furni calcarii*, Latin for the limestone kilns that the Romans hewed into the hillside.

Forcalquier boasts a clutch of reasonably interesting "sights": the **Couvent des Cordeliers**, a Franciscan convent, restored in the 1960s and now part privileged private housing, part visitable monument; the austere **Cathedral Church of Notre Dame** on the main square; and the 19th-century **chapel** on the hill above the old town with a *table d'orientation* to help you identify the surrounding mountains.

But the real flavour of Forcalquier can be tasted more sharply simply by taking an aimless wander around the splendid alleyways of the **old town**. Almost every narrow street here is lined with fine stone doorways and arches that are decorated with chiselled plaques, scrolls and intricate relief.

Forcalquier seems a place where the exigencies of the 20th century have had to work hard to dislodge a firm historic anchor. However, preservation of the cultural heritage that emanates so naturally from Forcalquier's people and buildings has its official home a few miles south of the town.

The **Priory of Salagon**, to be found just outside the village of **Mane**, has been converted into a major centre for local studies and research. As well as fascinating permanent exhibitions covering local history and a botanical garden planted with the medicinal plants that once played a significant role in the region's economy, serious lectures are given throughout the summer on aspects of local rural life, architecture and customs.

Salagon's principal aim is to inform and enrich the lives of the people of the region. As such, it is an unmissable detour for visitors looking for a real insight into the *Pays de Forcalquier*.

Those with a taste for imposing coun-try seats should combine Salagon with a visit to the **Château de Sauvan**, arguably the *département*'s finest 18th-century building. The Alpes-de-Haute-Provence is not an area renowned for its châteaux, and many are little more than small stately homes. Nonetheless, Sauvan possesses a classical elegance that merits its local title of "*Le Petit Trianon Provençal.*"

Other delights in the region include the small hilltop village of **Dauphin**, the pretty series of *pigeonniers* in and around **Limans**, and the **Observatory of Haute-Provence**, which attracts astronomers from all over France.

A boomtown: Manosque has an elegance and sense of refinement that sets it apart from the rest of the Alpes-de-Haute-Provence. Largely as a result of its position – a plum site on the Durance within easy reach of Forcalquier, the Montagne de Lure, the Valensole Plain and the Grand Canyon du Verdon – Manosque has become the principal economic axis of the *département*.

Twenty years ago, it was a sleepy

Dusk at Montfuron.

town with a population of less than 5,000. Today, that number has increased more than fourfold. Blossoming agriculture in the Durance Valley (Manosque is known for its yellow peaches), the proximity of the Cadarache nuclear research centre that has drawn scientists and their families to settle here, and the relentless flow of tourists have combined to give Manosque an energetic air of modernity.

Fortunately, progress has not seeped fully into the bricks and mortar of the town, which remains essentially medieval in layout and character. Manosque covers a small hill above the Durance; "a tortoise shell in the grass," in the words of Jean Giono.

Two imposing stone archways, the tall crenellated **Porte Saunerie** and the **Porte Soubeyran**, stand guard at the entrance to the **old town**. These are linked by the town's main artery, the Rue Grande. Encircling old Manosque is a busy ring road that has replaced the town's ancient ramparts.

Stepping through either of the *portes*

(gates) brings you into a pedestrian area of narrow streets, honey-coloured churches and fountain-filled squares. Outwardly, Manosque seems to have survived the onslaught of its astonishing growth, though the rows of chic modern shops and small pretty squares converted to parking lots jolt you back to the future.

Manosque *la Pudique* (the Modest), the nickname given to the town in the 16th century, seems rather inappropriate today. The name derives from a tale, almost certainly apocryphal, concerning a visit by François I. The young king showed more than a passing interest in the daughter of a local dignitary. To repel the king's advances and preserve her honour, the young girl promptly disfigured her face with sulphur.

Giono's magnificent friend: Giono, of course, is what most Frenchmen think of when they think of Manosque. It was here that he lived, wrote and died between 1895 and 1970. The sweep south from the Montagne de Lure, through Manosque, and west to the vast plains of

Inside Château de Sauvan.

Valensole and Puimoisson mark the boundaries of Giono's Provence.

Giono called the wide, flat **Valensole Plain** his "magnificent friend." Today, it is France's principal centre of lavender cultivation, but it wasn't always so. Lavender production is a 19th-century phenomenon, and the almond trees that blossom so spectacularly on the plain in early spring are a much more ancient element of the economy.

Summer is the time to see the Valensole in all its purple magnificence. On the cusp of July and into August, around the time of the harvest, the dusky violet rows stretch away to the horizon. The unmistakable odour, so redolent of a grandmother's linen cupboard, fills the air, while wooden trucks piled high with vast purple bunches lumber their way along the roads of the high plateau.

The few villages that huddle on the plain, surviving the winter lashings of wind and hailstorms, are for the most part unremarkable. The exception is **Riez**, notable for its four **Corinthian columns** – remains of a Roman temple of Apollo – standing alone in a field just outside the town. The ancient **Merovingian baptistry** is Riez's other great "sight." But what is most appealing about the town, particularly in its **old quarter**, is a pleasing scruffiness and an attitude of *laissez-faire* that pervades the old streets and makes the people seem relaxed and welcoming.

By contrast, **Digne-les-Bains**, capital of Alpes-de-Haute-Provence and last stop on the Train des Pignes, is not scruffy at all. A genteel spa town, spacious and airy but without much architectural distinction, it lies northeast of Riez in the imposing Pré-Alpes de Digne. It was here that Hugo set the first chapters of *Les Misérables*.

But Digne is not simply a town of fictional *malheureux*, rheumatics and departmental officials. The shady **Boulevard Gassendi** tempts with the pleasant cafés along its length and, in early August, Digne asserts its position with a boisterous festival and procession called the *Corso de la Lavande*.

Four days of revelry climax in a grand

Alpine peaks north of Digne.

procession. An array of huge flower-bedecked floats, some modern in theme, some traditionally Provençal, glide down the main boulevard to uproarious applause, preceded by the town's sanitation department trucks, which douse the streets with lavender water. Cunning Dignois reserve their tables at the boulevard's cafés for lunch and a good view of the parade.

Lavender, or its more common hybrid *lavandin*, is sold in Digne in every conceivable form. Soap, essence and sachets of the dried plant are all worth buying.

Those with no wish to take the waters, either of the thermal or lavender varieties, should head south towards the outskirts of town to Digne's eccentric **Alexandra David-Néel Foundation**. The woman who gives her name to this cultural-centre-*cum*-museum was a Parisian adventurer who spent much of her life travelling in remote parts of Asia, including perilous trips to the forbidden Tibetan capital of Lhasa. Seduced by the beauty of the Alpes-de-Haute-

n-residence ˉibetan nonk at the Javid-Néel ˉoundation.

Provence, which she called a "Himalayas for Liliputians," she bought a house in Digne in 1927 and named it *Samten Dzong*, meaning "the fortress of meditation."

When she died in 1969, aged 101, this remarkable woman left the house and its fascinating contents to the city of Digne. As in her lifetime, the Foundation continues to attract visitors and Buddhist pilgrims to view the collection of objects and documents that she acquired during her peripatetic existence.

Architecturally, Digne's greatest attraction is the Lombard-style **Cathedral Church of Notre-Dame-du-Bourg**, north of the Boulevard Gassendi on the outskirts of town. Look for the 13th-century portals in stunning blue and white limestone. Digne also boasts an averagely interesting municipal museum with local history exhibits and a collection of butterflies (for which the area was once well known).

More specialised is the well-ordered **Centre de Géologie**, signposted on the opposite bank of the Bléone, with an astonishing range of fossils and animal skeletons from prehistoric times.

Natural wonders: Near the southern borders of the Alpes-de-Haute-Provence lies the *département*'s greatest natural site, the **Grand Canyon du Verdon**. Even if you see little else in the area, on no account miss this. Natives of Arizona may find the name unlikely, but this massive crevice scored deep into the limestone is one of the most breathtaking of natural phenomena, at least in the Old World.

First stop on the Canyon trail is **Moustiers-Ste-Marie**, where an astonishing backdrop of craggy cliffs provides a taste of the glories to come. Moustiers is an attractive small town perched on the edge of a ravine. High up behind the town, the two sides of the ravine seem held together by a massive chain that is around 720 ft (220 metres) long. Suspended from the chain, like a pendant on a giant's necklace, is a man-sized metal star.

This curious piece of adornment has inspired poems by Mistral and Giono and all manner of speculation as to its origin. But local historians have settled on the legend that it was placed there by a knight returning from the Crusades, in fulfilment of a religious vow. In any event, the present star dates only from 1957, when the mayor of Moustiers decided that the town's most famous piece of jewellery was due for a facelift.

More obviously visible is Moustiers' major claim to fame – its *faïence*. The narrow village streets are crammed to bursting with shops and studios producing the white-glazed decorative pottery.

Established in the late 17th century by Antoine Clérissy, the recipe for the white glaze was said to have come via an Italian monk from Faenza. The industry prospered for the following 200 years, counting Madame de Pompadour among its customers. Changing fashions, however, brought about its decline in the 19th century, and the art was not revived until the mid-1920s.

Sadly, many of the items produced today have fallen prey to the depressing combination of high prices and low quality. Though it is still possible to

seek out good examples from among the vast range available, perhaps more rewarding is a visit to the **Musée de la Faïence** in the Placette du Prieuré.

Opposite the entrance to the museum, housed in a vaulted crypt, is the stunning three-tiered belfry of the Romanesque village church.

A fork in the road less than 2 miles (3 km) south of Moustiers offers a choice of routes to the Grand Canyon du Verdon. Heading south, the road skirts the spectacular man-made **Lac de Ste-Croix**, a 7-mile (11-km) stretch of perfect azure water created in the 1970s by the installation of a hydroelectric dam. The route then doglegs east to follow the southern ridge of the canyon, known as the **Corniche Sublime**. Alternatively, the old road to Castellane (D952) snakes along the northern ridge, veering away from the canyon edge around halfway along its length.

Both routes have their virtues. Choosing the Corniche Sublime means consistently spectacular views, most notably those at the **Balcons de la Mes-**

On the road to Annot.

cla, where the Verdon converges with the smaller canyon formed by the River Arturby. The left bank has its own impressive *belvédère* (viewing point), the **Point Sublime**, a dizzy 600 ft (180 metres) above the river, and offers two chances to climb down to the Canyon floor, at Chalet de la Maline (branch off from the village of La Palud) and just east of the Point Sublime (follow signs for Couloir de Samson). Both routes require at least a half-day trip.

Statistics on the Grand Canyon only hint at its magnificence. Twelve and a half miles (21 km) in length and 5,000 ft (1,500 metres) deep, the vertiginous limestone cliffs are gouged by the waters of the Verdon River, in turn glassy and crystalline or tumbling in white-water chaos. Colours are unreal: jewelled emerald and turquoise contrast in autumn with the ochres and russets of surrounding deciduous trees.

Less than a century ago, the canyon was largely deserted, with only a few local peasants still eking out meagre livings as woodcutters. By the late 1940s, the touristic potential of the canyon was accelerated by the construction of the Corniche Sublime. Tourism has now moved in wholesale, and those in the know make strenuous efforts to avoid the area completely during the month of August.

Nowhere are the crowds of summer visitors more oppressive than in **Castellane**. Like Moustiers-Ste-Marie, proximity to the canyon has brought welcome prosperity to the locals, at the expense of over-commercialisation. Queues of cars choke Castellane's narrow streets, beachballs and hiking paraphernalia fill its shops, and the native hospitality becomes, at times, understandably strained.

Seasonal demands aside, Castellane has a pleasing, if small, **old quarter**, lying to the north of the town's bustling hub, Place Marcel-Sauvaire. Market days (Wednesday and Saturday) enliven the town throughout the year, and the *Fête des Fétardiers*, held annually on 31 January, commemorates the lifting of a Huguenot siege in 1586. The

chapel of **Notre-Dame-du-Roc**, perched daringly on a high rocky outcrop, makes Castellane's skyline its most appealing feature.

On to higher ground: The Verdon River, so resplendently enclosed by the Grand Canyon in the south, keeps its luminous colour in its northern reaches. The **Lac de Castillon**, in the upper Verdon Valley, has much in common with its larger cousin, the **Lac de Ste-Croix**. Also man-made, it was created by a dam that was constructed and managed by Electricité de France. The dam was completed in 1947, making it the first of five built to harness the waters of the Verdon. Ste-Croix, completed in the 1960s, is the most recent.

The lakes that have resulted (Chaudanne, Ste-Croix, Castillon) perform the dual function of conserving precious water for this region of Provence and attracting tourism. Edging the Lac de Castillon, bizarre vertically grooved rock formations alternate with dazzling white sand spits that provide pleasant spots for swimming in summer.

In a broad valley of orchards and lavender fields at the head of the lake sits the small summer resort of **St-André-les-Alpes**, a haven for windsurfers, hang-gliders, anglers and *sportifs* of all sorts. This small village has not a great deal to recommend it architecturally or historically but is redeemed by the genuine hospitality of its small population. In summer, the village somehow manages to find room for four times its normal number of inhabitants. Nonetheless, tourism has not left as deep a scar here as in Moustiers or Castellane.

St-André's tiny station forms a stop on the route of the Train des Pignes. In addition, a *Belle Epoque* steam train, dating from 1909, rattles through on its way from Puget-Théniers to **Annot** every Sunday in summer.

East of St-André, the route to the charming small town of Annot leads through one of the many *cols* (high passes) that pepper this mountainous eastern side of the Alpes-de-Haute-Provence. Moving north and east, towards

Summer bubbles.

the "Grands Alpes" and the Alpes-Maritimes respectively, the *cols* increase in frequency and, at times, almost alarmingly in altitude. The **Col de Toutes Aures** (Pass of All Winds), however, is a relative small-fry, at a mere 3,688 ft (1,124 metres) high. Towering over it is the massive **Pic de Chamatte** which, at 6,160 ft (1,878 metres), dwarfs even the Montagne de Lure in the west.

This is a richly forested landscape, in marked contrast to the bleak beauty of the canyon region. Shaley precipitous slopes are cloaked with vast sweeps of dark evergreens parading down the steep cliff faces. Minuscule villages such as **Vergons** and **Rousine**, consisting of little more than a handful of drystone houses protected by weathered shutters, prefigure the Alpine experience to come.

Annot in the Vaire Valley is typical of this area's dual aspect – warmly Provençal yet markedly Alpine. Its wrought-iron balconies and stone *lavoirs* are as classically Provençal as

anything found further south. But the majesty of the Alps leaves its mark in the pure clarity of the air and the steely grey waters of the numerous streams that tumble through the town.

In winter, Annot sleeps under thick coverings of snow. Although the oldest populated centre in the area, Annot was unreachable by carriage as recently as 1830. In common with much of the rest of the Alpes-de-Haute-Provence, access was provided only by the network of mule tracks that crisscrossed the mountainous landscape.

For years the town has attracted painters. East of the sizeable main square, planted with a fine esplanade of ancient plane trees, the narrow streets of the picturesque **old town** climb steeply in medieval formation. Vaulted archways and a predominance of carved stone lintels bearing their 17th and 18th-century dates of construction line the tall houses of the Grand Rue. At the top of the old town, the narrow streets converge on a pretty square with the parish church and surrounding houses

e-Croix de erdon on e Lac de e-Croix.

painted in many different pastel hues.

The quaintly picturesque lure of Annot is not simply confined to its evocative old quarter. Just outside the town to the south is a vast cluster of massive rocks scattered far across the hillside. Known as the **Grès d'Annot,** these house-sized sandstone boulders seem to have been flung to earth from the cliff behind by an angry giant. Locals have built houses directly beside them, often using their sheer faces as an outside wall. Local legends, featuring troglodytes and primitive religions, surround them to this day.

Annot's local industry is based on two thriving factories: producing biscuits and, more traditionally, meat products. The town is also a popular centre for summer excursions and, like St-André, a stop on the route of the Train des Pignes.

Those with stout hearts and boots can follow the spectacular hiking trails into the nearby high-altitude **Coulomp Valley**. Alternatively, the Vaire Valley, running due north from Annot, is the setting of the typical mountain village of **Méailles**, perched high above the river. Still further north lies the ancient village of **Peyresq**, in ruins until 1955 when a group of Belgian students decided to transform it into a tiny but thriving cultural centre.

Into the past: Cross the drawbridge of the **Porte Royale** into the fairytale town of **Entrevaux**, and the 20th century recedes as if by magic. Situated on the eastern fringes of the Alpes-de-Haute-Provence and for centuries a frontier post defending Provence from Savoy, Entrevaux exudes a history more redolent than any town in the *département*. Seventeenth-century ramparts (the work of Louis XIV's masterful engineer, Vauban), turrets, drawbridges and a deep moat formed by the Var River cocoon the town. Cars are firmly relegated to the busy Nice road on the opposite bank of the river.

Like the ramparts, the majority of Entrevaux's houses, together with its cathedral church, date from the 17th century. A **citadel**, testimony to the

The fairytale town of Entrevaux.

town's key strategic position, is reached by an ascending path of nine zig-zag ramps, a remarkable feat of engineering that took 50 years to complete.

As well as with its history, Entrevaux entices with cultural and folkloric events. In August, a two-week music festival of 16th and 17th-century music is organised by an English resident of the town. The festival of John the Baptist, held annually on the weekend closest to 24 June, sees locals in traditional costume celebrating with a mass, dancing and a procession to the isolated **Chapel of St-Jean-du-Désert**, 4 miles (7 km) to the southwest. The popularity of the saint is such that similar festivals on a smaller scale are held concurrently in many of the small villages nearby, each with its procession to a chosen chapel "in the desert."

One delightful curiosity brings the visitor to Entrevaux back into the modern age. The minuscule **Musée de la Moto** is devoted entirely to the history of the automobile. Run by a former Grand Prix mechanic, it houses more

then 70 machines dating from 1905, all still in working order.

Entrevaux also boasts a thriving Centre of Mycology and Applied Botany, which attracts mushroom experts from all over France in the autumn. But perhaps of greater interest to the casual visitor is the tiny main square, **Place St-Martin**. It boasts one pleasant café, a clutch of pretty chestnut trees and a butcher who dispenses the local speciality, *secca de boeuf*, a type of dried salt beef, delicious when eaten with olive oil and lemon juice.

If Entrevaux seems uniquely untouched by the proximity of the Alps, **Colmars**, 18 miles (30 km) to the north, could hardly be more Alpine. Colmars is a fortified town crowned by two massive medieval castles, and, like Entrevaux, a former frontier post between Provence and Savoy. But there the similarity ends.

Approaching Colmars along the attractive D908 from St-André, the sloping roofs of wooden Alpine chalets seem a universe away from the dry-

stone *bories* of the Lure or the long, low *mas* of the Var.

Inside the well-preserved ramparts of the town, once again the work of the architect Vauban, the Alpine feel only increases. Houses are constructed with tidy wooden balconies, known as *solerets* (sun traps), locals sport jaunty Alpine caps that would not seem out of place in Bavaria and shop windows display amber bottles of *génépi* liqueur, made from Alpine flowers. Only the small fountains and the geraniums that line the balconies in summer confirm that this is Provence.

Colmar's name stems from Roman times when a temple to the god Mars was erected on the hill (*collis Martis*) that today forms the backdrop to the town. Of the two castles that dominate Colmar's skyline, the Fort de Savoie is the more imposing. Reached by a covered alleyway, the fort is a fine piece of 17th-century military engineering.

Sleepy in winter, Colmar's unspoilt charm and beautiful setting make it a popular centre for family holidays, particularly among residents of the major coastal cities. A *bravade*, more rooted in tradition than the celebrated St-Tropez version, takes place in June.

The French Alps proper lie hidden behind the **Col d'Allos**, 15 miles (25 km) north of Colmars, The high-altitude **Lac d'Allos**, ringed by snow-capped mountains and the breathtaking **Col de la Cayolle** (7,635 ft/2,327 metres) form stunning diversions along the route to the Alps, though they are frequently inaccessible in winter.

Barcelonette, squeezed into a narrow glacial valley surrounded by towering peaks and completely Alpine in character, is the northernmost town in Provence. It owes its unlikely name to its 12th-century rulers, the counts of Barcelona, who originally christened it Barcelona.

The Hispanic connection does not end there. Early in the 19th century, a period of migration to Mexico began, prompted by the success achieved by three local brothers who opened a textile shop there. Many followed, some of whom later returned to Barcelonette to build the incongruous Mexican-style villas for which the town is famous.

Less than a century ago, the villages of the Ubaye Valley remained spectacularly remote, ancient traditions persisted and locals spoke *le gavot*, an Alpine version of Oc. The **Musée de la Vallée**, on the Avenue de la Libération, provides fascinating accounts of the region's chequered history.

Today, though the "Mexican connection" remains strong, with frequent cultural exchanges and shops selling Mexican artifacts, a new flavour has emerged to dominate the atmosphere and preoccupations of the town: skiing. From December to April the modern ski resorts of **Super-Sauze** and **Pra-Loup,** just south of Barcelonette, pack the Ubaye Valley with international tourists and bring a welcome upturn in local fortunes.

In many ways, the history of Barcelonette is the history of the Alpes-de-Haute-Provence in microcosm: poverty, migration, gradual prosperity. It is an evolution that continues today.

Left, mountain wildflowers. Right, minstrel in Entrevaux.

Reillanne

Puimoisson

Caste

Moustiers-Ste. Marie

PARC

Valensole

Point
Sublime

Manosque

Riez

REGIONAL

Allemagne-
en-Provence

la Bastide-
-des-Jourdans

Lac de
Ste. Croix

Grand Canyon
du Verdon

Gréoux-
les-Bains

St. Martin-de-Brômes

Ste. Croix-de-
Verdon

LUBÉRON

Falaise des
Cavallèrs

Mirabeau

Vinon-sur-Verdon

Verdon

GRAND PLAN DE CANJUERS

MONTAGNE DE BARJAUDE

Montmeyan

la Verdière

Aups

Tavernes

Grottes
(Cave)

Rians

Tortour

Fox-Amphoux

Château du
Picasso
(Castle)

Barjols

Salernes

Draguignan

Vauvenargues

MONTAGNE STE. VICTOIRE

Cotignac

Entrecasteaux

Lorgues

Ollières

Châteauvert

Carces

Argens

Abbaye du Thoronet
(Romanesque Church)

Vidauban

St. Maximin-
la-Ste. Baume

Trets

le Vieux Cannet

Châteauneuf

Brignoles

le Luc

le Cannet-
des-Maures

Montagne
de la Loube
▲
830

Besse-
sur-Issole

Aille

la Ga
Fre

Roquevaire

St. Pilon

la Roquebrussanne

Gonfaron

Gémenos

MASSIF DE LA SAINTE BAUME

Carnoules

MAS

Signes

Méounes-
lès-Montrieux

Aubagne

Chartreuse-
Montrieux-le-Vieux

Gapeau

Collobrières

Chartreuse-
Montrieux-le-Jeune

Cuers

Pierefeu-de-Var

Chartreuse
de la Verne

la

le Castelle

Môle

Solliès-Pont

Bormes-les-
Mimosas

Cavalière

La Ciotat

les Lecques

Mt. Faron
▲
542

le Lavandou

Corn

Bandol

Ollioules

ILE DE BENDOR

La Seyne

Toulon

Hyères

Port-de-
Miramare

Cap Blanc

Sanary-sur-Mer

Carqueiranne

Six-Fours-les-Plages

les Sablettes

la Garonne

Rade d'Hyères

ILE DES EMBIEZ

N.D. du Mal
(Church)

Golfe de Giens

ILES D'HYÈRES

Cap Sicié

Giens

ILE DE
PORT-CROS

ILE DE
PORQUEROLLES

Porquerolles

PARC NATIONAL

Cap d'Arme

DE PORT-GROS

Var

20 km

214

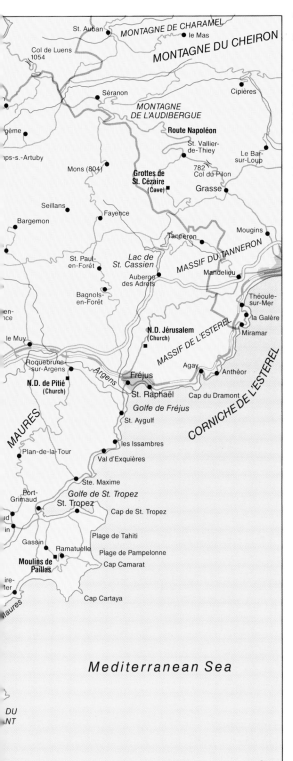

Mediterranean Sea

THE VAR

The Var is a palette of varied landscapes that connect the sea with the mountains and plains of the north. The richly forested *massifs* of Ste-Baume, Maures and Esterel that dominate the bottom section by the coast give way to acres of vineyards in the centre of the region. Further north, substantial hills are studded with small hilltop villages, waterfalls, caves and more vines. Here, in the least spoilt section of the *département*, the atmosphere of relative calm is sharply different from the noise and frenzy of the coast.

The coastal area is a broad spectrum of sights and sounds: the cosmopolitan urban sprawl of Toulon, the wild natural beauty of the Iles d'Hyères, the pleasing gentility of summer resorts such as Hyères, Sanary-sur-Mer, and Bandol, the Riviera splash of St-Tropez.

Tourism, of course, stands on an equal footing with wine production in the list of the Var's major industries. Many *visages pâles* (or "pale faces" – a local appellation for summertime visitors) never venture north of the busy A8 autoroute that bisects the *département* from east to west. However, a multitude of restored farmhouses and elegant modern villas serve as summer homes in the hills from St-Tropez to Aups. In central and upper Var alone, the number of *résidences secondaires* is estimated at more than 25,000.

Nonetheless, inland Var still offers a multitude of quiet secrets to those prepared to explore beyond the autoroute.

The Var lacks none of the Provençal clichés: pretty squares dappled by the shade of plane trees, clusters of medieval architecture, limpid pastel light. As they say in Lorgues, "*Ici on vit vieux et heureux*" (Here you live a long and happy life). Few would disagree.

The big city: The *préfecture* of the Var, **Toulon** is a major port and urban centre and, as such, not subject to the seasonal ebb and flow of population experienced

Preceding pages: the Massif des Maures.

by much of the rest of the *département*.

Clustered round a deep natural harbour and enclosed by a crescent of high hills, Toulon is also France's leading naval base. Many tourists bypass it, however, for its fetid narrow alleyways and chaotic suburban sprawl offer little enticement to the casual visitor. What they don't realise is that, along with all the low-life trappings of a major seaport, Toulon has its own share of grand buildings, chic boutiques, lively fishmarkets and a sense of cosmopolitan energy matched only by Marseille.

The main route through the city, the **Boulevard de Strasbourg**, bisects the grid of tall apartment blocks, department stores and imposing administrative buildings that make up 19th-century Toulon. South of the **Place Victor Hugo**, with its fine theatre and opera house, lies the seamier side of the city – a warren of narrow streets leading down to the **old port** (*darse vieille*). Unsalubrious bars rub shoulders with dingy restaurants that dispense the Toulon version of *bouillabaisse* (made with

potatoes) and North African specialities. Scruffy kids play football in the shadow of peeling tenements, and Arab *chômeurs* (unemployed workers) watch the world go by.

But the *basse ville*, as the Toulonnais call it, is not all sleaze. Small attractive squares (such as the Place Puget, Place Trois Dauphine and Place Camille Ledeau) draw elegant locals and some tourists to their designer shops and shaded cafés. Superb fish, vegetable and flower markets characterise mornings in the **Cours Lafayette**. And the patchwork streets lead inexorably towards Toulon's *raison d'être*: the port.

In fact, much of the *basse ville*'s bad press undoubtedly comes from the Avenue de la République, a filthy swarming roadway lined with hideous concrete post-war architecture. Damage caused by Allied bombings and the German razing of the harbourfront "for reasons of hygiene" hasn't been well-disguised. Historically, Toulon's era of major expansion occurred during the 17th century, though it was a base for

Shell girls welcome tourists to Toulon.

the royal navy as early as 1487. Under the orders of Louis XIV, the arsenal was expanded and the city's fortifications enlarged. A century later, the city unwisely took the side of the English against the Revolutionary government and was promptly brought to heel by a young Napoleon Bonaparte. The English fleet was roundly defeated in 1793, ensuring that Napoleon's name would never be forgotten.

High on the list of Toulon's many visitable sights are the comprehensive **Musée Naval**, the excellent contemporary art collections of the **Musée de Toulon** and the evocative, writhing figures of Puget's sculpted *atlantes*, now affixed unceremoniously to the modern façade of the city hall annex on the Quai Stalingrad.

For an excellent overall look, take the cable car ride at **Mont Faron**, just outside the city. From the top you will have a terrific bird's-eye view of Toulon, its satellite towns and the sea.

Calm resorts: To either side of the steamy cityscape of Toulon lies a trio of attractive coastal resorts. Bandol and Sanary to the west and Hyères to the east can't claim to be as lively or as chic as St-Tropez and Cannes, but many prefer them for that very reason.

Screened from the ravages of the mistral by an arc of wooded hills, **Bandol** has attracted numerous visitors to its sandy coves and pleasant promenades since the beginning of the 20th century. Among its more famous guests have been New Zealand author Katherine Mansfield, who wrote *Prelude* in the quayside Villa Pauline in 1916, and the celebrated Provençal actor Raimu. His cliffside villa, the Ker-Mocotte, is now a luxury hotel.

Modern-day visitors, a large proportion of them French, come for the town's three sandy beaches, lively harbour and air of calm sophistication. Another plus is Bandol's vineyards, which produce wines (particularly reds) rated among the best in Provence.

About a mile (2 km) off the coast of Bandol lies the tiny island of **Bendor**, enterprisingly transformed into a holi-

Toulon boy scouts.

day village by the pastis magnate Paul Ricard in the 1950s. On the island is a hotel, a clutch of rather expensive cafés, a recreation of a Provençal fishing village and Ricard's pride and joy – a museum devoted to the pleasures of alcohol. The grandly titled Exposition Universelle des Vins et Spiritueux contains more than 8,000 bottles of wine and spirits from all over the world, plus a selection of glassware. Though the island has an air of artificiality, its shady paths, lined with mimosa and eucalyptus, and its tiny sandy beach are reason enough for a summer excursion.

Just 3 miles (5 km) from Bandol is the pretty pink-and-white resort of **Sanary-sur-Mer**. Like its neighbour, Sanary benefits from a sheltered position supplied by its backdrop of hills, known as the Gros Cerveau. A number of *pointus* (old fishing vessels) add spice to its attractive harbour.

Artists and writers began to flock to Sanary in the early 1930s, inspired by Aldous Huxley's presence there. They were soon joined by a group of German intellectuals, headed by Thomas and Heinrich Mann, who fled to the town after Hitler's rise to power in 1933.

The nearby **Sicié Peninsula** makes for a worthwhile trip from Sanary. At its southern point, the **Chapel of Notre-Dame-du-Mai** sits on a high clifftop that drops sharply towards the sea. The view from here takes in *calanques* and the Iles d'Hyères.

To the east is **Hyères**, the most substantial of the three major resorts that surround Toulon and, in many ways, the most interesting. Hyères was the first resort to be established on the Côte, setting a trend that spread rapidly east from the late 18th century onwards. The list of famous consumptives, or merely pleasure-seekers, drawn to its balmy winter climate reads like an international Who's Who: Queen Victoria, Tolstoy, Pauline Bonaparte, Aubrey Beardsley, Edith Wharton, etc. Robert Louis Stevenson, though desperately ill during his stay, wrote: "I was only happy once – that was at Hyères."

By the 1920s, however, medical opinion had switched its allegiance to the curative properties of mountain, rather than sea, air. This and the increasing popularity of the "real" Riviera to the east swiftly relegated Hyères to a distinctly unfashionable position.

In many ways, the town's lack of chic has become one of its most attractive qualities. Busy all year round, Hyères plays host to several sporting and cultural events (such as the sailing regatta and the festival of cartoon animation) and has a thriving agricultural economy (peaches and strawberries) independent of tourism. The **vieille ville** is an appealing small medieval quarter, topped by a park and a ruined 14th-century castle with the spacious, flag-stoned **Place Massillon** at its heart.

Modern Hyères has an elegant *Belle Epoque* feel and some interesting examples of neo-Moorish architecture. A 19th-century taste for things "oriental" (inspired by Napoleon's Egyptian campaign) led to the construction of **La Mauresque** (Avenue Jean Natte) and **La Tunisienne** (Avenue de Beauregard) in the 1870s. Minarets, Arab

The island of Porquerolles.

arches and tropical date palms add a taste of the exotic.

Outside the town lie the vestiges of ancient Hyères (called Olbia), once an important Phocaean and Roman port. Antiquities excavated from the site can be seen in the **municipal museum**.

Isles of gold: Jutting out into the sea, the **Presqu'île de Giens** is a joyless, flat peninsula composed of salt marshes and some good beaches surrounded by ugly campsites. Salt collection, a local industry since pre-Roman times, continues today at the Côte's only remaining productive marsh, the Marais Salins des Pesquiers.

The main reason for taking this uninspiring route is to catch a boat from **La Tour-Fondue** at the southeastern tip to the **Iles d'Hyères**. (Boats also sail from Le Lavandou and Cavalaire).

This group of three subtropical islands, also known as the **Iles d'Or** (Isles of Gold**)**, is a haven of unspoilt natural beauty. **Porquerolles**, the largest and most accessible, has a small town with cafés and some fabulous beaches amidst dense vegetation. **Port-Cros**, more rugged and mountainous, is one of only six designated national parks in France. The third, **Levant**, is 90 percent inhabited by the French military and, therefore, mostly out of bounds. All that exists on it is a small nudist colony known as **Héliopolis**, founded in the 1930s and clinging to the bare and dramatic island's western tip.

Unless you're a naturist or a botanist, Porquerolles is probably the best choice for a visit. Its village, established as a small military base in the 19th century, is more colonial than Provençal in character. From here, you can hire bicycles to tour this eucalyptus and pine-clad island where cars are not allowed. Major spots of beauty include the lighthouse at the **Cap d'Arme** and **Plage Notre-Dame**, which is also excellent for swimming.

On Port-Cros, the terrain is much more challenging, and strict rules against smoking and the lighting of fires must be observed. A small **tourist centre**, open in summer, provides maps and

La
Mauresque
in Hyères.

guidelines. Perhaps the most rewarding walk (around two hours for a roundtrip) is along the **Vallon de la Solitude** that cuts across the southern end of the island. At its start, the island's only hotel, the 18th-century **Manoir d'Hélène**, serves a fine lunch.

Flower Village: Back on the mainland, a number of towns line the coastal road that leads inexorably to St-Tropez. This is not, strictly speaking, the Riviera, but you'd be hard pressed to tell the difference. A case in point is fashionable **Bormes-les-Mimosas**, a hilltop village enjoying stunning views of the Iles d'Or and the sea.

Recent critics have accused it of being over-prettified, but Bormes remains, despite the rather precious tag of "Les Mimosas" that was added to its name in 1968, one of the jewels of Provence. Bougainvillea, mimosa and eucalyptus (some of which sadly was destroyed by the harsh winters of 1984 and 1985) make this the archetypal *village fleurie*.

The names of the picturesque narrow streets – for example, Roumpi-Cuou (neck-breaker) and Plaine-des-Anes (donkey's sorrow) – colourfully suggest their steepness. Look out for the painted sundial on the **Eglise St-Trophime**, the fine medieval château at the top of the old town and the small museum on the Rue Carnot that contains some terracottas by Rodin.

South of Bormes, connected to the exclusive promontory of Cap Benat by a dyke, **Fort de Bregançon**, the "Camp David" of the French president, sits proudly on its own islet. Understandably, it can't be visited.

Dark forests: The **Massif des Maures**, a splendid tract of mysterious deep forest, much of it inaccessible, stretches roughly from Hyères to Fréjus and from the A8 autoroute down to the Mediterranean. Its name comes from the Provençal word *maouro*, meaning dark.

The Maures, together with the neighbouring Esterel *massif*, are components of the oldest geographical area in Provence. Schist, shot through with sparkling mica, makes up the high hills

Wine country above the coast.

and deep ravines of the massif. Cork oaks, Aleppo pines and chestnut trees form its dense vegetation.

The area was ruled by invading Saracens for more than 100 years, beginning in the early 9th century. Pillaging the countryside as far afield as Lake Constance, their reign of terror lasted until 972 when Count Guillaume destroyed their bastion at La Garde-Freinet.

In more recent times, the area has been ravaged no less destructively by the constant plague of forest fires, sparked spontaneously or by human carelessness. The desiccated forests quickly transform into monstrous walls of flame, leaving nothing but charred scrub in their wake. More than a million acres of the Var – France's most forested *département* – have been destroyed in the last 50 years. Preventative measures, such as the creation of firebreak paths and radical pruning of vegetation have had an impact since their introduction, but the light aircraft of Canadair scooping water from the sea to douse flames remains a common sight.

It is an annual battle, still being fought.

The Massif des Maures has few towns of any size, though its wooded hills conceal the private estates and villas of the rich and sometimes famous. **La Garde-Freinet**, an ancient Saracen stronghold and, in a sense, the capital of the Maures, is little more than a large village. Its traditional industry of cork production was a skill acquired from the otherwise barbaric Saracens in the ninth century. By 1846, the town produced more than three-quarters of France's bottle corks but, like many traditional industries, decline set in after the 1950s. Since the early 1980s, however, the industry has diversified into other uses of cork, and neatly stripped trunks of cork oaks line the *massif*'s serpentine roads and tracks.

In the town, the only obvious evidence of cork production are the cork bowls and ornaments on sale to tourists in the pricey boutiques of the Rue St-Jacques. St-Tropez chic has left its mark here, accelerating particularly in the last decade. Arty café loungers at the **Claire**

Firefighters in the Maures Forest.

Fontaine, epicentre of the village, are now more likely to read the trendy national newspaper *Libération* than the local *Var-Matin*. And existence of a "cocktail bar" – once an impossibly foreign concept – testifies to the proximity of the Côte.

Mercifully, La Garde-Freinet still has a stunning setting, charming stone *lavoirs* and unpretentious back streets. "Real" Garde-Freinet congregates in the **Cercle des Travailleurs Bar** on Place Neuve, where local men drink pastis under the watchful eye of a splendid Marianne bust.

South of the village, a walk to the ruins of the **Saracen fortress** is rewarded with great views of the massif and the sea. Recent archaeological digs have unearthed a collection of pottery and stoneware that are now on display in the tiny **Musée du Freinet** at the lower end of the village.

The rollercoaster road heading south from La Garde-Freinet cuts through the centre of the Maures towards the peninsula of St-Tropez. *En route* is the picture-postcard hilltop village of **Grimaud**, a maze of pretty streets awash with bougainvillea and oleander. Wander along the Rue des Templiers, for its medieval arcades, then up to the evocative ruined castle, destroyed on the orders of Cardinal Richelieu.

Cogolin, 1¾ miles (3 km) to the south, is a lively small town known for the manufacture of briar pipes and carpets. It is also a considerable producer of good quality wines. Visits can be made to the pipe and carpet factories.

Once on the peninsula, resist the magnetic pull of St-Tropez and head inland to investigate two perfect *villages perchés*, **Gassin** and **Ramatuelle**. Both have stunning views over the Baie de St-Tropez and numerous tiny streets, some no more than an arm's length across. Between the two villages, on the highest point of the peninsula, are a group of ancient windmills, the **Moulins de Paillau**, and a superb panorama.

Chestnuts and Carthusians: While the eastern section of the Maures is tinged with the atmosphere of the Côte, the

The Cercle de Travailleurs bar in La Garde-Freinet.

villages to the west remain largely un-scathed. **Collobrières**, bisected by a small river, is shady and peaceful even in August. This town is famous for its *marrons glacés*, along with all manner of confections made from the local chestnuts. Unlike the nougat of Montélimar or the *faïence* of Moustiers, Collobrières keeps its most famous export well hidden, but a small shop, the **Confiserie Azuréenne**, attached to the main factory, is a good source for buying chestnut delicacies.

Deep in the forest east of Collobrières is one of the real treasures of the Maures: the **Chartreuse de la Verne**. Founded in the 18th century, the Carthusian Charterhouse suffered centuries of fires and Protestant attack. The majority of the still existing buildings date from the 17th and 18th centuries, though the medieval cloisters and a sparsely restored monk's cell are evidence of more ancient origins. The various signs enjoining visitors to silence are a reminder that, after years of neglect, the Chartreuse is now occupied by nuns from the Order of Bethlehem.

Squeezed between the Maures and Esterel massifs are the major resorts of **Fréjus** and **St-Raphael**. For many years these towns were playgrounds for the rich, but today the choking traffic that pours through them during summer has dissolved much of their appeal. Unfortunate high-rise developments have aggregated the two towns together into one urban mass that is overcrowded in the summer and grim in the winter.

Of the two, Fréjus, 1½ miles (3 km) inland, is certainly the more interesting, largely because it contains more vestiges of the Roman past that both towns share. The **amphitheatre** on Rue Henri Vardon, though substantially damaged, is still in use as a setting for rock concerts and bullfights. Here, those with a taste for the drama and cruelty of the *corrida* can watch a spectacle with all the trappings of its Spanish equivalent. And, in the centre of town stands a medieval **cathedral**, begun in the 10th century and bordered by fine 12th-century cloisters that feature a fantastical ceiling decorated with animals and chimera. Also within the cathedral complex is an unmissable 5th-century **baptistry**, one of the three most ancient in France. All are reached from an entrance on Place Formigé.

Having devoted time to Fréjus's Roman and medieval attractions, it would be a shame to miss a couple of very unGallic curiosities nearby. A **Buddhist pagoda**, just off the N7 to Cannes, commemorates the death of 5,000 Vietnamese soldiers who perished in World War I. And a prettily faded and dilapidated Sudanese **mosque** lies unprepossessingly in the middle of an army camp off the D4 to Bagnols.

Swimming beaches can be found south of the town at Fréjus-Plage, though they are as crowded and unappealing as anywhere else you might go on the Côte in high season.

St-Raphael's rail terminus accounts for much of its liveliness, though it fell out of fashion as a tourist base some years ago. Around the middle of the last century, its attractions were much vaunted by the journalist Alphonse

Priest at the Chartreuse de la Verne.

Karr, whose enthusiasm lured the likes of Dumas and Maupassant to winter here. Now, though less trendy, St-Raphael has no lack of visitors, even if they're just here to lose a few francs at the rather hideous casino on the seafront. A **Museum of Underwater Archaeology**, close by a Romanesque parish church, is probably the town's only worthwhile "sight." It contains a good collection of Roman amphorae and a display of underwater equipment.

Heading west along the Gulf of St-Tropez, **Ste-Maxime** offers a taste of what St-Raphael was like in the not-too-distant past. The archetypal Côte resort, its palm trees, promenades and parasols offer the classic *corniche* experience. Though suffering as much as its neighbours from accelerating suburban sprawl, Ste-Maxime's neat marina and relatively golden beaches are still undeniably attractive. When quayside strutting and café lounging loses its appeal, head just north to visit the **Museum of Sound and Mechanical Instruments** in the Parc de St-Donat. It houses a unique collection of old phonographs, bizarre music boxes and a turn-of-the-century dictaphone.

More forests: Highwaymen and sundry criminal types ruled the impenetrable reaches of the **Massif de l'Esterel** for many centuries. Separated from the neighbouring Massif des Maures by the Argens Valley, the Esterel is more sparse in vegetation – a result of the devastating forest fires that swept the area in 1964. In addition, a disease has decimated the indigenous sea pines. But you will still find it an appealingly wild region only steps from the glitter of the Côte.

The red porphyry rock of the Esterel tumbles down to the sea in a dramatic sweep of high hills and ravines. The coastal road, the **Corniche d'Or**, is one of the least crowded sections of the Côte, though the familiar pattern of private villas and large hotels blocking views and access to the sea can be terribly frustrating even here. Head to the section from Cap Roux to Anthéor for some welcome relief and to the inviting

Along the Côte d'Or.

coves around Agay for swimming.

Inland, panorama lovers should head for **Mont Vinaigre** (at 2,060 feet/628 metres, the highest point of the massif) or, for wonderful sea views, the **Pic de l'Ours**. Skirting the northernmost section of the Esterel along the N7 brings you to the marvellous **Auberge des Adrets**, an authentic 17th-century coaching inn and one-time haunt of Gaspard de Besse, the Robin Hood of the Esterel. Gaspard spent many profitable years ambushing the mail and passenger convoys that plied the routes southeast of Mont Vinaigre. He was arrested with his accomplices in 1780 and executed the following year.

Central Var: The central area of the Var is dominated by the fertile **Argens Valley**, which runs horizontally across the *département*. To the south and north are the wooded, vine-covered hills that produce the majority of the A.O.C. Côtes-de-Provence rosés and reds. To most tourists, however, the area is little more than a transport corridor *en route* to the Côte. **Le Luc**, where the autoroute and N7 intertwine, is a small market town which has been sadly overrun, like many of its neighbours, by the pressure of passing traffic. Its rich history as a Roman spa town and Protestant refuge can be traced in the local museum, the **Musée Historique du Centre Var**, housed in the 17th-century **Chapel of Ste-Anne**. Look out, too, for Le Luc's best-known landmark, a 16th-century hexagonal **tower**.

As well as its wine, olives and chestnuts, Le Luc gained fame during the 1800s for the health-giving purity of its mineral water, *eau de Pioule*, which is still bottled at source on a small scale today. Perhaps less medically sound was Le Luc's reputation two centuries earlier as the centre for what was considered to be the most effective cure for whooping cough. Provençal superstition maintained that children could be cured by being passed seven times under the belly of a donkey. Le Luc's donkey had such prestige that children from Draguignan and even Cannes were brought to suffer the ordeal.

Harbourfront in St-Tropez.

Outside Le Luc is **Le Vieux Cannet**, one of the prettiest of the region's hill villages, clustered around an 11th-century church.

Further west along the autoroute lies **St-Maximin-la-Ste-Baume**. Pilgrims have poured in to this town since the fifth century to view one of the greatest of all Christian relics – the presumed bones of Mary Magdalene. After the so-called Boat of Bethany supposedly landed in the Camargue, its saintly crew dispersed to preach the word of God throughout Provence. Mary Magdalene is said to have made her way to the Massif de la Ste-Baume where she lived in a dank cave for more than 30 years. She died in the town of St-Maximin, where her remains were jealously guarded by the Cassianites.

Work began on the magnificent **basilica** that now contains the relics during the 1200s. It is considered to be one of the most impressive examples of Gothic architecture in Provence. Inside, a tiny blackened crypt, etched with centuries of grafitti, houses the relics. Visitors peer through iron bars to catch sight of the holy remains, wedged into a somewhat macabre gold setting.

The 19th-century writer Prosper Mérimée, in his role as inspector of monuments, dismissed St-Maximin as a dreary place and, excluding the basilica, it's tempting to share his view. But the *vieille ville* does have some worthwhile medieval arcades (Rue Colbert) and the interesting remains of a small Jewish community.

To the south of St-Maximin, in the ancient limestone mountain range of Ste-Baume, is the even more evocative cave where Mary Magdalene is said to have spent those last years. Reaching its entrance involves a strenuous climb through dense forest. This forest, in particular the reaches lying below the holy cave, was a magic and sacred place to Ligurians, Gauls and Romans, and the towering beech trees and lush undergrowth still seem bewitchingly sylvan today.

One hundred and fifty stone steps lead up from the shade of the forest to

Tilemaker and son.

the cliffside cave. Inside the vast dark recess, now filled with altars and saintly effigies, the old stones drip water. A final effort will bring you to St-Pilon, which is nearly the highest point of the *massif*. Mary Magdalene was said to have been lifted up to this peak by angels seven times a day during her years of cave-dwelling.

North of the autoroutes: Located in the northwest corner of the Var and dubbed the "Tivoli of Provence," **Barjols** is a small industrious town filled with streams, fountains and masses of peeling plane trees. In fact, what is reputedly the largest plane tree in France, 40 feet (12 metres) in circumference, casts its shade over the most famous of Barjols's 25 fountains, the vast moss-covered **"Champignon" fountain** in the tiny Place Capitaine Vincens.

Though the Tivoli tag attracts a good number of summer visitors, Barjols is in reality more of a unpretentious, workaday town than a successful tourist trap. Its prosperity was originally based on its tanneries, the last of which closed in 1986. Barjols is still, however, known for the manufacture of the traditional Provençal instruments, the *galoubet* (a three-holed flute) and *tambourin* (a narrow drum), which are played simultaneously by a single musician.

Barjols's **old quarter** is being extensively renovated and, as such, is in a state of flux. Ancient cobwebbed hovels alternate with low medieval archways in the dusty alleyways around the former college **Chapel of Notre-Dame-de-l'Assomption**. The church is all that remains of what was during the Middle Ages the favoured school for the children of the counts of Provence.

An undistinguished square close to the chapel hides one of Barjols's best treasures, the magnificent entrance to the **House of the Postevès**. The impressive entrance was sculpted during the Renaissance.

Barjols's claim to fame rests largely on its Fête de St-Marcel, which is arguably the most ancient and picturesque festival in Provence. Held on the weekend nearest to 16 January, the Fête des

The flutes of Barjols.

Tripettes celebrates the town's victory over the rival village of Aups in securing the relics of Saint Marcel for its own chapel. The day that the relics arrived, in 1350, just happened to coincide with the long-standing pagan practice of sacrificing an ox for a village feast. Eventually, secular and Christian festivities were combined into a single ecstatic festival.

Today, the festival consists of noisy processions to the sound of *galoubets* and *tambourins*. Every four years (1994, 1998, etc.) an ox is roasted on the Place de la Roquière and shared out among the revellers.

The real Var: Between the empty northern expanses of the **Canjuers Plain**, occupied by the French military, and the autoroute to the south lies a string of towns that come closest to representing the "authentic" Var.

Aups, on the fringes of the plain, is an access point for the Gorges du Verdon (on the Var's northern border) and a busy market town in its own right. The town is crowned by a lovely 16th-century clocktower decorated with a sundial. Aups, and the northern part of the Var in general, has a strong tradition of republican resistance and was the scene of many popular uprisings in the mid-19th century. The portal of the town's **Church of St-Pancrace** proudly bears the republican inscription: *Liberté, Egalité, Fraternité*.

Salernes, 6 miles (10 km) to the south, is a larger and more sprawling town with one of the best markets in the area. Like Aups, the town has been a centre of political resistance, especially during World War II. Above all, though, Salernes is known for its tile-making, the most prolific in the *département*. Around 15 factories still function today, many using traditional wood-fired kilns.

Salernes itself lacks the classic Provençal prettiness of many of the towns further east, but nearby are some unmissable gems of hilltop village architecture which are worth seeking out. Minuscule **Fox-Amphoux** crouches on a high hill to the west, its pretty streets

Tiled kitchen in Salernes.

clustered round a Romanesque church.

More commercial, but even more spectacular, is **Tourtour**, "the village in the sky." An irresistible *mélange* of breathtaking views and medieval vaulted passageways keeps its appeal even in the crowded summer months. Sadly, Tourtour's finest "monument" – two venerable elms planted in the main square to commemorate the birth of Louis XIV – recently fell prey to disease. They have been replaced by olive trees.

From **Cotignac**, a superb collection of 16th-century houses dominated by two ruined towers, the D50 snakes east to **Entrecasteaux**. The elegant **château**, centrepiece of this small village, was built for a local nobleman in the 1600s. Scandal ruined the family during the next century, when the residing *seigneur* shot his wife, and the château fell into disrepair.

Then, in 1974, it was bought by painter, soldier and adventurer Ian McGarvie-Munn, a larger-than-life Scotsman who married into the Ecua-dorean political hierarchy. The family set about the castle's restoration, de-spite the death of McGarvie-Munn in 1981 and considerable local hostility.

Today, it is a delightfully eccentric combination of architectural monu-ment, art gallery, hotel and private resi-dence. Wander through the family's kitchen to airy rooms hung with modern art and filled with McGarvie-Munn's collections of artifacts from around the globe. Only the gardens disappoint.

South along the **Bresque Valley** from Entrecasteaux stands what is in-disputedly the most beautiful building in the Var. The austere simplicity of the **Abbaye de Thoronet** is enough to turn non-believers into pilgrims. Together with Senanque and Silvacane, the ab-bey is one of the Provençal trio of so-called "Cisterian sisters," built in the 12th century to the ascetic precepts of the Cistercian Order. Only the play of light and shadow decorates the per-fectly proportioned chapel, cloisters and chapterhouse.

Neglected since before the Revolu-

Bathroom at the Château d' Entrecasteaux.

tion, the abbey was saved from ruin by Prosper Mérimée who urged its restoration in the 1840s. Work continues today, but a new threat to the abbey has surfaced in recent decades. Bauxite mining, the lynchpin of the local economy, has destabilised the abbey's foundations. A pressure group based in St-Raphael is currently campaigning for its protection.

Once a capital: Draguignan, the Var's only major inland town, was capital of the *département* until 1975, when it lost the title to Toulon. Its name recalls a dragon that was said to have terrorised the town in the 5th century. For this reason, the mythical creature can be seen in stone crests on many of the town's medieval gateways and houses.

The small city's greatest attractions lie in the tiny **medieval quarter** beyond the grid of 19th-century boulevards, designed by Baron Haussmann. The Rue de la Juiverie still has the remains of a synagogue facade, a relic of the important Jewish community that thrived here in the Middle Ages. Nearby is an attractive clocktower built in 1663, with a classic wrought-iron campanile.

After the sure delights of Draguignan's bustling market days, head out of town for an eclectic collection of visitable sights. Just to the northwest on D955 is the mysterious stone monolith of the **Pierre de la Fée** (the "fairy stone"), a vast slab of neolithic rock on three mighty stone legs. Following this road further north brings you to the verdant **Gorges de Châteaudouble**, a smaller version of the Verdon Gorges, cut by the River Naturby.

East of Draguignan, on the D59, is an **American military cemetery**, a legacy of the bitter fighting that raged around Le Muy in August 1944.

Nearby **Trans-en-Provence** boasts a cascading waterfall, a delicately painted Hôtel de Ville and a truly original curiosity on its outskirts. The "airborne well" (follow signs out of Trans for the *puits aérienne*) was conceived in 1930 by an eccentric Belgian inventor as a moisture-capturing solution to the region's thirst. The bizarre, beehive structure never fulfilled its laudable aim

and exists now as a unique and entertaining folly.

The northeastern Var: The villages of eastern Var catch much of the appealing flavour of the Alpes-Maritimes. **Fayence**, the largest town in the area and a major centre for hang-gliding, has little overt charm, but its satellite villages are among the prettiest in Provence.

The German artist Max Ernst made **Seillans** his home, spending the last years of his life in a villa at the top of the village. An atmospheric, painterly place, Seillans tumbles down a sheer hillside in a mass of pink and ochre stone and steep cobbled streets. Its boundaries are marked by the hilltop château, and the cool, shady Place du Thouron at the lower end of the village. Cars are banned within the ramparts.

The town, whose name is derived from the "pot of boiling oil" they poured over the heads of unwelcome Saracens, is known for its perfume-making and flower cultivation, a thriving industry since 1884. In recent years, Seillans has instituted an annual flower festival, a suitably chic affair for this attractive and prosperous village. Visit the **Eglise de Notre-Dame-de-l'Ormeau**, moments away on the low road, for its stunning colourful altarpiece, carved from wood by an unknown 16th-century Italian artist.

Less exclusive, but equally tempting, are the villages of **Bargemon** to the west of Seillans and **Mons** and **Bargème**, north of Fayence. Mons has all the ingredients of a perfect Provençal village, plus a superb view from the Place St-Sebastien of the Italian Alps, the Iles de Lérins and Corsica. Bargème, much more spartan, is splendidly isolated. It is the highest village in the Var, perched on a peak of the **Montagne du Brouis**.

Here, the surrounding landscape is sparse and dreary, and the resulting poverty gave locals a sorry reputation for crime and dishonesty in the last century. A decade ago towns like Bargème were virtually deserted, but the energetic restoration now being carried out in so much of the Var signals a future more shining than its past.

Right, the original Statue of Liberty stands in St-Cyr.

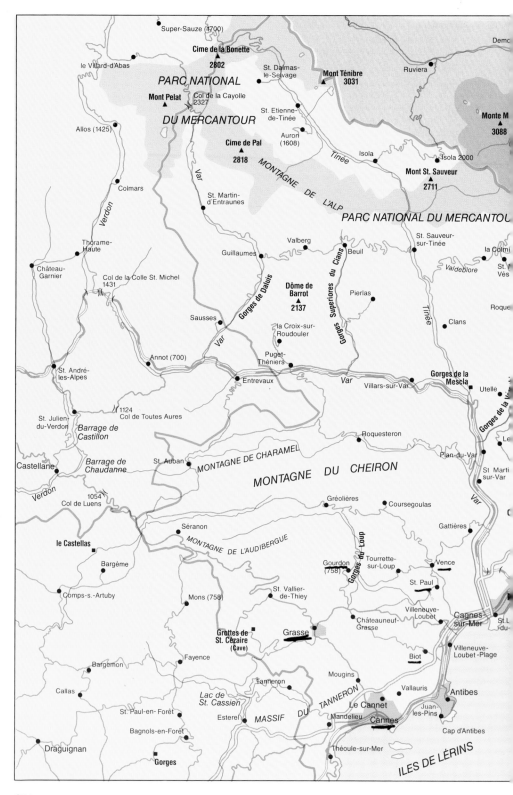

Super-Sauze (1700)

Cime de la Bonette
2802

le Villard-d'Abas

PARC NATIONAL

St. Dalmas-le-Selvage

Mont Ténibre
3031

Ruviera

Demc

Mont Pelat
Col de la Cayolle
2327

DU MERCANTOUR

St. Etienne-de-Tinée

Monte M
3088

Allos (1425)

Auron
(1608)

Cime de Pal
2818

MONTAGNE DE L'ALP

Tinée

Isola

Isola 2000

Var

Colmars

Mont St. Sauveur
2711

St. Martin-d'Entraunes

Verdon

PARC NATIONAL DU MERCANTOU

St. Sauveur-sur-Tinée

Thorame-Haute

Valberg

la Colmi

Château-Garnier

Guillaumes

Gorges du Cians

Beuil

Valdeblore

St. V
Vés

Col de la Colle St. Michel
1431

Dôme de
Barrot
2137

Gorges Superiores du Cians

Pierlas

Roque

Gorges de Daluis

Sausses

la Croix-sur-Roudouler

Tinée

Clans

Var

Annot (700)

Puget-Théniers

St. André-les-Alpes

Entrevaux

Var

Villars-sur-Var

**Gorges de la
Mescla**

Utelle

1124
Col de Toutes Aures

Gorges de la Va

St. Julien-du-Verdon

*Barrage de
Castillon*

Roquesteron

Plan-du-Var

Le

Castellane

*Barrage de
Chaudanne*

St. Auban

MONTAGNE DE CHARAMEL

MONTAGNE DU CHEIRON

St Marti
sur-Var

Verdon

1054
Col de Luens

Gréolières

Coursegoulas

Var

Séranon

Gattières

le Castellas

MONTAGNE DE L'AUDIBERGUE

Bargème

Gorges du Loup

Gourdon
(758)

Tourrette-sur-Loup

Vence

Comps-s.-Artuby

Mons (758)

St. Vallier-de-Thiey

St. Paul

Villeneuve-Loubet

Cagnes-sur-Mer

St.L
du-

Grottes de
St. Cézaire
(Cave)

Grasse

Châteauneuf-Grasse

Bargemon

Fayence

Biot

Villeneuve-Loubet-Plage

Callas

Tanneron

Mougins

Vallauris

Antibes

St. Paul-en-Forêt

*Lac de
St. Cassien*

DU TANNERON

Le Cannet

Juan-les-Pins

Bagnols-en-Forêt

Esterel

MASSIF

Mandelieu

Cannes

Cap d'Antibes

Draguignan

Gorges

Théoule-sur-Mer

ILES DE LÉRINS

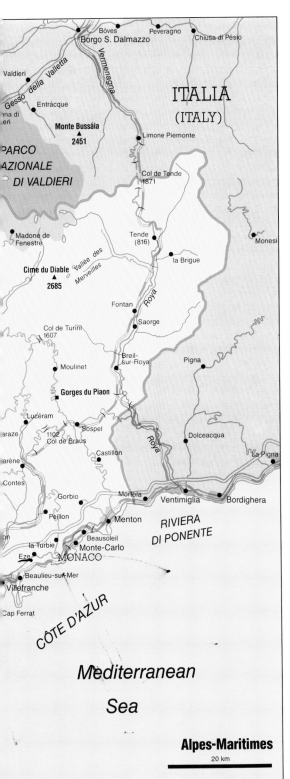

Map labels:
Bóves · Peveragno · Chiusa di Pésio · Borgo S. Dalmazzo · Valdieri · Gesso della Valletta · Vermenagna · Entrácque · ITALIA (ITALY) · Monte Bussáia ▲ 2451 · Limone Piemonte · PARCO NAZIONALE DI VALDIERI · Col de Tende 1871 · Madone de Fenestre · Tende (816) · Monesi · Cime du Diable ▲ 2685 · Vallée des Merveilles · la Brigue · Fontan · Roya · Saorge · Col de Turíni 1607 · Breil-sur-Roya · Pigna · Moulinet · Gorges du Piaon · Lucéram · Sospel · Dolceacqua · 1102 Col de Braus · Castillon · La Pigna · araze · arène · Contes · Gorbio · Mortola · Ventimiglia · Bordighera · Peillon · Menton · RIVIERA DI PONENTE · Beausoleil · Monte-Carlo · la Turbie · MONACO · Eze · Beaulieu-sur-Mer · Villefranche · Cap Ferrat · CÔTE D'AZUR · Mediterranean Sea · Roya

Alpes-Maritimes
20 km

THE ALPES-MARITIMES

It would come as a surprise to many of the tourists who regularly fight for a deck chair on the Côte d'Azur to find that the Riviera has a peaceful back garden. Not a typically French garden, of the geometrically trimmed and designed variety that the nobility used to keep by their châteaux in the Loire Valley. Nor, despite the Riviera's British patronage, one of those rambling but manicured gardens to be found at a country manor. Instead, a neglected and untidy garden of a character all its own.

Ninety percent of the *département* of the **Alpes-Maritimes** is forgotten. During the summer months, a combination of heat haze and smog along the overburdened Côte hides the *arrière-pays* (or back country). The rugged hills and snow-capped Alpine peaks are only revealed during other seasons, affording a tempting peek at what the rest of the region has to offer.

And yet, getting to this peaceful hinterland from the Côte takes but a matter of minutes. The **Vallée des Merveilles** (Valley of Wonders) lies barely 40 miles (70 km) north of Nice, close by the Italian border. Its solitary population of ibex, goats and the occasional lynx are hidden from prying eyes by rugged mountains that shelter a remarkable display of the prehistoric version of graffiti: rock drawings. In fact, 35,000 such drawings were etched into these rocks from the Bronze Age through to medieval times.

The valley is accessible only by foot, preferably for those with limbs and lungs strong enough to endure a day or two of solid walking and with a stock of hiking gear to match. There are no four-star hotels, luxury flats or villas with swimming pools here. If an overnight stay is necessary, the solid virtues of a mountain refuge will have to do. You will find no buses or trains to hop on to if you get tired and no cafés to stop at if you get thirsty. And, in many cases,

Preceding pages: Saorge perched village.

there aren't even any paths, let alone signposts to look at if you get lost.

For the inexperienced, a mountain guide is essential, and the tourist offices in **St-Dalmas** and **Tende** will help with this. Hardened hikers, on the other hand, can probably make do with a small scale map. They should head between the ominous Mt-Bégo and the 9,626-ft (2,934-metre) **Grand Capelet** and if they stumble across several lakes on the way, they'll know they can't be far wrong. There are mountain refuges on either end of this 40-mile (60-km) valley. If a thunderstorm strikes, don't panic. For the shepherds working in the valleys below over 3,000 years ago, Mt-Bégo was like a temple, a place where sheep were sacrificed in an attempt to appease terrifying storms. In our contemporary and less mysterious terms, it simply acts as a lightning conductor.

The Vallée des Merveilles is the centrepiece of the **Parc National du Mercantour**, a huge national park that cloaks the northern edge of the Alpes-Maritimes. As a whole, it is rather less foreboding than the Vallée, but it is still a deserted mountain area and comes with the same warnings. Snow and ice are present from October through June, and the weather can change without warning or be different from one valley to the next. Even in summer the local newspaper, *Nice-Matin*, is full of stories of those lost for days and of the injured and even the dead. The locals and the gendarmerie will not laugh at people wearing heavy gear in summer, nor will they shrug at those asking about a mountain guide.

The Mercantour is the lifeblood of the Alpes-Maritimes. The sources of all the rivers that flow through the *département* can be found here – the Tinée, the Vésubie and the Var, which after successive re-drawings of departmental boundaries is now located outside the *département* to which it gave its name. Yet, for all its rigour, the Mercantour is now much more civilised than when it was the protected hunting ground of the kings of Italy.

Although the Comté de Nice was re-

Hotel sign near St-Etienne-de-Tinée.

turned to France in 1860, the Mercantour remained an Italian enclave until 1946. After it was seceded, however, hunting was banned and the whole of the park became a nature reserve. Botanists now believe that over half of the 4,000 or so species of wildflowers to be found in France grow in the Mercantour. Equally, of course, another reason for the survival of such natural treasures is the minimal impact that human civilisation has had on the region – so far.

To get around the Alpes-Maritimes, some form of personal transport is essential. Public transport is sparse, centred on coach routes to some of the larger towns and the skiing resorts. Only two railways cut their way inland. One runs from Nice to Sospel and Breil and on to Cuneo in Italy, with about four trains a day. The other, dubbed the Petit Train des Pignes by the locals, is a more occasional route running from Nice up the valley of the Var River towards Levens. Attempts to revive it in recent years have stumbled.

Train travel inland is a commodity

that has been neglected by the regional council – thankfully. Soon after the first trains crossed the Massif de l'Estérel in 1863, the Côte d'Azur began to take the crowded appearance that it revels in today. But in the *arrière-pays* there are plenty of ruined railway viaducts and stretches of disused track to testify to a different attitude. The most striking is the Pont du Loup, which straddles the southern edge of the Gorges du Loup. It was bombed by the retreating German army at the end of World War II and never revived.

Travel up the main road – the N202, nicknamed the Route d'Hiver des Alpes – from the coastal town of St-Laurent-du-Var, and the reasons for the absence of public transport become clear. Nearer the coast, the highway on the eastern bank of the Var River is wide and straight, but as you gradually move inland it becomes narrower and starts to wind. Within 15 miles (25 km) you find yourself at the base of a gorge, one of the chief geological features of the *département*. These sheer valleys carved by

torrents are the only way for transport to reach the north.

From Plan-du-Var northwards, N202 gives off into several smaller roads, following tributaries of the Var, which head down the narrow gorges and into the mountains to the skiing resorts. All are dead ends or circular routes that eventually return to the N202 as it heads east to the Lac de Castillon, in the neighbouring *département* of the Alpes-de-Haute-Provence. The way out of the north of the Alpes-Maritimes is blocked by mountains.

This upper limit of the Alpes-Maritimes is marked by the medieval town of **Entrevaux**. Its fortress, with walls running up the hillside, was designed by Vauban, who was also responsible for the fort overlooking the port at Antibes. Entrevaux's violent history gives a rough guide to the many different nationalities that have had an influence on the region. The town's roots are to be found among the Ligurian tribes, with the area subsequently invaded by the Greeks, the Celts and the Romans. Christianity took hold but only survived until the 10th century, when the Saracens invaded the region. Entrevaue became Spanish for a few years in the 16th century, only to end up in French hands a few years later.

In summer, the N202 is virtually deserted. But, in winter, the 85 percent of the population of the Alpes-Maritimes that lives near the coast suddenly acquires a taste for the wilderness of the *arrière-pays*. The right bank of the Var becomes a fashionable artery on weekends as the Niçois head to the skiing resorts: **Auron** and **Isola 2000** for the *sportif* in search of a conversation piece; **Valberg** and **Beuil** for the less pretentious or those more inclined to cross-country skiing.

Auron lines up a full range of slopes and trails for the inveterate skier, as does Isola 2000. However, modern chalets and flats are not what the back country is about. It may be fun for a while, but mountains that have had trees and rocks gouged out, with ski lifts dotting the pastures, are the inland **Ski chalet in Auron.**

equivalent of the concrete structures on the coast.

Isola 2000 has no history beyond skiing. It borrowed its name from the village below and added a futuristic sounding number – the station's altitude – to match the space-age architecture of the buildings. It seems lurid next to the charms of other more historic villages in the area that double up as ski resorts. Beuil, for example, was once the seat of the Grimaldi family. During the Middle Ages, it was also the capital of the region.

Head down the mountain from Auron into the old town of **St-Etienne-de-Tinée**, and you rediscover rural France, with stone buildings and churches that enclose the most anonymous forms of artwork the region has to offer. The **Chapel of St-Sebastian** hides some of the frescoes that are the unsung treasures of the Alpes-Maritimes. They may be a far cry from the Picassos on the coast, but the artist was undoubtedly aware of their presence and value.

Most of the frescoes are hidden inside the simple stone churches found in villages all over the Alpes-Maritimes, such as the **Chapelle St-Antoine** in **Cians**. Many were painted on ceilings and walls by artists whose names have not survived the five centuries that their masterpieces have endured. Others are by figures whose fame has not gone beyond the art world, such as Louis Bréa, possibly because their work lacks the transportability of framed canvas. This makes it all the more unique. Few museums in capitals of the world can boast of having a Bréa. And the work of other Provençal artists such as Giovanni Canavesio or Baleison is not to be found in a Sistine Chapel.

The isolated **Chapel of Notre-Dame des Fontaines** represents another common feature of the *arrière -pays*. There is every chance that a visitor will have to ask for the entrance key to the chapel at one of the two inns in nearby **La Brigue**. In this understated region, if a visitor finds a chapel locked, the normal procedure is to ask about the key at a nearby restaurant or *mairie*.

The greatest pieces of art in the region, however, have to be attributed to Mother Nature. One of her more unique works can be found on the way to the ski slopes at Beuil and Valberg. The **Gorge du Cians** makes a change from the usual – though inevitably spectacular – narrow limestone rift valley, with deep red slate as its main material. The mix of red from the slate and the green from the vegetation makes for a colourful contrast that does not abate even when the weather is dull; elsewhere, grey limestone bears an uncanny resemblance to grey clouds.

From here the **Vallée de la Tinée** becomes disappointing, though the **Gorges de la Mescla** at its southern end have spectacular slabs of rock overhanging the road and the river. But it does enjoy the saving grace of having been visited by the Provençal artists, as nearly every village church will testify.

To revive one's enthusiasm for the area, the **Vésubie Valley** is on hand. Within easy reach of the coast, it takes you from a Mediterranean landscape (pines rooted on parched rock and dusty

Après-ski in Auron.

soil, olive trees) into a fresher Alpine scenery (tall dark-green pines, waterfalls near La Boréon and Roquebillière, green pastures).

A few miles to the east of St-Martin-Vésubie is **Valdebore** and the small skiing resort at **La Colmiane**, complete with a few old chalets. Visitors like to call the area "Little Switzerland," which produces a quizzical look on the face of many locals – if only because the translation, *"Petit Suisse,"* is a brand name for a type of cottage cheese. But it is, in fact, an apt reminder that the region north of Nice was part of the kingdom of Savoy for several centuries. The same kingdom covered what is today the western half of Switzerland.

The valley is rich in revolutionary history as well. Republican soldiers on their way south to Nice in 1793 were attacked here by a small local army, which used the area's geography to its advantage. They literally sneaked up behind the enemy and pushed them off the cliff face. The location of this minor setback to the French Republic is known as the Saut des Français, or "the Frenchmen's Leap."

The Vésubie Valley is also lined by several crumbling and precarious mule tracks once used by smugglers. One of the substances transported along the tracks was salt, brought in by traders from Italy anxious to avoid the *gabelle*, a tax on salt imposed shortly after the Revolution.

St-Martin-Vésubie offers cool respite as a mountaineering centre in summer. It is a sleepy and unpretentious small town disturbed only by the rush of water down a one-metre-wide canal that bears a distinct resemblance to an overgrown gutter. All its native inhabitants seem to have the rough and thick skin that goes along with decades spent in the mountains, yet are unmistakably Mediterranean by dint of their olive complexion.

In summer, they sit by and watch the hikers leave the Bureau des Guides de la Haute-Vésubie, generally on a trip into the nearby Mercantour. Their winter routine changes little, though much of

The Madone d'Utelle.

the watching is done from behind closed windows (temperatures can be over 27 degrees centigrade colder than in the warm season). Summer for a Vésubian starts on 2 July, when a procession wends its way out of St-Martin carrying an 800-year-old wooden statue of Notre-Dame-de-Fenêstre 7 miles (12 km) to the sanctuary at **Madone de Fenêstre**. Winter begins when the procession makes the return journey in the third week of September.

Utelle, at the foot of the Vésubie Valley, has a similar religious vocation. Its sanctuary, the **Madone d'Utelle**, is on the hill above the village, at a height of 3,786 ft (1,154 metres). The view is impressive, taking in the whole of the south and west down to the coast. Looking to the north and up the valley, you can see the gradually increasing height of the mountains.

The areas nearer the coast are already becoming more developed. The greater width of the lower valleys has allowed for the sprawling and ramshackle development of large towns like **Grasse**. On a day without wind, Grasse lives up to its reputation as the perfume capital of France; a sweet aroma lingers in the air from the three large perfume factories dotted around the town.

Fragonard, **Galimard** and **Molinard** offer guided tours for visitors, but much of the finely tuned creation of scents for the Paris couturiers is carried out in small unnoticed laboratories on the Cours Honoré-Cresp. And don't expect much antiquity beyond the huge copper vats used to distill perfume. Their modern factories have to keep up with a cost-efficient 20th century. History is provided at the **Museum of Perfume** – another of those sights where, if the door is locked, a call 50 metres down the road at the **Musée de l'Histoire de Provence** gains admission.

Beyond perfume, Grasse is little more than a provincial town. Social climbing is literally that in Grasse. The rich live further up the hill, cloistered in red villas surrounded by cypress trees, peering out occasionally at a panorama of Cannes. Down below, in the dark-ened narrow alleyways of the **Old Town**, urchins scurry from one set of steps to the next, occasionally tripping over the odd shopper. Washing hangs from windows, and families gather outside doorways to chat.

Grasse suffers from faded glory; the days when it welcomed regular holiday visits from the British monarch, Queen Victoria, or Napoleon's sister, Princess Pauline, are distant. The elegant cypress trees are confined to the gardens of the villas above and the remaining palms are scraggy. The casino is being rebuilt in a bid to recapture some of that swinging clientèle that made the Côte d'Azur a cliché.

Grasse may sound unprepossessing, but it acts as a useful start for the art-lover's trip through the Alpes-Maritimes. Famous artists came and went through the region, leaving their mark in the form of museums and collections. Several are to be found in the lower part of the *département*; the civilised flower beds in the garden, there only to be shown off to visitors.

The altar within.

To go with the lavender, mimosa and jasmine that grows on the surrounding terraced hills is the town's **Fragonard Museum**. Jean-Honoré Fragonard was as torn between Paris and Grasse (where he was born and where he died) as he was torn between the charms of several wealthy consorts. Paris offered life, while Grasse offered light. But Grasse has managed to hold on to many of the 18th-century artist's floral and voluptuous works, thanks to a series of paintings commissioned by Madame du Barry. They also possess the *oeuvres* of his less-renowned son and grandson.

All in all, this is not a town that shouts its interest at you. You have to find the hidden gems. In a dark corner of the **Cathédrale Nôtre-Dame-de-Puy** hang two Rubens paintings that have belonged to the town for over 150 years.

If the tourist had not been invented, towns like nearby **Vallauris** would not exist. And, if Pablo Picasso had not lived, the tourist would never have come to Vallauris. Today, Vallauris is a largely residential town, hidden in a valley of its own barely two miles from the sea. The mimosa on the surrounding hillsides struggles for a revival after having suffered the winter of 1984, the sharpest known to a living Azuréen. At least the orange groves survived, leaving some idea of the summer light that lured Picasso away from the more arid inland sprawl of Mougins.

Ceramics have been the livelihood of Vallauris for four centuries. The main shopping street is thick with tacky shops selling plates, bowls and other artifacts. Uphill, the Place de la Libération contains Vallauris's two museums. The **Musée National Picasso**, with the *War and Peace* mural that the artist finished in 1952, is one. (Not to be confused with the larger Picasso Museum in Antibes. Picasso left some 60,000 works of art altogether and a will worth over 1,200 million francs when he died in 1973 – more than enough to fill several museums.)

Next door, the other, the **Musée Municipal**, devotes itself to "*l'art ceramique*," and exhibits some of the work

Painting
perfumed
soaps in Eze.

242

that the effusive Catalan artist accomplished during his six years on the Rue de Fournas. The Madoura Pottery – a few yards away from the summer bustle on the main Avenue Clemenceau – retains the copyright to Picasso's ceramics, dating from the friendship between the artist and the workshop's owners, the Ramie family.

Fernand Léger adopted **Biot**, a *village perché* (perched village) in a valley about 2 miles from the sea, as his outpost. Shortly before his death, he bought the land that was later used by his wife, Nadia, to build a museum for his works. The **Musée National Fernand Léger** is a cubist temple, with a vast ceramic mosaic on the outside, and the permanent home to nearly 400 of the artist's paintings, carpets, stained glass and ceramics.

The stark features of the Léger museum, the creation of a Niçois architect, stand out against the impractical charm of the perched village of **Biot** – 500 years old, maybe, but also lived in, which explains why all the houses are restored. The steep cobbled alleyways are lethal once the rain falls, allowing the visitor to slip and slide with his precious cargo of Biot glass and pottery. Biot is now built on *l'artisanat*, and sells to tourists.

Yet, a brief look through one of the gaps between the ramparts shows still another landscape for the Alpes-Maritimes. Its own private valley with a view reminiscent of Tuscany: cypress trees, the occasional goat wandering in between the villas and swimming pools.

St-Paul-de-Vence, though further inland, shares a similar view. Countless celebrities chose the valleys below Vence and St-Paul to live in – a cheaper alternative to the hills of pricey Cannes. The Mediterranean vegetation is still there, emphasised at times by the cultivated sprawl of cyclamen and primula in the gardens. The curious bright blue dots add to the impression of colour brought by the flowers in the spring and summer light, though the feeling dwindles somewhat when a more attentive glance reveals that they are swimming pools.

St-Paul is a larger version of Biot, albeit with more cachet. Rather than pottery, the emphasis here is on artists' studios and medieval history. There should be no fear of the cannon that menacingly points towards you at the entrance to the village; the favourite ammunition in one minor skirmish with the inhabitants of Vence was cherry stones. Nevertheless, the village had a more serious function through the centuries as a fortress guarding the entrance to the Var region.

Art has lived with St-Paul for hundreds of years. The church houses a Murillo, a Tintoretto and works by other Italian masters. Nevertheless, it wasn't until the 1920s that the village became known as a centre for art. The **Auberge de la Colombe d'Or** was a meeting place for a bevy of artists – including Picasso, Utrillo, Bonnard, Chagall, Modigliani, Soutine – who left behind canvasses, as the tale goes, sometimes to settle long-running accounts. Whatever the truth, the Colombe d'Or has now assembled its own priceless – and private – collection of paintings and its own ceramic mural by Léger. It would have pains, however, to rival the collection to be found further up the hill.

The **Fondation Maeght**, arguably the most interesting of all the museums that the Côte d'Azur has to offer, rivals the best art collection in the world. It is unique in that the whole place was created as a temple of modern art and that many of its works were specially commissioned.

The building's brick and white concrete exterior was designed by the Spanish architect Jose-Luis Sert, who was heavily influenced by Le Corbusier, and is partnered by Miró sculptures. Indeed, all the structural features were devised to promote an understanding of 20th-century art, and the architect worked directly with some of the artists, principally Miró and Chagall.

Aimé Maeght's position as an art dealer undoubtedly helped him in his efforts to assemble the collection by 1964. Few people can boast of having a Chagall with the personal dedication "*à Aimé et Guigette (Marguerite)*

Maeght." Fewer still could have had the friendships, knowledge and money to integrate mosaics by Miró and Braque or a garden full of Giacomettis into the whole and then to continue collecting works of the following younger generations. Some of the holdings move out on special exhibitions, but the collection is so vast there is always something to replace it. Equally, there are special exhibitions from February to October.

Back in St-Paul, lesser mortals can at least sit opposite La Colombe at the **Café de la Paix**, which looks as if it provided the model for the French café in countless Hollywood productions. Amid all the contemporary richness and revelry, it is worth remembering that St-Paul's history is rather more killjoy. When King François I built the ramparts of the village in the 16th century, he uprooted all the inhabitants and packed them off to live in nearby La Colle-sur-Loup.

Over 100 years later, new residents arrived in the form of the monks of the Ordre des Pénitents Blancs. The order, created by the Bishop of Grasse, lent its name to countless chapels and churches throughout the region. Mercifully, the monks, clad in hooded white gowns, no longer parade eerily through the streets to celebrate the Lord's Supper.

Although **Vence** is larger and less artistic than St-Paul, the modern-day art pilgrim will end his or her journey by making straight for its **Chapelle du Rosaire**. Designed by Henri Matisse in 1951, the chapel is probably the most recent example of the kind of religious patronage that brought artists like Michelangelo to decorate churches throughout Italy.

In design it is Provençal and simple. Rows of tall and narrow arches form the windows, and the tiled roof is dominated elegantly by a tall and thin wrought-iron cross. Overall it is strikingly pure and bright, with the only colour in its white interior brought by the stained-glass windows. Matisse called it his most satisfying work.

Vence is a large town (21,000 inhabitants) that is lively all year round. Its

Vallauris master potter, Roger Collet.

244

origins date back to the 5th century, and its turbulent history matches that of Entrevaux: Ligurians, Lombards, Romans, countless Christians and Saracens plus the Germans and Italians of World War II all passed through the town, and some destroyed (the Lombards flattened the town on the two occasions that they occupied it). The 15th-century walls of the *vieille ville*, within the modern town, betray its former feudal vocation.

Yet, the historical instability of the town has lent it curiosity value. The **Cathedral** in Place Clemenceau was built on the site of the Roman temple and mixes a patchwork of styles and eras. It possesses a simple baroque facade, some Byzantine stonework, Gothic windows, Roman tombs and a mosaic by Chagall. Indeed, Vence's religious offerings are as refreshing as the fountain in the Place du Peyra and the bright atmosphere in the summer. Despite its popularity, the town retains a purer feeling of southern France, with its vegetable and fruit markets and the restaurants spilling into the squares. For once, the tourist becomes incidental.

Tourette-sur-Loup apparently has found a simple way of keeping the hordes at bay. Traffic can only pass through and is prevented from venturing into its steep and narrow alleyways, allowing geraniums to flower on the stone walls in the spring and summer. This *village perché* overlooks the southeastern end of the Loup Valley, though the Loup River itself is a short distance further down through olive trees and, in spring, fields of violets.

Actually, the reason behind Tourette's relative emptiness, even in the height of summer, is probably just that it lives in the shadow of its more illustrious neighbours, Vence and St-Paul. Arts and crafts are carried out without the glare of renown, although with equal skill. The potters, painters and wood-carvers have to be sought out. Most welcome the public, but their only sign is normally the open door of a village house. Few attempt the external displays to be found in Vallauris or Biot.

Dubuffet fountain in the Foundation Maeght.

The town's history is more tranquil as well, having attracted few of the attacks by Saracens or Lombards experienced by its other perched neighbours. Today, the only time the village ventures to cry its fame comes with the Festival des Violettes in March, a processional celebration of the flowers in the surrounding countryside. But March is still the low season as far as tourism is concerned, with only a trickle of outsiders making their way to Tourette for the festivities.

There are no ramparts, walls or battlements surrounding Tourette. The only war-like evocation comes with the 15th-century château, once the entrance to the village and now in the middle and occupied by the Mairie. A belfry marks the archway that leads through to the cobbled hills of the **Old Village**. The church stands in the main square and houses a Bréa triptych – an apt reminder that Tourette is on the edge of the *arrière-pays*.

Descending into the river valley at Pont-sur-Loup, you find yourself at the mouth of the imposing **Gorges du Loup**, the nearest of the inland rift valleys to the coast. It is also one of the most spectacular, with the torrential river scything its way through a deep gorge of grey rock and lush vegetation.

The **Cascade de Courmes** is halfway along the gorge, a waterfall that drops about 160 ft (50 metres) into a pool by a roadside tunnel. A pathway runs underneath the cascade of water, but years of erosion have made it mossy, smooth, slippery and treacherous. The start of the path is about 65 ft (20 metres) to the right of the waterfall, the steps sealed off by a rusting metal barrier. Another path, for the agile, begins on the opposite side of the road by the tunnel entrance and affords a different view of the waterfall after a short scrambled climb. Both are dangerous ventures.

Continuing north, the road crosses to the other side of the gorges. A glimpse of the river from the bridge that links the cliffs (be careful that you don't lean against a barrier that is rickety and rusting) bears witness to the link between the spectacular and the dangerous.

Forty metres below, the Loup plunges through the rocks while the rusting hulk of a car's wreckage lies beside it.

More pleasant thoughts are revived by the smaller **Cascade des Desmoiselles**. And further up are nice spots for trout fishing. Trips in the river valley are punctuated by warning signs about sudden rises in the water level, depending on the mood of a small hydroelectric station upstream.

If the term *village perché* needed a perfect example, it would find it in **Gourdon**. One whole side of the town teeters on the edge of a rocky cliff, a natural rampart obviating the need for any fortress walls to repel invaders. The feudal **château** was restored most recently in the 16th century. Inside you are treated to a display of all the charms of feudality: weaponry, a dungeon – complete with a bed, apparently to let the torturers' victims rest in between sessions – and a small collection of medieval art and memorabilia.

The château is reached after a brief walk (no cars allowed) up into the village. A few steps more allow you to run the gauntlet of the main street, lined with small shops full of crafts and postcards. The main square lies just down this way, with an anonymous and simple 11th-century church. But the view from the end of the square is Gourdon's real delight: the Loup Valley to the sea, the Massif de l'Estérel to the mouth of the Var, hills and valleys. Apart from defensive reasons, the *villages perchés* were placed as they were so as to have a clear line of sight to allied villages, to signal impending invasions. But, nowadays, the small terrace next to the square has been taken over by a nice little French restaurant.

The road from Gourdon winds down to Grasse. It's narrow at the top as might be expected and at the bottom too. Curiously, in the middle, it widens into a large expanse of smooth pitch-black tarmac, though the road never takes on the kind of traffic that could warrant such an extension. A freak of planning, and a warning for the future.

In 1988, several villages around the Loup Valley began to voice concern at projects for a new autoroute running inland, ostensibly to relieve the load on the coastal motorway and to ease access to the Côte d'Azur. Flysheets on the matter stuck to local telegraph poles will undoubtedly be a feature of the region for years to come.

Finding a straight stretch of road on the eastern side of the River Var, where the Alps spill down into the sea, is virtually impossible. Immediately behind Nice, a cluster of rocky hills surround the **Mt-Chauve** (or "bald mountain"). The name was aptly chosen. Vegetation stops dead partway up, leaving a bald patch at the top.

The "monk's head" is occupied by a disused fort with a 360-degree view. From here, the distance between villages appears short, and you may optimistically think of a quickly completed excursion through the dusty hills. But you will find that the miles are often tripled as you slowly swing through a pitted series of hairpin turns from one commune to the next.

A Renaissance fountain in the Place Republicaine of **Contes** offers some refreshment. And therein hangs a tale of how the God-fearing inhabitants of this small village tried to chase the devil away. The devil, being a thirsty soul, was known to quench his dry palate at the village fountain. The Contois conspired to capture him by smearing glue over the square, and he was banished from the town.

Contes is rare in that it is not at the top of a hillside but on a spur that juts out into the Valley of the Paillon. The château is at the bottom of the village and retains its Provençal name, Lou Castel. But Contes and its neighbours have grown. The area is more densely populated than the rest of the inner reaches of the *département*, as the villages within 15 miles (25 km) of Nice begin to assume the role of dormitories.

Few hamlets have stranger names than Coaraze, a derivation of the Provençal for *queue rasée*, or "shaved-off tail." Here, the devil appears anew. In search of a new home after his banishment from Contes, he entered this medi-

Puppy love in Utelle.

eval village. The inhabitants once again took exception to his presence and this time captured him by his tail. He managed to struggle free, but his tail was ripped off in the process.

Despite its medieval setting, Coaraze has taken on an artistic zest that is more akin to the towns on the other side of the Var River. On the wall alongside the cobbled stairway leading up to the church are three ceramic sun-dials, one by Jean Cocteau, the writer, filmmaker and artist.

On the edge of the village, the **Chapelle Bleue** furthers the strange mix. From the outside, it appears to be no more than one of the interminable number of ageing chapels in the area. But the inside has been well-restored, with post-war frescoes decorating the walls. Everything, including the light through the stained-glass window, is blue, which is a reminder of the Côte d'Azur rare in these parts – here, the light rarely takes on the clarity for which the region is famous.

Peillon offers far more classical charms. It is medieval once again, a period of history that seems rather sombre and full of strife. Peillon is painfully thrust on to the jagged edge of a small mountain side, the houses clustered together in such a way that from a distance the village appears to be a castle, with the church standing proud in the middle like a turret. Barely 9 miles (15 km) from the avenues of Nice, the little town has no streets, just alleyways and steps.

West of Peillon, within reach of the international border, the Italian influence starts. **Tende** actually was Italian for a long time – the town was handed back to France in 1947 after a plebiscite – but its inhabitants always professed to feel French. It looks Italian, however. The atmosphere is medieval, but not with the dismal stone walls of so many of the neighbouring villages.

Many houses have plastered walls, painted with matt colours that fade under the onslaught of the sun. Others use a green-hued schist, as befits an Alpine area using local materials. Indeed, the style is more Romanesque, and each has

Farmers' wives in Berthmont-les-Bains.

a balcony and an overhanging roof.

Tende, like any self-respecting town in a predominantly Catholic region has a church. But it is a different type than its western neighbours, with a belfry shaped like two stacked barrels and a small roof. Built in the 15th century, green columns protect its doorway.

La Brique, a brief excursion away, offers a similar history. In fact, so does most of the **Roya Valley**. This valley, which heads south from Tende towards Breil, was retained by the Italians until October 1947, because it was the only link with the Mercantour and the hunting grounds of the king of Italy. The current border has been designated according to the water table. No tributaries cross the frontier on either side.

Saorge is a spectacular sight. Squeezed onto a cliff face at the entrance of a gorge, it is the only town in the region to have lent its name to a gorge. It takes a trek by foot to reach the centre, through some of the steepest cobbled alleyways one could imagine in an urban, albeit small, area. Some people do still live here, but the young are quick to move out. The contemporary exodus contrasts with ancient times, when it seemed like everyone was trying to invade the fortified village – unsuccessfully. Such was its reputation for impregnability that they eventually all stopped trying.

The steepness does not rule out the existence of a Renaissance church, **St-Sauveur**, with an altar of red and gold. Bear in mind that the church organ dates from the 19th century, and some poor mules had to carry it up the hill. Saorge has not forgotten the contribution the animals made (and still make) to life in the village. One of the village festivals is dedicated to Saint Eloi, patron saint of the mules.

Visitors may moan about the steep alleyways but, for the Franciscan monks that dwell in the monastery, it helps create a tranquil and serene atmosphere. The monastery rests in a small square at the top of the village, among a cluster of olive trees. Below it, the valley apparently has a good echo, a feature that allowed 20th-century soldiers to communicate with a nearby château from the ruined castle above. The Franciscans only returned to their home in 1969.

By some quirk of administration and diplomacy in 1947, the frontier south of Breil was not arranged according to the border rules applied to the section further north. The Roya flows happily through the Italian border and into the sea at Ventimiglia. So does the main road, and **Breil-sur-Roya** is the last chance to turn off to head towards Sospel and Nice.

Breil produces olive oil and is the centre for a type of olive that is only found in the Alpes-Maritimes, *the cailletier*. The *département* is also unusual in that it cultivates olives up to a height of 2,600 ft (800 metres), twice as high as anywhere else. Production of olive oil, however, is quite limited, about 285 tonnes per year. Most of it is used to make high-quality cooking oil, and little of the production falls to industrial use. Breil itself lays claim to more than 40,000 olive trees and cel-

Saorge-style ravioli.

ebrates a lively grand Fête de l'Olive at harvest time, some time in October.

The town of Breil makes for a restful stop. The drama of Saorge is past, and here the urban centre lies on a flat expanse of valley, with the Roya running wide and calmly through it.

Sospel shares the tranquillity and the olive groves, if not the river. The Bevera, a tributary of the Roya, runs through Sospel instead, leaving a series of islets around an old bridge. The bridge is an oddity, with a toll gate in the middle that was reconstructed after World War II, when it was destroyed in a bombing raid. North of the bridge is the oldest part of the town, a close cluster of buildings with wooden balconies. By the river there is still an old sheltered washing trough filled with water even at the height of summer.

The setting for Sospel is Italian: the valley with its olive groves, the rivers meeting at the town with their islets, the toll gate on the old bridge. The impression is reinforced on the southern side by the square around the church. Of no particular shape and bare, it boasts a baroque church on one end. All the buildings are plastered and painted in weathered shades of orange, yellow, ochre or red, with contrasting green shutters. This is a style predominant in the east and all the way down through Italy, but which disappears just a few miles to the west.

The trick is to head south towards the coast at Menton, a town with similar architectural appeal. The road climbs to the **Castillon Pass** then winds interminably through a small dry valley. Along the way, **Piène** offers a reminder of the relatively underdeveloped world we are leaving. An Italianate square similar to Sospel but smaller, its unkempt buildings only escape tattiness by virtue of being baked by the sun. The church is odd on the outside, possessing a bell tower with strange pointed horns on all four corners. And tacked beneath the arch of the belfry is a modern clock. The rest of this dusty, deserted and humble village, however, seems to have missed modernity.

Winter's dusk.

250

Twelve miles (20 km) beyond the Castillon Pass, you drop below the motorway into the populous Menton, a shock after the quiet villages of the interior. You might prefer to rise away from the coastal sprawl towards the sanctuary of villages like **Castellar**. Moving west, with the ridge overlooking the Mediterranean on your left, you pass simple hillside villages like **Ste-Agnès** and **Gorbio**.

Here, within a few kilometres of one another stand two different worlds. To the south is the developed coast, peppered with villas and shops in between the pine trees. Just north perches the simplicity, quietness and relative poverty of the back country.

La Turbie is on the edge of the over-developed world. Sometimes it is caught in the swirl of clouds, lending a rather more sinister vein to the ruin of the **Trophée des Alpes** and its demonstrations of trained eagles. Set on the Grand Corniche (known as the Via Julia by the Romans and Napoleon's favourite way to Italy), the Trophée is the bait,

Villa in La Turbie.

and the Grande Corniche is the fishing line. The tourists reel themselves in.

The Trophée des Alpes originally was presented as a reward by the Roman Senate to the Emperor Augustus for his successful campaign against the remaining rebellious tribes of Gaul. Only one side with four columns remains to bear witness to the imposing 50 metres the monument used to measure. This section was restored by archaeologists, using original stones, at a height of 105 ft (32 metres). Inscribed inside are tributes to Augustus and a list of the 44 conquered tribes. Adorning the Trophy's walls are quotes from Virgil and one from Dante's *Purgatory*.

Below the monument lies the **Eglise St-Michel**. This church is a recent 18th-century offering, with a domed top to the bell tower and a clock. Baroque styles use more colour, and this one is no exception. Inside, the red marble is extensive, bordering on the gaudy, insolent style that might befit a film star's villa in St-Tropez.

The Grande Corniche is the highest of

the three corniches that run parallel to the coast. Of them, it's also the longest route from Monaco to Nice, though not the slowest since heavy traffic clogs the coast road.

The Moyenne Corniche is the quickest and probably the most stylish of the three routes. Alfred Hitchcock once caught a bus here, playing an extra in one of his films, *To Catch a Thief*. In that same movie, Cary Grant lived alongside the road, a retired cat burglar, residing in this part of the Côte d'Azur because he wanted to avoid the bustle of the coast and the big towns. Who could forget Grace Kelly – the Hollywood star who was having a real-life romance at the time of filming in 1956 with Prince Rainier of Monaco – as she swooped along the curves of the Moyenne Corniche in her roadster? She died tragically on that same corniche in 1982.

Whether Hitchcock stopped and wondered if he should fit the village of **Eze** into his film is not recorded. Eze village is impaled on a rocky spike by the road, a dramatic location suited to cinema's master of suspense. It is about 1,300 ft (400 metres) above the sea, which in summer shimmers silently and distantly below. Corsica is said to be visible from the highest point.

The German philosopher Friedrich Nietzsche is thought to have found the inspiration for his final book, *Thus spake Zarathustra*, while walking down a pathway to the sea here. Nietzsche retired from active life in 1869 due to syphilis and spent the rest of his time in Italy, with winters in Nice. By the time he started writing *Zarathustra*, he was already edging into insanity, as illness ate away at his brain.

Nietzsche's presumed path took him through an area of bushes and pine that is now bare, with a yellowing and, in parts, charred appearance. In 1986, the area's worst forest fire swept along this part of the coast. Its flames crossed the Moyenne Corniche, and the blackened landscape of sparse pine it left behind serves as a tragic reminder. The Alpes-Maritimes suffers less from forest fires than the neighbouring Var, but fires are still a summer hazard in this tinder-dry landscape – often fuelled by no more than a castaway dog-end.

The entrance to Eze through a small and easily lost archway comes after a short winding climb from the main road. Few other *villages perchés* command the popularity of Eze, and pushing through the narrow streets at the height of summer can be trying. The architecture (that medieval stone is familiar) hasn't changed, it has just been restored and cleaned up to house the souvenir shops. Where Eze gains is with the smell that lingers in its confined space. There are several restaurants in the town and a *crêperie* and bakery. They don't need to advertise – by the time you have been through the church and the chapel and the famed **exotic garden** at the summit of the hill, you'll be at their doorsteps, no matter how expensive the visit may be.

Eze also houses at least one expensive hotel. Honeymooners need look no further. The rooms match the price, as does the splendid view over the sea

Boules player.

from the windows. Breakfast? Why, "*croissants sur la terrasse, bien sûr,*" as the air warms up in the sun, and the turquoise water glimmers silently below. There are only two real reasons to stay in this hotel: frivolous indulgence and romance.

The strategic skills of the medieval architects who built the *villages perchés* are to be admired. But their efforts seem to have been somewhat wasted. Few of the villages were impregnable and, like Eze, most were at varying times occupied by the region's invaders. In the case of Eze, the multitude of change-overs has left historians confused about its actual origins. Some say the site was found by the Ligurians in 500 BC and the village built later during the Roman occupation. Others believe the village was founded by the Saracens. At the very least, all agree that the latter occupied it at some point.

A more recent creation for this part of the back garden of the Côte d'Azur is Eze's cactus patch, or "*jardin exotique.*" This garden was planted in 1950 around the ruins of the château, which had been dismantled under the orders of Louis XIV in 1706. Round cacti, hairy cacti, bristling cacti and flowering cacti share the garden with one-inch-long ants and the snails that have managed to snuggle in between the plants prickly spines.

Five items characterise the Côte d'Azur: the sea, the light, the weather, the culture and the crowds. Inland, you simply take away the sea and the crowds and add the feudal history that created the *villages perchés* owned by the fiefdoms: the Grimaldis, the Lascaris around Tende and the Villeneuves near Vence. But if war and religion moulded the development of the area, so did its natural wilderness. By simply being mountainous and rugged, it has preserved its beauty and kept crowds away.

In 1988, the regional council decided to promote tourism in the *arrière-pays*, in an attempt to revive the impoverished economy of the area. Fortunately for those who do visit the area, their effort has so far failed.

Corniche above Monte Carlo. Following pages: the "nose" at Fragonard; bottles of Orange blossom perfume.

THE PERFUMES OF PROVENCE

As you drive down the Autoroute du Sud, the first anticipatory whiff of Provence wafts in through the car window – air laden with the scent of yellow broom, thyme, mimosa, lavender. More than anything, it is this heady scent for which Provence is known by poets and tourists. So, it is entirely appropriate that the Provençal town of Grasse has been the centre of the world's perfume industry for the past four centuries.

The gentle climate, rich soil and cradle of mountains that protect it from the north wind make Grasse an ideal place for flower production almost all year round. Golden mimosa blooms in March. By early summer, there are acres and acres of fragrant roses, ready to be picked. Jasmine appears in the autumn. And, high above the town, the mountains are terraced with row upon row of purple lavender.

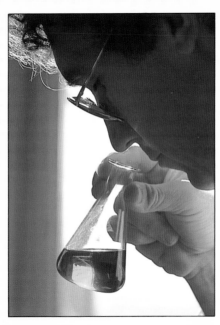

The perfume industry in Grasse originated with an immigrant group of Italian glovemakers in the 16th century. They discovered the wonderful scents of the flowers in the area and began perfuming their soft leather gloves, a favourite way to use perfume (along with pomanders and scented handkerchiefs) at a time when the odour of the general populace definitely required masking.

Demand for the floral perfumes steadily grew in the 18th and 19th centuries, and Grasse as a perfume mecca prospered. But local production of raw material declined after World War II. Competition from countries such as Turkey, Egypt and Bulgaria, where labour costs are much cheaper, proved decisive, and the gentle climate – so ideal for growing flowers – attracted many wealthy people to the area, pushing the price of land sky-high and causing many acres to be sold off as building plots.

Today, Grasse is better known for improving raw materials imported from other countries. Nonetheless, you can still see vast mountains of rose petals, vats of mimosa or jonquils and spadefuls of violets and orange blossom just picked and waiting to be processed each morning.

The flowers must be picked early, when the oil is most concentrated, and delivered immediately. It takes enormous quantities of the blooms to produce even the tiniest amounts of "absolute" perfume: about 750 kilos of roses for just one kilo of rose "absolute," about 4,000 kilos to produce one kilo of "essential oil."

There are a number of different methods used to create the "absolutes" or "essential oils," which the perfumer combines to create a fragrance. The oldest method is steam distillation, which is now used mainly for orange blossom. Water and flowers are boiled in a still, and the essential oils are extracted by steam – the heat breaks open the cells of the petals and leaves, and the essential oil floats on top while the water sinks to the bottom.

Another ancient method still used today, though it is very expensive, is "enfleurage." The flowers are layered with a semi-solid mixture of lard, spread over glass sheets and stacked in wooden tiers. When the fat is thoroughly impregnated with the perfume, the scent is separated out by washing the axonge with alcohol. Enfleurage is used particularly for jasmine and tuberose.

A more modern method is extraction by volatile solvents. Perfume can be extracted from flowers and plants by immersion in alcohol or a volatile hydrocarbon solvent such as petroleum ether. Only the perfume, colour and natural wax dissolve, leaving behind the cellulose and fibre components of the plant. After recovery of the solvent by distillation, the product is perfume. The wax is separated, leaving a final concentrate called the "absolute."

The highly trained perfumers or "noses" of Grasse can identify and classify hundreds of fragrances. In creating a fragrance, a perfumer is rather like a musician, using different "chords" of scent to blend together in harmony. The desired result is a complex perfume that will radiate around the body in a slow process of diffusion – what the French call "sillage."

A good perfume may include hundreds of different ingredients to achieve the correct balance, using powerful animal fixatives like ambergris, civet and musk to capture the delicate, ephemeral fragrances of the Provençal hillsides.

THE CÔTE D'AZUR

The French Riviera – that fabled stretch of Mediterranean seaside that runs from St-Tropez to the Italian border – is more steeped in myths, sensuality and surprise than just about anywhere else on earth. The name alone seems to excite the senses, and almost everyone, whether they are long-time residents on the Côte or they merely once spent a week in Cannes in the 1960s, likes to boast familiarity with the territory.

Whatever their experience and exposure, most people are confident they can recount the myth and recognise the reality of the Riviera. And, at any rate, the components of the myth are easy enough to enumerate.

Great Gatsby parties at private villas, with vast lawns sloping down to the deep blue sea at Cap Ferrat and the Cap d'Antibes. Breaking the bank at the casino in Monte Carlo, before returning to a luxurious suite (with a view of the château, *bien sûr*) at the Hôtel de Paris. Getting a *laissez-passer* (general pass) to the Cannes Film Festival each May and basking in the late afternoon sun in Nice's Cimiez Arena every July while listening to laid-back jazz.

The stories go on and on. Living next door to Brigitte Bardot in St-Tropez and descending to the Place des Lices for an afternoon game of *boules*. (Officially the French Riviera is in the Alpes-Maritimes *département* of France, but both friend and foe tend to include St-Tropez, which is in the Var, and Monaco, which is an independent principality, when they throw the term around.) Or, for the artistic, enjoying the light (Renoir said it was "the light, the light" that made the Riviera so special) and striving to become an artist to rival Matisse, Picasso, Signac and other past painters of the region.

The myth is, in fact, still reality. All of the above occur, or exist, today as much as they did in the past. Jet-setting, party-

Preceding pages: Menton. **Left, Rivieran sisters on the go.**

ing, gaiety, artists, casinos and Brigitte herself are not yet dead.

Not long ago, everyone who's anyone showed up dressed for the 1920s at a Great Gatsby party given at the Villa Araucaria in Cannes, a humble Riviera home that went on the market for US$8 million. American television superstar Bill Cosby regularly vacations at the luxurious Hôtel du Cap on the Cap d'Antibes and feasts on fresh, albeit expensive, fish at the nearby Bacon Restaurant. Princess Caroline spends a healthy part of the summer yachting on the Mediterranean, and Palm Beach in Cannes continues to feature cabarets under the full moon. Most people who live here don't even pinch themselves to make sure they're not dreaming.

Indeed, even its detractors agree that – from the point of view of weather, transport, services and, yes, light – the Riviera is certainly one of the best places to live or visit in Europe. The views, whether of distant corniches or near nude bathers, are splendid. The rocky cliffs, the hilltop towns, the markets, the national parks and a vast number of other amenities transform even the least romantic tourist into an unquenchable poet. Dufy's seascapes actually come to life.

When you have arrived for an afternoon of Alpine skiing in March, at the small resort of Gréolières, which is a mere 45-minute drive from Cannes, and you look down from the top of the mountain and see spring blossoming on the hills and summer at the beach, you have to marvel at your good fortune. The Riviera, myth and all, is quite a piece of work.

Relaxed but state of the art: It's no problem getting to the Riviera, because the Nice-Côte d'Azur International Airport, just a five-minute drive from the centre of Nice, is the second largest in France. Or you can arrive by the highways that link southern French cities with every neighbouring European country. Or take the high-speed train (TGV) from Paris or the milk train in from Italy or Spain.

Once you're here, for business or fun, you will be surprised by the modernity to be found around every corner. Telephone density in the region is among the highest in France, the number of hospital beds per inhabitant is well above the norm and there are excellent educational facilities, including American and international schools.

But the myth is not damaged by these state-of-the-art banalities. Even obstinate Parisians admit the pace is slower, the food is healthier and the grass is greener (everyone has automatic sprinkler systems, although these do nothing

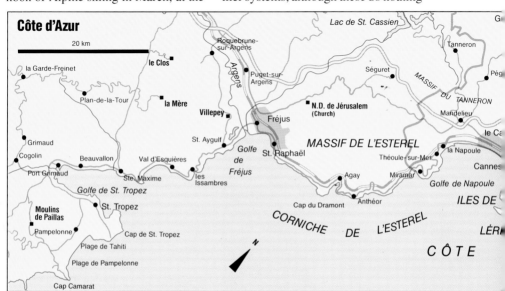

to combat the serious fires that occur every few years).

The relaxed pace is the key, of course, and both business and pleasure usually involve a round of golf, a sail on the Mediterranean or a run on the ski slopes rather than simply a sedate dinner at a restaurant (though there is no shortage of noteworthy business lunch and dinner spots) or a chat in an office (yes, there *are* offices).

Things are so easy going that the general mood is often referred to as "Mediterranean mellow." No one dares to look unduly hurried. Most local businessmen take their ties off between May and September and work in their shirtsleeves. Frenchmen on the coast, largely because of the exposure they have had to an international population since the days of Queen Victoria, are much more likely to invite you to their homes for a pastis or Perrier than their Parisian counterparts.

And everyone still takes the traditional Mediterranean late-afternoon stroll along the palm-lined Promenade des Anglais in Nice or the Croisette in Cannes – those stretches of street paralleling the usually azure sea where fashionable swimwear (or the lack of it) is constantly on parade.

And everyone can get by here – although there's no question that this is one place where the rich really are different from the rest of the world.

The Riviera, its beauty so democratic in nature, is a great equaliser between the rich and the poor. You can spend a fortune on a meal at the Louis XV in Monte Carlo (indisputably the top restaurant on the Riviera and much better than the over-touted Moulin des Mougins) or get a perfectly enjoyable pizza and *salade Niçoise* or a catch-of-the-day almost anywhere – though there are frequent exaggerations about the freshness of the fish.

You can get a suite at the Byblos in St-Tropez, the Negresco in Nice, La Reserve in Beaulieu or the Hermitage in Monaco for a small fortune, or you can camp in the delightfully rustic Estérel (the comparatively virginal coast between Cannes and St-Raphael) for a pittance. You can shop on chic streets – the Avenue des Beaux Arts in Monaco, the Rue d'Antibes in Cannes, the Rue de France in Nice – or find lively, colourful vegetable markets and hidden antique stores in the smaller villages.

But is the Riviera really this seductive? Would Picasso have been more productive had he not spent much of his creative life in Vallauris and Mougins? Would Anthony Burgess and Karl Lagerfeld have been less flamboyant if they hadn't lived in Monaco? Would

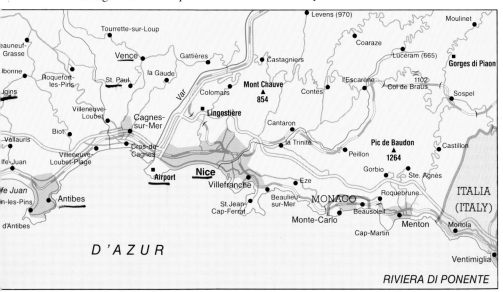

Einstein have been more creative if he were working with the many scientists and boffins based at Sophia Antipolis, the booming and fascinating 10,000-acre (4,000-hectare) technology park located just off the autoroute between Nice and Cannes?

No place for paleskins: Most inhabitants of the Riviera don't hide their pleasure in being able to boast the distinction of residing here throughout the year. While they each may have their own pet peeves (for example, it is virtually impossible to find a resident who doesn't complain about the influx of summer visitors), they generally tend to enjoy reinforcing Riviera myths and often make pale-skinned visitors from the north feel a little unwelcome.

The first thing locals or foreigners living on the Riviera let visitors know is just how *nice* it is to live down here. They enthusiastically recite the professional and personal conveniences of the area and immediately make you feel like an idiot for commuting in New York or London, contending with the traffic problems in Los Angeles or living with lousy weather in Paris, Stockholm or Moscow. But, face it, they're right. The Riviera *is* a good place to live and work, because most professionals (artists, bankers, brokers and lawyers) have chosen, and often claim they have made serious professional sacrifices, to make it home (which the French refer to as a "principal residence," in contrast to the many "secondary residences," or vacation houses, also to be found on the Riviera). Very few people are here against their will, which makes it both a productive and fun area.

The Riviera may not yet have turned into California, but the differences are fading fast, thanks to the preponderance of fast-food havens and autoroutes. The people aren't quite as beauty and health conscious as their sun-loving brethren in southern California, but the skin cancer scare certainly has not hit and being white and fat is definitely *out* between May and October. It is only a bit less *out* during the winter, when you can get by, just, with a facial tan from skiing.

A business lunch.

Indeed, there is even some slight discrimination on the Riviera if you show up at the beach in the middle of summer without a suntan and noticeably overweight. How much? Best not to try to find out unless you're one of the many northern businessmen with a good expense account to shield you.

At the same time, fortunately, the people living in the south are not sports fiends. They don't bore you with how far they have jogged or with what's new in weightlifting equipment. But it's rare to find someone who is not at all interested in one sport or another: The opportunity for exercise is so vast that it's hard to pass up.

In fact, it's difficult not to be tanned and in relatively good health when you pass a lot of time in the south of France, because so much of Rivieran life is spent outdoors. Even the most highly stressed businessman (there may be two or three around) will spend enough time in the sun to protect his tan.

The Mediterranean is itself the scene of numerous sports antics. Although polluted in parts (the new water-treatment plant near the Nice airport is intended eventually to make everyone forget pollution), it is still ideal for diving, swimming (a favourite, non-polluted spot is on the Estérel) and windsurfing (the winds in the summer are not overly strong, and most locals prefer the Ile de Giens near Hyères). There are numerous marinas at which to keep, rent or buy a boat, and one popular and somewhat relaxing sport is, in fact, simply just walking through the docks to look at other people's crafts.

Of course, you don't need to go in for exerting activities at all, if you don't want to. The most relaxed sport is *boules,* and every year the local daily, *Nice-Matin*, features a large colour photograph of celebrities playing in front of the Café des Arts in St-Tropez. There are also fine marked hiking trails and numerous camping sites throughout the back country. You can either follow the national *grands randonées* or take a stroll along the Balcon de la Côte d'Azur.

Left, limos. **Right**, **Carlton Hotel**.

If you decide that all activity is too strenuous, you can just sit on a beach. There's no doubt that boy and girl watching is also a big sport, and a lot of people get exercise just hanging out at places with weird names like "Waikiki Plage." Naturally, not even hanging out comes free, and it can cost over 50 francs to get onto a private beach and lie on a mattress under an umbrella for a full day.

The downside of Paradise: The French Riviera may be more than the Cannes Film Festival, the celebrity-filled Principality of Monaco, the exquisite Chantecler Restaurant on the Promenade des Anglais in Nice and bronzed beauties sunning on the beaches near Antibes. But do keep in mind that there are always pimples in paradise and that even the Riviera has its sour spots. The people attracted by the myth is the major problem.

Northern Europeans traditionally scurry to the Mediterranean sun and beaches during their August vacation. The resulting congestion on roads, on beaches and in restaurants exasperates most local residents even if it titillates crowd-seeking tourists. Scandinavians, presumably alone and contemplative during their harsh winter, seem to get a particular thrill out of body-to-body sunbathing.

And, while the Riviera does have its share of splendid villas, the cramped little housing developments (read secondary residences) make parts of it resemble an upmarket Calcutta. The closest thing to a building code is the presence of the Mediterranean itself, which, fortunately, limits expansion to the south (though Nice, Monaco and other communities have worked around this inconvenience by building on reclaimed land).

The much-touted slow pace also means local services have their ups and downs. Anyone with a New York mindset had better quickly adopt a more Mediterranean-mellow mentality. Shops still close between noon and three, and no one would ever pretend to be in a hurry or unduly respect punctu-

Monte Carlo casino.

ality. The exception, of course, are the drivers. They tailgate and run red lights more consistently than any other nationality this side of Taiwan.

Naturally, the area, which has a number of inordinately wealthy inhabitants, has attracted more than its share of human sharks. Some are selling a load of questionable investment opportunities. Watch out. The sun has got to a lot of them, and the casinos (in Monaco, Nice, La Napoule, Beaulieu and other famous hot spots) may be a better bet for doubling your money than some of their risky ploys.

Build a house, for example, and you might find that many of the contractors go bankrupt during the construction phase and leave you holding the plans. Watch out for scams in the antique markets (the best and most reliable is on the Cours Saleya in Nice) and on the roads, where stolen goods, especially rugs, are sold for a pittance. Legal or illegal, smart or stupid, cash is preferred for most services, to avoid the value-added tax (TVA) and income declarations. In fact, it is rare to find the tradesman who prefers a cheque.

Even the beaches and sea aren't always what a lot of people expect. The beaches in Nice are covered with large flat rocks rather than sand, and some doctors advise against swimming in the sea despite the renowned new sewage disposal system. Nor is the weather all it is cracked up to be. It is extremely frivolous and can often be overcast, or pour, for days at a time. The mistral is a vicious wind, and snow has made seaside skiing possible for two out of three winters during recent years.

Indeed, some days the Riviera looks a bit worn and, like the rest of us, it is aging. In fact, you might even say it is over 100 years old. The name "Côte d'Azur" (somehow translated into "French Riviera") was coined by French poet Stephen Liegeard a century ago, and during the summer of 1988 the local authorities (headed by Jacques Médecin, mayor of Nice for almost 25 years until he fled to South America following corruption and embezzle-

Hanglider above Monaco.

ment charges) tried to create something special for visitors to the south. They acknowledged the "100th Year of the French Riviera" with a number of special events – and omnipresent flags, shirts, bumper stickers and billboards.

Take the best with the worst and, once you wind up, there is something for everybody on the Riviera.

The big olive: The geographical focal point of the summer frenzy is **Nice**. The city attracts a healthy share of the region's eight million annual visitors, is the area's administrative capital and is occasionally alluded to as "The Big Olive." Most visitors do not come to the Riviera just to see Nice, but few of them leave without having included it in their itineraries.

Nice is not nearly as chic as neighbouring Monaco, nor as quaint as perched villages like **Eze** (a delightful spot with no cars and intimate touches like the fact that your luggage is taken up to the hotel on the back of a mule). Nor is Nice as celebrity-filled as St-Tropez. But it is the Riviera's largest city (almost half of the area's one million people live in and around it) and in the midst of a noticeable transformation to increase its amenability.

Founded by the Greeks, Nice was first embraced by English lords and Russian aristocrats as a winter resort. The boom in bathing and summer tourism didn't begin until the 1920s. Today, it blends a traditional Mediterranean-mellow lifestyle with a big push towards conventions (it is France's second largest convention city after Paris) and high-tech business (income from which now rivals the Riviera's annual revenue from tourism).

The state-of-the-art Acropolis convention centre and the $200-million Arenas business complex, opposite the airport that was itself built on reclaimed land and is now the second busiest in France, have forced inhabitants to readjust their priorities. The result: improved services, more hotels and restaurants, and an increasing number of off-beat and inviting activities.

Like most French towns, Nice has also created downtown pedestrian zones. Many of the mod shops and fast-food outlets are on the chic cobble-stoned Rue de France, but the best way to discover the city is simply to get lost in the maze of narrow cool streets in the colourful **old city**, "le Vieux Nice," with its *trompe l'oeil* paintings, hole-in-the-wall boutiques selling perfume and carnival masks, and wealth of moderately priced restaurants featuring local specialities.

The **Cours Saleya**, filled with antique stalls and flower markets, is the centre of action in Old Nice. Locally grown flowers, olives, vegetables and herbs are sold, and early risers can hit the fish market on Place St-François.

Feeling hungry? Ilene Médecin, the American-born wife of the disgraced mayor, says the *trucha omelette*, made from pine nuts and a spinach-like vegetable called *blettes*, is out of this world at Le Safari on the Cours Saleya. But *trucha* is just a starter. *Socca* (a traditional Niçoise chick-pea pancake cooked in an enormous round dish), pizza, *salade Niçoise* and other garlic-

Quiet beach in Menton.

scented fare can also help fill up a dull afternoon and empty stomach.

Good, moderately priced restaurants featuring local fare include Acchirado (39 Rue Droite), Nissa-Socca (5 Rue Ste-Reparate), Le Demode (18 Rue Benoit-Bunico) and La Taverne (3 Rue St-François). For a more Michelin-starred cuisine go to Chantecler in the Hotel Negresco (37 Promenade des Anglais), where chef Jacques Maximin makes tantalising dishes using local ingredients, herbs and spices.

The only way to stay cool after dinner is at "in" discothèques like the usually private La Camargue (Cours Saleya), Chez les Ecossais (6 Rue Halévy) or L'Aventure (12 Rue Chauvain), all of which open around 11 p.m. Disco-goers usually leave at 4 a.m. and head to the beach for a pre-dawn dip, an act that reminds visitors to France that they are in Nice – not Paris.

The sun sets late during Niçois summer nights, and the promenade provides romantic views, despite occasional interruptions from landing aircraft.

Typical housing in Monaco.

Princes and tennis stars: Cannes and Monaco are Nice's biggest rivals and are somewhat similar to one another. If Nice is generally regarded as tough and feisty (which is an exaggeration), Monaco and Cannes are considered chic and chi-chi (in fact, another exaggeration).

Monaco, Europe's second smallest independent country after the Vatican – its 460 acres (186 hectares) make it smaller than New York's Central Park – has an idyllic perched-on-the-Mediterranean setting that makes it an unofficial part of the Riviera. But Monegasques go out of their way to stress their independence.

The Principality is often considered a hotbed of gossip, intrigue and royal shenanigans. But don't go to Monaco expecting theatrics – even though columnists certainly spare no ink regaling readers with tales of high-spending gamblers breaking the bank at the casino (almost never), beautiful princesses dancing into the night (rare), the rich and not-always-famous frolicking on and in the Mediterranean (occasion-

ally) and small apartments selling for big millions (almost always).

Contemporary Monaco is both a more sedate-than-scandalous playground in the sun and a serious business community. The streets can be safely walked at midnight (wearing real jewellery makes a part of the myth that is Monaco reality), the omnipresent police force is more helpful than intimidating, the public services are exceptional and even the discothèques (like The Living Room or Jimmy'z) are rarely raucous. There is a definite lack of violence, screeching police cars and dens of iniquity.

Monaco is still ruled by Prince Rainier, whose family, the Grimaldis, have been running Monaco since 1297, when François Grimaldi snuck in disguised as a Franciscan monk. Rainier gets through the year on a $7 million budget and shows little sign of wishing to relinquish power to his son, Prince Albert, who is the Riviera's most sought-after bachelor.

Meanwhile, since her mother's tragic death in an automobile accident in 1982, a maturing Princess Caroline, now mother of three, has assumed the role of being Monaco's most important cultural and social force. As head of a variety of organisations, like the Monte Carlo Ballet and the Princess Grace Foundation, she is often seen performing official functions about town.

Princess Grace, the former American actress Grace Kelly who married Rainier in 1956, is entombed in the cathedral located on "the Rock," as the hill dominating Monaco is called.

The complexion of Monte Carlo is changing. There are a dwindling number of ageing dowagers and wealthy Greek yacht owners (if you want to feel like Niarchos, who kept his yacht here, 200-ft/60-metre luxury vessels can be rented for $50,000 a day), but there is steady growth among members of the burgeoning financial community and there are still some star-studded foreign residents.

Monaco is worth a visit just to see the cool, cobble-stone streets on the Rock,

Waiting for the bus.

the luxurious suites in the Hermitage Hotel and Hotel de Paris, the basement aquarium at the majestic **Oceanographic Museum**, Charles Garnier's historic late 19th-century **casino** and Prince Rainier's pink-tinted **castle**, where there is a daily changing of the guard at 11.55am.

Sit on the terrace at the renovated Café de Paris in the Place de la Casino, rent a private *cabana* on the *plage* at the Monte Carlo Beach Hotel or drop in on the fascinating **Museum of Dolls and Automata**, with its miniature 18th- and 19th-century houses and collection of 400 dolls, and you might even want to make Monaco your own third or fourth residence.

Really want to live here? You'd be buying a veritable jewel on the Mediterranean. Twenty percent of Monaco is already built on reclaimed land, but even this unreal terrain constantly rises in value. A big penthouse (500 sq. metres) in Le Florestan sells for over $7.5 million. The many cranes in evidence are putting up new and luxurious apartment and business complexes like the "Monte Carlo Palace."

There are only 30,000 people in Monaco, of which an even smaller 5,000 are Monegasque citizens. Most of the working population arrive from France and Italy by car or train each day, but you can also get there by helicopter from Nice Airport. Among the new attractions is the **Princess Grace Rose Garden** in Fontvieille, the latest addition to the Principality built mostly on reclaimed land.

If you really want to partake of the myth that is Monaco, shop in the **Place du Casino** and on the **Avenue des Beaux Arts**, only 500 ft (150 metres) long, at Cartier, Bulgari, Buccelati, Ribolzi and other extravagant boutiques. Nabil Boustany, the Lebanese entrepreneur who has completely rebuilt the Metropole Hotel, also has a number of glittering boutiques in the adjoining marble-floored, chandelier-laden commercial gallery.

Want to blow a fortune before you go to the casino? The Louis XV Restaurant on the ground floor at the Hotel de Paris, which chef Alain Ducasse has wondrously transformed into the Riviera's culinary hotspot since it opened in May 1987, is actually worth its weight in gold (or French francs, which is what the Monegasque use for currency).

Other good places to be seen dining are the Roger Vergé Café in the Winter Sporting Club's shopping arcade (Vergé owns the three-star Moulin de Mougins) or at Rampoldi's (very "in"), Le Saint Benoit (good fish and a view of the palace), La Coupole (where Yves Garnier is probably the second-best chef in town), and the Grill Room on top of the Hotel de Paris.

More than 250,000 visitors flock to Monaco each year, and hundreds of day-trippers arrive in tour buses to look at the sights. The heavily touristed Monaco of today is more likely to include attendees at an insurance conference than gigolos and high rollers heading for the casino tables.

The chi-chi: Cannes, which got its name from the canes and reeds in surrounding marshes that no longer exist,

Facades of Villefranche.

is "twinned" with Beverly Hills and often puts on some of the same airs. But it is, in fact, a small manageable town with a nice shopping street (**Rue d'Antibes**) lined with both internationally known and locally based boutiques, a pleasant beachfront (**La Croisette**), a pretty **carousel** behind the municipal casino, and mythically named hotels like the Carlton and the Majestic.

Every visitor to Cannes should take a walk along the **old port**, mingle on the shopping streets in the **old town** (there is a calming view from the dominating citadel and an interesting selection of archaeological artifacts in the **Castre Museum**) and get in some beach time. During the high season you may want to head for the water early because by mid-morning the sea will already be spilling over with bathers. And, of course, finding a parking spot on those days becomes an all-day event.

Summer is not the only time to be wary of in Cannes. The town also tends to become obnoxiously overcrowded during the Film Festival in May. The latest attempt to control traffic by changing the one-way streets has done little to eliminate congestion.

The two best restaurants in Cannes are the Royal Gray, featuring *nouvelle cuisine* from a chef trained by Michel Guerard, and La Palma d'Or at the Martinez Hotel, where you can eat on the terrace on the first floor – and get above the traffic.

Chic getaways: Go outside these three "metropolitan" areas and you, like everyone else, will soon discover your own favourite town on the Riviera. Each little village, usually with cool squares and fountains, has distinctive characteristics and idiosyncracies that either attract or repel visitors.

Most of the towns on the Riviera have pleasant pedestrian zones, medieval architecture and exceptional views. Again, all this seems irrelevant when you can't find a parking place in the middle of summer. But during the winter they are, must one say it, quaint.

St-Tropez (generally referred to simply as St-Trop) still features the most

Beach vendor in St-Tropez.

celebrities *per capita* of any spot on the Riviera. Its 6,000 permanent residents (many of whom rely on tourism for a considerable portion of their income) take the summer fashion show in their stride and understandingly tolerate the gatherings at the Senequier Restaurant along the port and dancing until dawn at the Caves du Roy. Yes, Brigitte Bardot might have closed her fashion boutique, but she still protects her animals in her villa, La Madraque.

Ask the residents for the best restaurants, and they'll mention Le Chabichou (expensive) or Auberge des Maures, L'Escale and La Fregate. Culture in St-Tropez? There is the **Maritime Museum**, with everything you might want to know about Mediterranean shipping, and the "Annonciade" in the 16th-century **chapel**, along with a collection of modern French masters.

But St-Trop in the summer, when the population is about 100,000, is the Riviera at its worst. Beaches (with names like Tahiti Beach, Tropezin and Tabou) are polluted with bronzing bodies, and even the sea, the majestic Med, reeks of suntan oil.

Matisse would probably no longer title his painting of St-Tropez *Luxe, Calme et Volupté*, though he would presumably be pleased that there is still not a major highway or rail service into the town. If in St-Trop, the best time of day is dawn near the port or by the colourful markets in the **Place aux Herbes**. To get away, take a stroll in the nearby pine forests or the vineyards on the adjacent peninsula.

Another chic "getaway" (meaning place to be seen) spot is **Port Grimaud**, a modern city built to resemble a contemporary Venice that serves as a second home for the likes of actress Joan Collins. It was designed in 1966 and depicts the type of Venice that Walt Disney might have created. At least, however, there is no entrance charge.

Antibes (the name means "the city opposite," referring to its proximity to Nice), is more authentic and somewhat distant from the hustle-bustle. It has seafront **ramparts**, an old **fort**, (*see*

Sophia Antipolis.

INSIDE THE CANNES FILM FESTIVAL

The Cannes Film Festival ranks with the truffle as France's most misunderstood export item. Just as that fetid tuber, rooted out by swine, is erroneously viewed as an aphrodisiac, so too the Cannes Film Festival is falsely perceived as a leading event in the cultural life of the seventh art.

In fact, it is a gruelling two-week gathering each May of celluloid salesmen and a marathon homage to bad taste and conspicuous consumption that resembles nothing so much as the Loyal Fraternity of Water Buffalo assemblies once attended by Fred Flintstone and Barney Rubble.

If you're lucky, you've come to Cannes during one of the other 11 months. Consult your calendar. If you have erred, take the next train out to Nice. Should you choose to stay, there are a few things you should know. May weather in Cannes is cool and capricious. But the world's film industry doesn't throng to the city to catch rays and surf. Perhaps *you* do not tire of topless beaches and *bouillabaisse*, but those Riviera specialities retain little charm for the motion picture executives who have been coming to the festival year-in, year-out since it began in 1947.

One look at the row of tacky billboards that will disfigure the Croisette, Cannes's palm-lined main street, for the next fortnight should make things clear: for visiting movie moguls, Cannes is above all else a convention centre, complete with its very own casino, seasonal commerce and attendant sleaze.

Nonetheless, Cannes is a convention centre with a difference. Hoteliers will remind you that you are in the official "sister city" of Beverly Hills – usually when you mention the exorbitant price of rooms. However, it also goes a long way toward explaining life in Cannes. As in that pricey L.A. suburb, snootiness and exclusivity come a-tumblin' down when a paying customer comes to town. Where else could the likes of Pia Zadora hold a group of adults in thrall?

Thus Cannes, the jewel of the Riviera, plays fickle host year round to trade events in the advertising, television and recorded music industries. To the executives who attend them, these acronym happenings (with names like MIPTV, MIDEM and SPONCOM) spell an extended opportunity to cut deals and take advantage of the swollen expense accounts that have helped make show business legendary for its vulgarity.

But none of these events manage to excel the *Festival international de film* – as your haughty hotelier will undoubtedly call it – in the sway it holds over the popular imagination. Nor can they touch its sales volume, conservatively estimated at $3 billion each year.

And still it remains misunderstood, this most famous festival. When it comes down to it, the uninitiated have only an inkling as to the real reason why over 12,500 film producers, directors, distributors and actors, over 3,000 journalists and no less than 2,500 hangers-on are attracted to the French Riviera every year for two weeks.

Common fallacies attribute these attendance figures to the allure of celebrities or the opportunity for participants to appear important for those few brief days. But these explanations leave many questions unanswered. All those ruthless women and cynical men with name tags, the mountains of printed hokum, the watts and volts squandered in an effort to keep Pia Zadora and her ilk illuminated during their press conferences – what does it all mean? Why doesn't the whole place just turn into a pillar of salt?

The answer is held in the palm of the invisible hand of capitalism.

Sure, there are movies here, hundreds of them – without question, the widest selection available anywhere in the world at any one time. (Yet it is possible – indeed, not uncommon – for a film executive to serve the industry's obligatory two-week May sentence here and not see a single one in its entirety.) Sure, there's the prestigious Golden Palm competition, the countless retrospectives and the priceless photo opportunities. Even the world's press is out in force – more often than not at the Press Bar, wrestling with their daily deadline for copy.

But all the cloying puffs about "art" and "culture" that billow around Cannes for two weeks, like so much smoke from a clove cigarette, don't emanate from the real fire at the festival. That inferno is located in the belly of the beast known by regulars here as "The Bunker" – that is, at the film market or *marché du film*, located in the basement of that unsightly concrete convention centre that dominates the coastal landscape of this little harbour town.

For the film market is, ultimately, the force that drives the motion picture industry and the real reason that everyone who's anyone in show business is present in May. Indeed, sellers and would-be sellers of motion pictures from countries the world over come here to hawk their wares like so many carpet merchants at a Turkish bazaar.

But how can you tell the players from the fans in the basement, what with everybody smiling incessantly? Lucky for you, the name tags will be colour-coded. Don't worry about recognising any faces – none of the real celebrities would be caught dead down here in the basement. The stars only give press conferences and an occasional photo session on the beach. And the big-fish producers do business over cocktails at the Carlton, Martinez or Majestic. (Go, *have* a drink or two for $10 a pop at one of these elegant *Belle Epoque* hotels, and appreciate too just how much an expense account separates the men from the boys in filmdom.)

No, down in the basement what you'll find are the official representatives of national film industries taking savage bites out of their countries' GNPs, faceless salesmen from assembly-line celluloid factories the world over and mustachioed peddlers who keep their collection of film reels underneath their trench coats.

Pity the first-time Cannes festival-goer who makes the mistake of breaking his piggy bank to bring his "personal statement" film here in search of an appreciative audience.

We're talking about the small-potatoes producer. He's the one who went way over his small-potatoes budget, renting equipment and making prints of his film. He never got around to paying his technicians or actors. But he doesn't really care. He's finished his film, and now it's for sale and that's what matters. Maybe he takes out more advertising than he can afford in the daily trade papers here like *Screen International*, the festival's journal of record. Next there's the question

of whom to invite to the screenings. One problem is all those damn journalists trying to see movies for free. Of course, they, too, have their place in the film industry. But down in the basement, journalists are viewed less as paying customers than simple freeloaders. To enhance their discredit, they're likely to be staying at flea-bag flophouses far from the Croisette. Producers never shake the journalist's hand at the market if they can avoid it.

The hand they seek is that of the distributor, typically the least interesting person from the point of view of conversation but the most important in terms of box-office receipts. The distributor's the one who puts the film into theatres, thereby enabling the public to pay to see it. (And if they pay enough, maybe, someday, the aforementioned technicians and actors will see some remuneration for all their efforts.)

The distributor plays for keeps: He or she is too busy brooding over *Screen International*'s list of yesterday's box-office figures even to crack a smile at the latest Pia Zadora story going around. This one silently emerges from the screening room and shakes his or her head – or sits down to sign a contract with the producer. If the latter, the producer may join the hard-working journalists at the Press Bar and apologise profusely for not shaking their hands earlier.

Now, you, like our neophyte producer friend, know where it's at in Cannes at this, the mad, lecherous, granddaddy of all film festivals. And, also like our novice, you shouldn't go away disappointed, now that you've frittered away the last of your piggy-bank savings in this overpriced seaside resort.

If you came to rub shoulders with the stars, don't let a line of truncheon-wielding *gendarmes* stand between you and Miss Zadora. If the flicks are your game, don't be put off by the fact that all accreditation for the festival is arranged out of Paris six months in advance. After all, you're in Cannes, the closest thing in Europe to Sunset and Vine. And anything is possible in the cinema.

Above all, remember: it's never too late. In the month of May, there are at least a dozen daily trains that can get you out of here and safely to Nice in an hour.

page 274) tree-lined avenues and a splendid cobble-stoned **old town** with a seductive array of markets.

Picasso lived here, in the **Château Grimaldi**, for six months in the 1940s, and the château now houses his famous *Joie de Vivre* (the term that many people use to define the allure of the Riviera). Another famous visitor to Antibes was Napoleon, who was imprisoned in Fort Carré.

The nearby **Cap d'Antibes** features the jet-setters' favourite, Hotel de Cap, and Bacon, a great fish restaurant. **La Garoupe**, the beach on the Cap d'Antibes that Gerald and Sarah Murphy used to rake clean every morning, is still *the* place to enjoy the sun. **Juan-les-Pins**, like Nice, has an annual jazz festival and dozens of discothèques, but it is too congested nowadays to be considered similar to the fashionable resort it was in the 1920s when the "Lost Generation" of Americans flocked here.

Other towns are much less congested and worth dropping into during a drive along the Med. **Villefranche** has a sur-prising fishing village charm, Henry Crews's château is still a site to see in **La Napoule**, **Cap Ferrat** has its charming port of St-Jean and **Beaulieu** is still the closest thing to the *Belle Epoque*. Here there are, at dusk, intimations of Somerset Maugham. Inhabitants often refer to the part of the coast between Nice and Monaco as "little Africa" in reference to its bougainvillea, palm trees and other vegetation.

Menton holds an annual lemon festival when floats parade through the town, but its waterside Promenade du Soleil and 17th-century fort containing the **Jean Cocteau Museum** are away from the glamour.

To avoid the crowds, head for an island, like the **Iles de Lerins** off Cannes. Frequent boats go to **Ste-Marguerite**, the larger island where stands the fortress of "Man in the Iron Mask" fame, and to the smaller **St-Honorat**, with a guest-accommodating Cistercian monastery. Many visitors, though, prefer the islands off **Hyères**, which boast a nudist colony.

Rivieran business executive.

Tomorrow's Riviera: Though the myth lives on, the Riviera is in the midst of a major transformation which will, one day, perhaps, put the fabled days of yore to rest once and for all.

The Riviera has become the frontier of new business. As already noted, income from science, service industries and light industry now rivals the $2 billion annual revenue from tourism that has been the area's long-time economic mainstay.

During the 1970s and 1980s the flamboyant if ultimately corrupt mayor Jacques Médecin led a concerted effort towards diversification away from tourism and towards educational institutions, scientific ventures and light high-tech industry. They encouraged the construction of industrial zones, created the financial structure to attract large and small companies and gave a special boost to science and education.

Today, there is a pleasant blend of Mediterranean climate and lifestyle with state-of-the-art technology, enlightened business attitudes and a well-established communication, educational and scientific infrastructure. Even Cannes is setting aside some land for high-tech industries.

Want to go to school here? It's almost free if you're French and much less than an American university if you're not. The University of Nice, with a student body of 20,000, sets the pace for higher education (about 10 percent of the students are foreign), and numerous graduate schools – such as the renowned Ecole des Mines – round out the educational opportunities on the Riviera.

There is also competition between the different cities, towns, technology parks and industrial sites to attract tourism and new industry. Municipal and local agencies will sell you on the investment potential of the Riviera for your company – though they admit that there are not the government subsidies you will find in Ireland or other parts of France. The "quality of life," rather than financial incentives, are the main selling points.

Besides business in general, business

Promenade des Anglais in Nice.

tourism is also budding, and companies flock to the Riviera for conferences and conventions. The **Acropolis** – the Nice arts and convention centre – actively competes with the **Palais de Festival** in Cannes, which hosts the Cannes Film Festival, for international conferences.

But even smaller communities – like Menton, Grasse, Beaulieu, Sophia Antipolis and Antibes – have their own conference facilities, and visitors are accommodated in numerous hotels (there are 1,680 hotels on the Riviera) of varying price. For these and other reasons, American and British firms, scattered in different towns along the Mediterranean, contend that there is little strain adapting to the environment.

Merrill Lynch and Citicorp are located in Monaco, and the Coopers and Lybrand accountancy firm is represented by an associated firm in Nice. NCR, Rank Xerox and other high-tech leaders have sales offices in the region, while the UNISYS International Management Centre is in St-Paul-de-Vence.

Monaco, due to its relaxed tax laws, is the centre of most financial activity, while **Sophia Antipolis** is already home to numerous international advanced technology companies, service and engineering firms, educational and training centres, research laboratories and light production facilities.

There are about 10,000 people living and working within Sophia Antipolis (combining the Greek word for wisdom and the name of the nearby city of Antibes), in around 500 companies, and this figure has been steadily increasing. Sophia Antipolis has generated service industries, including travel agencies, public relations companies, banks, conference centres and a 35-court tennis club.

Mediterranean salad: The new Riviera could, in fact, turn out to be better than the old. One positive aspect is the mix of professionals who are making the place a permanent home. There is an engaging blend of French and international business people (Merrill Lynch in Monaco has 27 employees representing 12 different nationalities) in a wide variety of industries ranging from perfume (which still accounts for over 25 percent of all exports from the Riviera) to fashion (among which are Chacok and Jitrois) to multinationals like Air France, IBM, Digital Equipment Corp., Texas Instruments, Wellcome and numerous others.

In addition, the Riviera's service sector, employing two-thirds of the population, has kept up with the economic growth. This transformation is beginning to wipe out the "resort" feel of the region – except during the summer. For example, the area has a banking network employing almost 6,000 people at over 440 branches.

Want to settle here? If you've got venture capital, there are a number of worthwhile young start-up companies on the look-out for funding. Entrepreneurs flock to southern France because of the large affluent market, its talented labour pool and available financing.

There's no question that the Riviera will keep moving in a business-oriented direction. And what this does to the myth remains to be seen.

Left, chic visitor. **Right**, Givenchy shop window in Monaco.

277

A SHORT HISTORY OF THE BIKINI

"For the first time in history, the entire staff of the European edition and the foreign service of the *New York Herald Tribune* now in Paris insisted yesterday on covering the same assignment. Each was so determined to do that job that, for the sake of organisational morale, they were all assigned to the story. It turned out to be an exhibition of the world's smallest bathing suit, modeled at the Piscine Molitor."

– *Paris Herald Tribune*, 1946.

When the first two-piece bathing suit was unveiled in Paris on 5 July 1946, it had such an impact that its designer, Louis Réard, named it "bikini" after a recent atomic explosion in the Pacific Ocean. Its arrival launched the beginning of a new era in bathing attire and a new attitude towards women's bodies. Today, it seems amazing that such a small amount of fabric could be interpreted in so many different ways and at the centre of so much controversy.

In the late 19th century, bathing suits came in two pieces, but they were very different. Composed of a long tunic and knickers – generally of wool or serge – their integral purpose was to cover up the body. In fact, for a long time, bathing suits were designed for beachwear rather than for swimming.

It was only at the turn of the century that one-piece garments appeared. The first rib-knit, elasticised, one-piece bathing suit was made in the United States in 1920 by the Jantzen Company. This change of attitude from prudishness to practicality can be attributed largely to swimmer Annette Kellerman, who joined many competitions against men in swimming events held in the River Thames in London, the Seine in Paris and in the English Channel.

In 1924, designer Jean Patou added a fashionable touch by introducing bathing suits bearing Cubist-inspired designs. And, of course, the ubiquitous Coco Chanel was also instrumental in the bathing suit revolution. During her much publicised affair with the Duke of Westminster, she was one of the first women to sport a tan, acquired during long vacations in Spain and on the Riviera, where she wore the most up-to-date swimsuits and beachwear.

But, of the many designers who contributed to promoting the bikini over the years, Jacques Heim was the most innovative. Having opened a chain of boutiques selling sportswear as early as 1946, he popularised the use of cotton for beachwear when he used the fabric in his couture collections.

With the end of World War II, beaches on both sides of the Atlantic reopened and seaside vacation became once again possible. But, although dressier swimsuits in brighter colours were emerging, as well as backless models in the new lightweight fabrics, the attitude towards baring one's skin was still prudish. Peggy Guggenheim told of being fined on a Spanish beach where she was vacationing with painter Max Ernst in the early 1940s. The local *carabinieri*, having gone to the trouble of measuring her back *decolleté*, deemed it indecent.

American *Vogue* began giving advice on how to choose a good suit: "Don't spoil the looks of your perfect dive with a fluggy-ruffles, cutie-pie suit…don't go in for violent water sports in a suit with trick fastening…take off your girdle before you try it on for it's likely to give you delusions of grandeur about your figure…don't overdo the little girl angle when you are chronologically or anatomically unsuited …don't stop at one bathing suit…"

But it was really only in the 1950s that the attitude towards the bathing suit started to

Early ad for Jantzen one-pieces.

Ladies Worsted Bathing Suits
Special Designs and Colors Made to Order

SWIMMING is rapidly becoming a national sport and we have never been able to supply the demand for these bathing suits

ease. Even though Esther Williams and her nautical extravaganzas did a great deal for the glamour of sophisticated swimming attire, it was not until Brigitte Bardot came on the scene that bikinis found their role model.

Right from the start, the French Riviera was the focal point of the bikini's development, particularly in St-Tropez. In 1956, Bardot was photographed there wearing a gingham bikini decorated with frills. Instantly, gingham became the rage.

During the 1960s, swimwear was designed to emphasise the body with underwiring for the bosom. "The new way for a bikini," said British *Vogue* in 1963, "is little-boy shorts and a built-up bra." But, by the end of the decade, when smaller busts became the look, the costumes were more severely cut.

And bikinis were designed at their scantiest: "the minimum two-piece for a perfect tan, leaving the least possible marks from sunbathing" (French *Vogue*, 1969). The arrival of nylon also was important: "The quick-change *maillot* – when it's dried in the sun it's a sinuous velvety black, and when it's soaked with water it glistens like a seal on the rocks. In the miracle fibre Vyrene." (British *Vogue*, 1965).

Brigitte Bardot.

In keeping with the hit song "She wore an itsy-bitsy, teeny-weeny, yellow, polka-dotted bikini," two-piece suits inched their way to nothingness. By the mid-1970s the more daring sunbathers had even begun to remove their tops. The arrival of the monokini (just a bottom) was inevitable.

While going topless is still taboo in many countries, it is accepted easily in most of Western Europe, especially on the French Riviera. However, the one-piece is finding new interest. Take it from Felix Palmari, the knowledgeable owner of the Tahiti beach club, one of the oldest "private" beaches on the "Route des Plages." When Felix opened his concession on the 6-mile (10-km) stretch of pure white sand, he was alone. Today, it is staked out with sprawled bodies in every stage of undress and dozens of exotically named concessions renting parasols and mattresses.

"We've seen it all," says Felix, who remembers how beautifully deserted the beach was when he arrived here 40 years ago. "Fashions move, but I think that women today are less into showing off their nudity. They take off their tops in order to tan, but there is a definite comeback of the one-piece bathing suit."

FOR THOSE
WITH MORE THAN
A PASSING INTEREST
IN TIME...

Before you put your name down for a Patek Philippe watch *fig. 1,* there are a few basic things you might like to know, without knowing exactly whom to ask. In addressing such issues as accuracy, reliability and value for money, we would like to demonstrate why the watch we will make for you will be quite unlike any other watch currently produced.

"Punctuality", Louis XVIII was fond of saying, "is the politeness of kings."

We believe that in the matter of punctuality, we can rise to the occasion by making you a mechanical timepiece that will keep its rendezvous with the Gregorian calendar at the end of every century, omitting the leap-years in 2100, 2200 and 2300 and recording them in 2000 and 2400 *fig. 2.* Nevertheless, such a watch does need the occasional adjustment. Every 3333 years and 122 days you should remember to set it forward one day to the true time of the celestial clock. We suspect, however, that you are simply content to observe the politeness of kings. Be assured, therefore, that when you order your watch, we will be exploring for you the physical—if not the metaphysical—limits of precision.

Does everything have to depend on how much?

Consider, if you will, the motives of collectors who set record prices at auction to acquire a Patek Philippe. They may be paying for rarity, for looks or for micromechanical ingenuity. But we believe that behind each $500,000-plus

bid is the conviction that a Patek Philippe, even if 50 years old or older, can be expected to work perfectly for future generations.

In case your ambitions to own a Patek Philippe are somewhat discouraged by the scale of the sacrifice involved, may we hasten to point out that the watch we will make for you today will certainly be a technical improvement on the Pateks bought at auction? In keeping with our tradition of inventing new mechanical solutions for greater reliability and better time-keeping, we will bring to your watch innovations *fig. 3* inconceivable to our watchmakers who created the supreme wristwatches of 50 years ago *fig. 4.* At the same time, we will of course do our utmost to avoid placing undue strain on your financial resources.

Can it really be mine?

May we turn your thoughts to the day you take delivery of your watch? Sealed within its case is your watchmaker's tribute to the mysterious process of time. He has decorated each wheel with a chamfer carved into its hub and polished into a shining circle. Delicate ribbing flows over the plates and bridges of gold and rare alloys. Millimetric surfaces are bevelled and burnished to exactitudes measured in microns. Rubies are transformed into jewels that triumph over friction. And after many months—or even years—of work, your watchmaker stamps a small badge into the mainbridge of your watch. The Geneva Seal—the highest possible attestation of fine watchmaking *fig. 5.*

Looks that speak of inner grace *fig. 6.*

When you order your watch, you will no doubt like its outward appearance to reflect the harmony and elegance of the movement within. You may therefore find it helpful to know that we are uniquely able to cater for any special decorative needs you might like to express. For example, our engravers will delight in conjuring a subtle play of light and shadow on the gold case-back of one of our rare pocket-watches *fig. 7.* If you bring us your favourite picture, our enamellers will reproduce it in a brilliant miniature of hair-breadth detail *fig. 8.* The perfect execution of a double hobnail pattern on the bezel of a wristwatch is the pride of our casemakers and the satisfaction of our designers, while our chainsmiths will weave for you a rich brocade in gold *figs. 9 & 10.* May we also recommend the artistry of our goldsmiths and the experience of our lapidaries in the selection and setting of the finest gemstones? *figs. 11 & 12.*

How to enjoy your watch before you own it.

As you will appreciate, the very nature of our watches imposes a limit on the number we can make available. (The four Calibre 89 time-pieces we are now making will take up to nine years to complete). We cannot therefore promise instant gratification, but while you look forward to the day on which you take delivery of your Patek Philippe *fig. 13,* you will have the pleasure of reflecting that time is a universal and everlasting commodity, freely available to be enjoyed by all.

Should you require information on any particular Patek Philippe watch, or even on watchmaking in general, we would be delighted to reply to your letter of enquiry. And if you send us

fig. 1: The classic face of Patek Philippe.

fig. 4: Complicated wristwatches circa 1930 (left) and 1990. The golden age of watchmaking will always be with us.

fig. 2: One of the 33 complications of the Calibre 89 astronomical clock-watch is a satellite wheel that completes one revolution every 400 years.

fig. 5: The Geneva Seal is awarded only to watches which achieve the standards of horological purity laid down in the laws of Geneva. These rules define the supreme quality of watchmaking.

fig. 3: Recognized as the most advanced mechanical regulating device to date, Patek Philippe's Gyromax balance wheel demonstrates the equivalence of simplicity and precision.

fig. 6: Your pleasure in owning a Patek Philippe is the purpose of those who made it for you.

fig. 7: Arabesques come to life on a gold case-back.

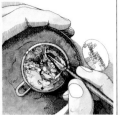

fig. 8: An artist working six hours a day takes about four months to complete a miniature in enamel on the case of a pocket-watch.

fig. 9: Harmony of design is executed in a work of simplicity and perfection in a lady's Calatrava wristwatch.

fig. 10: The chainsmith's hands impart strength and delicacy to a tracery of gold.

fig. 11: Circles in gold: symbols of perfection in the making.

fig. 12: The test of a master lapidary is his ability to express the splendour of precious gemstones.

PATEK PHILIPPE
GENEVE
fig. 13: The discreet sign of those who value their time.

your card marked "book catalogue" we shall post you a catalogue of our publications. Patek Philippe, 41 rüe du Rhône, 1204 Geneva, Switzerland, Tel. +41 22/310 03 66.

Reality check. Call home.

—— *AT&T USADirect® and World Connect®. The fast, easy way to call most anywhere.* ——

Take out AT&T Calling Card or your local calling card.** Lift phone. Dial AT&T Access Number for country you're calling from. Connect to English-speaking operator or voice prompt. Reach the States or over 200 countries. Talk. Say goodbye. Hang up. Resume vacation.

Austria⁺†††...	022-903-011	Luxembourg...	0-800-0111	Turkey*...	00-800-12277
Belgium*...	0-800-100-10	Netherlands*...	06-022-9111	United Kingdom...	0500-89-0011
Czech Republic*...	00-420-00101	Norway...	800-190-11		
Denmark...	8001-0010	Poland†◆¹...	0◊010-480-0111		
Finland...	9800-100-10	Portugal†...	05017-1-288		
France...	19-0011	Romania*...	01-800-4288		
Germany...	0130-0010	Russia*†(Moscow)...	155-5042		
Greece*...	00-800-1311	Slovak Rep.*...	00-420-00101		
Hungary*...	00◊-800-01111	Spain●...	900-99-00-11		
Ireland...	1-800-550-000	Sweden...	020-795-611		
Italy*...	172-1011	Switzerland*...	155-00-11		

AT&T
Your True Choice

**You can also call collect or use most U.S. local calling cards. Countries in bold face permit country-to-country calling in addition to calls to the U.S. World Connect® prices consist of USADirect® rates plus an additional charge based on the country you are calling. Collect calling available to the U.S. only. *Public phones require deposit of coin or phone card. † May not be available from every phone. †††Public phones require local coin payment during call. ◆ Not available from public phones. ◊ Await second dial tone. ¹Dial 010-480-0111 from major Warsaw hotels. ●Calling available to most European countries. ©1995 AT&T.

For a free wallet sized card of all AT&T Access Numbers, call: 1-800-241-5555.

Getting Acquainted

The Place

Language: French.
Religion: Roman Catholic.
Time zone: Central European Time (GMT plus one hour).
Currency: French franc (ff).
Weights and measures: Metric.
Electricity: 220–230 volts AC.
International dialing code: 00 33.

Provence is located in the southeastern corner of France. It is bordered to the west by the Rhône River, to the north by the Baronnies Range and the Hautes-Alpes, to the east by Italy and to the south by the Mediterranean Sea. It comprises five different *départements:* the Bouches-du-Rhône, the Vaucluse, the Alpes-de-Haute-Provence, the Var and the Alpes-Maritimes. The Bouches-du-Rhône contains an area frequently referred to as a region in its own, the Camargue.

The landscape is widely varied – from seaside cliffs and sandy beaches to dry wide plains and salt marshes to opulent Alpine reaches and jagged limestone mountains. Much of this land is sparsely populated with heavy concentrations of people in the major cities. For example, the Bouches-du-Rhône (the largest of the Provençal *départements* and third largest in all of France) possesses some 1,700,000 inhabitants – however, over a million of them live in Marseille alone.

Special Attractions

Provence not only attracts the rich and famous to its glamorous resorts such as St Tropez and Juan-les-Pins, it also draws many people to the unspoilt villages, particularly the perched villages of the hinterland, just a few miles up from the coast. Here there are many attractions too for the more hardy tourists, with miles of hiking and cycling trails and opportunities for all kinds of outdoor pursuits. The light and the colours of the region have been a magnet for artists as can be seen in the many museums and galleries displaying the works of Matisse, Picasso and several other famous names.

Climate

Provence is renowned for its sunshine. There are 300-plus sunny days a year and less than 800 mm each year of rain, but, when it rains, it pours. Average temperatures range from 45°F (7°C) in winter to 76°F (24°C) in summer. Winters are mild and sunny, and summers hot and dry with long days.

Climate will vary, of course, between the high country and low country. Nonetheless, all the region experiences the sporadic virulence of the legendary northwest wind, the mistral, during the late autumn to early spring.

The People

The Provençals may at first appear standoffish, but persevere and they will become the friendliest and most generous people you could hope to meet.

Never forget that the Provençals spent very many centuries as an independent nation and are fiercely proud of their rich heritage. They behave as any modern Western Europeans, but don't be surprised to find even the more cosmopolitan folk adhering to old superstitions and rites. You can't be expected to know them all, so just be polite, respectful, willing and friendly, and – unlike the Parisians – they'll forgive you any gaffes.

The Government

Provence is one of the 22 separate regions that make up France and comprises five of the country's 96 *départements*. Its capital is Marseille – France's largest seaport and second largest city, with a population of over 1 million.

France itself is a republic, led by a president elected popularly for a term of seven years, a prime minister who heads the government and its ministries, and a parliament (or government) composed of the National Assembly and the Senate. Provence, of course, sends representatives to the national parliament as well as having local bodies of its own. It has traditionally been a seat for communism although facets of the radical right also have a strong following.

Each *département* (roughly comparable to an English county) is divided into a number of disparately-sized communes whose district councils control a town, village or group of villages under the direction of the local mayor. Until recently, France was ruled largely by central government, but the Paris-appointed *préfets* lost much of their power under the socialists (1981–86) when the individual *départements* gained their own directly elected assemblies, giving them far more financial and administrative autonomy. Each *département* still has a *préfet*, but the role is now more advisory than executive; the *préfecture* is based in the principal town of each *département*. Communes are now responsible for most local planning and environmental matters; decisions relating to tourism and culture are mostly dealt with at regional level, while the state controls education, the health service and security.

French *départements* are identified by an individual number which is used as a convenient reference for administrative purposes, for example it forms the first two digits of the postcode in any address and the last two figures on vehicle licence plates. The *département* numbers follow a simple alphabetical order:

Alpes-de-Haute-Provence – 04.
Alpes-Maritimes – 06.
Bouches–du–Rhone – 13.
Var – 83.
Vaucluse – 84.

The Economy

For centuries, Provence's economy has been agriculturally based, producing a lion's share of the country's fruits, vegetables, herbs, olive oil, rice, sheep, etc. Many of these products are, in turn, used in such local industries as soapmaking. Provence also has vital interests in fishing and oil refineries. Over the last century, the economy has been overwhelmingly assisted by a growth in tourism. The Côte alone acquires about 10 billion ff annually from the millions of tourists who visit it each year.

Planning the Trip

What to Bring & Wear

What you will want to bring depends on your plans. No matter what, you will probably need good walking shoes or sneakers and, if you're coming during the warmer season, pack a bathing suit.

Even in the larger cities, modes of dress are more casual than you would find further north. For fine dining, however, you will want something respectable. Keep in mind that the hinterland of Provence is fairly conservative, though Aix-en-Provence, Avignon and Marseille are cosmopolitan. On the Côte d'Azur anything goes – as long as it is *à la mode*.

If you are going in the winter or early spring be sure to bring some warm clothes and windbreakers to protect you against the fierce mistral wind. Any Alpine or elevated destination will be chilly at night.

Maps

A first essential in touring any part of France is a good map. The Institute Géographique National is the French equivalent of the British Ordnance Survey and their maps are excellent; those covering the region are listed below:

Red Series (1:250,000, 1 cm to 2.5 km) sheet No. 115 covers the region at a good scale for touring.

Green Series (1:100,000, 1 inch to 4 miles or 1 cm to 1 km), are more detailed, local maps. Sheet Nos. 67 and 68 cover the coast and the south, 60 and 61 the north of the region. The Green Series are quite good for walking too, although serious walkers will need IGN's highly detailed 1:50,000 and 1:25,000 scales (**Blue Series**).

Another particularly good series for touring are the Telegraph (**Recta Foldex**) maps which cover France on four maps.

Michelin Regional maps are published at a scale of 1;200,000 (1 cm

to 2 km) both in the regional and local series.

Town plans are often given away free at local tourist offices, but if you wish to purchase them in advance, they are available from Michelin or Blay.

Stockists in London are Stanfords International Map Centre, 12–14 Long Acre, Covent Garden WC2, tel. 0171-836 1321; The Travel Bookshop, 13 Blenheim Crescent, London W11 2EE, tel: 0171-229 5260; Travellers' Bookshop, 25 Cecil Court, London WC2N 4EZ, tel: 0171-836 9132; and The European Bookshop, 5 Warwick Street, London W1, tel: 0171-734 5259.

World Leisure Marketing, PO Box 245, Derby DE23 7ZZ, tel: 01332 272020, are the UK agents for IGN and offer a mail order service. To order from IGN's Blue Series tel: 01629 826262.

Compass Books, 32 Bertie Ward Way, Rash's Green, Dereham, Norfolk NR19 1TE, tel: 01362 691623, offers a mail order service (7-day money-back guarantee) and carries a wide range of maps and guides for the whole of France. Alternatively, France House, Digbeth Street, Stow-on-the-Wold, Gloucester GL54 1BN, tel: 01451 870871; fax: 01451 830869 carries the most comprehensive stock of French publications in the UK.

In France, most good bookshops should have a range of maps, but they may cost less in hypermarkets or service stations. Motorway maps can often be picked up free of charge at rest areas.

Entry Regulations

All visitors to France require a valid passport and a visa (except nationals from EU countries, Andorra, Monaco and Switzerland. If in any doubt check with the French consulate in your country, as the situation may change from time to time. If you intend to stay in France for more than 90 days at any one time, then a *carte de séjour* must be obtained (again from the French consulate) – this also applies to EU members until restrictions are relaxed.

Animal Quarantine

The French are fanatical dog lovers, so don't be startled if you find pooches in

even some of the better restaurants. Likewise, many hotels accept pets for a slight additional cost.

Nonetheless, there are certain restrictions regarding bringing pets into the country. Animals under three months old are not allowed in at all. Owners are allowed to bring in a maximum of three pets (dogs and/or cats) of which only one can be a puppy. Each animal should be accompanied by a rabies vaccination certificate or an official statement that the animals are in good health and that they are coming from a country free from rabies for more than three years.

If for some reason you feel the need to bring in more than three pets, your request must be addressed to: **Ministère de l'Agriculture**, Direction de la Qualité, Bureau des Echanges Internationaux, 175 Rue du Chevaleret, 75646 Paris Cedex 13, tel: (1) 45.84.13.13.

Customs

There are few limitations on what can be brought into France. Any items destined for personal use (including bicycles) are admitted without formality provided the quantity or type of good does not indicate an intention to carry out a commercial transaction. Also, there are no particular customs formalities for small quantities of food products brought into France by tourists.

The following items are subject to special formalities: gold currency may be brought in only with special permission from the Banque de France. Other articles of gold (i.e. jewellery) should not exceed 500 grams in weight. Arms and ammunition can only be brought in only with an import authorisation issued by the customs headquarters, after approval by the appropriate ministry. For pets, see notes in the previous section.

The following items are strictly prohibited: narcotics, copyright infringements, fakes and counterfeits, and weapons and ammunition (unless an import authorisation is shown).

From 1 January 1993, custom barriers within Europe for alcoholic drinks and tobacco (bought and duty paid in France) practically ceased to exist, but for goods bought at duty-free shops on the ferry or aeroplane the old restrictions still apply. The current allowances are shown below (with on-board duty-free shop allowances in brackets). If you are in doubt, check with your local customs office (in the UK: HM Customs and Excise, Dorset House, Stamford Street, London SE1 9NG, tel: 0171 928 3344).

Customs allowances, for each person over 18 years of age:
10 litres (1 litre) of spirits or strong liqueurs, over 22 percent volume.
20 litres (2 litres) fortified wine.
90 litres (2 litres) wine (of which no more than 60 litres may be sparkling wine).
200 cigars (50) **or** 400 cigarillos (100) **or** 800 cigarettes (200).

Health

Don't be surprised if you return home from Provence *healthier* than when you left. Plenty of exercise, fresh food, stress-reducing wine and general calm are a way of life in Provence, and most visitors find themselves quickly adapting. Only those with high cholesterol should (as ever when in a French region) be wary, although the emphasis on fish and away from cream sauces helps that too.

On a technical level, the water is safe to drink, and fewer pesticides and preservatives are used on the vegetables and fruit than in many other countries. If you buy directly from the greengrocer, you will find indicated those foods that have been treated, and at a market you can ask. Nonetheless, always wash or peel them before eating.

The greatest peril that the newcomer to Provence faces – and it *is* a serious one – is over-exposure to the immensely powerful sun. A bad sunburn or sunstroke can ruin an entire trip, not to mention your skin and health permanently. Bring a sunblock of 15, even if you're going specifically to get a St-Tropez tan (the lotion will only prevent you from burning, not from tanning) and buy a big hat as soon as you arrive. Try to avoid major sightseeing outings on foot or bike at midday.

The International Association for Medical Assistance to Travelers (IAMAT) is a non profit-making organisation which anyone can join, free of charge (although donations are requested). Benefits include a membership card, entitling the bearer to services at fixed IAMAT rates by participating physicians, and a Traveller Clinical Record, a passport-sized record completed by the member's own doctor prior to travel.

EU nationals should check before leaving for France that they qualify for subsidised treatment under the EU (most British nationals do: check with the Department of Health and acquire from them the form E111). The E111 does not cover the full cost of any treatment so you may find it worthwhile to take out private insurance too.

Money

The Franc is divided into l00 centimes – a 5-centime piece being the smallest coin and the 500 ff note the highest denomination bill. Banks displaying the *Change* sign will change foreign currency and in general, at the best rates (you will need to produce your passport in any transaction). If possible avoid hotels or other independent bureaux which may charge a high commission.

Credit cards are widely accepted, but Visa is by far the most common and can now be used in petrol stations, hypermarkets and many supermarkets. Access (Mastercard/Eurocard) and American Express are also accepted in many establishments. Credit cards and cash cards from many European banks can also be used to obtain cash from cashpoints outside banks, using a PIN number.

Eurocheques, used in conjunction with a cheque card, drawn directly on your own bank account, can be used just like a cheque in the UK and are commonly accepted. Apply for these, or if you prefer, travellers' cheques, from your own bank, allowing a couple of weeks before your departure.

Public Holidays

It is common practice, if a public holiday falls on a Thursday or Tuesday, for French business to *faire le pont* (literally "bridge the gap") and have the Friday or Monday as a holiday too. Details of closures are normally posted outside banks etc. a few days before the event but it is easy to be caught out, especially on Assumption Day in August, which is not a holiday in the UK.

New Year's Day   1 January

Easter Monday (but not Good Friday)
Labour Day   Monday closest to
                  1 May
VE Day   8 May
Ascension Day
Whit Monday Pentecost
Bastille Day   14 July
Assumption Day   15 August
All Saints Day-   1 November
Toussaint
Armistice Day   11 November
Christmas Day   25 December
(but not Boxing Day, 26 December).

Provence is the land of fêtes. Check locally for events and stock up on petrol and provisions.

Getting There
By Air

It used to be that travelling to Provence meant time, and visitors either had to board a train, a yacht or a motor car (and sometimes all three) before arriving at their destination. Those days are long gone. Nice airport is now the busiest French airport after Paris, welcoming more than 4 million passengers a year.

Thirty regular airlines link Nice to 79 towns in 34 countries, with direct flights to and from New York, Los Angeles, Frankfurt, London (up to 24 a week) and Paris (up to 113 a week), not to mention Beirut, Abidjan and 73 other regional and international destinations. The national airline, Air France, is just one of many good places to check when looking for one of these direct flights.

If you plan to visit the eastern part of Provence rather than the Côte d'Azur or Alpes-Maritimes, you may want to fly into the Marseille-Provence airport. Although also international, this airport is slightly smaller than its Riviera cousin, and some passengers may need to arrange connecting flights through Paris. Truly small airports also exist in Nîmes, Toulon and Fréjus. Air Inter is the usual carrier to contact for any internal flights (book through Air France).

Travellers planning to connect with one of these smaller airports, fans of the picturesque and speedy train, those on a tight budget or those determined to visit the city of lights before heading to the region of light will want to fly into Paris first. Numerous airlines service both the Orly and Charles-de-Gaulle airports, and all are very close in price and service.

One of the best airlines offering flights to Paris, at least for travellers from the United States, is Continental Airlines. Scheduled flights between New York and Paris leave daily. They are no more or no less comfortable than any of the other American airlines, but Continental's prices are very competitive with those of its peers.

By Sea

There are several ferry services operating from the UK, the Republic of Ireland and the Channel Islands to the northern ports of France. All of them carry cars as well as foot passengers. Hovercraft crossings are fast, but more dependent on good weather than the ferries. The new Seacat catamaran service offers the quickest crossing but, like the hovercraft, can only carry a limited number of cars. The ports of Boulogne, Calais and Le Havre offer direct access by motorway to Paris; there is almost direct motorway access also via Dunkerque and Caen.

Brittany Ferries sails from Portsmouth to Saint-Malo and Caen, Plymouth to Roscoff, Cork (Eire) to St Malo and Roscoff, and a cheaper Les Routiers service from Poole to Cherbourg (summer only). Details from Wharf Road, Portsmouth PO2 8RU, tel: 01705 82770I; or from Millbay Docks, Plymouth PLI 3EW, tel: 01752 22I32I.

Hoverspeed operates hovercraft from Dover to Calais and Boulogne (crossing time approximately 30 minutes). The Seacat catamaran runs between Boulogne and Folkestone. Details of all services from Hoverspeed Ltd, Marine Parade, Dover CT17 9TG, tel: 01304 240241.

North Sea Ferries connect travellers from the north of England and Scotland to France, via their Hull-Zeebrugge route. Situated 56 km (35 miles) from the French border, Zeebrugge gives good motorway access to Paris region. The overnight services offer entertainment and a five-course dinner and breakfast are included in the fare. Contact the company at King George Dock, Hedon Road, Hull HU9 5QA, tel: 01482 795141.

P & O European Ferries operate the short sea routes from Dover to Calais, as well as Portsmouth to Le Havre and Cherbourg. Fares and schedules from P&O, Channel House, Channel View Road, Dover CT16 3BR, tel: 01304 203388.

Sally Line ferries use the smaller ports of Ramsgate and Dunkerque. Details from 81 Piccadilly, London W1V 9HF, tel: 0171-409 2240; for reservations: Argyle Centre, York Street, Ramsgate, Kent CT11 9DS, tel: 01843 595522.

Sealink Stena Line ferries operate from Dover to Calais (the fastest shipping route at 90 minutes), Southampton to Cherbourg, and Newhaven to Dieppe. Details and reservations for all services are available from Charter House, PO Box 121, Park Street, Ashford, Kent TN24 8EX, tel: 01233 647047.

Irish Ferries offer a service from Rosslare to Le Havre and Cherbourg, with ferries leaving daily from 1 April to mid-September to one of the two ports. It currently runs a service once weekly from Cork to Le Havre and Cherbourg from June–August. Contact them at 2–4 Merrion Row, Dublin 2, tel: 661-511.

True romantics may want to sail into Provence, and there is no better way than on a yacht. There are no formalities for arrivals at a sea port, but be sure to have the registration certificate of your craft on board. Once there, you will find no shortage of mooring space along the coast, with 126 yachting ports and 20,416 berths in all. Nonetheless, in high season, if you have your heart set on a spot along the Croisette, you should reserve ahead.

For further information and a complete list of places from where to rent a yacht, contact:

Syndicat National des Loueurs de Bâteaux de Plaisance, Port de la Bourdonnais, 75007 Paris, tel: (1) 45.55.10.49; telex: 203963 F.

Those without a little sloop of their own and no wish to lease one should check with one of the larger cruise lines. Ports of call for cruise ships and shipping companies include Marseille, Toulon, Nice, Cannes, Villefranche and St-Tropez.

By Rail

The Société Nationale des Chemins de Fer (SNCF), with its ultra-modern trains, offers without question one of the nicest ways to go anywhere in France. The trip down into Provence is particularly pleasurable. From your comfortable window seat, you will get a chance to experience the incredible change in light and landscape as your train plunges into the south.

Your trip will also be incredibly fast – possibly almost as fast as flying if you count getting to and from the airport, waiting for your bags, etc. SNCF is the proud parent of the fastest train in the western world, the Train Grand Vitesse (TGV), and its incredible 162 mph (270 kph) service includes Paris to Nice. The cost is a bit higher, and you do have to reserve your seats ahead of time.

SNCF's Motorail service is particularly convenient for Europeans – including residents of the British Isles. Chances are that you will want a car to get around in Provence, and the Motorail service allows the visitor to enjoy a berth on a train-auto-couchette while his/her own vehicle occupies a nook on the same train. Motorail is even offered for the train-ferry-train route from Great Britain.

SNCF has also designed a service for cyclists. Under the Train & Velo system, you register your bicycle half an hour before leaving, for a cost of 30 ff, and it's transported with you. It will take about half an hour to retrieve it once you've arrived. For an additional 25 ff, SNCF will collect your bike from your home and/or deliver it at your destination.

One last advantage in taking the train is the number of discount fares available. The France-Vacances pass (sold outside France only) allows adults to travel for either 4, 9 or 16 days of unlimited travel at a discount. Americans can also purchase France Rail 'n' Drive passes, which offer couples a flexible schedule of combined second-class train travel and car rental. And SNCF honours the Eurailpass and Eurail Youthpass.

Some tips for travelling by train: don't forget that you need to punch your ticket into the little orange boxes (marked *compostez votre billet*) stationed at the platform entrances before boarding the train. When reserving for the TGV, be sure to indicate whether you want *fumeurs* (smoking) or *non-fumeurs* (non-smoking). Also, if you wish to have breakfast on the TGV, you would do well to reserve it (the cost will be additional to the cost of your ticket). Finally, be sure to keep an eye on your suitcases when the train is waiting in a station, if you've left them in one of the between-car baggage nooks. Although the trains are clean and civilised, it is not unknown for thieves to hop on and off during stops.

For further information, passes or tickets, you can contact:

Paris: SNCF, 10 Place de Budapest, 75436 Paris, tel: (1) 45.82.50.50.
London: SNCF Rail Shop, 179 Piccadilly, London W1 0BA, tel: 0345 300003 (reservations); tel: 0891 515477 (information).
New York: French National Railroads, 610 Fifth Avenue, New York, NY 10020, tel: (212) 582 4813.
Los Angeles: 9465 Wilshire Boulevard, Beverly Hills, CA 90212, tel: (213) 274 6934.
San Francisco: 360 Post Street on Union Square, San Francisco, CA 94102, tel: (415) 982 1993.
Chicago: 11 East Adams Street, Chicago, IL 60603, tel: (312) 427 8691.
In Miami: 2121 Ponce de Leon Boulevard, Coral Gables, Miami, FL 33134, tel: (305) 445 8648.
In Eastern Canada: 1.500 Stanley Street, Suite 436, Montreal, Quebec H3A IR3, tel: (514) 288 8255.
In Western Canada: 409, Granville Street, Suite 452, Vancouver, BC V6C 1T2, tel: (604) 688 6707.

By Bus

Eurolines is a consortium of almost 30 coach companies operating in France and throughout Europe. Coaches run from London three times a week to Marseille, Toulon, Hyères, Fréjus and St Raphael from April–October; also July–October to Sisteron, Grasse, Cannes, Juan-les-Pins and Antibes. Discounts are available for students and senior citizens. Book through Eurolines, 52 Grosvenor Gardens, Victoria, London SW1W 0AU, tel: 0171-730 0202. Connections are bookable to London from many British towns via National Express.

Several bus companies operate coach services between Provence and

other international destinations. Here are two Nice-based lines that have stops in Barcelona, Brussels, Geneva, London, Madrid, San Remo, Valencia, Ventimiglia and, by extension, Morocco, Portugal and southern Spain:

Intercars Euroline: Gare Routière de Nice, Promenade du Paillon, 06000 Nice, tel: 93.80.08.70.
Phocéens Cars: 2 Place Massena, 06000 Nice, tel: 93.85.66.61.

By Car

It is not a bad idea for Europeans to drive down into Provence, since they will probably want to have a car once they arrive. One extremely comfortable way to do this is by the aforementioned Motorail service offered by SNCF, where your automobile is stored upon the same train where you are given a couchette. This service is available on ferry routes as well.

If you would rather drive yourself, you will find that the autoroutes of Provence are swift and well-maintained and provide easy connections with the rest of Europe. Tolls are, however, both frequent and very expensive – the total for the trip from Calais to the Meditterean is over 400 ff. (You don't just pay once when you get off, but rather in stages *en route*.)

There are a couple of popular scenic routes that tourists might want to take, although they aren't as fast as the Autoroute du Soleil. The most famous of these is the Route Napoleon, tracing the path that the emperor himself once took on his march into the Alps. It follows from Digne to Grasse to Cannes and is indicated on most maps. A second route originating in Digne goes through the Vallée du Var and takes you by Puget-Theniers into Nice. Travelling laterally, the Route Nationale 7 (RN 7) will give you a look at many pretty towns.

Travelling with Children

In some ways, Provence is an ideal spot to bring children. It is inexpensive, very safe and spacious. And, although a lot of the things that make Provence so special – the sensuousness, the smells, the great food, the fascinating folklore – may be less appealing to your average toddler or adolescent, they will probably find the bright festivals and ethnic museums

more tolerable than they would La Scala or the Louvre.

Most of the larger towns have a *Centre Jeunesse* or youth centres. There, they should be able to advise you of special events or attractions for younger people, although they tend to cater to adolescents and teenagers rather than kids.

A lot of families enjoy the many opportunities to camp in Provence. This is a particularly inexpensive way to accommodate an entire family, and kids quickly make friends with the kids of other campers. Another affordable way to house a brood is by renting one of the *gîtes ruraux*. If you want to stick to hotels, you will find that most have some sort of reduction for families – particularly if they stay in an extra bed in your room.

Little children generally enjoy amusement parks, and in Provence there are a few:

OK Corral, Cuges-les-Pins, tel: 42.73.80.05. Amusement park along an (American) Western theme with a Wild West show. Open: March–October; daily May– 31 August otherwise weekends only.
Eldorado City, Chateauneuf-les-Martigues, tel: 42.79.86.90. Another amusement park with a Western theme. Open: 1 June–15 September.
Marineland, Carrefour RN 7/Route de Biot, Antibes, tel: 93.33.49.49. Marine zoo with dolphins, killer whales and sea elephant shows. Admission and show costs 60 ff. Open: all year. Also aquatic park with 12 giant water toboggans and a wave pool. 68 ff. Open: June–September.
Parc de Loisirs de Barbossi, Domaine de Barbossi, RN 7/Route de Fréjus, tel: 93.49.64.74. Wild West train, electric cars, motorbikes for kids, puppet theatre, pony club, tennis, bowling alley, mini-zoo.

Students

The university in Aix is one of the very best in France, and other universities and academic institutions exist in Marseille and along the Côte d'Azur. For more information:

United Kingdom

French Embassy, Service des Echanges Extra-Universitaires, 22 Wilton Crescent, London SW1.

Central Bureau for Educational Visits and Exchanges, Seymour Mews House, Seymour Place, London W1H 9PE, tel: 0171-486 5101.

United States

American Youth Hostels, Spring Street, New York, NY 10012, tel: (212) 431 7100.

Council on International Exchange, 205 East 42nd Street, New York, NY 10017, tel: (212) 661 1414.

FACETS, 989 Sixth Avenue, New York, NY 10017, tel: (212) 475 4343.

French Embassy, 4101 Reservoir Road NW, Washington, DC 20007, tel: (202) 944 6000.

French Cultural Attaché, French Embassy, 40 West 57th Street, 21st floor, New York, NY 10019. Open: 2–5pm, weekdays.

Canada

French Embassy, 464 Wibrod, Ottawa Ontario 6M8 KIN, tel: (613) 238 5715. Cultural attachés in Edmonton, Montreal, Moncton, Quebec, Toronto, Vancouver and Winnipeg

Comité d'Accueil Canada France (CACF - OTU), 1183, Rue Union, Montreal H3B 3C3, tel: (514) 875 6172; telex: (055) 62015; or 17 St Joseph, Suite 311, Toronto M4Y 1JB, tel: (416) 962 0370.

Australia

French Cultural Attaché, French Embassy, 6 Darwin Avenue, Yarralumia, ACT 2600, tel: (062) 705111.

France

CÔTE D'AZUR

Some academic institutions located on the Côte d'Azur that offer language courses:

College International de Cannes, 1 Avenue du Docteur Pascal, 06400 Cannes, tel: 93.47.39.29; telex: 214 235 ATT College INT. Courses all year round, minimum age 16 yrs. Accommodations, full board or day school.

Alliance Française, Centre Regional d'Examens de l'Allliance Francaise de Paris pour le Côte d'Azur, 1, Rue Vernier, 06000 Nice, tel: 93.87.42.11. All year round, min 16 years. Optional accommodation.

Centre International d'Etudes Françaises, Université de Nice, Faculte des Lettres, Boulevard E.-Herriot, 06000 Nice, tel: 93.86.66.43 Two summer sessions, minimum age 18 years.

Ecole du Château, Château Notre-Dame-des-Fleurs, 06140 Vence, tel: 93.58.28.50; or

FIVE, 1 bis Rue Molière, 06000 Nice, tel: 93.52.42.82; telex: 460000. Courses from February–December, minimum age 18 years.

Institut de Français, 23, Avenue Général Leclerc, 06230 Villefranche-sur-Mer, tel: 93.01.88.44; telex: 970989. Four- or eight-week programmes all year round, minimum age 21 years.

Centre International de Formation Musicale, Conservatoire National de Region, 24 Boulevard de Cimiex, 06000 Nice, tel: 93.81.01.23. Courses 7–22 July, 24 July–8 August, minimum age 16 years. French language, music, dancing, plastic arts.

PROVENCE

Provence is famous for its many artistic schools and colonies. **The Centre National d'Information et de Documentation sur les Métiers d'Art (CNIDMA)** regularly updates a catalogue (90 ff) that lists all available programmes in France, including prices. Some operate only during the summer. **CNIDMA**, Musée des Arts Décoratifs, 107 Rue de Rivoli, 75001 Paris.

Below are some suggestions for studying arts, crafts and music in the Vaucluse:

● Pottery
Michel Delsarte, Chemin des Chinaïes, Plan de Saumane, 84800 Isle-Sur-La-Sorgue, tel: 90.20.33.17.
Gabriel Vorburger, Mas Mabelly, 84360 Puget-Sur-Durance, tel: 90.68.32.08.

● Lace-making, Spinning, Dying & Weaving
Mya Lagas-Muller, Le Rocasson, Chemin de Combemiane, 84400 Apt, tel: 90.74.32.83.

● Drawing, Painting & Sculpture
Bernard Pfriem, Foreign Study/Lacoste, Cleveland Institute of Art, 11141 East Boulevard, Cleveland, Ohio 44106, tel: (216) 421 4322.
Hélène Marion, Atelier du Beffroi, Les 4 coins, 84330 Caromb.

Marion Lamy, Grande Rue, Cabrières d'Avignon, 84220 Gordes, tel: 90.76.92.53.
Daniel Robert, Les Compagnons du XXè siècle, Mas de la Rouvière, 84210 Venasque.
Monique Labarthe (Ceramics, Sculpture), 75 Rue Antoine de Très, 84240 La Tour d'Aigues, tel: 90.77.50.13.

● Fine Arts Restoration
Michel Hebrard, 3 Rue du Puit de la Tarasque, 84000 Avignon, tel: 90.82.02.68.

● Basket-making & Caning
Jean Claude Mangematin, Atelier du vannier, 84730 Cabrières d'Aigues.

● Photography
Jean-Pierre and Claudine Sudre, 84710 Lacoste, tel: 90.75.82.70.
Jean Raffegean, Le Jas, Roussillon, 84220 Gordes, tel: 90.75.62.83.

● Ironwork
Gérard Besset, Prats des VAllats, 84240 Grambois, tel: 90.77.93 84.

● Music
Deller Academy of Early Music – Summer course in Lacoste. 61 Oxenturn Road, Wye, Ashford, Kent, England.

Travellers with Special Needs

Most less able travellers will be keen to book accommodation in advance rather than arriving "on spec". Most of the official list of hotels (available from the fGTO or the regional tourist office – *see Useful Addresses*) include a symbol to denote wheelchair access, but it is always advisable to check directly with the chosen hotel as to exactly what facilities are available. Balladins is a chain of newly-built, budget-priced hotels throughout France which all have at least one room designed for disabled guests and restaurants and all other public areas are accessible. For a complete list, contact Hotels Balladins, 20 rue du Pont des Halles, 94656 Rungis Cedex, tel: (1) 49.78.24.61; fax: (1) 46.87.68.60.

Handicapped tourists can also check with the departmental tourist offices and should contact the regional tourist board of the Côte d'Azur for the Riviera–Côte d'Azur Hotel Guide's list of rooms with easy access. A couple of places on or near the Riviera specialise in the disabled guest:

Arc Vacances Association, Le Delta, Avenue des Mouettes, 06700 St-Laurent-du-Var, tel: 93.07.20.84.

Le Beau Soleil, 12 Boulevard J-Crouet, 06310 Grasse, tel: 93.36.01.70. Centre for the disabled and the mentally handicapped. Open: all year round with a capacity of 100–150 people.

France has established a handful of national organisations that assist disabled visitors. For information about accommodation, means of transport, recreational activities and access to historical monuments, museums, theatres, etc., contact:

Comité National Francais de Liaison pour la Réadaptation des Handicapes, Service Accessibilité, 38 Boulevard Raspail, 75007 Paris, tel: (1) 45.48.90.13.

La Maison de la France, 8 Avenue de l'Opéra, 75001 Paris, tel: (1) 42.96.10.23.

An information sheet aimed at disabled travellers is published by the French Government Tourist Office; for a copy, send an SAE. There is a guide, *Où Ferons Nous Etape?* (published in French only) which lists accommodation, throughout France, suitable for the disabled, including wheelchair users, but again if you have specific needs you would need to double check when booking. It is available (for 40 ff by post) from the Association des Paralysés de France, Service Information, 17 Boulevard August Blanqui, 75013 Paris, tel: (1) 40.78.69.00. This organisation may also be able to deal direct with specific enquiries and can provide addresses of their branches throughout France. The *Rousseau H Comme Handicapé* guide may also prove useful. It is available from Hachette bookshops or at SCOP, 4 Rue Gustave-Rouanet, 75018 Paris, tel: (1) 42.52.97.00.

The Michelin Red Guide *France*, for hotels and their *Camping-Caravanning – France* both include symbols for disabled welcome.

The Royal Association for Disability and Rehabilitation (RADAR), 25 Mortimer Street, London WIN 8AB, tel. 0171-637 5400, has some useful information for tourists, including a guide book, *Holidays and Travel Abroad*. This is a general country by country guide and provides information about France as a whole, including hotel chains offering suitable accommodation, and tour operators offering specialist holidays.

France's sister organisation to RADAR, the Comité National Français de Liaison pour la Réadaption des Handicapés (CNFLRH), is based at 38 Boulevard Raspail, 75007 Paris, tel: (1) 45.48.90.13. It offers a good information service for visitors with special needs to France, although they do not have an specific information about the region itself.

For young people, the Centre d'Information et de Documentation Jeunesse, 101 Quai Branly, 75740 Paris Cedex 15 provides information on services for young less able travellers. It publishes *Vacances pour Personnes Handicapées* and annual leaflets on acitivity and sports holidays for young disabled people. Parents may also find the following organisation helpful: Union Nationale des Associations de Parents d'enfants Inadaptés (UNAPEI), 15 Rue Coysevox, 75018 Paris, tel: (1) 42.63.84.33.

The Comité de Liaison pour le transport des personnes handicapées, Conseil National des Transports, 34 avenue Marceau, 75009 Paris publishes a booklet called *Guide des Transport à l'usage des Personnes à Mobilité Réduite*. This gives brief information on the accessibility and arrangements for less able passengers on all forms of public transport and contacts for special transport schemes throughout France.

The Holiday Care Service offers free information on travel, accommodation and counterpart associations in France. Send a large SAE to them at 2 Old Bank Chambers, Station Road, Horley, Surrey RH6 9HW, tel: 01293 774535; fax: 01293 784647; Minicom: 01293 776943.

For young people, the Centre d'Information et de Documentation Jeunesse, 101 Quai Branly, 75740 Paris Cedex 15 provides information on services for young less able travellers. It publishes *Vacances pour Personnes Handicapées* and annual leaflets on activity and sports holidays for young disabled people. Parents may also find Union Nationale de Associations de Parents d'enfants Inadaptés (UNAPEI), 15 Rue Coysevox, 75018 Paris, tel: (1) 42.63.84.33 useful.

The Comité de Liaison pour le transport des personnes handicapées, Conseil National des Transports, 34 avenue Marceau, 75009 Paris publishes a booklet called *Guide des Transport à l'usage des Personnes à Mobilité Réduite*. This gives brief information on the acessibility and arrangements for less able passengers on all forms of public transport and contacts for special transport schemes throught France.

Some cessionary ferry fares are available for members of the following organisations:

The Disabled Drivers Association, Ashwellthorpe, Norwich NR16 1EX, tel: 01508 41449.

Disabled Driver's Motor Club, Cottingham Way, Thrapston, Northants NN14 4PL, tel: 01832 734724.

Disabled Motorist's Federation, Unit 2a, Atcham Estate, Shrewbury SY4 4UG, tel: 01743 761889.

More information about air and sea travel is also available in a guide entitled Door-to-Door. For a free copy write to Department of Transport, Door-to-Door Guide, Freepost, Victoria Road, South Ruislip, Middlesex HA4 0NZ who can also provide copies on cassette for the vision-impaired.

In the US, the following organisations offer services to disabled travellers:

Travel Information Service, Moss Rehabilitation Hospital, 1200 West Tabor Road., Philadelphia, PA 19141-3099, tel: (215) 456 9600 – has general information for would-be travellers.

Society for the Advancement of Travel for the Handicapped (SATH), 26 Court Street, Brooklyn, New York 11242, tel: (718) 858 5483 – offers advice and assistance in travel matters.

Accessible Journeys, 35 W Sellers Avenue, Ridley Park, Philadelphia, 19078-2113 – offers tours using wheelchair accessible transport in Europe.

In Canada the following organisation may be of help:

Canadian Rehabilitation Council for the Disabled, 45 Sheppard Avenue E, Toronto, Ontario, M2N 5W9, tel: (416) 250 7490 – national organisation producing some material relating to travel.

Practical Tips

Business Hours

Shops: are generally open from 9am–noon and 2–7pm with the prerequisite two-hour midday break for lunch and siesta. Everything except a handful of ambitious *boulangeries* and greengrocers will be closed on Sunday, and many stores will be closed on Monday as well.

Banks: are open Monday through Friday from 8.30am–12 noon and 2.30–4pm, but watch for long weekends.

Post offices: are open from 8am–5pm; all but the largest branches are closed from noon–2pm. If you get desperate, Telecom Service, 12, Boulevard Charles-Nedelec, in Marseille is open all night for telephone, telegram and postage stamp services.

Tipping

Tipping follows much the same rule as in the rest of France. Taxi drivers get about 10–15 percent of the amount marked on the meter. Hotel staff expect 5–10 ff for every item of baggage. You can leave 5–10 ff for the chambermaid daily, but you don't necessarily have to tip the concierge. Restaurants generally include tips in the bill *(service compris)* at 15 percent, so you don't have to worry about this. The same goes for café waiters. Do not aggravate your waiter by calling him *garçon*, always *monsieur* and waitresses either *Mademoiselle* or *Madame*. Hairdressers get about 10 percent with another 10 ff to the shampooist and the manicurist.

Porter Services

In the airports, you can generally hire your own baggage trolley for free or a few francs. Just look for the trolley corrals. Trains are more difficult. In general, porters have their own official scale for tips, but it is usual to give them about 5 ff extra.

Complaints

Complaining is a way of life all over France, so don't expect to have your own complaints greatly honoured. If you really are aggrieved, take it to your local tourist board and be polite but persistent and firm. This goes for your concierge if you have problems with a bill.

Weights & Measures

The metric system is used in France for all weights and measures, although you may encounter old-fashioned terms such as *livre* (about 1 pound weight – 500 grammes) still used by small shopkeepers.

For quick and easy conversion remember that 1 inch is roughly 2.5 centimetres, 1 metre roughly equivalent to a yard, 4 ounces is just over 100 grammes and a kilogram is just over 2 lbs. As a kilometre is five-eights of a mile, a handy reckoning is to remember that 80 kilometres = 50 miles, thus 40 kilometres = 25 miles. Accurate conversions are given below:

Weight:

3.5 ounces (oz)	=	100 grammes (g)
1.1 pound (lb)	=	500 g
2.2 lb	=	1 kilogram (kg)

Length:

0.39 inch	=	1 centimetre (cm)
1.094 yard	=	1 metre (m)
0.62 mile	=	1 kilometre (km)

Liquid:

2.113 pints	=	1 litre (l)
0.22 Imp gallon/ 0.26 US gallon	=	1 litre
2.2 Imp gallons/ 2.6 US gallons	=	10 litres

Temperature:

Temperatures are always given in celsius (centigrade). Here are some fahrenheit equivalents:

0°C = 32°F; 10°C = 50°F; 15°C = 59°F; 20°C = 68°F; 25°C = 77°F; 30°C = 86°F; 35°C = 95°F

Religious Services

Roman Catholicism is the predominant religion in Provence, as in all of France. However, all religions are represented and in most cities possess places of worship.

Pilgrimages

There are a number of pilgrimages made to spots in Provence throughout the year. The most famous of these is, of course, the gypsy pilgrimage to Les Stes-Maries-de-la-Mer 24–25 May. During this period, gypsies from all over Europe make their way to the seaside town in pilgrimage to their patron saint, Sarah. A large mass is held followed by a procession to the sea carrying the statue of Saint Sarah – plus there is a great deal of dancing and singing and general partying. Some others:

Allauch: Notre-Dame-du-Château – 8 September.

Beaucet: Eglise St-Gens May and September.

Boulbon: St-Marcelin (Procession of the Bottles) – 1 June.

Marseille: Notre-Dame-de-la-Garde – 14 and 15 August.

Marseille: Notre-Dame-de-la-Calline – 8 September.

St-Etienne-du-Grès: Notre-Dame-du-Château – end of May.

Ste-Etienne-les-Orgues: Notre-Dame-de-Lure – 8 September.

Stes-Maries-de-la-Mer: Saints Mary Jacoby and Salome – Sunday by 22 October.

Stes-Maries-de-la-Mer: invention of the hunt – Sunday by 4 December.

Media

Radio & TV

You will find a wide selection of different radio stations, some of them very good. In English, along the Côte d'Azur, is the Radio Riviera. French television is improving, but don't expect to find channels in your native language or to find TVs in any small to mid-size hotels.

Newspapers & Other Publications

Train stations are good places to find large selections of international publications. Otherwise, *tabacs* and kiosks will have all the local and national dailies. Widely available (in English) is the *International Herald Tribune*. London papers are sold on the Côte.

Libraries

Keep in mind that the word *librairie* in French means bookshop and *bibliothèque* means library. Aix-en-Provence, with its university, has no shortage of libraries, unlike Marseille or Avignon. The Inguimbertine Library in Carpentras is world famous, comprising some 230,000 volumes plus musical scores, 14 to 16th-century Book of Hours and 19th-century prints and drawings. Check with your local tourist office for a *bibiliothèque* that might contain books in your language.

Bookshops

Unsurprisingly, the university town of Aix-en-Provence is an absolute mecca for bookshops. Indeed, due to its proud cultural heritage, most of Provence's larger towns have a nice selection of bookstores, many of which carry ancient, priceless editions. As ever, check with the local tourist office.

Anglophones will like: the English Bookshop, 23 Rue de la Republique, 2nd floor in Avignon; the Paradox Bookstore, 2 Rue Reine Jeanne in Aix-en-Provence; and the Cannes English Bookshop, 10, Rue Jean-de-Riouffe in Cannes.

French speakers should check out Les Arsenaulx, 25 cours d'Estienne d'Orves in Marseille. After selecting a book from their well-chosen collection of upscale books, you can settle down at the adjacent teashop and read.

Postal Services

Provincial post offices – *Postes* or PTTS (pronounced *Pay-Tay-Tay*) are generally open Monday–Friday 9am–noon; 2–5pm and Saturday 9am–noon (opening hours are posted outside); in the cities and main towns they are generally open continuously from 8am–7pm. Inside major post offices, individual counters are marked for different requiremetns – if you just need stamps, go to the window marked *Timbres*. If you need to send an urgent letter overseas, ask for it to be sent *partexprès*, or through the Chronopost system which is faster but very expensive.

To cut down queues, many post offices have now installed coin-operated franking machines which produce franked stickers. These machines, marked *Libre service affranchissement*, are easy to operate and have instructions (similar to bank cash machines) in English.

Stamps are usually available at tobacconists (*tabacs*) and normally at shops selling postcards and greeting cards.

Telegrams (*cables*) can be sent during post office hours or by telephone (24-hours); to send a telegram in English dial 16-1 42 33 21 11. Expect to pay around 75 ff for a minimum of 15 words to the US, Canada or the UK.

For a small fee, you can arrange for mail to be kept *poste restante* at any post office, addressed to Poste Restante, (Poste Centreale – for main post offices) then the town's post code and name e.g. 06000 Nice. A passport, or identity card is required when collecting mail.

Many post offices have coin-in-slot photocopying machines and fax facilities.

Telecoms

The French telephone system, once quirky, is now one of the most efficient in the world. That is not to say that you can be guaranteed to find telephone boxes (*cabines publiques*) that are always operational, but most are. Telephone numbers have been rationalised to eight figures, given in sets of two, e.g. 99.44.63.21., the only codes necessary are for dialling into or out of Paris or overseas. To dial Paris from the provinces, dial 16.1, then the subscriber's number; to dial out of Paris, just dial 16 then the number.

International calls can be made from most public booths, but it is often easier to use a booth in a post office – ask at the counter to use the phone, then go back to settle the bill – but you have no record of the cost of the call until the end.

Coin-operated phones take most coins and card phones are now very common and simple to use. It is worth purchasing a phone card (*une télécarte* – currently 50 ff or 120 ff) if you are likely to need to use a public call box, as many are being converted to take cards and in some towns are far more numerous now than coin-operated ones. Cards are available from post offices, stationers, railway stations, some cafés and tobacconists. Several main post offices now also have telephones that can be used with credit cards.

If you use a phone (not a public call box) in a café, shop or restaurant you are likely to be surcharged. Some hotels and cafés now have computerised public telephones whereby the caller receives a printed statement of the details of his call on payment of the bill at the bar – a useful asset for business travellers.

To make an international call, lift the receiver, insert the money (if necessary), dial 19, wait for the tone to change, then dial the country code (*see below*), followed by the area code (omitting any initial 0) and the number. International dialling codes:
Australia 61.
Canada 1.
Ireland 353.
UK 44.
US 1.
Useful numbers:
Operator services 13.
Directory enquiries 12.

Note that numbers will be given in pairs of figures, unless you ask for them to be given *chiffre par chiffre* (singly).

If using a US credit phone card, dial the company's access number:
Sprint, tel: 19 00 87.
ATT&T, tel: 19 00 11.
MCI, tel: 19 00 19.

Most post offices in France have now replaced their traditional telephone directories with the computerised **Minitel** system. Members of the public can use this free of charge to look up any number in the country. The instructions (in French) are fairly simple to understand, and you simply tap in the name of the town, *département* and person (or company) whose number you seek for it to be displayed on the small screen, connected to the telephone. It can also be used in the same way as yellow pages to find, for example, all the dry cleaners listed in a particular town.

If you need to make a phone call in rural areas, or small villages with no public phone, look out for the blue plaque saying *téléphone publique* on private houses. This means the owner is officially required to allow you to use the phone and charge the normal amount for the call.

You cannot reverse charges (call collect) within France but you can to countries which will accept such calls. Go through the operator and ask to make a PCV (pronounced *pay-say-vay*) call. Telephone calls can only be received at call boxes displaying the blue bell sign.

To take advantage of cheap rates, use the telephone weekdays between 10.30pm and 8am and at weekends after 2pm on Saturday when you will have 50 percent more time for your money.

The cheapest times to use the telephone are weekdays between 10.30pm and 8am, and at weekends, after 2pm Saturday and all day Sunday.

Tourist Offices

Regional Tourist Offices

CRT Provence–Alpes-Côte d'Azur, Immeuble CMCI, 2 Rue Henri-Barbusse, 13241 Marseille Cedex 01, tel: 91.39.38.00; fax: 91 56 66 61.

Department Tourist Offices (CDT)

Alpes de Haute-Provence: 42 Boulevard Victor Hugo, BP170, 04005 Digne Cedex, tel: 92.31.57.29; fax: 92.32.24.94.

Alpes-Maritimes: 2 Rue Deloye, 06000 Nice, tel: 93.80.84.84.

Bouches-du-Rhône: 6 Rue du Jeune Anarcharsis,13001 Marseille, tel: 91.54.92.66; fax: 91.33.01.82.

Var: Conseil Général, 1 Boulevard Foch, BP9, 83300 Draguignan, tel: 94.68.58.33; fax: 92.47.08.03.

Vaucluse: La Balance, Place Campana, BP 147, 84008 Avignon Cedex, tel: 90.86.43.42; fax: 90.86.86.08.

Bouches du Rhône offers a service **Reservation Loisirs Acceuil** for booking all kinds of accommodation and activity holidays: **Domaine du Vergon**, 13370 Mallemort, tel: 90.59.18.05; fax: 90.59.16.75.

The Var offers a similar services, particularly for actitivity holidays: **AVDTR**, conseil Généneral du Var, 9 Avenue Colbert, 83000 Toulon, tel: 94.89.14.44.

Tourist Information

Every town in Provence has an Office du Tourisme or a Syndicat d'Initiative. They can tell you anything you need to know. In the cities they often speak a number of languages.

BOUCHES-DU-RHONE

Esplanade Charles de Gaulle, 13200 Arles, tel: 90.96.29.35.

Mairie et Syndicat d'Initiative, 13570 Barbentane, tel: 90.95.50.39.

Hôtel de Manville, Les-Baux-de-Provence, 13520 Maussane-les-Alpilles, tel: 90.97.34.39.

Mairie et Syndicat d'Initiative, 13990 Fontvieille, tel: 90.97.70.01.

Rue Lamartine, 13910 Maillane, tel: 90.95.74.06.

Place Jean Jaurès, 13210 St-Rémy-de-Provence, tel: 90.92.05.22.

59 Rue des Halles, B.P. #9, 13150 Tarascon, tel: 90.91.03.52.

56 Cours Gimon, 13300 Salon-de-Provence, tel: 90.56.27.60; fax: 90.56.77.09.

Place du Général-de-Gaulle, 13100 Aix-en-Provence, tel: 42.26.02.93.

4 La Canebière, 13001 Marseille, tel: 91.54.91.11; telex: 430.402.

Place P. Baragnon, 13260 Cassis, tel: 42.01.71.17; telex: OFTOUCA 441287.

CAMARGUE

Avenue Van Gogh, 13460 Les-Stes-Maries-de-la-Mer, tel: 90.47.82.55.

ALPES-DE-HAUTE-PROVENCE

Hôtel de Ville, 04200 Sisteron, tel: 92.61.12.03.

Place du Bourguet, 04300 Forcalquier, tel: 92.75.10.02.

Place Dr P. Joubert, 04100 Manosque, tel: 92.72.16.00; fax: 92.72.58.98.

Le Rond-Point, 04000 Digne, tel: 92.31.42.73; fax: 92.32.27.24.

Syndicat d'Initiative, Moustiers 04360, tel: 92.74.67.84.

Rue Nationale, 04120 Castellane, tel: 92.83.61.14.

Rue Principale, 04170 St-Andre-les-Alpes, tel: 92.89.02.46.

Place Revelly, 04240 Annot, tel: 92.83.21.44. Syndicat d'Initiative, Old Forge, 04320 Entrevaux.

Syndicat d'Initiative, 04370 Colmars-les-Alpes, tel: 92.83.41.92.

4 Avenue des 3 Frères Arnaud, 04400 Barcelonette, tel: 92.81.03.68; fax: 92.81.15.26.

VAR

8 Avenue Colbert, 83000 Toulon, tel: 94.22.08.22; fax: 94.22.30.54.

Allées Vivien, 83150 Bandol, tel: 94.29.41.35; fax: 94.32.50.39.

Jardins de la Ville, 83110 Sanary-sur-Mer, tel: 94.74.01.04.

Rotunde Jean Salusse, BP 721, 83400 Hyères. Tel 94.65.18.55; fax: 94.35.85.05.

1 Place Gambetta, 83230 Bormes-les-Mimosas, tel: 94.71.15.17; fax: 94.64.79.57.

Place de la Mairie, 83680 La Garde-Freinet, tel: 94.43.67.41.

Place Republique, 83310 Cogolin, tel: 94.54.63.18; fax: 94.54.10.20.

Place Hôtel de Ville, 83470 St-Maximin-la-Ste-Baume, tel: 94.78.00.09; fax: 94.78.09.40.

Boulevard Grisolle, BP 18, 83670 Barjols, tel: 94.77.20.01.

Place F. Mistral, 83630 Aups, tel: 94.70.00.80; fax: 94.84.00.87.

Rue Victor Hugo, 83690 Salernes, tel: 94.70.69.02.

9 Boulevard Clemenceau, 83300 Draguignan, tel: 94.68.63.30; fax: 94.47.10.76.

Le Valat, 83440 Seillans, tel: 94.76.96.04.

ALPES-MARITIMES

La Ruade, 06660 Auron, tel: 93.23.02.66.

Place de la Chapelle, 06410 Biot, tel: 93.65.05.85.

Mairie, 06360 Eze, tel: 93.41.03.03.

Mairie, 06620 Gourdon, tel: 93.42.54.83.

Place de la Foux, 06130 Grasse, tel: 93.36.03.56.

Mairie, 06620 Gréolières, tel: 93.59.95.16.

Maison d'Isola, 06420 Isola 2000, tel: 93.23.15.15.

Avenue Mallet, 06250 Mougins, tel: 93.75.87.67.

L'Escarène, 06440 Peira Cava - Turini Camp d'Argent, tel: 93.91.57.22.

Place Felix-Fauré, 06450 St-Martin Vésubie, tel: 93.03.21.28.

2 Rue Grande, 06570 St-Paul-de-Vence, tel: 93.32.86.95.

Mairie, 06470 Sauze, tel: 93.05.52.62.

Centre Administratif, 06470 Valberg, tel: 93.02.52.77.

Boulevard Gambetta, 06560 Valbonne, tel: 93.42.04.16.

Square 8 mai 1945, 06220 Vallauris, tel: 93.63.82.58.

Place du Grand-Jardin, 06140 Vence, tel: 93.58.06.38.

CÔTE D'AZUR

11 Place de Gaulle, 06600 Antibes, tel: 92.90.53.00.

Palais des Festivals, Esplanade Georges Pompidou, 06401 Cedex, Cannes, tel: 93.99.19.77.

51 Boulevard Guillaumont, 06160 Juan-les-Pins, tel: 93.61.04.98.

274 Avenue Henry-Clews, BP 947, 06210 Mandelieu, tel: 93.49.95.31.

Palais de l'Europe, 8, Avenue Boyer, 06500 Menton, tel: 93.57.57.00.

2A Boulevard des Moulins, 98000 Monaco, tel: 92.16.61.16.

SNCF Station, 06000 Nice, tel: 93.87.07.07.

Avenue Dénis-Semeria, 06230 St-Jean-Cap-Ferrat, tel: 93.76.08.90.

Quai Jean-Jaurès, BP 183, 83992 St-Tropez, tel: 94.97.45.21; fax: 94.97.82.66.

Consulates

American : 2 Rue St-Florentin, 75001 Paris, tel: (1) 42.96.14.88. In Marseille, tel: 91.54.92.00.

Australian: 4 Rue Jean-Rey, 75015 Paris, tel: (1) 45.75.62.00.

British: 9 Avenue Hoche, 75008 Paris, tel: (1) 42.66.91.42. In Marseille, tel: 91.53.43.32.

Canadian: 35 Avenue Montaigne, 75008 Paris, tel: (1) 44.43.29.00. In Marseille, tel: 91.37.19.37.

Irish Embassy: 12 Avenue Foch, 75116 Paris, tel: (1) 45.00.20.87.

Emergencies
Security & Crime

Aside from the port cities (notably Marseille and Toulon) and along the Côte d'Azur, where you need to take extra care, Provence tends to be filled with poor but honest folk. It is always wise to exercise caution. In particular, *never* leave anything behind in a car or unattended in a station.

If you do run into trouble, you should inform the local police – but don't expect too much. You might also want to contact the local tourist board. For grave problems, you should not delay in calling your nation's consulate.

Medical Services

The International Association for Medical Assistance to Travelers (IAMAT) is a non-profit-making organisation which anyone can join, free of charge (although a donation is welcome). Benefits include a membership card, entitling the bearer to services at fixed IAMAT rates by participating physicians, and a Traveller Clinical Record, a passport-sized record completed by the member's own doctor prior to travel. A directory of English-speaking doctors, belonging to IAMAT, and on call 24 hours a day, is published for members' use.

IAMAT offices:

US: 736 Center Street, Lewiston NY 14092, tel: (716) 754 4883.

Canada: 1287 St Claire Ave W.,Toronto M6E 1B9, tel: (416) 652 0137; 40 Regal Road, Guelph. Ontario N1K 1B5, tel: (519) 836 0102.

New Zealand: PO Box 5049, Christchurch 5.

Switzerland: 57 Voirets, 1212 Grand-Lancy, Geneva.

For minor ailments it may be worth consulting a pharmacy (recognisable by its green cross sign), which have wider "prescribing" powers than chemists in the UK or US. They are also helpful in cases of snake or insect bites and identifying fungi.

If you need to see a doctor, expect to pay around 100 ff for a consultation, plus a pharmacist's fee for whatever prescription is issued. The doctor will provide a *feuille des soins* which you need to keep to claim back the majority of the cost (around 75 percent) under EU agreements. You have to attach to the *feuille* the little sticker (*vignette*) from any medicine prescribed to enable you to claim for that too. Refunds have to be obtained from the local *Caisse Primaire* (ask the doctor or pharmacist for the address).

In cases of medical emergency, either dial 15 for an ambulance or call the Service d'Aide Médicale d'Urgence (SAMU) which exists in most large towns and cities – numbers are given at the front of telephone directories.

The standard of treatment in French hospitals is generally high, and you should be able to find someone who speaks English to help you. You may prefer to try to get to either the Ameri-

can Hospital at 63 Boulevard Victor-Hugo, 92292 Neuilly, tel: (1) 46.41.25.25; or the British Hospital Hortford, 3 Rue Barbes, 92300 Levallois, tel: (1) 46.39.22.22, both just outside Paris. Show the hospital doctor or authorities your E111 and you will be billed (once you are back home usually), for approximately 25 percent of the cost of treatment.

IN AN EMERGENCY

Marseille

SOS Doctor, tel: 91.52.91.52.

SOS Cardio, tel: 91.52.84.85.

SOS Pediatrics, tel: 91.26.19.19.

SOS Centre Antipoison, tel: 91.75.25.25.

SOS Dentists, tel: 91.25.77.77.

SAMU (for serious medical emergencies), tel: 91.49.91.91.

Aix-en-Provence

SOS Doctor, tel: 42.26.24.00.

Antibes

SOS Doctor, tel: 93.33.40.20.

Nice

SOS Doctor, tel: 93.83.01.01.

Cannes

SOS Doctor, tel: 93.38.39.38.

Lost Property

If property is lost in a subway or on a bus, go to the terminal point and, if you're lucky, it will be waiting for you there. Otherwise, ask a conductor for the number of the lost and found. For property lost on a train, ask the conductor or general information officer for assistance.

For lost credit cards, it is important to notify the authorities straight away on the following numbers:

Visa/Carte Blance, tel: 54.42.12.12 or (1) 42.77.11.90 (Paris).

Diner's Club, tel: (1) 47.62.75.00.

American Express, tel: (1) 47.77.72.00; traveller's cheques, tel: (1) 05.90.86.00.

Contact your airline or local train station as appropriate for any luggage forgotten while in transport. In the case of the train, don't be surprised to discover that you must pay for a ticket and travel personally to the spot where your bag is being held. For luggage forgotten in a hotel, contact the concierge.

Getting Around

Provence is in the southeastern corner of France. While there are several cities along the coast and the Rhône River, much of the region is not reachable by train or plane. Tiny hillside hamlets, forgotten plains' towns and mountain-perched villages make for some of the most rewarding visits but can only be reached by car or bicycle.

Maps

The regional Michelin maps are without question the handiest and most thorough maps available. You will find them all over, in bookshops, tabacs, train stations, etc.

From the Airport

If you fly into the Nice Airport, you can rent a car, hail a cab or take the STANCA bus, tel: 93.21.30.83, to: Cros de Cagnes, Villeneuve-Loubet Plage, Antibes, Juan-les-Pins, Golfe-Juan, Villefranche, Beaulieu, Eze-sur-Mer, Cap-d'Ail, Monaco, Roquebrune, Menton or Cannes. The bus also services the Monaco and Menton Airports.

The Auto Nice Transport (ANT), tel: 93.96.31.51, will bring you from the airport to Nice's Place Massena or harbour.

ANT will also take you from the airport to the railway station. To go from the train to the airport, contact Transport Benavent, tel: 93.88.14.02, departures on arrival of every train.

Finally, to go from the Nice Airport to the Marseille Airport, there is Phocééns Cars, tel: 93.85.66.61. They also serve Nice to Aix-en-Provence.

Public Transport

Some of the towns in Provence linked by train are Nîmes, Arles, Avignon, Arles, Tarascon, Marseille, Aix-en-Provence, St-Auban, Digne, Toulon, Hyères, Cannes, Nice, Menton and Breil. Stations are generally conveniently located, with taxis and buses waiting for the weary or heavily laden.

Nonetheless, tourists wishing to get into the many wonderful nooks of Provence will need another means of transportation. Bikes are popular, but that both limits the area you can cover and the time you have to spend on important Provençal activities like site exploring and café sitting. It is best either to bring a car or rent one once you've arrived. (For more information about renting, see below Private Transport.)

Buses run between most towns. They won't all be as fast or air-conditioned, but they will get you to wherever you are going.

AIX

Phone the bus station (tel: 42.27.17.91) or try Compagnie Autocars de Provence, 10 Avenue de-Lattre-de-Tassigny, 13100 Aix-en-Provence (tel: 42.23.14.26) whose regular service to many places in Provence may be what you need.

MARSEILLE

Either phone the bus station (tel: 91.08.16.40) or contact aTRC, 300 Avenue du Prado, 13008 Marseille (tel: 91.76.55.35).

NICE

Phone the Gare Routière (tel: 93.85.61.81) for departures from Nice.
Elsewhere, enquire at the local Syndicate d'Initiative for information.

Private Transport

Car hire is can be rather expensive if rentals are organised locally, but bikes (vélos) are fairly readily available for hire, often from cycle shops. Local tourist offices keep information on hire facilities. French Railways generally have them for hire at several stations in the region; they do not necessarily have to be returned to the same station. Bikes can be carried free of charge on buses and some trains (Autotrains), but on many of the other, faster services you will have to pay. Travelling by a combination of bike and bus or train can be an excellent way of touring, and relieves you of some of the legwork. For further information see Outdoor Activities.

Driving

British, US, Canadian and Australian licences are all valid in France and you should always carry your vehicle's registration document and valid insurance (third party is the absolute minimum, and a green card – available from your insurance company – is strongly recommended).

Additional insurance cover, which can include a get-you-home service, is offered by a number of organisations including the British and American Automobile Associations and Europ-Assistance, Sussex House, Perrymount Road, Haywards Heath, Sussex RH16 1DN, tel: 01444 442211; in the US – Europ Assistance Worldwide Services Inc., 1133 15th Street, Suite 400, Washington DC 20005., tel: (202) 347 7113. The Automobile Club National is the umbrella organisation of France's 40-odd motoring clubs. They will assist any motorist whose own club has an agreement with it. Contact them at 9 rue Anatole-de-la-Forge, 75017 Paris, tel: (1) 42.27.82.00; fax: (1) 40.53.90.52.

Rules of the Road

Britons must remember to drive on the right: it doesn't take long to get used to, but extra care should be taken when crossing the carriageway, for instance, to use a service station. It is very easy to come out and automatically drive on the left – especially if there's no other traffic around.

The minimum age for driving in France is 18; foreigners are not permitted to drive on a provisional licence.

Full or dipped headlights must be used in poor visibility and at night; sidelights are not sufficient unless the car is stationary. Beams must be adjusted for right-hand drive vehicles, but yellow tints are not compulsory.

The use of seat belts (front and rear if fitted) and crash helmets for motorcyclists is compulsory. Children under 10 are not permitted to ride in the front seat unless fitted with a rear-facing safety seat, or if the car has no rear seat.

Priorité à la Droite: An important rule to remember is that priority on French roads is always given to vehicles approaching from the right, except where otherwise indicated. In practice, on main roads the major road will normally have priority, with traffic being halted on minor approach roads with one of the following signs:

Stop
Cedez le passage – give way
Vous n'avez pas la priorité – you do not have right of way
Passage protégé – no right of way

Particular care should be taken in towns, where you may wrongly assume you are on the major road, and in rural areas where there may not be any road markings (watch out for farm vehicles). Note that if a driver flashes the headlights it is to indicate that *he* has priority, not the other way round. Priority is always given to emergency services and also public utility vehicles e.g. gas, electricity and water companies.

The French changed the rules concerning roundabouts – drivers already on the roundabout have priority over those entering it, but beware; some drivers still insist that priority belongs to the drivers entering a roundabout.

Speed Limits

Speed limits are as follows, unless otherwise indicated: 80 mph (130 kph) on toll motorways; 68 mph (110 kph) on other motorways and dual carriageways; 56 mph (90 kph) on other roads except in towns where the limit is 30 mph (50 kph). There is also a *minimum* speed limit of 50 mph (80 kph) on the outside lane of motorways during daylight with good visibility and on level ground. Speed limits are reduced in wet weather as follows: toll motorways: 68 mph (110 kph), dual carriageways: 62 mph 100 kph, other roads: 50 mph (80 kph).

On-the-spot fines can be levied for speeding; on toll roads, the time is printed on the ticket you take at your entry point and can thus be checked and a fine imposed on exit. Nearly all *autoroutes* (motorways) are toll roads.

Autoroutes are designated "A" roads and national highways "N" roads. "D" roads are usually well maintained, while "C" or local roads, may not always be so.

Carry a red warning triangle to place 55 yards (50 metres) behind the car in case of a breakdown or accident (strongly advised, and compulsory if towing a caravan). In an accident or emergency, call the police (dial 17) or use the free emergency telephones (every 1 mile/2 km) on motorways. If another driver is involved, lock your car and go together to call the police. It is useful to carry an European Accident Statement Form (obtainable from your insurance company) which will simplify matters in the case of an accident.

Unleaded petrol (*essence sans plomb*) is now widely available in France. If in doubt, a map showing the location of filling stations is available from main tourist offices.

For information on current road conditions, telephone the Inter Service Route line on tel: (1) 48.94.33.33 (this is a recorded anouncement in French and not always terribly clear).

Car Hire

As previously mentioned, hiring a car is an expensive business in France, partly because of the high VAT (TVA) rate – 33 percent on luxury items. Some fly/drive deals work out reasonably well if you're only going for a short visit. French Railways offer a good deal on their combined train/car rental bookings. Weekly rates often work out better than a daily hire and it can be cheaper to arrange hire in the UK or US before leaving for France. The minimum age to hire a car is 18, but most companies will not hire to anyone under 23, or 21 if paying by credit card and the hirer must have held a full licence for at least a year. Apart from Avis, most companies have an upper age limit of 60–65.

Listed below are the major agent's central reservation offices in Paris. They all have offices in the region:
Avis: tel: (1) 49.06.68.68; fax: (1)47.78.98.98.
Budget/Millebille: tel: (1) 46.86.65.65; fax: (1) 46.86.22.17.
Europcar/National/Interrent: tel: (1) 46.09.92.21; fax: (1) 49.10.55.00.
Hertz: tel: (1) 30.45.65.65; fax: (1) 47.48.51.51.

Taxis

Taxis are normally readily available at railway stations and at official taxi ranks in city centres. Taxis can be a convenient method of travel in the cities, but don't expect to use many in the countryside.

Tel: 42.26.29.30; tel: 42.27.71 (day) or 42.26.29.30 (night); tel: 42.21.61.61.

MARSEILLE
Tel: 91.02.20.20; tel: 91.06.15.15; tel: 91.49.91.00; tel: 91.49.20.20; or tel: 91.05.80.80.

Motorcycles & Mopeds

Rules of the road are largely the same as for car drivers. The minimum age for driving machines over 80cc is 18. GB plates must be shown and crash helmets are compulsory. Dipped headlights must be used at all times. Children under 14 years are not permitted to be carried as passengers.

Bicycles

Bicycles are a favourite means of getting around all over Provence. Those visiting steeper areas or who are less athletically ambitious may want to rent mopeds instead. They are inexpensive, easy to rent and popular with the locals.

To take your own *vélo* to France is easy – they are carried free on most ferries and trains – or you can rent cycles for a reasonable cost; main railway stations usually have them for hire and you can often arrange to pick up at one station and leave the bike at a distant one. Alternatively, try bicycle retailers/repairers or ask at the local tourist office.

Some youth hostels rent cycles and also arrange tours with accommodation in hostels or under canvas. For more information, contact the YHA in your home country. French Routes, 1 Mill Green Cottages, Newbridge, Yarmouth, Isle of Wight, PO41 0TZ, tel: 01983 78392, offers a route planning service for individual tourists and will arrange bicycle hire and accommodation if required.

Cycling holidays are offered by various organisations; with campsite or hotel accommodation there is the added advantage of knowing that your luggage is often transported for you to your next destination. Some operators are listed below:
Fédération Française de Cyclotourisme, 8 Rue Jean-Marie-Jégo, 75013 Paris, tel: (1) 44.16.88.88; fax: (1) 44.16.88.99. More than 60 guided tours offered each year, all over

France, 60–100 km (40–60 miles) per day. Bring your own bike.

Fédération Française de Cyclisme, Bâtiment Jean-Monnet, 5 Rue de Rome, 93561 Rosny-Sous-Bois, tel: (1) 49.35.69.00.

Bicyclub SA, 8 Place de la Porte-Champerret, 75017 Paris Cedex, tel: (1) 47.66.55.92 fax: (1) 48.94.09.97.

Vélo-Relais/Hexaclub, 38 Rue du Mesnil, 78730 St-Arnoult-en-Yvelines, tel: (1) 30.59.34.09.

Cresta Holidays, 32 Victoria Street, Altrincham, Cheshire WA14 1ET, tel: 0161-927 7000.

Cyclists Touring Club, Cotterell House, 69 Meadrow, Godalming, Surrey GU7 3HS, tel: 01483 417217.

Headwater Holidays, 146 London Road, Northwich CS9 5HH, tel: 01606- 8699. Hotel accommodation, and your luggage transported.

Susi Madron's Cycling for Softies, 2–4 Birch Polygon, Rusholme, Manchester, M14 5HX, tel: 0161-248 8282. Well-established company offering holidays with good hotel accommodation.

It is advisable to take out insurance before you go. Obviously the normal rules of the road apply to cyclists. Advice and information can be obtained from The Touring Department of the Cyclists Touring Club (*see above*). Their service to members includes competitive cycle and travel insurance, free detailed touring itineraries and general information sheets about France. The club's French counterpart, Fédération Française de Cyclotourisme offers a similar service. Rob Hunter's book *Cycle Touring in France* is also extremely useful as a handbook and the IGN Cyclists' Map No. 906 *France Vélo* carries a mass of information.

Such is the French passion for cycling that local clubs organise many trips lasting a day or more and visitors are welcome to join in. Weekend or longer tours are organised by the national Bicyclub (*address above*). Lists of clubs and events are also organised by local members of the Fédération Française de Cyclotourisme (*address above*), write to them for regional or departmental offices. They also produce leaflets giving suggested cycle tours for independent travellers, ranging from easy terrain to very hard going for the more experienced cyclist, with details of accommodation, cycle repairers and other facilities en route.

Unlike the rest of France, Provence is not dissected by many waterways. The three main bodies of water that can be used for transportation are the Rhône River, the Durance River and the Mediterranean Sea.

Travel by water is both necessary and pleasant to visit any of the many offshore islands. You will find services ferry and boat companies easy to locate and reasonable.

For the **Ile de Bendor**, boats leave from Bandol at least 25 times a day, tel: 94.29.44.34. For the **Iles d'Hyères**, boats leave for Porquerolles from Tour Fondue between six and 19 times a day depending on the season. Boats to Port-Cros and Le Levant from the Port d'Hyères leave slightly less frequently – up to four times a day. The times vary according to the month, so get a schedule from SNCF or the tourist board. You can also take an all-day cruise to the islands from the Toulon Port on the Quai Stalingrad. Finally, in the summer, you can also sail to Porquerolles from Le Lavandou with one trip a day leaving at about 9am and returning in the evening. More frequent boats leave from the same port to Port-Cros and Levant in season.

You can also rent sailboats and yachts along the Mediterranean and the mouth of the Rhône. For example: **Eagle Yacht Charters**, 150 Main St, Port Washington, New York, NY 11050, tel: (516) 883 3033. Luxury crewed yachts for charter from any port in the Mediterranean. Bare boats from major Rivieran ports.

Or join a cruise along the Rhône or Camargue in a boat with or without living accommodation:

Tiki III, Capitaine Edmond Aupy, Rue de Petit-Rhône, 13640 Les-Stes-Maries-de-la-Mer, France, tel: 90.97.81.22; fax: 90.97.99.47.

Les 4 Maries, 29 Rue Mistral, 13450 Les-Stes-Maries-de-le-Mer, tel: 90.97.81.96; fax: 90.97.87.78.

L'Arlène, 30 Avenue Franklin Roosevelt, 75008 Paris, tel: (1) 43.59.37.41; fax: (1) 42.25.06.49.

Le Cyne, Rue Fourrier, 30300 Beaucaire, tel: 66.59.45.08. Seven-hour trips from Avignon down the Rhône through Arles to Aigues-Mortes. Discounts for senior citizens.

If you wish to navigate yourself on the Rhône, boats can be hired from:

Au Fil de l'Eau, 1 Rue Emile Zola, 94400 Vitry-sur-Seine, tel: (1) 46.80.60.70; fax: (1) 46.81.96.70. Camping boats based near Béziers.

DNP France, 20 Quai du Canal, 30800 Saint-Gilles, tel: 66.87.27.74; fax: 66.87.08.59.

Blue Line, 2 Quai de Canal, 30800 Saint-Gillies, tel: 66.87.22.66; fax: 66.87.15.20.

Some distances in spread-out Provence may seem daunting; however, once in a town or city, most sites are within easy walking distance from one another. Also, in certain parts of Provence, particularly the northern regions, the land is liberally crossed with wonderful walking and hiking trails.

The French Ramblers' Association, FFRP, publishes Topoguides (guide books incorporating IGN's 1:50,000 scal emaps). For information Sentiers et Randonnées, 64 Rue Gergovie, 75014 Paris, tel: (1) 45.45.31.02; fax: (1) 43.95.68.07.

The AVDTR in the Var (*see above*, Toursit Office addresses), publishes booklets of hiking trails and organises rambling holidays.

Tour operators offering packaged walking holidays include:

Clés de France, 13 Rue Saint-Louis, 78100 St-Germain-en-Laye, tel: (1) 30.61.23.23.

Ramblers Holidays, Box 43, Welwyn Garden City, Hertfordshire AL8 6PQ, tel: 01707 331133.

Sherpa Expeditions, 131a Heston Road, Hounslow, Middlesex TW5 0RD, tel: 0181-577 2717.

Waymark Holidays, 44 Windsor Road, Slough, Berkshire SL1 2EJ, tel: 01735 516477.

Hitchhiking is never the best means of travel. If you are determined to thumb it, however, you probably will find it relatively safe and easy.

Hitchhiking is forbidden on motorways, but you can wait at slip roads. **Allostop Provoya**, tel: (1) 42.46.00. 06, is a nationwide organisation which aims to connect hikers with drivers (you pay a registration fee and a contribution towards fuel).

Where to Stay

Hotels are plentiful in the main towns and along the main highways, but those in the smaller country villages can be the best. All hotels in France conform to national standards and carry ☆-ratings, set down by the Ministry of Tourism, according to their degree of comfort and amenities. Prices (which are charged per room, rather than per person) range from as little as 90 ff for a double room in an unclassified hotel (i.e. its standards are not sufficient to warrant a single star, but is likely to be clean, cheap and cheerful), to 550 ff for the cheapest double room in a ☆☆☆☆ luxury hotel.

Hotels are required to show their menus outside the hotel and details of room prices should be visible either outside or in reception, as well as on the back of bedroom doors. It is possible for a hotel to have a one-☆ rating, with a ☆☆ restaurant. This is ideal if you are on a budget and more interested in food than fading wallpaper or eccentric plumbing.

When booking a room, you should normally be shown it before agreeing to take it; if it doesn't suit you, ask to be shown another (this may sound odd advice, but rooms can vary enormously within the same building). Prices are charged per room; supplements may be charged for an additional bed or a cot (*lit bébé*). You may be asked when booking if you wish to dine, particularly if the hotel is busy – preference should not, but may in fact be given to hungry customers as there is not a lot of profit in letting rooms alone. Also the simple request, "*On peut dîner ici ce soir?*" will confirm that the hotel's restaurant is open (many are closed out of season on Sunday or Monday evenings).

Lists of hotels can be obtained from the French Government Tourist office in your country or from regional or local tourist offices in France. It is also worth buying from your local French Tourist Office the *Logis et Auberges de France* guide. This is an invaluable guide to a very good and reasonably priced network of family-run hotels who aim to offer a friendly welcome and good local cuisine. The guide can be bought in bookshops in France but it is more expensive. It can be used to book hotels before travelling (for the central reservation office in Paris, tel: (1) 45.84.83.84). Some tourist offices will make hotel bookings for you, for a small fee (usually around 15 ff).

Several hotel chains and associations offer central booking facilities. These range from the very cheap and simple groups such as the Balladins chain, which has almost 100 modern ☆ hotels, to the Concorde group of 28 ☆☆☆☆ and de-luxe hotels. A list of central booking offices is given below:

Altéa/Mercure, 7 Allée du Brévent, 91021 Evry Cedex Résinter, tel: (1) 60.77.27.27; fax: (1) 60.77.21.08. 160 ☆☆☆ hotels.

Balladins, 20 Rue du Pont-des-Halles, 94656 Rungis Cedex, tel: (1) 46.87.51.93; fax: (1) 46.87.68.60. ☆ budget-priced hotels.

Campanile, 31 Avenue Jean-Moulin, 77200 Torcy, tel: (1) 64.62.46.46; fax: (1) 64.62.46.61. 225 ☆☆ to ☆☆☆☆ hotels.
UK office: Red Lion Court, Alexandra Road, Hounslow, Middlesex TW3 1JS, tel: 0181-569 6969; fax: 0181-569 4888.

Climat de France, 5 Avenue du Cap-Horn, ZAC de Courtaboeuf, BP 93, 91943 Les Ulis, tel: (1) 64.46.01.23 or 05.11.22.11 (toll-free in France); fax: (1) 69.28.24.02. 150 ☆☆ hotels.
UK office: Voyages Vacances International, 34 Saville Row, London W1X 1AG, tel: 0171-287 3181.

Concorde Hotels, 35–37 Grosvenor Gardens, London SW1W 0BS, tel: 0171-630 1704; fax: 0171-630 0391.

Formule 1, Immeuble le Descartes, 29 Promenade Michel-Simon, 93163 Noisy-le-Grand, tel: (1) 43.04.01.00; fax: (1) 43.05.31.51. 178 ☆ budget-priced hotels, offering a booking service from one hotel to another in the chain.

Ibis/Arcade, 6–8 Rue du Bois-Briard, 91021 Evry Cedex, tel: (1) 60.77.27.27; fax: (1) 60.77.22.83. 170 ☆☆ hotels.
UK office: Resinter, 1 Shortland,s London W6 8DR, tel: 0171-724 1000; fax: 0181-748 9116.

Minotels France Accueil, 163 Avenue d'Italie, 75013 Paris, tel: (1) 45.83.04.22; fax: (1) 45.86.49.82. 150 ☆☆ and ☆☆☆ hotels.
UK office: France Accueil, Westfiled House, Bratton Road, Westbury, Wilts BA13 3EP, tel: 01373 824490; fax: 01373 825674; **or** Minotels Great Britain, 37 Springfield Road, Blackpool, FY1 1PZ, tel: 01253 292000; fax: 01253 291111.
US office: Minotels Europe, 683 South Collier Boulevard, Marco Island, Florida 33037, tel: (813) 394 3384 (toll free: 1-800-336 4668); fax: (813) 394 3384.
Canadian office: Tours Chanteclerc, 65 Rue de Brésoles, Montréal, Québec H2Y 1V7, tel: (514) 845 1236; fax: (514) 845 5794.

The following hotel groups do not have central booking facilities. Most of these groups offer something other than the average hotel. Each group produces its own brochure or list of hotels, available from the addresses below, but bookings have to be made with the individual establisments.

Châteaux-Demeures de Tradition et Grandes Etapes de Vignobles, BP 40, 13360 Roquevaire, tel: 42.04.41.97; fax: 42.72.83.81. 120 elegant ☆☆☆ hotels, particularly in wine-growing regions.

Moulin Etape, Moulin de Chameron, 18210 Bannegon, tel: 48.61.83.80; fax: 48.61.84.92. 48 former mills offering ☆ to ☆☆☆☆ accommodation.

Les Nids de France, 15 Rue Verdun, 78800 Houilles, tel: (1) 39.68.95.41. 43 ☆☆☆ family hotels.

Rand'Hotel, Chamina, BP 21, 8 Rue de Verdun, 15130 Arpajon-sur-Cère, tel: 71.64.54.23; fax: 71.63.53.58. 18 ☆ to ☆☆☆ hotels in the Massif Central, catering particularly for hikers.

Relais et Châteaux, 9 Avenue Marceau, 75116 Paris, tel: 47.23. 41.42; fax: (1) 47.23.38.99. 153 independently-owned hotels and restaurants in former castles and other historic buildings (guide available from French Government Tourist Offices abroad). UK information office: 28 Basil Street, London SW3 1AT.

Les Relais du Silence, 2 Passage Duguesclin, 75015 Paris, tel: (1) 45.66.77.77; fax: (1) 40.65.90.09. Over 200 ☆☆ to ☆☆☆☆ hotels in particularly tranquil settings.

Hotels

The following is a selective list of recommended hotels in Provence, arranged by *département*. For more information, you should contact the tourist office for your destination.

Vaucluse

Cité des Papes, 1 Rue Jean Vilar, 84000 Avignon, tel: 90.86.22.45; fax: 90.27.39.21. 65 rooms. If you are determined to stay next door to the lovely Palais in Avignon, consider the Cité des Papes. Be sure to request one of the quiet back rooms from where you get a palatial view. 450–550 ff

Ferme Jamet, Chambre d'Hôtes, Ile de Barthelasse, tel: 90.86.16.74. The Ferme Jamet stands on the Ile de Barthelasse some 3 miles (5 km) from the centre of Avignon. Simple, calm and pleasant, its five bungalows and two apartments share a tennis court, pool and fields of cereals, pine trees and vineyards.

Le Hameau-de-la-Lauze, Villes-sur-Auzon, tel: 90.61.83.23. A good starting point for hiking excursions around the Gorges de Nesque. Hidden among the woods, this *ferme-auberge* (farm-inn) is the essence of rusticity. It's charming, but don't expect silk sheets.

Hostellerie Le Beffroi, 84330 Caromb, tel: 90.62.45.63; fax: 90.62.30.15. 10 rooms. Comfortable and affordable rooms with picturesque beamed ceilings – it also boasts a first-class restaurant much admired by the locals.

Hôtel de Garlande, 20 Rue Galante, 84000 Avignon, tel: 90.85.08.85; fax: 90.27.16.58. 12 rooms. In the old town of Avignon, situated by the Place St-Didier, it is comfortable, straightforward and reasonable. 220–380 ff

Hôtel-Restaurant La Magnaneraie, 37 Rue Camp de Bataille, 30400 Villeneuve-les-Avignon, tel: 90.25.11.11; fax: 90.25.46.37. 25 rooms. When visiting Avignon, you may want to stay in nearby Villeneuve. The hotel is quiet and conveniently situated with an excellent restaurant, a swimming pool and tennis courts. It's not priced to fit into everyone's budget. 500–950 ff

Mas de la Tour, 84400 Gargas, tel: 90.74.12.10; fax: 90.04.83.67. 33 rooms. The *mas* is the traditional Provençal farmhouse, and a stay in one during your visit is *à propos*. Built in the 12th century, the Mas de la Tour now sports a swimming pool and is convenient to the Cavaillon region. 250–400 ff

La Mayanelle, 84220 Gordes, tel: 90.72.00.28; fax: 90.72.06.99. 9 rooms. Closed: 2 January–1 March. Excellent small hotel with a wonderful view of the Luberon. 320–420 ff

Le Mignon, 12 Rue Joseph Vernet, 84000 Avignon, tel: 90.82.17.30; fax: 90.85.78.46. 15 rooms. P-star, but surprisingly adequate for its category. It's not luxurious, but its location is central and its bathrooms sparkle.

The Squash Club, 32 Boulevard Limbert, 84000 Avignon, tel: 90.85.27.78. For inexpensive, barebones (but decent) accommodation in Avignon. Bed and breakfast are offered for under 60 ff.

Bouches-du-Rhone

Golf Club de Mouriès, 13890 Mouriès, tel: 90.47.59.95. A real find. Set in an old château, with a swimming pool and nice views, it is also very inexpensive. Mouriès is just to the east of Arles and a good back up when the latter town becomes overbooked.

Hôtel D'Arlatan, 26 Rue du Sauvage, 13200 Arles, tel: 90.93.56.66; fax: 90.49.68.45. 46 rooms. A very popular hotel. 250 ff

Hôtel des Quatre Dauphins, 54 Rue Roux Alpheron, 13100 Aix-en-Provence, tel: 42.38.16.39; fax: 42.38.60.19. 12 rooms. Inexpensive but comfortable accommodation in Aix. 290 ff

Hôtel Le Cloître, 18 Rue du Cloître, 13200 Arles, tel: 90.96.29.50; fax: 90.96.02.88. 33 rooms. Closed: January–February. Arles makes the perfect centre for any visit to the western part of the Bouches-du-Rhône or the Camargue. And, within Arles, you won't find a more conveniently located, pleasantly run and well-priced hotel. Set on a narrow street just a stone's throw away from the Roman theatre, you will feel Provençal without any discomfort. 222–320 ff

Hôtel Liautaud, 2 Rue Victor-Hugo, 13260 Cassis, tel: 42.01.75.37; fax: 42.01.12.08. 32 rooms. Although Cassis is somewhat more modest than Cannes, it still falls into the Côte d'Azur summer frenzy. Book well in advance, and you will find this water-front hotel a reasonably priced and accommodating place to stay. Whatever you do, however, don't wind up at the less salubrious, less well managed and less keenly priced Cassitel across the street. 260 ff

Hôtel Peireiro, Avenue des Baux, 13990 Fontvieille, tel: 90.97.76.10; fax: 90.54.76.10. 40 rooms. For those who prefer to stay outside the town centre of Arles. Lovely veranda and pool. 260 ff

Le Globe, 74 cours Sextius, 13100 Aix-en-Provence, tel: 42.26.03.58; fax: 42.26.13.68. 45 rooms. Guests generally consider themselves quite lucky to have found such nice rooms at reasonable prices. 220 ff

Pension Maguy, Avenue du Revestel, Cassis 13260, tel: 42.01.75.37. Inexpensive and centrally located.

Sofitel Vieux-Port, 36 Boulevard Charles Livon, 13001 Marseille, tel: 91.52.90.19; fax: 91.31.46.52. 130 rooms. Set right on the old harbour with wonderful porches that look out over the yachts and fishing boats, it is within reasonable walking distance of many of Marseille's major attractions. There is a small pool and several restaurants for afternoons when you're too hot to go anywhere. Its unparalleled elegance offers the visitor a great haven from the less-lovely aspects of this city and, at the same time, it manages to retain a real French flavour. 660 ff

Camargue

L'Auberge de la Fenière, RN 453, Raphèle, Arles, tel: 90.98.47.44; telex: 441 237. 25 rooms. Visitors to the Camargue may well want to make Arles their home base. This attractively converted farmhouse, conveniently located on N 453, just east of Arles and *en route* to the Camargue, has the added plus of a restaurant that serves both traditional French and Camarguais specialities. 210–488 ff

Alpes-de-Haute-Provence

Auberge Charembeau, N 100, 04300 Forcalquier, tel: 92.75.05.69. 11 rooms. Its claim to fame is its excellent home-cooking restaurant, which is open only to those staying in the hotel. 235–305 ff

Auberge du Parc, Place Charles Bron, 04170 St-Andre-les-Alpes, tel: 92.89.00.03. 12 rooms. Actually in

the town of St-Andre. Good restaurant.
Le Barrasson, 04160 Château-Arnoux, tel: 92.64.17.12. 12 rooms. 8 miles (14 km) from Sisteron in Chateau-Arnoux. Comfortable and inexpensive hotel, with a very good restaurant.
Francois 1èr, 18 Rue Guilhempierre, 04100 Manosque, tel: 92.72.07.99; fax: 92.72.14.34. 25 rooms. Basic, friendly hotel. 150–250 ff
Hostellerie des Deux Lions, 11 Place du Bourguet, 04300 Forcalquier, tel: 92.75.25.30. 15 rooms. Set on the main square of Forcalquier. Medium-priced, authentic 17th-century coaching inn. Has a good restaurant. 260–360 ff
Hôtel Coin Fleuri, 9 Boulevard Victor Hugo, 04000 Digne, tel: 92.31.04.51. 15 rooms. Visitors to Digne travelling on a more modest budget will find the Coin Fleuri a pleasant hotel and restaurant. 130–230 ff
Hôtel Honnoraty, Les Scaffarels, 04240 Annot, tel: 92.83.22.03. 10 rooms. Located just over 1 mile (2 km) outside of Annot. Charming, cheap and friendly – and its restaurant serves very good food. 150–240 ff
Hôtel le Chamois, 04370 Colmars-les-Alpes, tel: 92.83.43.29. 26 rooms. A nice place to make your base for sporting activities in the Colmars region. Pleasant and inexpensive, it also has its own restaurant. 170–280 ff
Hôtel le Colombier, Route d'Allos, 04170 St-Andre-les-Alpes, tel: 92.89.07.11. 24 rooms. Le Colombier offers a swimming pool and restaurant without being too pricey. The downside is that it is located about a mile outside of town. 150–300 ff
Hôtel Le Grand Paris, 19 Boulevard Thiers, 04000 Digne, tel: 92.31.11.15; fax: 92.32.32.82. 30 rooms. The place to stay in Digne for those with discerning taste and large wallets. Its restaurant is excellent. 400–460 ff
Hôtel Pyjama, Super-Sauze, tel: 92.81.12.00; fax: 92.81.03.16. 10 rooms. Open: 15 December–Easter and July–August. Ski buffs should head on up to the winter sports hotel. Geared for the snow seeker, it is also open in July and August. 320–420 ff
Hôtel St-Clair, Chemin du Serre, St-Etienne-les-Orgues, tel: 92.73.07.09. 28 rooms. Just over a mile south of St-Etienne-les-Orgues. In delightful surroundings, the hotel has a restaurant

and swimming pool. 172–373 ff
Hôtel Tivoli, Place du Tivoli, 04200 Sisteron, tel: 92.61.15.16. 19 rooms. A pleasant, medium-priced hotel with a well-above-average restaurant.
Ma Petite Auberge, Avenue F. Mistral, 04120 Castellane, tel: 92.83.62.06. 18 rooms. A modest, reasonably priced hotel in Castellane.

Var

Auberge des Adrets, RN 7, 83600 Fréjus, tel: 94.40.36.24. 10 rooms. In the heart of the Massif de L'Esterel. Luxurious coaching inn placed in a fabulously isolated location, it boasts a tennis court, swimming pool and nearby golf course and riding.
Auberge de la Tour, 83630 Aups, tel: 94.70.00.30. 24 rooms. Near the church in Aups. A comfortable spot with the bonus of a restaurant that serves local specialities.
Bastide de Tourtour, 83690 Tourtour, tel: 94.70.57.30; telex: 970 827; fax: 94.70.54.90. 26 rooms. Probably the most expensive and palatial place in the Var. 650–1,350 ff
Château d'Entrecasteaux, Entrecasteaux, tel: 94.04.43.95. Quite expensive but certainly the most unusual place to stay in the area. It offers a sort of bed-and-breakfast – but only in three rooms. The setting is, to put it mildly, sumptuous.
Hostellerie Allegre, 20 Rue J.J. Rousseau, 83690 Salernes, tel: 94.70.60.30. 26 rooms. A simple but comfortable hotel.
Hôtel Bel Ombra, Rue La Fontaine, 83150 Bandol, tel: 94.29.40.90. 20 rooms. Very reasonable in cost.
Hôtel Belle-Vue, Place Gambetta, 83230 Bormes-les-Mimosas, tel: 94.71.15.15. 14 rooms. If you are appalled by the high prices of the Côte will be relieved by those at this lovely hotel.
Hôtel La Claire Fontaine, Place Vieille, 83310 La Garde-Freinet, tel: 94.43.63.76. 8 rooms. Those wishing to escape the craze of St-Tropez should head up to the pretty, tiny La Claire Fontaine, set on the small main square. 180–240 ff
Hôtel des Deux Rocs, 83440 Seillans, tel: 94.76.87.32. 14 rooms. Set in a lovely spot above the town. Converted 18th-century manor house, complete with terrace and fountain outside. The price is medium-high, and it has a res-

taurant.
Hôtel Europe, 7 bis Rue Chabannes, 83000 Toulon, tel: 94.92.37.44. 30 rooms. Less expensive and close to the tourist office.
Hôtel Du Portalet, 4 Rue Limans, 83400 Hyères, tel: 94.65.39.40. 18 rooms. Pleasant, centrally located and easily affordable.
Hôtel du Parc, 21 Boulevard de la Liberté, 83300 Draguignan, tel: 94.68.53.84. 20 rooms. An ordinary but reliable hotel outside the old town. 250–300 ff
Hôtel Ker-Mocotte, Rue Raimu, 83150 Bandol, tel: 94.29.46.53 telex 400 383. 19 rooms, 210–285 ff. The sea-perched Ker-Mocotte was once home to the Provençal-born movie star Raimu. It's restaurant is open only to guests staying at the hotel.
Hôtel Pins d'Argent, Port St Pierre, tel: 94.57.63.60. 20 rooms. More expensive but by the beach. With a swimming pool and restaurant. 300–550 ff
Hôtel Pont d'Or, Route St-Maximin, 83670 Barjols, tel: 94.77.05.23. 16 rooms. Pleasant, inexpensive hotel.
Hôtel Tour, Quai General de Gaulle, 83110 Sanary-sur-Mer, tel: 94.74.10.10. 30 rooms. Located right next to the Saracen tower. Inexpensive but good value.
New Hôtel Amirauté, 4 Rue Adolphe-Guiol, 83000 Toulon, tel: 94.22.19.67. 64 rooms. A lovely hotel, centrally located. Medium-range price.

Alpes-Maritimes

Auberge de la Roya, Saorge, tel: 93.04.50.19. Comfortable, cheap hotel run by lovely people.
Au Logis du Puei, 06450 Bollène-Vésubie, tel: 93.03.01.05. 16 rooms, 150–260 ff w/o pension, 565–685 ff w/pension. Quiet hotel with 16 rooms and an excellent restaurant.
Château de la Chevre d'Or, Rue de Barri, 06360 Eze, tel: 93.41.12.12; fax: 93.41.06.72. 20 rooms. Open: March–November. An unforgettable experience. Its four-star restaurant offers a magnificent view of the coast from Nice to Monaco, and its hotel combines a warm provincial elegance with Riviera élan. 1,700–3,200 ff
Domaine du Foulon, Route de Gourdon, 06620 Gréolières, tel: 93.59.95.02. 13 rooms. Pleasant hotel beside a park about 2½ miles (4

km) outside Greolieres.

Las Donnas, Rue Marie Madeleine, 06660 Auron, tel: 93.23.00.03; fax: 93.23.07.37. 48 rooms. Comfortable. Moderate rates. 225–425 ff

Hôtel Les Prés, 06670 Levens, tel: 93.79.70.35. 8 rooms. Small, quiet hotel. 230 ff

Pinatelle, Boulevard d'Auron, 06660 St-Etienne-de-Tinée, tel: 93.02.40.36 fax: 93.02.47.90. 14 rooms. Very inexpensive and not exactly deluxe – but more than acceptable.

Cote d'Azur

Auberge Les Santons, Colline de l'Annonciade, 06500 Menton, tel: 93.35.94.10. Has a great view of the Riviera.

Bel Air du Cap Ferrat, Boulevard Général de Gaulle, 06290 St-Jean-Cap-Ferrat, tel: 93.76.50.50; fax: 93.76.04.52. 59 rooms. Open: July–October. Exclusive is this hotel's middle name. Its first name is expensive. 950–8,900 ff

Hôtel Byblos, Avenue Paul Signac, 83990 St-Tropez, tel: 94.97.00.04; fax: 94.97.40.52. 107 rooms. Open: March–November. Another place to throw some money around. 700–4.500 ff

Hôtel Frisia, 2 Boulevard E. Gauthier, 06310 Beaulieu-sur-Mer, tel: 93.01.01.04; fax: 93.01.31.92. 35 rooms. Closed: November. Not too bad – for the Côte – in price and set across from the port in Beaulieu-sur-Mer. Best are the rooms with terraces. 280–570 ff

Hôtel Rialto, 55 Rue de la Buffa, 06000 Nice, tel: 93.88.15.04. 105–180 ff (all doubles), no credit cards. Only two of its eight rooms have their own showers, but it does have the distinction of being only two blocks from the ocean. Also, most rooms have kitchenettes.

Relais du Postillon, 8 Rue Championnet, 06600 Antibes, tel: 93.34.20.77. 14 rooms. It's hard to find a bargain in high season on the Côte d'Azur, but Postillon in the old town of Antibes is pretty close to one. It's pleasant enough – but not by the sea. 240–350 ff

Sofitel-Mediteranée, 2 Boulevard Jean Hibert, 06400 Cannes, tel: 93.99.22.75; fax: 93.39.68.36. 152 rooms. Standing on the tip of the Croisette, its beautifully appointed rooms, looking out over the sea, seem

right out of a fine country home. Swimmers can enjoy the beachfront across the street and the rooftop pool. Everyone enjoys the excellent and courteous service. This is a first-class business and luxury hotel all the way. 590–790 ff

Sofitel Splendid, 50 Boulevard Victor Hugo, 06048 Nice, tel: 93.16.41.00; fax: 93.87.02.46. 130 rooms. Close to the city centre and only 440 yards (400 metres) from the sea. 690–1,060 ff

---

The *Gîtes Ruraux* (farmhouse accommodations) are a great way to dig right into Provençal life. Basically, the *gîtes* are traditionally arranged houses or flats situated nearby a farm or village. They can be rented for anything from a weekend to several weeks and are a great alternative from the hotel circuit for those (especially with children) looking for a peaceful respite in the countryside.

To rent a *gîte*, you first buy a catalogue appropriate to the region from that *département's* Reservations Service. Inside you will find descriptions, photos, prices and phone numbers for a large selection of farmhouses. When you've found one that appeals to you, you can either contact the owners directly or go through the departmental Reservation Service.

Vaucluse

Gîtes de France, Chambre Départementale de Tourisme, Place Campana La Balance, BP 147, 84008 Avignon Cedex, tel: 90.85.45.00; fax: 90. 85.88.49. Catalogue: 37 ff.

Bouches-du-Rhône

Gîtes de France, Domaine du Vergon, 13370 Mallemort, tel: 90.59.18.05; fax: 90.59.16.75. Catalogue: 35 ff.

Alpes-de-Hautes-Provence

Gîtes de France, Maison du Tourisme, Rond-Pont du 11 Novembre, BP 201, 04001 Digne Cedex, tel: 92.31. 52.39; fax: 92.32.32.63. Catalogue: 50 ff.

Var

Gîtes de France, Conseil Général, Rond-Point du Draguignan, BP125, 41274 Draguignan Cedex, tel:

94.67.10.40; fax: 94.68.69.84. Catalogue: 66 ff.

Alpes-Maritimes

Gîtes de France, 55 Promenade des Anglais, BP 602, 06011 Nice Cedex 1, tel: 93.44.39.39; fax: 93.86.01.06. Catalogue: 66 ff.

If you do not wish to book direct, there is a booking service in London, **Gîtes de France**, 178 Piccadilly, London W1V 9DB, tel: 0171-493 3480. Alternatively, the main ferry companies offer gîte holidays inclusive with channel crossing.

The regional tourist offices (*see above* Useful Addresses) each produce their own lists of all recognised sites, with details of ☆-rating and facilities.

As with other types of holiday accommodation, the sites can get booked up in high season, so do consider advance booking. Members of the Camping Club or Camping and Caravanning Club of Great Britain may make use of their booking services. The Michelin Camping/Caravanning Guide lists sites which accept (or insist on) pre-booking.

The Camping Service at 69 Westbourne Grove, London W2 4UJ, tel: 0171-792 1944, can book sites either from their own brochure of ☆☆☆ and ☆☆☆☆ sites or certain others and will also book ferries. A camping *carnet* is useful (some sites will not accept a booking without one).

Campsites, like hotels have official classifications from ☆ (minimal comfort, water points, showers and sinks) to ☆☆☆☆ luxury sites with more space to each pitch, and offer above-average facilities, often including a restaurant or takeway food, games areas and swimming-pools. The majority of sites nationwide are ☆☆. Average prices are around 20 ff per person per night at a ☆ site, to around 45 ff at a ☆☆☆☆ site.

If you really like to get back to nature, and are unimpressed by the modern trappings of hot water and electric power, look out for camp-sites designated *Aire naturelle de camping* where facilities will be absolutely minimal and prices to match. These have a maximum of 25 pitches so offer the opportunity to stay away from some of the more commercial sites (which can be huge).

The French Federation of Camping and Caravanning Guide (FFCC) can be obtained from Springdene, Shepherd's Way, Fairlight, East Sussex TN3 4BB. The guide lists over 2,000 sites and includes details of sites accessible to disabled people.

Some farms offer "official" sites too under the auspices of the Fédération Nationale des Gîtes Ruraux – these are designated *Camping à la ferme*, again facilities are usually limited but farmers are only allowed to have six pitches and if you are lucky you will get to know and enjoy the farm life and some of its produce.

Packaged camping holidays are now very popular with British holidaymakers and ideal for other overseas visitors too, as all the camping paraphernalia is provided on the site – you only have to take your personal luggage. Many companies now offer this type of holiday, mostly with ferry travel included in the all-in price. Most of the companies have couriers on the sites to help with any problems.

It is interesting to note that where such companies have taken over sections of existing sites, that facilities have improved to meet the demands of their customers and so benefit all campers. Many companies offer good opportunities for sports and leisure, such as wind-surfing or surfing; often the equipment, and sometimes instruction too is covered by the cost of the package. Be warned, though, that some of the sites are very large, so might not suit those who wish to get away from it all.

Tour operators include:

Canvas Holidays, 12 Abbey Park Place, Dunfermline KY12 7PD, tel: 01383 62100. Pioneers in the field; offers a nanny service.

Euroecamp Travel, Canute Court, Toft Road, Knutsford, Cheshire WA16 0NL, tel: 01565 626262.

Keycamp Holidays, Ellerman House, 93–96 Lind Road, Sutton, SM1 4PL, tel: 0181-394 4000.

Youth Hostels

Holders of accredited Youth Hostel Association cards may stay in any French hostels which are in fact run by two separate organisations; Fédéra-

tion Unie des Auberges de Jeunesse (FUAJ), 27 Rue Pajol, 75018 Paris, tel: (1) 44.89.87.27; fax: (1) 44.89.87.10 which is affiliated to the International Youth Hostel Federation; and the Ligue Française pour les AubergesÁ de Jeunesse (LFAJ), 38 Boulevard Raspail, 75007 Paris, tel: (1) 45.48.69.84; fax: 45.44.57.47. Expect to pay around 60 ff per night.

The British **Yough Hostel Association** publishes the *International Youth Hostel Handbook, Vol. I* (revised each March), which includes all the hostels in the region. Contact the Youth Hostel Association, 8 St Stephen's Hill, St Alban's, Hertofrdshire, tel: 01272 845047 or person from: 14 Southampton Street, London WC2E 7HT, tel: 0171-836 8541. They also handle membership queries, tel: 0171-836 1036.

In the US apply to the **American Youth Hostels Inc**, PO Box 37613, Dept USA, Washington DC 20013/7613, tel: (202) 783 6161.

Gîtes d'Etapes

Gîtes d'Etapes offer hostel accommodation and are popular with ramblers, climbers and horse riders (some offer stabling). All official *Gîtes d'Étapes* come under the auspices of the Relais Départementaux des Gîtes Ruraux. These are a popular form of cheap accommodation particularly in the national parks. Prices are similar to youth hostels – around 50 ff per night for basic accommodation, but up to 110 ff or more in the more luxurious establishments which may be on farms offering riding facilities and/or stabling. You do not have to be a member of any organisation to use them.

University Residences

To arrange a stay in a university residence, you should go through the "Crous" university extension service.

AIX-EN-PROVENCE

Crous, Cité "Les Gazelles", Avenue Jules-Ferry, 13621 Aix Cedex 1, tel: 42.26.33.75.

MARSEILLE

Crous, 38 Rue du 141 e-RIA, 13331 Marseille Cedex 3, tel: 91.95.90.06.

Food Digest

What to Eat

In place of France's traditional rich cream sauces (although you can always find these, if it's what you want), Provençal cuisine uses only the freshest of pungent herbs, garlic and olive oils to enhance meals of the most delicate local meat, fish or shellfish served with the most succulent, sun-bursting tomatoes, eggplant or asparagus. It is hard to imagine anyone, no matter what the taste or diet, going hungry in Provence.

Among the specialities of Provence are:

gigot de mouton	leg of lamb, especially that of Sisteron
daube	beef braised with spices and red wine
gardianne	a strictly Camarguais bull stew with olives
pieds-paquets	tripe stuffed with garlic, onion, etc.
anything *farci*	stuffed meat, fish, fowl or vegetable
ratatouille	vegetable stew
bourride	white fish served in a clear soup with *aioli*
soupe au pistou	a herby vegetable soup with beans
soupe de poisson	an all-liquid fish soup, served with a spicy mayonnaise called *rouille* and croutons
poutargue	mullet eggs grated in oil – "white caviar"
anchoïade	crushed anchovies and olive oil on bread
brandade	crushed cod with olive oil
tapenade	cream of black olive, served on bread
aïoli	garlic-mayonnaise condiment

goat cheese	a gaggle of different
bouillabaisse	rockfish such as
	rascasse, fielas
	(eel) and *St-Pierre*
	served whole in a
	bath of *soupe de*
	poisson

Perhaps the most celebrated aspect of the cuisine is its use of the *herbes de Provence* – wildly aromatic herbs like basil and oregano, grown all over the dry and sun-parched Provençal countryside.

Of course, where exactly you are in Provence will determine the local speciality. Along the coast it may include fish and crustaceans, while lamb and *farcis* are found inland. The Camargue has its own, exceedingly exotic cuisine, as seems appropriate for the cowboy life.

The Vaucluse and Bouches-du-Rhône are particularly famous for their abundance of luscious produce – the melons of Cavaillon, cherries of Malaucène, strawberries of Carpentras, peaches of Cabannes, olives of the Crau Plain, etc. – but, everywhere, the fruit and vegetables will be fresh.

Various areas are known for their desserts:

Carpentras:	*berlingots* (a sort of caramel candy); and chocolate truffles.
Aix:	*calissons* (an almond-paste confectionery).
Marseille:	*navettes* (a sweet biscuit shaped as a boat); and *pompes à l'huile*.
Puyricard:	chocolate.
Allauch:	*suce-miel* (honey-based candy).
Alpes-Maritimes:	honey cakes and candy.
From all over:	*nougat* (a sugar-paste candy with nuts); and *fougasses* (bread with nuts, olives or cheese).

Where to Eat

Look for basic, family-run restaurants with fresh-daily menus, and you can't go wrong. Markets are another great place. Bring a knife and wander.

Vaucluse

La Fourchette II, 17 Rue Racine, 84000 Avignon, tel: 90.85.20.93. For contemporary bistro-style food with a Provençal touch. The menu of the day is always affordable.

Hostellerie la Magnaneraie, Rue de Camp de Bataille, 30400 Villeneuve-les-Avignon, tel: 90.25.11.11. Even if you don't choose to stay at the hotel, you can still enjoy a sumptuous feast on its well-shaded pleasant porch.

Hostellerie Le Beffroi, 84330 Caromb, tel: 90.62.45.63. You must be sure to make reservations ahead of time, for the locals are committed fans of its delicious menu.

Les Lavandes, Place Leon Doux, 84390 Monieux, tel: 90.64.05.08. A spectacular view, and its charm is enhanced by the many riders who come into the mountain to dine here, tying their horses in the square adjacent to the restaurant.

Lou Barri, Seguret. A charming tea room with a very pretty view.

Le Mas de Cure Bourse, Route de Caumont, RD25, 84800 L'Isle-sur-la-Sorgue, tel: 90.38.16.58. For a delicious traditional Provençal meal in a cozy, restored *mas*.

Le Mesclun, Rue des Poternes, 84110 Séguret, tel: 90.46.93.43. You can sit on the tranquil dining terrace and point to the vineyard whose wine you would like to have with your meal. In addition, the portions are lavish and the desserts simply irresistible.

Le Saule Pleureur, Le Pont des Vaches, Route dAvignon, 84170 Monteux, tel: 90.62.01.35; fax: 90.62.10.90. This little restaurant well deserves the reputation that keeps guests coming out of their way to dine here.

Restaurant de France, 12 cours Joel-Estève, Serignan, tel: 94.70.06.83. A bit off the beaten track but worth a stop (just northeast in Serignan near Orange).

Tante Jeanne, on an unmarked dirt road, near Buoux. No telephone. Tante Jeanne's address is a well-guarded secret near Apt and not far from the hamlet of Buoux (*see article on cuisine*) with no telephone. Nonetheless, true fans of Provençal cuisine should consider the search a small price to pay for having Sunday lunch here. The meal begins at 11.30am precisely.

Bouches-du-Rhone

For regional specialities Aix-en-Provence-style try **Le Félibre**, hidden away on one of the old town's myriad back streets. To begin, choose the sampler of local appetisers.

More Provençal cuisine can be sampled at **Côte d'Aix**, also in the town centre.

Le Miramar, 12 Quai du Port, 13002 Marseille, tel: 91.91.10.40. Only 14 restaurants belong to the "Guild of the Bouillabaisse Marseillaise" – 12 of which are in Marseille. Always phone ahead of time since the dish takes hours to prepare. It's served elegantly here – for a hefty price.

Chez Fonfon, 140 Vallon des Auffes, 13007 Marseille, tel: 91.52.14.38. Another guild member, located by the edge of the Marseillaise seaside.

L'Epuisette, Vallon des Auffes, 13007 Marseille, tel: 91.52.17.82. A third guild member. The establishment's fresh fish, and *bourride*, served on an open terrace, make for a nice alternative to *bouillabaisse*.

Chez Gilbert, Quai Baux, 13260 Cassis, tel: 42.01.71.36. Most of the harbour-front restaurants can be counted on to serve excellent fresh fish. Outstanding among them, however, is the delectable Chez Gilbert. And, for the quality of the meal, the price is not outrageous.

Les Arsenaulx, Restaurant-Salon de Thé, 25, cours d'Estienne d'Orves, 13001 Marseille, tel: 91.54.77.06; fax: 91.54.76.33. Excellent and inspired menu, it is imaginatively located within an ancient stone arsenal adjoined to a bookstore and tea house. Much of the fare is fresh fish but It's not wildly expensive (120–150 ff) and it's a real find. Ultra-cool as only Marseille can do it – hip without being at all adolescent.

Le Cave de Mon Oncle Tam, Aix-en-Provence. An excellent and slightly more atmospheric spot for traditional French food.

Le Gibassier, 46 Rue Espariat, 13100 Aix-en-Provence, tel: 42.27.53.54. Late-night *boulangerie* (bakery). Insomniacs will appreciate their 2am–1pm and 2–8pm hours.

Le Madeleine, Place de Verdun, 13100 Aix-en-Provence. A good old stand-by. It's not exotic, but you can be confident that you will eat well.

La Presqu'île, Route de Port-Miou, Les Calanques, 13260 Cassis, tel: 42.01.03.77; fax: 42.01.94.49. Fabulous view of the cliffs in Cassis. Its menu, also, is pretty special, although some might say pretentious. Expensive.

La Regalido, 13990 Fontvieille, tel: 90.97.60.22. The restaurant is set in a restored olive-oil mill brightly decorated with flowers. Not only a culinary but an aesthetic treat. The menu is fairly costly, but they do take American Express, Diners Club and Visa.

Le Temps de l'Heure, Rue Vauvenargues, 13100 Aix-en-Provence. Does not serve dinner or any hard alcohol and the service can be unbelievable slow, but it's still an extremely popular place for tea and dessert, a cold beer or glass of wine. Its *tarte maman* (apple tart) is not to be beaten.

Le Vaccarès, Place Forum, 13200 Arles, tel: 90.96.06.17; fax: 90.96.24.52. The perenially popular Vaccarès counts among its illustrious clientele writers Michel Tournier, Yvan Audouard and Daniel Boulanger as well as fashion designer Christian Lacroix. Menu at 145–180 ff.

Les Thes-Tard, 2 Rue Vian, 13001 Marseille, tel: 91.42.29.74. Each table and chair bears a unique design *à* Picasso, and the clientele is generally equally artsy. The food is earthy in a very French way, and on Sunday mornings you can enjoy a musical brunch American or Viennese style for 50 ff. A la carte menu 45–70 ff, set menus at 35 and 40 ff. Open: 11am–2am. Closed: Tuesday.

Lou Gardianoun, Rue Noguier, 13200 Arles, tel: 90.93.66.28. Another well-liked restaurant that specialises in Camargue cuisine. Menu 75–150 ff.

O'Stop, Place de l'Opéra, 13001 Marseille, tel: 91.33.85.34. An all-night restaurant with a charming, rustic atmosphere. 50–80 ff. Open: 3pm–6am.

Oustau de Baumanière, 13520 Maussane-les-Alpilles, tel: 90.97.33.07. One of France's very best restaurants. It is also priced accordingly. Here, you won't find any hearty stews, although the basis is still strictly Provençal, with an emphasis on fresh local produce.

Restaurant Le Saigon, 8 cours Jean-Ballard, 13001 Marseille, tel: 91.33.21.72. Excellent Vietnamese food, served with traditional grace and at attractive prices. Best are the innovative dishes that blend Oriental and Provençal styles. Open: noon–2pm and 7–11pm. Closed: Monday.

Rizerie du Petit Manusclat, Le Sambuc, 13200 Arles, tel: 90.98.90.29. Rice is what makes the Camargue go round. For some delicious examples in a very interesting place.

Vitamine, Rue Dr Fanton, 13200 Arles, tel: 90.93.77.36. If you're dying for fresh salad, American health-food style, and don't mind putting up with an uppity owner and slightly inappropriate prices.

Camargue

Le Bistro du Paradou, Avenue de la Vallée des Baux, 13125 La Paradou, tel: 97.32.70. A genuine country café, with one daily meal, one price and a real homespun atmosphere. Unsurprisingly, the cuisine is Provençal.

Boduc Lighthouse, south along the road to salins-de-giraud. Make a stop to try Juju's fresh fish.

La Camargue, Rue Republique, 30220 Aigues-Mortes, tel: 66.53.86.88. A good local restaurant.

La Fenière, RN 453, Raphèle, Arles, tel: 90.98.47.44. A pretty farmhouse conveniently located right outside Arles. It offers both *Camarguais* and traditional French cuisine. 120–170 ff.

Hôtel Le St-Gilloir, St-Gilles. Vegetarians are in for a treat. The menu offers some tasty vegetable-based local dishes, especially during asparagus season.

Alpes-de-Haute-Provence

André, 21 bis Place Terreau, 04100 Manosque, tel: 92.72.03.09. A good, inexpensive restaurant.

Auberge Charembeau, 04300 Forcalquier, tel: 92.75.05.69. Offers good homecooking to the guests in its hotel.

Auberge de Reillanne, 04110 Reillanne, tel: 92.76.45.95. For high-class country-style cooking in a beautiful setting.

Le Grand Paris, 19 Boulevard Thiers, 04000 Digne, tel: 92.31.11.15; fax: 92.32.32.82. Serves pricey regional dishes that have been critically acclaimed.

Hostellerie de la Fuste, Route D4, La Fuste, tel: 92.72.05.95; fax: 92.72.92.93. If something special is what you're after, reserve a table for an all-out meal at the beautiful Hostellerie de la Furste just outside Manosque.

La Mangeoire, Place 4-Vents, 04400 Barcelonette, tel: 92.81.01.61; fax: 92.81.01.61. Although it is closed most of June, Sunday nights and all of Monday, La Mangeoire is a popular place.

Les Santons, Place de l'Eglise, 04360 Moustiers-Ste-Marie, tel: 92.74.66.48. Reserve a table for a pleasant, medium-high priced meal.

Var

Auberge de la Rade, Bord de Mer, 83700 Agay, tel: 94.82.00.37. Restaurants in the Massif d'Esterel are generally more expensive than their northern brethren, but this one is both good and quite reasonable.

Auberge du Vieux Fox, Place de l'Eglise, Fox-Amphoux, tel: 94.80.71.69. A real find.

Auberge la Verdoyante, 83990 Gassin, tel: 94.56.16.23. Also in Gassin is a small *auberge* with good quality meals (but no rooms).

Au Sourd, 10 Rue Molière, 8300 Toulon, tel: 94.92.28.52. A good standby, unless you are there in July when it is, rather inconveniently, closed.

Bello Visto, Auberge la Verdoyante, 83990 Gassin, tel: 94.56.16.23. Aptly named – drinks and/or meals served on its terrace are accompanied by a fabulous view. The establishment also has nine rooms for overnight guests.

Chez Nous, Boulevard Jean Juarès, 83470 St-Maximin-la-Ste-Baume, tel: 94.78.02.57. You'll be assured of a civilised, respectably priced dinner.

Le Delphin, 7 Rue Roux-Seigneuret, 83400 Hyères, tel: 94.65.04.27. Quality dining.

Les Deux Cochers, Boulevard G-Peri, 83300 Draguignan, tel: 94.68.13.97; fax: 94.70.82.40. Has a pleasant terrace.

La Faucado, Route Nationale, 83310 La Garde-Freinet, tel: 94.43.60.41. Has the special benefit of a beautiful open-air terrace.

Le Lézard, 7 Place du Marché, 83310 La Garde-Freinet, tel: 94.43.62.73. A trendy restaurant/bar.

Lou Calen, 1 cours Gambetta, 83570

Cotignac, tel: 94.04.60.40; fax: 94.04.76.64. Deservedly one of the most popular quality restaurants in the north central Var. It is set within an equally well-liked hotel, and both are a good find.

Parc, Corniche Bonaparte, 83150 Bandol, tel: 94.32.36.36; fax: 94.32.56.29. Enjoy a medium-priced meal. Fish specialities.

Pascal, Square L.-Varane, 83000 Toulon, tel: 94.92.79.60. You will find an good selection of North-African residents' cuisine in this interesting part of the old town.

Alpes-Maritime

Auberge de la Madone, Peillon Village, L'Escarène, 06440 Peillon, tel: 03.79.91.17. For a well-prepared, unpretentious dining experience at reasonable prices.

Château de la Chèvre d'Or, Place Felix-Fauré, 06450 St-Martin Vésubie, tel: 93.41.12.12; fax: 93.41.06.72. A PPPP-star restaurant with a view from Nice to Monaco.

Chez Henri, Place du Village, 06570 St-Paul-de-Vence, tel: 93.32.82.75. Pleasant, mid-priced restaurant. No reservations.

Le Feu-Follet, Place de la Mairie, 06250 Mougins, tel: 93.90.15.78; fax: 93.75.72.83. Next door to Le Relais and much less frightening prices. Reserve a few days ahead of time.

Moulin de Mougins, Quartier Notre-Dame de Vie, 06250 Mougins, tel: 93.75.78.24; fax: 93.90.18.55. Roger Vergé, the chef, is the most influential of all the great chefs of the Côte d'Azur. A visit to his restaurant is certainly to be cherished. In summer, reserve at least two or three weeks ahead of time and, whenever you go, bring a good 600 ff.

Le Relais à Mougins, Place de la Mairie, 06250 Mougins, tel: 93.90.03.47; fax: 93.75.72.83. Stressful to the wallet is Le Relais à Mougins. In summer, reserve at least ten days ahead of time.

Les Plantanes, 17 route Nationale, 06540 Fontan, tel: 93.04.53.06. Les Plantanes, "Chez Mario," offers the specialties of the Saorge Valley: Raviolis!

Cote d'Azur

La Barale, 39 Rue Beaumont, 06300 Nice, tel: 93.89.17.94. "La Mère Barale", *restauratrice extraordinaire*, is probably one of the best-known personalities in Nice. Anything out of the kitchen tastes fabulous, but specialities include *estocaficada* and Provençal ravioli *(ralhola)*. They serve dinner only, for a menu under 200 ff that includes wine. Closed: Sunday, Monday and all of August.

Le Chicorée, 5 Rue du Lieutenant Colonelli, 06310 Beaulieu-sur-Mer, tel: 93.01.01.27. There is no fixed menu, since all depends on the day's catch.

La Mère Besson, 13 Rue des Frères Pradignac, 06400 Cannes, tel: 93.39.59.24; fax: 93.99.10.48. For a bit of Provençal along the Riviera. They do not serve lunch in July and August and are always closed on Sunday.

La Merenda, 4 Rue Terasse, 06000 Nice. A strictly unpretentious bistro with terrific regional food. It makes for a nice change after the touristic fanfare found in many places along the Côte. Closed: Saturday night, Sunday, Monday and all of February and August. No phone.

Le Pizza, Quai St-Pierre, 06400 Cannes. For the best flame-oven-cooked pizza in Cannes, maybe anywhere. The tiny, tight-shirted proprietors, with classically "Italian" temperaments they do nothing to hide, also offer a wide variety of Italian favourites that anyone can afford.

Le Portofino, Beaulieu Port, 06310 Beaulieu-sur-Mer, tel: 93.01.16.30. The excellent *soupe de poisson* is a bargain at 60 ff. Be sure to order the day before since it is made fresh for you.

Restaurant Bacon, Boulevard Bacon, 06600 Cap d'Antibes, tel: 93.61.50.02; fax: 93.61.65.19. Reserve a week ahead and ask for a table with a view. (Keep in mind that they only take Diners Club and Visa, and lunch alone starts at 250 ff.)

La Saleya, 06300 Nice, tel: 93.62.29.62. Funky brasserie, set in a great place to hang out – Nice's flower market.

Vien Dong, St-Tropez, tel: 94.97.09.78. The food is very good, but that's only half the attraction. Its owner is the other half – a former Mr Universe.

Les Vieux Murs, Avenue Admiral-de-Grasse, 06600 Antibes, tel: 93.34.06.73; fax: 93.34.81.08. A great and fairly reasonably priced meal can be had whilst sitting comfortably along-side the ancient sea wall. Moderately priced.

Drinking Notes

Provençal vineyards are rich and varied, producing reds, whites and rosés of decent to superb quality.

The most famous wines made in Provence come from the *département* of the Vaucluse and are more properly classified under the "Côtes du Rhône." Among these, Châteauneuf-du-Pape is the most celebrated. Full-bodied with a fruity flavour, the reds, in particular, are considered among the top French wines. Also excellent are the slightly lesser-bodied reds of Gigondas, the Vaqueyras and Séguret wines, and sweet muscat wine from Beaune de Venise.

The "Côtes de Provence" comprises the region between Aix and Nice, of which the most famous are the Bandols. Aix-en-Provence and the Baux-de-Provence vineyards have their own *appellation*. These wineries are situated between Mount Ste-Victoire and the Rhône in the Arles district. The best of their wines are the delicious whites from Cassis and Palette.

In Aigues-Mortes of the Camargue, the local wine is Listel. It is remarkable for being a *vin de sable*, which means, literally, that it is made from vines that grow directly out of the sand. The white is called *gris de gris* and the red is called *rubis*.

Provence also is the home of the famed *pastis*, which is an anise-flavoured aperitif.

In the wine-growing region of the Vaucluse, you will find numerous *caves* open for wine-tasting. For example:

La Domaine les Palliers, 84190 Gigondas, tel: 90.65.85.07. Prop. M. Roux.

A couple from the Bouches-du-Rhône are:

Château d'Estoublon-Mogador, 13990 Fontvieille, tel: 90.54.64.00. Prop. M. Lombrage père & fils. Open for on-site sale of their wines and a chat with the long-time owner who speaks French and English and is very talkative.

Château Revelette, 13490 Jouques, tel: 42.63.75.43. Prop. Peter Fischer. Open: Monday, Wednesday and Saturday for tasting, a tour of their cave and on-site sale of their young wines. The chateau is located just south of the Durance.

Attractions

Museums

A complete list of museums worth visiting in Provence and along the Côte d'Azur would be endless. Most museums charge an entrance fee, but are often free or half-price on Sunday. As a rule, national museums are closed on Tuesday, municipal museums on Monday. Opening times vary. Most close for a long lunch break, noon–2pm or noon–2.30pm, although major sites are often open continuously, especially in summer. Listed below are some of the more well-known sites.

Pays d'Arles

Musée Réattu in Arles. Open: October–March 10am–12.30pm and 2–5.45pm; April–May 9.30am–12.30pm and 2–7pm; June–September 9.30am–7pm.

All other museums in Arles. Open: November–February 9am–noon and 2–4.30pm; March 9am–12.30pm and 2–6pm; April 9am–12.30pm and 2–6.30pm; May 9am–12.30 and 2–7pm; June–9 August 8.30am–7.30pm.

Château Barbentane in Barbentane, tel: 90.95.51.07. Outside season: open only on Sunday. In season: July–September, open every day 10am–noon and 2–6pm at 30-minute intervals.

Cathédral d'Images in Les Beaux. Open: 18 March–11 November 10am–7pm (after October closes at 6pm and on Tuesday). Les Beaux has several other museums.

Musée des Alpilles in St-Rémy: tel: 90.92.13.07. Open: dail 10am–noon, 2–6om (3–8pm July and August).

Aix

Musée Granet, tel: 42.38.14.70. Open: 10am–noon and 2–6pm. Closed: Saturday.

Musée du Vieil Aix, tel: 42.21.43.55. Open: 10am–noon and 2.30–6pm. Closed: Monday.

Museum d'Histoire Naturelle, tel: 42.42.26.23.67. Open: 10am–noon and 2–6pm. Closed: Sunday morning.

Musée Paul-Arbaud, tel: 42.38.38.95. Open: 2–5pm. Closed: Sunday and holidays and all September.

Pavillon Vendome, tel:42.21.05.78. Open: 8.30am–noon and 2–6pm. Closed: Tuesday.

Atelier Cézanne, tel: 42.21.06.53. Open: 10am–noon and 2.30–6pm. Closed: Tuesday and holidays.

Fondation Vasarely, tel: 42.20.01.09. Open: 9.30am–12.30pm and 2–5.30pm. Closed: Tuesday (except July and August). (A bus leaves from the Boulevard de la République every half hour.)

Marseille

Musée d'Histoire de Marseille, tel: 91.90.42.22. Open: noon–7pm. Closed: Sunday. Métro: Vieux-Port. Admission: free Wednesday afternoon.

Musée Cantini, tel: 91.54.77.75. Open 11am–6pm. Métro: Vieux Port-Hôtel de Ville.

Musée de Vieux Marseille, tel: 91.90.80.28. Open daily. Métro: Vieux Port-Hôtel de Ville.

Docks Romains, tel: 91.91.24.62. Open daily. Métro: Vieux Port-Hôtel de Ville.

Musée d'Archéologie (Borély), tel: 91.79.29.10. Open: 9.30am–noon and 1–5.30pm. Bus: #44 (enter Avenue Clot-Bey) or #19 (enter Parc Borély).

Musée des Beaux-Arts: tel: 91.62.21.17. Open daily. Métro: Longchamp-Cinq Avenue.

Musée d'Histoire Naturelle, tel: 91.62.30.78. Closed Tuesday and Wednesday morning. Métro: Longchamp-Cinq Avenue.

Musée Grobet-Labadie, tel: 91.62.21.82. Open daily. Métro: Longchamp-Cing Avenue.

Musée de Château-Gombert, tel: 91.68.14.38. (Museum of Popular Arts and Traditions of Marseille Area). Open: every afternoon except Tuesday. Métro: Frais-Vallon, then bus #5.

One very special exhibition hall is the **Maison de l'Artisanat et des Métiers d'Art** (21, cours Honoré d'Estienne d'Orves, 13001 Marseille, tel: 91.54.80.54). The objective of this institution, which represents working artisans throughout the Provence–Alpes–Côte d'Azur region, is to serve as a marketing outlet for and information centre about regional artists and craftspeople.

Camargue

La Palissade Nature Museum, outside Salin de Giraud, tel: 42.86.81.28. On the Route de la Plage de Piemancon. Open: 9am–5pm Monday–Friday 11 June–1 September.

Musée Camarguais, Mas du Pont de Rousty. Open: 1 October–31 March daily except Tuesday 10am–5pm; 1 April–30 September 9am–6pm.

Réserve Nationale de Camargue, La Capelière, Route d.36B. Open: Monday–Saturday 9am–noon and 2–5pm. Admission: free.

Alpes-de-Haute-Provence

Natural History Museum in Riez. Open: April–Oct am and pm, only am the rest of the year. Closed January to mid-February.

Musée Municipal in Digne, tel: 92.31.45.91. Closed: Monday and every morning September–June. Admission: free on Sunday.

Alexandra David-Neel Foundation in Digne, tel: 92.31.32.38. Visits by guided tour only. Open: daily.

Musée de la Faïence (pottery museum) in Moustiers-Ste-Marie, tel: 92.74.61.64. Open: April–October. Closed: Tuesday.

Musée de la Vallée (Museum of Regional History) in Barcelonette, tel: 92.81.27.15. Open: afternoons only.

Toulon

Naval Museum, tel: 94.02.10.61. Open: 10am–noon and 1.30–6pm. Closed: Tuesday out of season.

Musée du Vieux Toulo, tel: 94.92.29.23. Open: 2–6pm. Closed: Sunday.

See too the **Memorial to the Landing** in Provence, at the Old Fort, Tour-Beaumont, tel: 94.65.39.67. Open all year.

Elsewhere in the Var

Municipal Museum in Hyères, tel: 94.65.39.67. Closed: Tuesday.

Musée du Freinet in La Garde-Freinet, tel: 94.21.81.32. Open: afternoons Wednesday–Saturday, also Sunday morning.

Musée des Arts et Traditions Populaires de Moyenne Provence in Draguinan, tel: 94.47.05.72. Closed: Sunday morning and Monday.

Alpes-Maritimes

Musée Fernand Leger in Biot, tel: 93.65.05.85. Open: April–September 10am–noon and 2–6pm; October–March 10am–noon and 2–5pm. Closed: Tuesday.

Musée Picasso *(La Guerre et la Paix)* in Vallauris. Open: 1 October–31 March 2–5pm; 1 April–30 September 10am–6pm. Closed: Tuesday.

Musée Municipal in Vallauris, tel: 93.64.18.05. Closed: Tuesday.

Musée de l'Automobile in Mougins, tel: 93.69.27.80. Closed: 15 November–15 December.

Musée d'Art et d'Histoire de Provence in Grasse.Closed: November and on weekends.

Villa Fragonard in Grasse, tel: 93.36.01.61. Closed: Saturday and November.

Fondation Maeght in St-Paul-de-Vence. Open: every day.

Chapelle du Rosaire de Matisse in Vence. Open: Tuesday, Thursday and by appointment. Closed: 1 November to mid–December and holidays.

Nice

Musée Nationale Marc Chagall, tel: 93.81.75.75. Open: 1 July–30 September 10am–7pm; 1 October–30 June 10am–12.30pm and 2–5.30pm. Closed: Tuesday.

Musée d'Art Naïf Anatole Jakovsky, tel: 93.71.78.33. Closed: Tuesday and holidays.

Museum d'Histoire Naturelle. Closed: Tuesday, from mid-August to mid-September, and holidays.

Musée Matisse et d'Archéologie. Closed: Sunday morning, Monday and November.

Musée Massena. Closed: Monday, November and holidays.

Elswhere on the Côte

Musée d'Archéologie in Antibes. Closed: November; and Tuesday, except in summer.

Musée Grimaldi Picasso in Antibes, tel: 93.94.91.91. Closed: Tuesday;

November; and holidays.

Musée Renoir du Souvenir in Cagnes-sur-Mer, tel: 93.20.61.07. Closed: Tuesday; 15 October–15 November; and holidays.

Musée Cocteau in Menton, tel: 93.36.01.61. Closed: Monday, Tuesday; and holidays

Musée Ephrussi de Rothschild, 062330 St-Jean-Cap-Ferrat, tel: 93.01.33.09.

Galleries

The countryside of Provence has become somewhat of a mecca for painters and artist colonies, and art galleries exhibiting local painters abound. This is particularly true in the Lubéron area of the Vaucluse, the Pays d'Arles and lower Alpes-Maritimes. Larger cities have galleries with changing exhibitions. For names, addresses and current expositions check with the local tourist office.

Concerts

Although Provence boasts no well-renowned resident symphonies, music lovers will find no shortage of concerts – classical, traditional or jazz – during the summer here, due to the abundance of cultural festivals. Off-season, pickings become somewhat reduced except in the more cultural cities, such as Marseille, Avignon, Aix-en-Provence, Nice and Monaco, or in abbeys and churches. Following are some random suggestions:

Vaucluse

AVIGNON

Year-round musical soirées at Minit Conservatory.

Concerts by the Orchestre Lyrique de la Region d'Avignon Provence.

Festival of opera, music, etc., second week in July through first week in August (tel: 48.74.59.88).

LOURMARIN

Musique d'Eté au Château de Lourmarin, second week in July through August (tel: 90.68.15.23)

GORDES

Festival of jazz and classical music (plus theatre), end July through first week in August

Bouches-du-Rhone

AIX-EN-PROVENCE

Festival in July, then varied series from January–April, April–May, and in June.

ARLES

All types of music from classical to flamenco during the Festival d'Arles (contact: Hôtel de Ville, 13637 Arles, tel: 90.93.34.06).

MARSEILLE

The Orchestre Philharmonique de Marseille and sporadic and seasonal concerts at **Château Borély** (tel: 91.72.41.27); **Château Gombert**, **Cathédrale de la Major** (tel: 91.55.04.36); **Théâtre aux Etoiles** (mostly popular – tel: 91.33.47.97); Centre de la **Vieille-Charité** (some very prestigious orchestral visitors); **Abbaye St-Victor** (tel: 91.33.25.86); **Port Frioul** (tel: 91.91.55.56).

ST-RÉMY

Free organ concerts at the Collegiale St-Martin, every Saturday at 5.30pm from June–September.

The Music Conservatory, from mid-July to end-August, "L'Argelier," Route d'Avignon (tel: 90.92.08.10).

Concerts at Fondation Armand Panigel, Petite Route des Jardins (tel: 90.92.07.92).

SALON-DE-PROVENCE

Classical and jazz concerts at the Château de l'Emperi during the summer.

TARASCON

Year-round classical concerts and organ music at the Collegiale or the auditorium.

Var

EGUILLES

Sporadic classical concerts at the church.

ENTRECASTEAUX

Sporadic classical and jazz performances at the châteaux (tel: 94.04.43.95).

ST-MAXIMIN

Sporadic orchestral concerts at the Royal Convent.

TOULON

July music festival.

LE VAL

Festival d'Eté à la Campagne with choral music and operettas, during July and August (tel: 94.69.06.15).

Alpes-de-Haute-Provence

ROUSSET

Sporadic classical concerts at the church.

SISTERON

"Nuits de la Citadelle" music festival during July and August.

Along the Côte d'Azur

CANNES

Sacred music festival in December. Les Nuits Musicales du Suquet, second and third weeks in July, classical concerts held at Notre-Dame d'Esperance in the old town. (For information contact: Billetterie du Palais du Festival, La Croisette, 06400 Cannes, tel: 93.3944.44.)

JUAN-LES-PINS

The Antibes Jazz Festival, three weeks in July. (For information contact: Maison du Tourisme, 11 Place de Gaulle, Antibes 06600, tel: 93.39.44.44.)

MENTON

Music festival with performances outside the St-Michel church in the old town. (For information: Palais de l'Europe, 06500 Menton, tel: 93.33.82.22.)

MONACO

Symphony, particularly October–December.

Dance

Many of the summer festivals (see Diary of Events) incorporate classical and folkloric ballet companies into their schedules, while some actually focus on dance, such as the "Danse à Aix – Festival International" held end-June through the first two weeks in July. Avignon's summer festival has some excellent offerings, while Arles's summer festival attracts some of the most original, ethnic dance groups.

The summer Offenbach Festival in Carpentras lets ballet take up half its agenda and, year round, Monte Carlo is quite proud of its local troupe.

Opera

Established 200 years ago, the Marseille Opera was traditionally known as the European proving ground for divas. It was said that if a singer had a success there, he or she had "arrived," partly because of the opera house's prestige and partly because of the Marseillaise audience's reputation for being ruthless critics.

This is no longer quite as true – although supposedly the Marseillaise audience continues to make most singers apprehensive – but opera fans will still enjoy taking in one of their productions. For information, contact: **Opéra de Marseille,** 1 Place Reyer, 13001 Marseille, tel: 91.55.14.99.

During July and August, Orange boasts all-out opera productions during the "Chorégies d'Orange," poetically staged amidst Roman ruins. Slightly more modest, but still enjoyable, are the operas that form part of the Aix-en-Provence festival and the Offenbach festival in Carpentras.

Theatre

Practically every town in Provence has its own theatre. Almost all productions, are going to be in French, but even non-French-speaking audience members may find them enjoyable. Marseille has some of the most interesting theatres, including the celebrated La Criée (30, Quai de Rive-Neuve, 13007 Marseille, tel: 91.54.74.54) run by actor and director Marcel Maréchal. Fans of experimental theatre will find much to interest them in this city, and classicists will be thrilled to find full productions of Ancient Greek plays given in the original language during the summer "Festival des Iles."

Avignon and Aix-en-Provence offer worthwhile theatre all year round, and occasionally in English. In the summer, however, both cities really take off – as do half the towns in Provence – with special, high-quality productions as part of their summer festivals.

Cinema

Avignon has begun including a French-American Film workshop as part of their summer festival but, without question, the biggest cinema event to take place in Provence every year is the Cannes Film Festival in May. For information, contact: **Le Palais des Festivals,** Esplanade Président Georges Pompidou, La Croisette, 06400 Cannes, tel: 93.39.01.01.

As it happens, nearby Nice has also been steadily cementing some very well-equipped film studios over the past years. If you would like to use their facilities, contact one of the following:
Studio de la Victorine Côte d'Azur, 16 Av. Edouard Grinda, 06200 Nice, tel: 93.72.54.54; telex: 970056.
LTM, 10, Boulevard St-Denis, 92400 Courbevoie, tel: 47.88.44.50; telex: 630277.
LTM Corp. of America, 437 W 16th Street, New York, NY 10011, tel: (212) 243-9288.
LTM Corp. of America, 1160 N Las Palmas, Hollywood, CA 90038, tel: (213) 460-6166; telex: 677693.

Those more interested in seeing films than making them will find movie houses in most of the larger towns and all the cities. The schedules are geared for local French audiences, of course, but anglophones will probably find that about half the films shown are American or English productions with only the subtitles in French.

Things to Do
City

Every major city and many of the larger towns in Provence will have at least one museum worth visiting, usually one historical site and maybe also a prehistorical site, a summer music and/or theatre festival, a colourful market, a main boulevard lined with cafés for people watching, and an assortment of good restaurants. Unless you are looking for Monets and Davids (which you can find in some cities), you will find no shortage of interesting distractions.

Regional Attractions

The listing below covers some of the regions' main attractions; *see also* Travelling with Children (*above*) for more ideas:

Aquacity, Le Petit Péage, 13270 Les Pennes Mirabeau, tel: 91.96.12.13. Aquatic park with huge pools, slides, a "white water" river, restaurant and other attractions. Open early June–mid September.

Aqualand, Zac des Pradeaux, BP42, St-Cyr-sur-Mer, tel: 94.32.09.09. Leisure park with pools and rapid rivers. Open June–September.

Aquatica, on RN98 to Ste-Maxime, 83600 Fréjus, tel: 94.53.58.58. Park with wave pool, slides and other aquatic delights. Restaurant. Open daily June–October, weekends May–November.

La Barber Zoo, Route de Salon, 13330 Pelissanne, tel: 90.55.19.12. Over 800 animals.

Les Cordes Nature Reserve, on Route D17, Fontvieille-en-Provence, tel: 90.54.69.44. Archaelogical site and other attractions. Open April–October.

Mont-Faron Wild Animal Centre, 83000 Toulon, tel: 94.88.07.89. Breeding centre for wild animals.

Niagara, 83310 La Mole, on the road to Canadel, tel: 94.49.58.87. Water park with pools, including wave pools, slides and Jacuzzis. Restaurant and bar. Open 25 June–mid-September.

Parc Minifrance, on RN7 Nice–Brignoles road, tel: 94.62.26.00. France in miniature at the Nicopolis activity centre. Also brasserie and restaurant. Open until after midnight in summer, until dusk in winter.

Excursions

You will find that the Offices de Tourisme of most major touristic cities offer excellent sightseeing tours, although they do tend to be in French. They can also help you to find an organisation that does offer a tour for your specific destination and in the language of your choice. Otherwise, you can check with one of the local travel agents or one of the tour operators.

Following are a few, limited names:

In the Camargue

Mas Sauvage, Connaissance de la Camargue Sauvage, Le Paty de la Trinité, 13200 Arles, tel: 90.97.11.45.

Half- to whole-day guided trips in jeep or car or horseback, gypsy evenings, open all year round.

On the Riviera

Santa Azur, 11 Avenue Jean-Medecin, 06000 Nice, tel: 93.85.46.81; telex: 461029. Sightseeing by motorcoach.

CTM, 5 square Merimée, 06400 Cannes, tel: 93.39.79.40; telex: 470810. Sightseeing by motorcoach.

Palais Lascaris, 15 Rue Droite, 06300 Nice, tel: 93.62.05.54. Guided tours with cultural or historical themes.

Information desk at the train station, 33 Avenue Malaussena, 06000 Nice, tel: 93.88.28.56. Guided tours by train to Provençal villages.

Nightlife

Cafés & Bars

A good portion of social activity in Provence centres around the cafés. Much like pubs in England, cafés can be found in even the tiniest towns, filled with locals, a *bière*, a *ballon de rouge* or a *café* in hand, midday, after work, after dinner.

It would be, quite simply, impossible to list all the good cafés in Provence. Superficially, they are all more or less alike: small tables spilling out onto the street, an interior bar, serving mostly beer, wine, soda and coffee with a light menu of sandwiches, pizza and such. Of course, to the insider, each is infinitely different, frequented only by certain members of the town, except for the occasional unaware tourist.

Glance the clientele and patrons before sitting down. If they look like what you are looking for and you get a good feeling, you can't really go wrong.

Avignon

You'll find scores of open-air bars and cafés near the Palais des Papes, although, keep in mind that they will become less pricey the further you go from the palace.

Aix-en-Provence

Similarly, the large cafés right on the Place de la Libération in Aix-en-Provence will be outrageously expensive and rather touristy, but further up the Cours Mirabeau prices become more reasonable. Les Deux Garcons café is the local favourite for "cruising." (53, Cours Mirabeau. Open: 6am–1am).

Arles

Fans of the *cocarde* should visit Le Tambourin on the Place du Forum where the local toreadors hang out.

Marseille

Hipsters should head for the cafés along the Cours Julien, while a slightly older crowd may prefer one of those along the Place Thiars.

St-Tropez

Is famous for its "café society." Most famous of all is its Café Senequier (Quai Jean Juarès, open 8am–midnight), where you get a good chance to yacht- as well as people-watch. Another lively favourite is the Café des Arts (Place des Lices. Open: 8.30am–4am in July and August. Closes at 8.30pm September–June).

In general, cafés take the place of bars in Provence, but larger towns, major hotels and the cities do have fully-fledged bars. Just remember, that mixed drinks are not the local speciality. You might be wise to explain exactly what it is you want in your drink.

Discos

A surprising number of towns have discos, although they won't all be quite like Les Bains in Paris.

Pays d'Arles/Camargue

Most people in the Pays d'Arles either travel up to Avignon, to Montpellier (during the school year) or to Les-Stes-Maries-de-la-Mer to go dancing. Particularly "in" is **Le 13ème** in Les-Stes-Maries-de-la-Mer, Place des Gitans, tel: 90.97.88.79. Open: 10.30pm–4am.

Arles, Barbentane, Châteaurenard, Eygalières, Maussane, Orgon and St-Rémy-de-Provence all also have at least one discothèque, although their quality isn't guaranteed.

Cassis

Cassis's disco is called **Big Ben** and is located on the Place Clemenceau (tel: 42.01.93.79). It's a perfectly harmless sort of place – the kind of disco where everyone waits for someone else to start the dancing.

Cannes

In Cannes, the best-known disco is **Galaxy**, set above the municipal casino. Despite the fairly steep entrance fee, the interior is of the too-worn velvet type and the clientele seems to match. Locals and those in the know prefer **Le Blitz** at 22 Rue Masse.

ANTIBES

Further down the beach, **La Siesta** has acquired a certain popularity, despite their bizarre Polynesian theme – with flaming torches and interior concrete lily ponds – and extremely out-dated music. It can be found (if anyone cares to) along the Route du Bord de Mer in Antibes (tel: 93.33.01.18).

NICE

Has three particularly fashionable discos: **La Camargue** on the Cours Saleya (usually private), **Chez Ecossais** at 6 Rue Halévy, and **L'Aventure** at 12 Rue Chauvain.

Nightclubs & Cabarets

You will find a number of nice nightclubs and cabarets in the larger cities of Provence, particularly ones that have jazz. The **Piano Bar** at Hôtel Mercurie in Avignon is a time-honoured spot for enjoying a drink to the sound of casual piano music. One favourite among jazz lovers in Aix-en-Provence is **Le Jazz Club**. In Arles, jazz aficionados patronise **Pub le 37*2** (19 Place Honore Clair, tel: 90.96.11.44).

Marseille has any number of good jazz bars. Behind the Théâtre de la Criée is the **Golden Jazz Club** (40, Rue Plan Fourmiguier, Quai de Rive-Neuve, tel: 91.54.36.36). The towns along the Côte d'Azur also have their fair share. Best to check with your local Syndicat d'Initiative.

Gambling

There is no shortage of casinos along the coast of Provence, and Monte Carlo's is probably the world's most famous. To enter them you generally must have an ID card or passport and pay 50–55 ff. (Don't be confused by the widespread chain of supermarkets called "Casino.")

ANTIBES

La Siesta, Route du Bord de Mer, Pont la Brague, tel: 93.33.01.18. Boule, baccarat, roulette, *chemin de fer*, blackjack. Its adjacent nightclub spills out onto the beach and is decorated in a Polynesian themes – complete with torches.

BEAULIEU

Casino, 8 Avenue Blundell Maple, tel: 93.01.00.39. Roulette, baccarat, blackjack, 30/40, *chemin de fer*, *banque à tout va.*

CANNES

Palm Beach, Place Franklin D. Roosevelt, tel: 93.43.91.12. Boule, roulette, 30/40, blackjack, *chemin de fer.* Open: 1 June–31 October. Gambling begins at 5pm.. Also, dinner dances at the "Iron Mask" with terrace orchestras, etc., and a private nightclub called "Jack Pot". Lunch grill called the "Commodore" with a swimming pool.
Municipal Casino, La Croisette, tel: 93.38.12.11. Boule, roulette, *chemin de fer*, blackjack, 30/40, *banque à tout va.* Open: 1 November–1 May. Gambling begins at 4pm. Year-round (and slightly sleazy) nightclub, "Galaxy."

MENTON

Casino de Menton, Avenue Felix Fauré, tel: 92.10.16.16. Boule, roulette, blackjack.

NICE

Casino Club, 6 Rue Sacha Guitry, tel: 93.80.55.70. Boule. Entrance is only 10 ff, no passport required.
Casino Ruhl, 1 Promenade des Anglais, tel: 93.87.95.87.

MONACO

Monte-Carlo Casino, Place du Casino. Baccarat, roulette, *chemin de fer*, 30/40. Slot machines. Entrance fee of 50 ff, but free for American roulette, blackjack and craps.
Mandelieu-la-Napoule Loews, Boulevard Henri-Clews. American roulette, blackjack, craps.

BOUCHES-DU-RHONE

Aix-en-Provence, 2 bis Avenue Napoleon-Bonaparte, Aix-en-Provence, tel: 42.26.30.33. Boule, baccarat, roulette, 30/40, blackjack.
Carry-Le-Rouet, tel: 42.45.01.58. Boule, baccarat, roulette.
La Ciotat, Avenue Wilson, tel: 42.83.40.63. Boule. Open: all year round.
La Rostagne, Avenue Docteur Leriche, Cassis, tel: 42.01.78.32. Boule, baccarat, roulette, 30/40, blackjack. Open: all year except May, 3pm–2am.

Calendar of Events

The rich Provençal heritage has left in its wake an abundance of colourful festivals. With a little planning, you should have no trouble including at least one in your visit. Below is an extensive, though not exhaustive, list:

January

1–31 January to February: Maurel Pastoral, Marseille; Month of the Sea Urchin, Sausset-les-Pins; Equestrian Fair, Avignon; Music Convention, Cannes; Car Rally, Monte-Carlo; Mimosa Festival, Mandelieu.
6: Fête of St-Clair, Allauch.
17: Fête of St-Marcel, Barjols.
31: Fête des Petardiers Castellane.

February

Early February: Fête de la Chandeleur, Marseille; Antiques Fair, Avignon; Votive of Ste-Agatha, Maillane; Corso Carnavalesque, Pelissane; Mardi Gras, Corso Coudoux; Mimosa Festival, Cannes; Mardi Gras Lemon Festival; Menton.
4–14 February to March: International TV Festival, Monaco; Carnival, Chât.-l-Martigues.

March

4–14: Nice Carnival, Nice; Ski Yachting Cup, Cannes; Cycling Race, Paris-Nice; Mandelieu Festival of the Gourds, Nice.
25: Commemoration of Mistral Maillane.
26–29: Grand Prix of Magic, Monte-Carlo.
27: International Marathon, Nice
End month: Corso Fleuri, Pelissane.

April

April to October: Cocardes and Corridas Arles Art Festival at the Castle Mandelieu.
11–26: Antiques Fair, Antibes.

Second week: Spring Fête, Martigues.
13–17: Springtime of Arts, Monaco.
15: International Tourn. Water Polo, Antibes.
Last two weeks: Sailing Regatta, Hyères.
18–26: International Open Tennis Cham., Monaco.
18: Floral Symphony, Antibes.
25: Fête of St-Mark, Meyreuil.
Last Sunday: Fête of the Cowboys, Arles.
End month: Fête of St-Mark, Eyguières.
End month: Fête of St-Mark, Villen.-l-Avignon.

May

Beginning May to June: Fête of the Good Angel, Rognonas; International Film Festival, Cannes; Rose Festival, Grasse; Concours de Farandoles, Salin-de-Giraud.
1: Carreto dis Ases, St-Rémy-de-Prov.
First Sunday: Fête of Ste-Croix, Le Tholonet.
First two weeks: Fête de Mai, Nice.
9–17: Old Cars Rally, Antibes.
Second Sunday: Fête of the Horse, Barbentane.
Sunday & Monday after 15: Fête of St-Gens, Monteux-le-Baucet.
16: Vine Growers Festival, Antibes.
16–18: Bravade, St-Tropez.
Mid-May: Fête of Bresson Blazets, Salon-de-Provence.
24–25: Gypsy Pilgrimage, Stes-Maries-de-la-Mer.
25: Votive Fête, Peypin.
26: Baroncellienne Day, Stes-Maries-de-la-Mer.
Last Sunday: Fête of the Horse, Châteaurenard.
Second & third Sunday: Corso Fleuri, Lambesc.
28: Vow of the Echevins Mass, Marseille.
30–31: Racing Cars Grand Prix, Monaco.

June

1: Fête of the Grape Harvest, Boulbon; Fête des Barjaquets, Rognac.
Beginning of month: Lei Farandoulaire, Sestian Aix-en-Provence; Fête at the Windmill, Fontvieille; Fête des Chirons, Miramas; Fête des Canourgues, Salon-de-Provence.
First Sunday: Wine Festival, Courthèzon; Fête of St-Elgius, Mollèges; Courses de Vachettes,

Cabannes; Fête of the City, La Ciotat; Festivals de Quartier, Marseille; International Theater Festival, Antibes; Provençal Festival, Hyères; Spanish Bravade, St-Tropez; Fête of the Sea, Toulon.
June to July: Bullfighting, Barbentane.
June to September: Bullfighting, Nîmes.
11–14: Fête du Cordage, Tarascon.
13: Pilgrimage, Cuges-les-Pins.
14: Fête of St-Anthony, Meyreuil.
Mid-June: Grande Fête Votive, Stes-Maries-de-la-Mer.
22–24: Fête des Aires de la Dine, Salon-de-Provence.
23: Fête of St-John, Valrèas; Fête of St-John, Cabannes; Fête of St-John, Istres.
23–25: Fêtes, Martigues.
24: Fête of St-John, Entrevaux; Fête of St-John, Aubagne; Fête of St-John, Les Baux-de-Prov.; Fête of St-John, Eygalières; Fête of St-John, Fontvieille; Fête of St-John, Mallemort.
Sunday after 24: Fête of St-John, Allauch.
Third week: Fête des Carabins, Fos-sur-Mer.
29: Fête of St-Elgius, Eyrargues.
Last Sunday: Parrot Festival, Bollène.
Last Sunday: Fête of St-Peter, Menton.
Last week: Fête of the Sea, Cassis.
Last week: Fêtes Traditionelles, Arles.
End month: Music Festival, St-Rémy-de-Provence.
End month: Fête of St-John, La Ciotat.
End month: Fête Votive, La Gavotte.
Last Sunday: Country Festival, Salin-de-Giraud.
Last Sunday: Fête of the Tarasque, Tarascon.

July

July: Fête of St-Elgius, Maillane; Fête of St-Elgius, Rognonas; Music Festival , Uzès; Music Festival, Toulon.
July to August: Offenbach Festival, Carpentras; The Season at Aix, Aix-en-Provence.
16–17 July: C Music Festival, Entrevaux.
July and August: Cultural Festival, Vaison-la-Romaine; Jazz Festival, Cavaillon; Courses de Vachettes, Salin-de-Giraud; Music & Theatre Festival, Sisteron.
July to September: Bullfighting, Arles.
1–15 July: Local Festivals, Vauvenargues.

First week: Provençal Week, Aix-en-Provence; Cocarde d'Or, Arles.
First weekend: Fête de Bel Air, Salon-de-Provence.
First Saturday: Venetian Festival, Martigues.
First Sunday: Fête of St-Elgius, Châteaurenard; Local Festival, Cadolive.
Early July: Provençal Festival, La Ciotat.
Second weekend: Local Festival, Salon-de-Provence.
8–14: Garlic and Local Products Fair, Cabriés.
9: Annual Fête, La Ciotat.
10–24: Artisan's Fair, Riez.
11–14: Feria du Cheval, Méjanes.
14: Wine Festival, Vacqueyras; Arrival of the Bulls, Tarascon; Local Fête, Noves; Local Fête, Maillane; Grand Fête of Summer, St-Andiol; Grand Fête, St-Rémy-de-Prov.; Fête of Summer, Lamanon.
Weekend before 15: Linden, Lavender and Olivetree Festival Buis-les-Baronnies.
Second Sunday: Fête Votive, Carnoux.
Mid-month: Fête of the Sea, Fos-sur-Mer; Fête de Notre Dame, Carpentras; Flower Festival, Seillans.
Mid-July to August: Dance & Drama Festival Avignon; Music Festival, Aix-en-Provence; Festival of the Arts, Orange.
16–18: Fête of Ste-Severe, Villars-Colmars.
17–25: International Jazz Festival, Antibes.
Third week: Picodon Fête with Goat, Cheese Competition Saôu.
21–22: Fête of Mary Magdalene, Ste-Baume.
21–25 July: International Fireworks Festival, Monaco.
22: Fête of Ste-Madeleine, St-Maximin; Provençal Dance, Fontvieille.
Third Sunday: Fête Virginienco, Stes-Maries-de-la-Mer.
Fourth Sunday: Wine Festival, Cairanne.
Last Sunday: Fête of St-Elgius, Graveson.
28: Local Fête, Sanary.
29: Fête of St-Peter, Auriol.
End month: Festival of Folklore, Aubagne; Local Festival, Seillans.
Last week: Market of Provence, St-Rémy-de-Prov.

August

August: Jasmine Festival, Grasse; Music Festival, St-Maximin.

First two weeks: Fête of Hte-Provence, Forcalquier.

Early August: Fête of St-Elgius, Cuges-les-Pins; Fête of St-Stephen, Istres; Fête St-Peter, Marseille; Local Fête, La Garde Freinet.

First Sunday: Jasmin Festival, Grasse; Fête Votive, La Barben; Fête Voti ve, Fontvieille; Lavender Corso, Digne.

First weekend: Fête du Q. Fontsainte, La Ciotat.

First Sunday after 6: Grape Festival , Fréjus.

7–21: Artisan's Fair, Riez.

10–15: Local Festival, Fos-sur-Mer.

14: Fête des Facteurs, La Ciotat.

14–15: Pilgrimage to Notre Dame, Garde, Marseille.

14–17: Feria Saintoise, Stes-Maries-d-l-M.

15: Grande Corrida, Arles; Pilgrimage to N.D. de Lure St-Etien-l-Orgues; Fête Votive, Carry-le-Rouet.

Mid-month: Fête of St-Elgius, St-Etien.-du-Gré; Fête du Logis-Neuf, Allauch.

22–23: Rally Cross Int'l, Antibes.

24 : Garlic Festival, Hyères.

Third week: Festival Provençal, Séguret.

Third Sunday: Fête Votive, Meyrargues.

28–29: Fête of Notre-Dame, Maillane.

30 August–9 November: Holiday on Ice, Nice.

September

Early September: Fête Votive, Marignane; Fête of Ste-Rosalie, La Fare-l-Oliviers; Fête of Cassis Wines, Cassis; Festival of Animation, Hyères; Jazz Dixieland Festival, Mandelieu.

First weekend: Autumn Festival, Courthèzon.

First Sunday: Fête Votive, Graveson.

6–8: Fête for Mistral, Maillane.

8: Pilgrimage to N.D. Galline, Marseille; Fête of La Diane, Moustiers-Ste-M; Pilgrimage to N.D. de Lure St-Etien-l-Orgues.

Mid-month: Fêtes of the Rice, Arles; Fête for Mistral, Aix-en-Provence; Fête du Jumelage, Salon-de-Provence.

Second Sunday: Fête of St-Maurice, Pélissane.

Fourth Sunday: Fête Votive, St-Rémy-de-Prov.

End month: Fête of St-Michel, Mallemort; Fête for Grape Harvest, Auriol.

October

October: Niss'Artisanat Crafts, Nice.

First Sunday: Votive Fête of St-Batie, Jouques.

Beginning month: Provençal Day, Mallemort; Grand Fête of St-Hubert, Vauvenargues.

8 October: Car Rally of Antibes, Antibes.

14–18: Mountain Film Festival, Cannes.

Sunday closest 22: Blessing of the Sea, Stes-Maries-d-l-M.

November

November: Chestnut Festival, La Garde Freinet; International Crafts Show, Cannes.

1–7: Birds Exhibition, Antibes.

First or Second Sunday: Chestnut Festival, Isola.

Mid-month: Baptème des Côtes du Rhône, Avignon; Commemorative Ceremony, Stes-Maries-d-l-M.

18–19: Monaco Feast Day, Monaco.

End November–January: Santons Fair, Marseille.

December

December: Sacred Music Festival, Cannes; Italian Films Festival, Nice; International Circus Festival, Monaco.

2–6: Underwater Film Festival, Antibes.

5 December–10 January: Luna Park Fair, Nice.

Mid-month: Veillée Calendale, Martigues.

24: Provençal Midnight Mass Every Town & City; Shepherds Festival, Les Baux; Mystery Play, Séguret.

20 December–January: Crèche i.e. Arles, Auriol, Marseille, Allauch.

End month–January: Pastorales i.e. Barbentane, Marseille, Cassis.

The summer cultural festivals are terrific. Following is a list of names and addresses, from where you can get information or purchase tickets:

Aix-en-Provence: Festival International d'Art Lyrique et de Musique, Palais de l'Ancien Archevêche, 13100 Aix-en-Provence, tel: 42.23.34.82.

Arles: Dance, Music and Photo Festival, Bureau du Festival, 13200 Arles, tel: 90.96.47.00.

Avignon: Festival d'Avignon, Bureau du Festival, BP 92, 84006 Avignon, tel: 90.86.24.43.

Orange: Chorégies d'Orange, Maison du Théâtre, BP 180 - Place Sylvain, 84105 Orange Cedex, tel: 90.34.24.24.

Vaison-la-Romaine: Hôtel de Ville, Bureau du Festival de Vaison-la-Romaine, 84110 Vaison-la-Romaine, tel: 90.36.24.79.

Shopping

You will have no trouble finding wonderful gifts and mementos to take home from Provence, without having to spend a lot of money. The best things to buy are local crafts or products, for which the Provençals are so famous. Among these are: *santon*s (little figures from clay or sometimes dough used together to create a nativity scene); pottery; faïence (fine ceramics decorated with opaque glazes); brightly coloured fabrics (the Souleiado stores carry the most famous *tissu*s, but they are also the most costly); hand-woven baskets; and bath and toiletries made with local herbs like lavender. Or you might just want to pick up a bottle of lavender essence, a little bag of fresh Herbes de Provence or a bottle of delicately green olive oil.

Some towns are inextricably linked with particular products, like the wonderful handblown glass from Biot, the perfumes from Grasse or soap from Marseille. The same goes for certain regions: honey with the Alpes-Maritimes and Alpes-de-Haute-Provence; olive oil and *santon*s with the Bouches-du-Rhone; leather products with the Camargue and Alpes-de-Haute-Provence. And, if you're on the

Riviera – well, there really is no better place to buy a bikini.

Shopping Areas

Practically every town will give you an opportunity to shop – if not in a local atelier or store, at the market place. But, for some specific suggestions, see below:

Vaucluse

AVIGNON

A well-liked leathermaker in Avignon offering accessories, bags and belts in leather, is Vincenette Ranchet-Leron. **Zenaide**, 4 Rue Pavot, 84000 Avignon. **Souleiado**, 5 Rue Joseph Vernet, 84000 Avignon. Basically *the* shop for Provençal memorabilia. Located all over Provence and in many cities internationally as well, these stores are most famed for their beautiful fabrics done in bright traditional designs. You can buy the fabric in bolts or already decorating any number of different gift items such as address books or aprons. They also stock a few other random pieces of Provençal handicraft. Their stock is top of the line and you pay quite a lot for it, but to ease the pain they take several credit cards (AE, DC, EC and Visa) and ship internationally.

BONNIEUX

La Bouquière, 84480 Bonnieux. For wooden and educational toys, stop at the atelier of Xavier De Tugny.

GORDES

Souleiado shop for Provençal cloths, etc. Place du Monument.

LE THOR

Louis Ortiz, Chemin Croix de Tallet, Le Thor, tel: 90.33.91.30. It may seem silly to buy rush caning for chair bottoms while on vacation but, just the same, you might consider bringing some back from Louis Ortiz's workshop, to be attached once you get home. Done in any number of different patterns, it will last forever.

MALAUCENE

Emmanuelle Chouvion, Cours des Isnards, 84340 Malaucène. Deep blue tints, inspired by the colour of lavender, are among the themes chosen for

the contemporary tone of Emmanuelle Chouvion's smooth and polished pottery.

VAISON-LA-ROMAINE

This town is becoming a good place to purchase local pottery and paintings as the reputation for its artist community steadily grows.
Souleiado shop for Provençal cloths. 2, Cours J.H. Fabré, 84110 Vaison-la-Romaine.

VALREAS

Stop in at Revoul to buy truffles. **Revoul**, 84500 Valrèas, tel: 90.35.01.26.

Bouches-du-Rhône

AIX-EN-PROVENCE

Atelier Fouque, 65 Cours Gambetta, 13100 Aix-en-Provence, tel: 42.26.33.38. All visitors to Aix should make a point of stopping at the atelier Fouque. Here you can both purchase and watch the manufacture of *santons* by one of the craft, Paul Fouque, and his talented daughter, Mireille.
A La Reine Jeanne, 32 Cours Mirabeau, 13100 Aix-en-Provence, tel: 42.26.02.33. *Calissons*, the local almond-paste sweet, make a nice souvenir to take home. You can find them all over the place but the confectionary store A La Reine Jeanne is centrally located. Will ship internationally.

The old town boasts quite a few chic (and not inexpensive) shops, including designer clothing, baby things and antiques.
Souleiado shop for Provençal cloth, etc. Place des Tanneurs, 13100 Aix-en-Provence.

ARLES

L'Art du Bois, 29 Rue des Porcelets, 13200 Arles, tel: 90.96.77.17. Jesus Sendon's painstakingly handcarved woodworking carries on the traditions of the *style Provençale*. Smaller gift items can be purchased directly at his atelier while larger pieces must be comissioned. Not inexpensive but very hard to find elsewhere.
Souleiado shop, 4 Boulevard des Lices, 13200 Arles, tel: 90.96.37.55.
Atelier Jannin, 1 Rue du Bastion. 13200 Arles. Lovely contemporary designs on cotton worked by the owner, Juliette Jannin.

AUBAGNE

Poterie Provençale, Avenue des Goums, 13400 Aubagne, tel: (42.03.05.59. French visitors flock here to purchase their bargain-priced, hand-made cookware. Their casseroles etc., are the original sturdy and rustic Provençal dayware.

FONTVIEILLE

Li Mestierau, Val Parisot, 13990 Fontvieille, tel: 90.97.77.95. Here you will find beautiful painted silk garments and earthy handwoven wools. Clothing, upholsteries and murals can be bought on site or commissioned. A visit to the group workshop, set up commune-style, is itself worth the trip.
Atelier Monleau, Route d'Arles, 13990 Fontvieille, tel: 90.97.70.63. For beautiful handmade and hand-painted faïence, porcelain and ceramics visit the atelier of the multi-prize-winning Chantal Monleau and family.

Les Baiux-de-Provence

Like any good tourist centre, Les Baux has lots of shops. The quality is good although the prices are higher than you will find elsewhere.

MARSEILLE

Atelier Carbonel, 47 Rue Neuve Ste-Catherine, 13007 Marseille, tel: 91.54.26.58. Indisputedly one of the most famous and has the added attraction of a large workshop and small "museum."
Souleiado shop for Provençal cloths, etc. 101, Rue Paradis.

MEYRARGUES

Atelier Devouassoux, Legrand Vallat, 13650 Meyrargues, tel: 42.57.51.10. Huguette Devouassoux is famous for making *santons* in faïence rather than just plain red clay.

St-Remy-de-Provence

Known as the centre for the herb market, St-Rémy has many *herboristeries*. Most wonderful, with a colourful variety of bath items (made with local herbs and packaged aesthetically) and a complete selection of freshly dried herbs is: **L'Herbier de Provence**, 34, Boulevard Victor-Hugo, St-Rémy-de-Provence, tel: 90.92.11.96. Prop. Anne & Vincent du Rothazard.
Souleiado shop, 2 Avenue de la Résistance.

ST-ZACHARIE

La Petite Foux, RN 560, 83640 St-Zacharie, tel: 92.72.96.02. This roadside workshop/store of the talented young Voelkel offers unique hand-turned pottery to the public. The potter's personal favourites are his blossoming, Oriental-inspired vases and bowls.

Alpes-de-Haute-Provence

DIGNE

Maison de la Lavande, 58 Boulevard Gassendi, 04000 Digne-les-Bains, tel: 92.31.33.94. Lavender shop for soap, essence, etc.

FORCALQUIER

Atelier Le Point Bleu, 22 Rue Violette, 04300 Forcalquier. At the Atelier Le Point Bleu of Michele Paganucci, you will find painting on silk, scarves, cushions and more.

MOUSTIERS-STE-MARIE

This town is famous for elegant, handpainted faïence, known as "Moustier-ware." Probably the best (and most expensive) pottery in this style can be found at the Atelier Segriès. They take the major credit cards and are prepared to ship internationally.
Atelier Segriès, 04630 Moustiers-Ste-Marie, tel: 92.74.66.69.

RIEZ

G. Ravel, Allées Louis Gardiol, 04500 Riez. A good, old-fashioned store for lavender honey.

Var

CUGNES-LES-PINS

Quartier du Puits, Chemin de la Pujeade, 13780 Cuges-les-Pins. Alain Carbone handmakes his leather saddles.

DRAGUINAN

Philippe Rabussier, Lot. Les Faisses #13, 83300 Draguignan. Philippe Rabussier is another well-respected leathermaker, who fashions such objects as beautiful handbags, belts and wallets.

RAMATUELLE

Souleiado store, Rue des Sarassins.

Alpes-Maritimes

BIOT

La Verrerie de Biot, Chemin des Combes, 06410 Biot, tel: 93.65.03.00. No visitor to the Côte or Alpes-Maritimes should miss a visit to the Verrerie de Biot. Next to the large atelier where they give demonstrations of glassblowing methods is an even larger shop (they will ship overseas, it is costly but it means you don't have to pay the tax). They take American Express and Visa and are open on Sundays.

OPIO

If you don't know *what* you would like to bring home, except that you want it to be Provençal, stop at the **Huilerie de la Brague**. They stock all sorts of different local specialities, from olive oil to olivewood carvings to Provençal cloths.

VALLAURIS

Famous for its pottery since Picasso developed an atelier there, Vallauris is now a sink of trashy tourist shops. There's only one true potter left: Roger Collet, Montée Ste-Anne, 06406 Vallauris.

Markets

If there is one thing that symbolises Provence, it is the open-air markets. After cafés, they are the centre of social activity for the locals, as well as where the Provençal cook obtains the multitude of fresh ingredients that make up the delicious cuisine. Every town has its own – be it tiny or enormous.

Vendors of locally produced vegetables, fruit, herbs, cheese, sausage, meat, honey, flowers, soaps, lavender essence and fresh-baked breads set up their stands at daybreak. In addition, some towns have a *marché au brocante* (literally, junk market) which offers everything from priceless antiques to brand-new items like underwear to honest-to-god junk. If you want to get to know Provence, you have to go to one of their markets.

Here's a list of where and when:

Vaccluse

APT

Lively market – Saturday.

AVIGNON

Diverse – daily.
Produce and flea market – Saturday and Sunday morning.
Antiques 30 August–2 September.

BOLLÈNE

Lively market – Monday.

CAVAILLON

Produce and diverse – Monday.

CHÂTEANEUF-DU-PAPE

Diverse – Friday.

GORDES

Diverse – Tuesday.

ISLE-SUR-SORGUE

Antiquities and flea – Saturday and Sunday.

ORANGE

Produce and diverse – mid-April to mid-October.

ROUSSILLON

Diverse – Wednesday.

VAISON-LA-ROMAINE

Lively market – Tuesday.

Bouches-du-Rhone

AIX-EN-PROVENCE

Diverse – daily; largest diverse (Old Town) – Saturday.
Flowers – Monday, Wednesday, Friday, Sunday.

ARLES

Produce and diverse (Place Lamartine) – Wednesday.
Produce and diverse (Boulevard des Lices) – Saturday 7am–12.30pm.
Sheep – 3 and 20 May.

BARBENTANE

Diverse – Wednesday; goats – 19 and 20 May.

CASSIS

Diverse (Parking du Marché) – Wednesday and Friday.

CHÂTEAURENARD

Produce and diverse – Sunday 7am–12.30pm.

FONTVIEILLE

Produce and diverse (Place de l'Eglise) – Monday and Friday 8am–noon.

JOUQUES

Diverse (Parking Municipal) – Wednesday afternoon and Sunday.

LA CIOTAT

Diverse (Place Evariste Gras) – daily.

MAILLANE

Diverse (Place de l'Eglise) – Thursday.

MARSEILLE

Diverse – daily; flower and fish – daily except Sunday.

ST-ETIENNE-DU-GRÈS

Fruits and vegetables (Place du Marché) – daily 6am–8pm.

STES-MARIES-DE-LA-MER

Diverse (Place de la Mairie) – Monday and Thursday.

ST-RÉMY

Produce and diverse – Wednesday and Saturday 7am–1pm.
Animals – 25 April and 28 October.
Wine and Provençal – end July.

SALON

Diverse (Cours Gimon) – Wednesday; diverse (Canourges) – Friday.
Diverse (Quartier des Bressons) – Saturday.
Animals – 6 and 22 May, 29 September and 10 November.

TARASCON

Produce and diverse (Place des Halles) – Tuesday 7am–1pm.
Sheep and asses – first week September and first week October.

Alpes-de-Haute-Provence

BARCELONETTE

Diverse – Wednesday and Saturday.

CASTELLANE

Diverse – Wednesday and Saturday.

COLMARS-LES-ALPS

Diverse – Tuesday.

DIGNE

Diverse – Wednesday, Thursday, Saturday.

FORCALQUIER

Diverse – Monday.

MANOSQUE

Diverse – Saturday.

MOUSTIERS

Diverse – Friday.

SISTERON

Lively market – Wednesday and Saturday.

Var

BORMES-LES-MIMOSAS

Diverse – Wednesday.

COLOBRIÈRES

Diverse – Sunday.

DRAGUINAN

Vegetable – daily; produce and diverse – Wednesday and Saturday.

FAYENCE

Diverse – Thursday and Saturday.

HYÈRES

Major diverse (Place Lefevre) – third Thursday in month.
Fea market (Place Massillon) – most mornings.

LE LAVANDOU

Diverse – Thursday.

SALERNES

Diverse – Sunday.

SANARY

Diverse – Wednesday.

SEILLANS

Major diverse – first Sunday in July.
Flower fair – mid-July.

TOULON

Flower and vegetable (Cours Lafayette) – every morning.
Fish (Place de la Poissonerie) – every morning.

Alpes-Maritimes

GRASSE

Diverse – Tuesday.

VENCE

Diverse – Tuesday and Friday.

ST-ETIENNE-DE-TINÉE

Diverse – Friday and Sunday.

ST-JEANNET

Diverse – Thursday.

SOSPEL

Diverse – Thursday.

TENDE

Diverse – Wednesday.

VALLAURIS

Diverse – Wednesday and Sunday.

Côte d'Azur

ANTIBES

Diverse – daily except Monday and Friday.

CANNES

Diverse – daily except Monday.
Grand diverse – Saturday and Sunday.

MENTON

Diverse – daily; grand diverse – Saturday.

NICE

Lively market – daily except Monday.

ST-TROPEZ

Lively market – Tuesday and Saturday.

Export Procedures

On most purchases, the price includes TVA (VAT or Valued Added Tax). The base rate is currently 18.6 percent, but can be as high as 33 percent on luxury items.

Foreign visitors can claim back TVA; worth doing if you spend more than 4,200 ff (2,000 ff for non-EC residents) in one place. Ask the store for a *bordereau* (export sales invoice). This must be completed to show (with the goods purchased) to customs officers on leaving the country (pack the items separately for ease of access). Then mail the form back to the retailer who will refund the TVA in a month or two. Certain items purchased (e.g. antiques) may need special customs clearance.

If you have a complaint about any purchase, return it in the first place to the shop as soon as possible. In the case of any serious dispute, contact the local Direction Départementale de la Concurrence et de la Consommation et de la Répression des Fraudes (see telephone directory for number).

Outdoor Activities

Participant

Provence provides plenty of opportunities for the sporting-minded. Cycling, hiking, rock climbing, swimming, sailing, windsurfing, tennis, golf, riding, skiing and the local favourite of *boules* are some of the most popular athletic activities in the region. Also, if you'd prefer to sit back and watch someone else get sweaty, Provence has some very special offerings: bullfighting, motor rallies, yacht races, horseracing and the ubiquitous *boules*.

You will find that hiking is a predominant activity for the whole region, which is criss-crossed with *Grands Randonnées*. The GRs are national hiking paths along which you can walk from Nice to Holland or Menton to Spain. Maps by Les Cartes Didier Richard outline these routes and mark relay stations and spots for rock climbing. Of particular interest might be maps #1 Alpes-de-Provence, #9 Haut-Pays Niçois, #19 En Haute Provence and #26 Au Pays d'Azur.

Below are some suggestions as to what you can do where and how to get further information:

Vaucluse

HIKING

The Vaucluse is particularly tempting to the hiker because of the wonderful trails surrounding Mt-Ventoux. You can get information about trails, from the **Comité National des Sentiers de Grande Randonnée**, 8 Avenue Mar-

ceau, 75008 Paris, tel: 47.23.62.32 or local tourist boards.

HORSE RIDING

Riding is another big draw in the Vaucluse. For information about holidays geared towards the equestrian, hacking, trekking, riding excursions, etc, plus a free yearly folder with prices and programmes, contact:

Association Nationale pour le Tourisme Equestre, ANTE–Provence, 28 Place Roger-Salengro, 84300 Cavaillon, tel: 90.78.04.49.

AVIGNON

When in Avignon, you might try the olympic-sized pool at Ile de Barthelasse, the **Squash Racket Center** at 32 Boulevard Limbert, or the Golf Club at Chateaublanc.

Bouches-du-Rhone

AIR SPORTS

Air sports such as flying, parachuting, gliding, hang gliding and ballooning, earthy sports such as cycling, walking and riding , and watersports like swimming, sailing and waterskiing (on the coast) are some of the favourites in the Bouches-du-Rhône.

For information about all the different schools, clubs, courses, etc., contact:

Direction Départementale de la Jeunesse et des Sports, 20 Avenue de Corinthe, 13006 Marseille, tel: 91.78.44.88.

CYCLING

Despite the heat of the sun, and probably due to the flatness of much of the land, cyclists love the Bouches-du-Rhône. For information, contact:

Comité Départemental de Cyclisme, Maison du Quartier des Chutes Lavie, 10 Boulevard Anatole-France, 13004 Marseille, tel: 91.64.58.79.

Comité Départemental de Cyclotourisme, 15 Lotissment la Trevaresse, 13540 Puyricard, tel: 42.92.13.41.

DIVING

For information about the more-than-80 diving centres in the Bouches-du-Rhône, contact:

Comité Départemental de Sports Sous-Marins, 38 Av. des Roches, 13007 Marseille, tel: 91.52.55.20.

FISHING

One nice place to fish is the little lake outside St-Rémy-de-Provence. For other locations, contact:

Fédération Départ. des Assoc. Agrées de Peche, 30 Boulevard de la République, 13100 Aix, tel: 42.26.59.15.

GOLF

You will find a nine-hole golf course in Bouc Bel Air and 18-hole courses either just completed or almost completed in Les Milles, Cabriès, Allauch, Fuveau and La Valentine. For more information about local golf courses, contact:

Délégation Régionale de Golf, 82 Rue Breteil, 13008 Marseille, tel: 91.37.01.23.

HIKING

Although this is probably the least favourable of the five Provençal *départements* for hiking, there are some worthwhile inclines around Aix-en-Provence and Les Alpilles. Contact:

Comité Départemental de Montagne (Alpinism), M. Gorgeon, 5 Impasse du Figuier, 13114 Puyloubier, tel: 42.61.48.49.

Comité Départemental de Randonnée Pedestre (Hiking), 16 Rue de la Rotonde, 13001 Marseille, tel: 42.21.03.53.

SAILING

The following towns have marinas: Berre, Carro, Carry, Cassis, La Ciotat, La Couronne, Fos, Istres, Marignane, Marseille, Martigues, Port de Bouc, Port St-Lous, St-Chamas, Stes-Maries-de-la-Mer and Sausset-les-Pins.

For further information about sailing and windsurfing, contact:

Comité Départemental de Voile et Planche à Voile, SNE Mourièpiane, L'Estaque, 13106 Marseille, tel: 91.03.73.03.

SWIMMING

The following towns have municipal swimming pools, which can be a relief during long hot days: Aix, Arles, Aubagne, Châteaurenard, Fos, Gemenos, Istres, La Ciotat, Marseille, Martigues, Maussane, Rognac, La Roque d'Antheron, St-Martin de Crau, St-Rémy-de-Provence, Salon-de-Provence and Trets.

Alpes-de-Haute-Provence

As might be expected, the Alpes-de-Haute-Provence has many attractions for the alpinist. Rock climbing, hiking and mountain biking are key activities here, with all levels of difficulty to be found. Also, the rivers that snake between the gorges and the lakes that dot the mountains mean kayaking, rafting, sailing, fishing and all other types of fresh water sports. Finally, in the winter, there is always alpine skiing.

For information about renting kayaks and/or pedalos, details of *Grand Randonnées* (the national hiking paths) routes and rock faces for climbing, maps, etc., in the area of the Grand Canyon de Verdon, contact:
Syndicat Initiative, Rue Nationale, 04120 Castellane, tel: 92.83.61.14.

● Annot

Not far from Colmars, deeper into the mountains in the Vallée de l'Ubaye is another resort that beckons the athletic. Annot offers a municipal pool, four tennis courts, more *randonnées pedestres*, fishing, kayaking, cross-country skiing (with a special cross-country ski school) and an equestrian centre (in season). For information, contact:
Syndicat d'Initiative, 04240 Annot, tel: 92.83.23.03.

● Barcelonette

The two largest ski resorts in the area are Pra-Loup and Super-Sauze. For information on them, you can contact:
Syndicat d'Initiative, Place Sept Portes, 04400 Barcelonette, tel: 92.81.04.71.

● Colmars

Colmars is more or less a centre for sporting activities. Situated by the Verdon and Lance rivers and Allos, Encombrette and Lignin lakes and at the base of several mountain peaks, you can kayak (classed at a level of III and IV), windsurf and sail, hike over 150 miles of marked paths through forests and along mountain slopes, fish for trout and, from November–April, there is alpine or cross-country skiing at either Le Seignus d'Allos (4,500–8,200 ft/1,372–2,499 metres, with 24 miles/39 km of trails and 9 chairlifts) or La Foux d'Allos/Prloup (6,000–8,700 ft/1,829–2,652 me-

tres, with 72 miles/116 km of trails, 17 chairlifts, towlifts and gondolas). The town also has three municipal tennis courts, a municipal swimming pool, a sledding hill and a year-round judo school.

For information, contact:
Office Municipal des Sports et des Loisirs, Mairie de Colmars, 04370 Colmars-les-Alpes, tel: 92.83.41.92.

Var

Aside from cycling, hiking and riding, most of the Var's sportive activity takes place by the coast. There you will find all the usual water-related sports: suntanning, girl- and boy-watching, sailing, boating, swimming, parasailing, etc.

Two towns in upper Var have guides available and organise outings for walks and hiking – Val d'Entraunes and Beuil-Valberg. For information, contact:
Syndicat d'Initiative, Val d'Entraunes, tel: 94.05.51.04.
Bureau des Guides, tel: 94.02.42.34. A single organisation in the Var provides all the information you could need on trekking, whether by foot, bike or on horseback. Booklets of maps and circuits are available from them:
AVDTR, 9 Avenue Colbert, 83000 Toulon, tel: 94.89.14.44.

Alpes-Maritime

CLIMBING

There are fully equipped climbing schools in Cabris, Gourdon, St-Jeannet, La Loubière, St-Dalmas-de-Valdeblore, Le Boréon (by St-Martin-Vésubie), Roquebillière, Belvedere, Valberg, St-Etienne-de-Tinée, Auron, Isola 2000 and Tende. The Mercantour National Park offers a cornucopia of possibilities for outdoor enthusiasts with climbing ascents that range from difficult to very difficult.

HIKING

Hiking is also a big thing in the Alpes-Maritimes, and you can get a great little map called *The Hiker's Handbook* from the Comité Regional du Tourisme Riviera-Côte d'Azur (55 Promenade des Anglais, 06000 Nice, tel: 93.44.50.59). This will tell you everything you need to know – hostels and relay stations, hiking routes, park rules, and names and numbers for climbing schools, guides, regional

clubs and assocations. It also contains a good general map.

GOLF

There are five 18-hole golf courses in the Alpes-Maritimes, with average rates of 180 ff on weekdays and 250 ff on weekends:
Golf Bastide du Roy, 06410 Biot, tel: 93.65.08.48.
Monte-Carlo Golf Club, Mont-Agel, 06320 La Turbie, tel: 93.41.09.11.
Country Club de Cannes Mougins, 175 Route d'Antibes, 06250 Mougins, tel: 93.75.79.13.
Golf Club Cannes Mandelieu, RN 98, 06210 Mandelieu-La-Napoule, tel: 93.49.55.39.
Golf de Valbonne, La Bégude, route D 4, 06560 Valbonne, tel: 93.42.00.08.

HORSE RIDING

And, of course, there are lots of stables. Costs average about 50 ff per hour. For information:
ANTE Provence-Côte d'Azur, Mas de la Jumenterie, Route de St-Cézaire, 06460 St-Vallier-de-Thiey, tel: 93.42.62.98; or
Comité Hippique Départemental, Stand Municipal des Sports, Parc Layet, 06700 St-Laurent-du-Var, tel: 93.20.99.64.

MOUNTAINEERING

The best time for mountaineering is from June–October. Always be on your guard for violent late-afternoon storms and remember that bad weather here comes from the east. For mountain weather reports tel: 93.71.81.21.

Some addresses that might be of use:
Regional Council for Hiking Enthusiasts, 2 Rue Deloye, 06000 Nice. Written enquiries only. If within France, please include return postage.
French Alpine Club (FAC), 15 Avenue Jean Medecin, 06000 Nice.

SKIING

During winter, skiing becomes the most popular alpine activity in this department. Twelve smaller resorts exist, each ranging from about 4,500–6,500 ft (1,380–1,980 metres):
L'Audibergue, tel: 93.60.31.51.
Beuil-Les-Launes, tel: 93.02.30.05.
Le Boréon, tel: 93.02.20.08.
La Colmiane-Valdeblore, tel: 93.02.84.59.

Esteng-D'Entraunes, tel: 93.02.84.59.
La Gordoloasque-Belvedere, tel: 93.05.51.36.
Gréolières-Les-Neiges, tel: 93.59.70.12.
Peira-Cava, tel: 93.93.57.12.
Roubion-Les-Buisses, tel: 93.02.00.48.
St-Auban, tel: 93.60.43.20.
St-Dalmas-Les-Selvage, tel: 93.02.41.02.
Tende-Caramagne, tel: 93.04.60.91.
Turini-Camp-D'Argent, tel: 93.03.01.02.
Val-Pelens-St-Martin-D'Entraunes, tel: 93.05.51.04.

In addition, there are three major resorts – **Auron**, **Isola 2000** and **Valberg** – within easy driving distance from Nice. For information, contact:
Office du Tourisme/Auron, 06660 St-Etienne-de-Tinée, tel: 93.23.02.66; telex: 470300. 25 ski lifts, 44 trails, 75 miles (121 km) of slope. 5,300–8,200 ft (1,600–2,500 metres). Several winter packages are available from the tourist office. Also, summer packages including hiking', tennis courts, riding, fencing and judo.
Office du Tourisme/Isola 2000, 06420 Isola 2000, tel: 93.23.15.15; telex: 461666 F. 22 ski lifts, 40 trails, 70 miles (113 km) of slope. 6,000–8,600 ft (1,830–2,620 metres). Ice driving school and snow bike. Several winter packages available. Also, summer packages including tennis lessons, horseback riding lessons, hiking and swimming pool.
Office du Tourisme/Valberg, 06470 Valberg, tel: 93.02.52.54; telex: 461002 F. 21 ski lifts, 55 trails, 50 miles (81 km) of slope. 5,300–8,000 ft (1,620–2,440 metres). Also, 30 miles (48 km) of trail for cross-country skiing. One winter package consisting six nights "full ski" from January–March.

Côte d'Azur

If the French are known for being a fairly unathletic nation, the residents of the Côte d'Azur are an exception. After all, they have great beaches at their feet and sunny skies over their heads all year round. You can find all sorts of water-connected activity that might interest you, plus tennis courts galore, racquet clubs and miniature golf (full golf courses are located inland – *see under Alpes-Maritimes*). Some places to go or contact:

AVIATION

Aerodrome International Cannes-Mandelieu, 269 Avenue Francis Tonner, 06150 Cannes-La Bocca, tel: 93.47.11.00.

BOWLING

Bowling de Nice Acropolis, 5 Esplanade Kennedy, 06300 Nice, tel: 93.55.33.11. Bowling alley with 24 tracks. Open: all year from 11am–2am with a bar and cocktail lounge.
California Bowling, Route de Grasse, 06600 Antibes, tel: 93.33.23.95. Bowling alley with a roller-skate disco. Open: all year.

CYCLING

Comité Départemental, c/o F. Parcillie, Le Jura A, 12 Boulevard Henri Sappia, 06000 Nice, tel: 93.51.22.56.

DIVING

Comité Départemental, Fort Carré, 06600 Antibes, tel: 93.95.05.65. In general, many hotels, beaches and sports shops rent diving equipment. The best place to dive is along the Esterel.

HANG GLIDING

Ecole Francaise de Vol Libre, La Colmiane, tel: 93.02.83.50.
Fédération Francaise Vol Libre, 54 bis Rue de la Buffa, 06000 Nice, tel: 93.88.62.89. (The first is actually a school.) The wind currents are great all over, but the best locations are considered to be near Gourdon and Fayence.

HORSE RIDING

Association de Polo de Cannes-Mandelieu, tel: 93.36.81.93. For riding *see under Alpes-Maritimes*.)

FISHING

Fédération Départementale des Sociétés de Pêche, 20 Boulevard Victor Hugo, 06000 Nice, tel: 93.03.24.09. For fishing. You can rent boats at most marinas to go fishing in the Mediterranean, but locals prefer going into the mountains after trout. Get a permit or get arrested.

SAILING

There is no shortage of places from where to rent or buy sailboats. Almost every city on the Mediterranean has a port with boats for hire. To find out the going prices drop in on the yacht clubs or pubs. Many of the clubs also teach sailing.
Lique Provence Côte d'Azur, 20 Rue des Palmiers, 06600 Antibes, tel: 93.34.78.07.
Aquasport, Port Gallice, 06160 Juan-les-Pins, tel: 93.61.20.01.
Camper & Nicholson's Yacht Services, Port Canto, 06407 Cannes, tel: 93.43.16.75.
South of France Boating, Marina Baie des Anges, Villeneuve-Loubet, tel: 93.20.55.16.
Yacht Club Beaulieu/St-Jean, Quai White Church, Pourt de Plaisance, 06310 Beaulieu, tel: 93.01.14.44.
Yacht Club de Monaco, Cale de Halagé, Quai Albert 1èr, Monte Carlo, tel: 93.30.63.63.

SQUASH

All three clubs listed here are open all year.
Squash Club, Les Terriers, Route de Grasse, Sortie Autoroute, 06600 Antibes, tel: 93.33.35.33.
Squash Club Vauban, Avenue du Maréchal Vauban, 06300 Nice, tel: 93.26.09.78.
Squash Lou Pistou, Avenue du Zoo, 06700 St-Laurent-du-Var, tel: 93.31.05.44.

TENNIS

The Sophia Country Club is the newest and brightest club on the Côte, located among 31 acres of woodland far from the smelly and noisy autoroutes. Yannick Noah's coach, Patrice Hagelauer, is director here, and tennis holidays, junior tennis competitions, private lessons and training for players and coaches are available.
Ligue Côte d'Azur, 5 Avenue Suzanne Lenglen, 06000 Nice, tel: 93.53.92.98.
Sophia Country Club, Biot-Sophia Antipolis, 06560 Valbonne, tel: 93.65.26.65.
Tennis Ecole de Villeneuve-Loubet, Route de Grasse, 06270 Villeneuve-Loubet, tel: 93.20.60.09.

WINDSURFERS

These may be rented at many sports shops and almost every beach along the Côte. Rental costs range from 35–50 ff per hour, and lessons go for 75–90 ff per hour. A spin on water skis costs about 70 ff for six minutes.

Spectator
AUTO RALLIES

Particularly popular spectator sport along the Côte d'Azur. The most famous are, of course, the Grand Prix in Monaco at the end of May and the Monte-Carlo Car Rally in January. Other rallies are the Rally of the Roses in Antibes, beginning in October, the Golden Snail old cars rally in Antibes, mid-May, and the vintage car rally in Toulon, in May. For information about racing in the Bouches-du-Rhône, contact:
Ligue Regionale Provence, Course de Sport Automobile et Circuits Automobiles, 7 Boulevard Jean-Jaurès, 13100 Aix, tel: 42.23.33.73.

BOULES

Any time you see four or more men gathering around an open space, chances are good that they are going to embark on the Provençal sport of *boules*. Basically, *boules* is somewhat like bowling – you try to knock certain balls with other balls. You can join in and play, but don't unless you know what you're doing. Provençals can be as fervent about their *boules* games as some people are about soccer.

BRIDGE

If you are a bridge fan, you might want to head towards St-Tropez during April for the International Bridge Festival. A bridge tournament is held during mid-May in Antibes.

BULLFIGHTING

Full-fledged bullfights can be seen at various times during the warm months at the arenas in Arles, Nîmes, Les-Stes-Maries-de-la-Mer and Fréjus. At the *grand corrida* in Arles on 15 August, they don't kill the bull, but during Arles's Easter *feria*, Easter Saturday, Sunday and Monday, they do.
If bullfighting seems like more than you can stomach, you might want to take in one of the *cocardes* instead. In the *cocardes*, about 20 men dressed in white run around the ring badgering a series of bulls until they lose their tempers and charge. In the meantime, the men try to collect points by pulling strings and rosettes off their horns. The Society of Prevention of Cruelty to Animals might not love it, but there really is nothing bloody about it (unless one of the men doesn't move fast enough). And it's very much like what a baseball game is to an American – the Provençal folk arrive in droves on Saturday afternoons to cheer for the favourites, eat peanuts and drink beer. More bull-connected sports and events can be seen in other smaller towns in Provence, particularly those in or near the Camargue, such as the mid-June bull races in Les-Stes-Maries-de-la-Mer or *courses camarguais* in Tarascon.

HORSES

During May in Cannes you can see both an International Jumping show and the Spring Cup Regatta.
For horseracing addicts, the Cagnes-sur-Mer race track is open from 15 December–16 March and from 28 June–30 August, Tuesday, Friday and Sunday. This is subject to change from year to year, for information tel: 93.20.30.30.

TENNIS

Tennis lovers around the world direct their attention to Monaco every third week in April for the International Open Tennis Championship.

Photography

Just as painters once flocked to the south with their easels, photographers now find themselves seduced by the magical light and colours of Provence. There's no shortage of photo opportunities in the region, but you should keep in mind a couple of points:

1. By noon the sun is very strong. Unless you don't mind washed-out pictures, you should try to shoot early in the morning or at dusk. You may also want to buy a polarised filter before leaving home.
2. Because of the heat, film left in your car can be damaged. It is best to leave anything you aren't immediately using back at your hotel. Otherwise, try to get a protective and insulated pouch.
3. Unless you absolutely can't wait, you would do well to hold off until you get home to have your film developed. Especially in the smaller towns, the quality of development is not guaranteed and it will generally be quite pricey.
4. Similarly, film purchased in the small towns will be expensive and may be old.

The Pays d'Arles boasts two major events for photographers. The first is the Rencontres Internationales de la Photographie in Arles. The Rencontres include a photographic festival during the first week of July with soirées of photographic spectacles projected upon a giant screen in the Théâtre Antique; a selection of photographic exhibitions set up in varied spots around the town during the first two weeks of July; and over 40 different courses and lectures given by recognised professional photographers during the first three weeks of July. During this period, Arles overflows with photographers from around the world, from the most famous to the most humble.
For more information, contact:
Rencontres Internationales de la Photographie, 16 Rue des Arènes, BP 90, 13632 Arles Cedex, tel: 90.96.76.06.

The second event takes place from mid-September into early October. During this time, the renowned Maine Photographic Workshops take up residence in Fontvieille to offer a series of intensive week-long classes. Unlike the Rencontres, the Workshops concentrate on personalised interaction with the instructors and hands-on learning. They also take care of your lodging, etc., in the best of styles. Of course, you do pay for this.
For more information, contact:
Maine Photographic Workshops, Rockport, Maine 04856, United States, tel: (207) 236-8581.

Language

French, of course, is the official language of Provence, although the area does have its own regional dialect of "Provençal." Apart from encounters with older people deep in the country and the names of restaurants, Provençal won't impinge much on the average tourist and, if you speak at least some French, you shouldn't find communication impossible (although their lilting accent may take a while to get used to). The dialect is not an easy one to pick up, even if you speak other romance languages. One tip: *"Lou"* means "the" in Provençal and is used in the names of many establishments.

Useful Phrases

hello	*bonjour*
good bye	*au revoir*
please	*s'il vous plaît*
thank you	*merci*
thank you very much	*merci beaucoup*
you're welcome	*de rien*
Where is/are...?	*Où est/sont...?*
What is it?	*Qu'est-ce que c'est?*
How much?	*Combien?*
Do you have...?	*Avez-vous...?*
When?	*Quand?*
What time is it?	*Quelle heure est-il?*
with/without	*avec/sans*
the airport	*l'aeroport*
the plane	*l'avion*
the train station	*la gare*
the train	*le train*
the bus	*le car*
the car	*la voiture*
the subway	*le métro*
the bank	*la banque*
the exchange	*le change*
customs	*la douane*

the post office	*le bureau de poste*
the bathroom	*les toilettes*
room where the bath is	*la salle des bains*
the police station	*la gendarmerie*
Help!	*Au secours!*
the hospital	*l'hôpital*
the doctor	*le medecin*
the nurse	*l'infirmière*
the dentist	*le/la dentiste*
I am sick.	*Je suis malade*
the drugstore	*la droguerie/la pharmacie*
shampoo	*le shampooing*
soap	*le savon*
shaving cream	*la creme à raser*
toothpaste	*le dentifrice*
tampon	*le tampon (hygienique)*
I want to dial a number	*Je veux composer un numero*
...to call collect	*...téléphoner en PCV*
...make a person-to-person call	*...téléphoner avec préavis*
breakfast	*le petit déjeuner*
lunch	*le déjeuner*
dinner	*le dîner*
a cup	*une tasse*
a glass	*une verre*
a plate	*une assiette*
a bowl	*un bol*
a fork	*une fourchette*
a knife	*un couteau*
a spoon	*une cuillère*
a napkin	*une serviette*
the bill	*l'addition*
the waiter	*le garçon*
the waitress	*la serveuse*
I would like a coffee	*Je veux du café*
coffee with milk	*du café au lait*
tea	*du thé*
wine	*du vin*
beer	*une bière*
mineral water	*de l'eau minerale*
juice	*du jus*
ice cubes	*les glaçons*
butter	*la beurre*
salt	*le sel*
pepper	*le poivre*
sugar	*le sucre*

mustard	*la moutarde*
jam	*la confiture*
oil	*l'huile*
vinegar	*le vinaigre*
bread	*le pain*
eggs	*les oeufs*
vegetables	*les légumes*
salad	*la salade*
meat	*la viande*
beef	*le boeuf*
rib steak	*l'entrecôte*
lamb	*l'agneau*
leg of lamb	*le gigot d'agneau*
cold cuts	*la charcuterie*
ham	*le jambon*
pork	*le porc*
sausage	*la saucisse*
rabbit	*le lapin*
veal	*le veau*
chicken	*le poulet*
fish	*le poisson*
trout	*la truite*
salmon	*le saumon*
red mullet	*le rouget*
shellfish	*les fruits de mer*
lobster	*l'homard*
shrimp	*les crevettes*
dessert	*le dessert*
cheese	*le fromage*
fruit	*les fruits*
pastry	*la patisserie*
ice cream	*la glace*

Numbers

one	*un*
two	*deux*
three	*trois*
four	*quatre*
five	*cinq*
six	*six*
seven	*sept*
eight	*huit*
nine	*neuf*
ten	*dix*
twenty	*vingt*
thirty	*trente*
forty	*quarante*
fifty	*cinquante*
sixty	*soixante*
seventy	*soixante-dix*
eighty	*quatre-vingt(s)*
ninety	*quatre-vingt-dix*
one hundred	*cent*
one thousand	*mille*

Further Reading

Belles Letters

Two Towns in Provence, by M.F.K. Fischer. New York: Vintage Books, 1983.
Tender is the Night, by F. Scott Fitzgerald. New York: Scribner's
Giono, Jean, *Regain*.
Aspects of Provence, by James Pope Hennessy.
Le Clos du Roi, by Marcel Scipion.
Living Well is the Best Revenge, by Calvin Tomkins. New York: E.P. Dutton
Village in the Vaucluse, by Lawrence Wylie. Third ed., New York: Harper & Row, 1974.

Cuisine

La Veritable Cuisine Provençale et Niçoise, by Jean-Noel Escudier. France: Solar, 1982.
Recueil de la Gastronomie Provençale, by Monique Granoux. France: Delta 2000/Editions SAEP, 1983.
Cuisine of the Sun, by Roger Vergé. Edited and adapted by Caroline Conran, New York: MacMillan, 1979.

Other Insight Guides

There is a full range of books in the prestigious *Insight Guide: France* series. A companion guide to *Insight Guide: Provence* is *Insight Guide: Côte d'Azur*, with further stunning photographs taken by Catherine Karnow. Other titles are *Alsace*, *Burgundy*, the *Loire*, *Normandy*, *Paris*, as well as the entire country captured between the pages of *Insight Guide: France*.

Insight Pocket Guides offer travellers personal itineraries from a local host who recommends all the best places to visit during a short stay. The books include a full-size fold-out map. Titles in the France series include Alsace, Brittany, Corsica, Côte d'Azur, Loire Valley, Paris and Provence. *Insight Pocket Guide: Provence* is hosted by Mark Fincham, who has lived in the region for more than a decade. *Insight Pocket Guide: Côte d'Azur* is by Michaela Lentz, friend of many of the coast's celebrities, who lives in a farmhouse near Vence.

Insight Compact Guides are small in size but not lightweight in content. They give tours, with maps, of each destination, offering incisive details on all the key sites. Travel, restaurant and hotel accommodation details make these ideal on-the-spot mini-encyclopaedias. French destinations in the series include Brittany, Burgundy, Normandy, Paris and Provence.

Art/Photo Credtis

All photography by
Catherine Karnow

except for:
Ruth Aebi 104, 189
Douglas Corrance 8/9
Gavin Lewis 206
National Gallery of Art 50/51, 52
Rex Features 109, 111
Anne Roston 40, 46, 87, 200
Bill Wassman 2

Maps Berndtson & Berndtson

Visual Consultant V. Barl

Index

T

U–Z

A
B
C
D
E
F
G
H
I
J
a
b
c
d
e
f
g
h
i
j
k
l